PELICAN BOOKS
A372
CHAMBER MUSIC
EDITED BY ALEC ROBERTSON

Chamber Music

EDITED BY
ALEC ROBERTSON

PENGUIN BOOKS

Penguin Books Ltd, Harmondsworth, Middlesex, England
Penguin Books Inc., 3300 Clipper Mill Road, Baltimore, Md 21211, U.S.A.
Penguin Books Australia Ltd, Ringwood, Victoria, Australia

—

First published 1957
Reprinted 1960, 1963, 1967

—

Made and printed in Great Britain
by The Whitefriars Press Ltd
London and Tonbridge
Set in Monotype Baskerville

CONTENTS

PART TWO

PART THREE

INTRODUCTION

CHAMBER music is so comprehensive a term that it can be taken to include anything from a vocal or instrumental solo to such works as Bach's Brandenburg Concertos or Schönberg's first Chamber Symphony for fifteen solo instruments.

This book adopts the usually accepted limitations of the term: that is, instrumental ensemble music with one instrument to a part and for no body larger than a nonet, and therefore music for groups of players that can be accommodated in a fairly large room. (That the narrow living room of the flat-dweller would be overcrowded by a duo is a misfortune to be attributed to the modern way of life, and one that seems unlikely to be remedied.) The heart of this book, I want to emphasize, is the string quartet, as we know it in the great line of composers from Haydn to Bartók, and its allied forms, the string trio and quintet, piano trio, quartet, and quintet, etc.

Separate sections have been allotted to duet-sonatas (excluding works for piano duet) and to works with wind instruments, both to avoid congestion in other sections of the book and to make reference to those mediums easy for readers with a special interest in them.

As this book does not pretend to be any more consistent than its title the reader must not be surprised to find, for example, Schubert's Octet in the section devoted to its composer and not in the one dealing with works with wind instruments. There is also a certain amount of overlapping (which will do no one any harm, least of all the composers) and no apology need be made for including so lengthy a section on Bartók's six string quartets. He is, by general consent, the greatest composer of our time in this testing medium – some would hold the greatest since Beethoven in intellectual grasp and force – and the only one to have written a series of quartets that cover the whole span of his creative life.

Such are the main and most easily organized parts of the

book. As it would obviously not have been possible to deal with the chamber works of the huge concourse of late nineteenth and twentieth century composers separately in the space remaining, it seemed best to group those that are included in the sections concerned with their countries of origin.

In the painful matter of selection, America and England, in a book designed primarily for English-speaking readers, were obvious choices; and, because of their many and outstanding contributions to chamber music, so were France, and Germany. Of the numerous candidates for the remaining place Russia was chosen as possessing chamber music with the widest general appeal.

It has fortunately been possible to include, in the sections dealing with duet-sonatas and works with wind instruments, a number of compositions from the countries excluded – as the index at the end of the book will show – but this still leaves many regrettable omissions, particularly in the field of the string quartet.

Contributors were asked, in general, to select a few works in their respective sections for special analytical treatment, and they have, with one or two exceptions, followed the chronological method either throughout their whole section or within a group of works in a similar medium. Eric Blom's section on Mozart is the chief exception mentioned above. Dr Blom has chosen to deal with the various elements of Mozart's style – melody, harmony, rhythm, form, etc. – and by so doing presents an interesting and suggestive variation of the general chronological treatment, and one particularly suited to the year of the two hundredth anniversary of the composer's birth. Contributors were also asked to bear in mind the large and ever increasing repertoire of the long-playing record, which is continually opening up new fields of experience: the majority of the works mentioned in these pages has been recorded and most of the others are likely to follow. It is worth noting that the 'sleeves' of LP records usually carry analytical notes on the music and other information of value to the listener.

No list of records is given in this book – such lists are

necessarily out-of-date by publication time – but, in any case, the reader can easily find out what is available by consulting the quarterly catalogue of all 'classical' LP records issued by *The Gramophone* Magazine.

Miniature scores of a large amount of the music dealt with in this book, by both 'classical' and modern composers, are published by firms too numerous to mention here and can be ordered from any intelligent music dealer.* A growing number of people finds delight and profit in examining and following 'the map of the country', before, during, and after listening to a recording† : and even those who do not 'know their notes' may be assured that if they begin by studying a minuet or slow movement from such a work as Haydn's 'Emperor' Quartet (in which the tune of the slow movement, already well known, remains unchanged in the variations on it that follow) they will find the instrumental lines much easier to follow than they might imagine, and they will soon be able to move on to more complex textures.

The confused but very interesting history of the two and a half centuries or so of chamber music that preceded the first quartet for solo strings that Haydn composed in 1755 does not come within the scope of this book. It can be read about in any good musical dictionary or history of music, and it is to be hoped that the reader will feel tempted to explore this rich field, above all the lovely string works of Corelli and Purcell with which that period of history ends. The sections on duet-sonatas and works with wind instruments, in this book, begin with Bach; but as almost every composer, up to the middle of the eighteenth century, wrote chamber music, the authors of these sections have had to be rigorously selective.

While this book may confidently be expected to interest lovers of chamber music it is greatly hoped that it may also attract the attention of those who may have avoided this

* Penguin Scores provide considerably fuller biographical and analytical notes than any others; some of these have none at all.

† Scores (or programme notes) should not, in my opinion, be used in the concert hall during performance: one should be wholly allied with the performers in the bringing to life of the printed notes.

beautiful form of music by a mistaken notion that it is monotonous, or by a dislike of the tone of only a few strings playing together (how much leaders with whining or steely tone on their E strings have to answer for here!), or for any reason other than an ineradicable allergy.

The case for chamber music – if it must be presented – has been well put by Homer Ulrich, an American author, in his excellent book on the subject*, and I quote the following passage from the introductory chapter.

One of the most satisfying and stimulating fields of music lies before us.

Chamber music is a bountiful source of pleasure to those who know the field. It is at once one of the most enjoyable and the most dignified of literatures. The musical amateur often makes it his hobby and considers it the mainspring of his musical existence. The experienced layman finds himself richly rewarded for his intelligent listening. The professional musician turns to it for relaxation and for a kind of pleasure that no other field offers.

Furthermore it has challenged the greatest composers to their best efforts. ...

'E'en little things can yield a perfect pleasure, e'en little things can be supremely dear' – so run the lines of a Tuscan song beautifully set to music by Hugo Wolf. And of nothing is that so true as of the 'little things' of chamber music. One finds in that field no necessary correlation between size and quality.

Again chamber music provides a medium for the expression of particularly intimate ideas ... (and) it does not depend for its effects upon great splashes of sound, and great variety of tone-colour, or great virtuoso display. In chamber music there is room only for the essentials, all mere padding is avoided. One is aware of the musical essence, of the composer's inmost intentions. ...

In conclusion, may I express the hope that the enthusiasm with which the contributors to this book have carried out their tasks may be reflected in its readers, thereby furthering the deeper appreciation of chamber music which all of us concerned in the making of this book have so much at heart.

3 June 1955   ALEC ROBERTSON

* Columbia University Press, see Bibliography.

ACKNOWLEDGEMENTS

I WISH to thank the following publishers for giving me permission to reproduce extracts from their copyright publications:

Augener Ltd (Frank Bridge: Fourth String Quartet)

Boosey and Hawkes (Béla Bartók: Sixth String Quartet)

Columbia University Press (*Chamber Music, The Growth and Practice of an Intimate Art*, Homer Ulrich, 1948)

Durand & Cie, Paris [United Music Publishers, London] (César Franck: Sonata for Violin and Piano, Piano Quintet; Debussy: Sonata for Violin and Piano, Sonata for Cello and Piano; Fauré: Second Cello Sonata)

J. Hamelle & Cie, Paris (Fauré: First Piano Quartet)

Hinrichsen Edition Ltd, Bach House, 10–12 Baches Street, London, N.1 (Samuel Wesley: Quartet No. 1)

Alfred Lengnick & Co. Ltd. (Edmund Rubbra: Second Quartet)

Novello & Co. Ltd (Stanford: First Piano Trio, Op. 35; Elgar: String Quartet; Bliss: Second String Quartet)

Oxford University Press (Vaughan Williams: String Quartet; Walton: String Quartet)

G. Schirmer Inc., New York [Chappell & Co. Ltd, London] (Bloch: Third String Quartet)

Schott & Co. Ltd, London (Peter Racine Fricker: Wind Quartet; Hindemith: First String Trio)

Universal Edition A.G., Vienna (Alban Berg: Lyric Suite)

Universal Edition (London) Ltd, London (Béla Bartók: Second, Third, Fourth, Fifth Quartets; First and Second Sonatas for Violin and Piano)

Zenemükiadó Vállalat, Budapest V, Szent Istvántér 15 (Béla Bartók: First Quartet)

A.R.

PART ONE

—

I

Joseph Haydn (1732–1809)

ROSEMARY HUGHES

INTRODUCTION

IN 1805 Haydn, then aged seventy-three, compiled a thematic list of his works with the help of his copyist. It is not a complete list – his memory was failing by then – but it is beautifully neat and systematic. Symphonies and divertimenti – instrumental works smaller and lighter than the symphonies, for different combinations of instruments – string quartets and piano trios, trio-sonatas for two violins and string bass, songs, operas, sacred works – all are classified under their proper headings.

Forty years earlier, about 1765, he began to draw up such a catalogue. He had planned it no less systematically, each category of works beginning on a fresh page. Like the later catalogue, it starts off in style with the symphonies; the *divertimenti* are there, and the trio-sonatas. But for string quartets we look in vain. It is only when we run our eyes down its columns once more that a familiar pattern of notes catches the eye here and there, and we discover, tucked away among the divertimenti, over twenty of the earlier string quartets. One or two are labelled '*divertimento a quattro*'; but there is no attempt to treat them as belonging to a separate category with a distinctive character of its own.

To us this seems inconceivable – so completely has the string quartet come to be accepted not merely as a special and individual instrumental combination, but as the essence and archetype of all chamber music. That this was not always so, Haydn's two catalogues place on record for us, as quietly and impersonally as scientific charts registering the emergence of a new biological species. What they do not record is that it was Haydn himself who, more than anyone else, was responsible for bringing it into being. It did not come about consciously, or of set purpose; in that first catalogue the description '*divertimento*' is impartially applied both to the earliest and most rudimentary of the quartets and to those which are string quartets in the fullest sense of the word. But between the two lies a process of evolution, brought about by the act of writing for four stringed instruments in such a way that they gradually became a single entity, and one capable of every height and depth of musical utterance. One of the great scholars of our century, Marion Scott, summed it up in a just and memorable phrase: 'Haydn did not invent the form: he made it – an infinitely higher achievement.'

Haydn did not 'invent' the string quartet. Music for strings in four parts was already being written throughout his adolescence and young manhood: by Italians such as Tartini, Pugnani, and the Sammartini brothers, by the splendidly progressive group of composers working in Mannheim and led by Johann Stamitz and Franz Xaver Richter, by the much-admired Florian Gassmann in Vienna. But with all its variety and contrast of national and personal styles, even of name – *quadro, quatuor, sonata a quattro, sinfonia a quattro* – this four-part music for strings is not yet music for string quartet: and the distinction is vital. It falls into two main types, of which the first is orchestral in conception. Strings in four parts were the foundation of every orchestra: first and second violins, violas, cellos, with double basses an octave lower lending extra resonance and power to the bass line; so it is now, with one important difference – that the conductor of the orchestra directed the performance from the harpsichord and was counted on to support and fill in the harmony, playing his so-called *continuo* from the bass part only, with figures beneath the notes to indicate the harmonies required. And most of these eighteenth-century works for four-part strings belong to the orchestral category: they are in fact symphonies for string orchestra, whether styled *sinfonia a quattro* by Tartini or merely *quatuor* by the Viennese Gassmann. The violins (first and second frequently in unison) move with an un-mistakably orchestral gait, whether in vigorous *allegro* or flowing *cantabile* melody; the viola part – save in the fre-quent fugal movements – consists entirely of accompanying figures; the cello, yoked to the solid foundation-bass line and to the harpsichord *continuo*, never sings. Moreover, the viola line at times crosses that of the cello in such a way as to contradict the harmonic sense of the passage, showing that the orchestral double-bass, with its lower octave, was reckoned upon to maintain the balance, and there are bare passages in the harmony which the harpsichord is clearly counted on to fill out.

There is, however, another type of four-part music for strings belonging to the fifties and sixties of the eighteenth century. It is strongly represented in the work of the Mann-heim composers Richter and Johann Stamitz, and stands closer to the string-quartet style in that it is clearly designed for four solo players. The parts are richly ornate, all of practically equal interest – none are relegated to a merely accompanying role. But the parts are *too* interesting, too florid, like those of four independent concerto soloists. And such they are: these quartets clearly originated in the con-certo grosso of the Handel type, with its little *concertante* group of soloists set against the full orchestra. They may even have been performed in that way, for in some early printed sets of parts, prominent melodies or particularly florid passages are marked *solo*; although eventually the little *concertante* group may have 'hived off', in the imagina-tion of one or two composers, and set up on its own. That there was a recognized distinction between the orchestral and the *concertante* style in writing for four-part strings we learn from the French title page of a set of *Six Quatuors* by Johann Stamitz's son Karl, which are classified as being 'Two for full Orchestra, two *concertante*, and two in which the first parts may be played by a Flute, and Oboe or a Clarinet'. The world of music-making which this title-page conjures up is delightfully varied; but it is a world in which the string quartet, as such, is recognized by nobody.

Certainly it was not the normal, accepted chamber-music combination. That, for Haydn and for his generation, was the trio-sonata as we know it in the work of the great masters of the seventeenth and early eighteenth centuries – two violins, string bass, and harpsichord *continuo*. In his early years, Haydn – who, we should never forget, had one foot in the first half of the eighteenth century – wrote trio-sonatas as a matter of course, in which a keyboard continuo is as necessary as in any by Handel.* And had Haydn composed only indoor music – 'chamber music' in its original and literal sense – he might have remained yoked to this kind of texture, and to the harpsichord. But he was also writing outdoor music: those serenades and divertimenti for which, in eighteenth-century Vienna, any anniversary or festivity provided an excuse, and which often brought the price of a meal to young musicians, like Haydn in the 1750s, living precariously on casual earnings. They were cheerful, loosely-organized little works, usually in at least five movements, with two minuets as a general rule (and often other dance movements as well) and a melodious, florid *cantabile* slow movement which gave the leader a chance to shine as soloist. They were written for whatever instruments were available: violins, violas, wind instruments, a string bass. The one inevitable absentee, in an outdoor and mobile band, was the harpsichord. Thus it

---

* Six of these early trio-sonatas have been published in a modern edition by Peters and, though inferior in breadth to their spacious Italian models, their sense of movement and their sometimes remarkable freedom of form afford a delightful insight into Haydn's immature but vigorous mind.

was that Haydn, from his earliest days, wrote for combinations of instruments *without continuo*: learning (slowly, for his was a slow-moving mind) how to spread harmonic richness through the inner parts to replace the filling-out provided by the *continuo* player; discovering, too, that those parts in combination actually sounded as well, if not better, without the perpetual wash of harpsichord tone colouring the entire background.

OP. 1, 2, 3

IT was, if Haydn's memory can be trusted, an apparently chance series of circumstances that led him to write for a quartet of solo strings: a summer invitation round about 1755 from a Viennese nobleman, Count Fürnberg, who mustered four string players – including young Haydn – for the evening music-making at his country residence. Another composer in his place might well have written elaborate four-part works in the *concertante* style. But to Haydn four string players spelt an orchestra – the small flexible orchestra of his street serenading, with all that this implied: freedom from the harpsichord *continuo*, simplicity of treatment, and a succession of short movements (with dance movements well to the fore), rather than the three movements normal to the chamber sonata at that period: in short, the *divertimento*.

Here, then, is the explanation of Haydn's own classification of his earliest quartets and the key to their character. They are indeed *divertimenti*. The first dozen, those orginally published as Op. 1 and Op. 2, are all in five movements with two minuets apiece,* and – although written for solo strings – conceived in terms of a very small orchestra. The

---

* Opus numbers in the eighteenth century were merely publishers' groupings. The original 'Op. 1, No. 1', was the little five-movement quartet in E flat discovered in 1931 by Marion Scott; in later editions it was replaced by the present Op. 1, No. 5, in three movements, which is really a displaced symphony.

cello line is mainly 'foundation-bass', and the viola frequently crosses it, as if Haydn were unconsciously reckon-
ing on a phantom double-bass an octave lower. Indeed, so
fluid was the line of demarcation in the middle of the
century between chamber works and works for the orchestra that, when the Op. 2 set was brought out in Paris, the
publishers gave it the title *Six Sinfonies ou Quatuors Dialogués*
and two of them even had horn parts added – which
probably represent Haydn's original version. It is the
measure of Haydn's real achievement in 'making' the
string quartet that, starting with this *divertimento*-like conception of the quartet of strings, he should have realized
that it had other and profounder potentialities, and brought
them to fruition.

That, however, lies still in the future. What concerns us
now is the nature of these little *divertimento*-quartets and
what, for Haydn, resulted from their being rooted in the
divertimento rather than in the *concerto grosso* or the trio-
sonata. The first thing is simplicity. He starts with spare,
simple lines – almost bald at times; and thus, his growth is
not hampered by complexities; he has not to prune them –
only to let them flower. Notable here is the bold, effective
harmony which he creates by writing in two parts doubled
at the octave – usually between the upper and lower
strings. This is a type of scoring eminently suitable for outdoor serenades; we find it in the minuet of that best-known
of all serenades, Mozart's *Eine Kleine Nachtmusik*, and it
occurs repeatedly in the minuets of Haydn's early quartets.
This two-part harmony is something that to the end of his
life Haydn never ceased to use – but transmuted by his
greater experience and sensitivity into a texture of the utmost refinement: compare its first appearance, in the second
minuet of Op. 1, No. 3, in D, and a mature example from
the wonderful *Largo* of the E Flat Quartet, Op. 33, No. 2,
written over twenty years later.

Even from the outset, these simple textures are used with
astonishing skill and with an unfailing instinct – mostly
lacking in other composers who wrote quartets of the orches-

tral type – that each part must have something to say. Indeed, the French publisher's term, *quatuors dialogués*, is extraordinarily apt. The present Op. 1, No. 1, in B flat is full of such dialogue – the two-part harmony of the second minuet, the gentle answering phrases between upper and lower strings in the trio of the first, while in the last movement there is a brisk exchange of repartee between the first violin and the lower strings, and between middle and outer voices. Rudimentary though it all is, there is movement, vivacity, and variety in this and in all the other works of these two sets, and – save in the slow movements, which are mostly elaborate violin solos of the opera-aria type – there is no relapsing into mere accompaniment for anyone.

Then as regards general design, it was through the *divertimento* that the minuet was planted fairly and squarely among Haydn's quartets long before it was a regularly accepted part of the symphony. And this has a twofold importance. Firstly, and of more immediate significance, it is in the minuet that Haydn's own personality and originality first reveals itself. The other movements, for all their vivacity, tend to speak in clichés. But the minuets leave us in no doubt that here is a composer with a fresh and inexhaustible flow of melody and a vividly imaginative ear for tone colour. Compare the bold, sweeping melody of the second Minuet of Op. 1, No. 3 (Ex. 1 (*a*) above) with its ghostly, tiptoe Trio in the minor: an idea carried out, with fresh applications in detail, in the Trios of both Minuets of

Op. 2, No. 2. And the little G minor canonic Trio in the
second Minuet of Op. 1, No. 4, anticipates the famous
'Witches' Minuet' of the great D Minor Quartet, Op. 76,
No. 2, by a good forty years.

The contemporary habit of using a different key for the
trio likewise appealed to his strong, albeit immature, sense
of key contrast: in over three-quarters of these early minuets
the trios are either in the minor or in fresh major keys. But
more far-reaching in its ultimate effect is the fact that Haydn
now has within his grasp two distinct traditions with regard
to the character of the minuet and its actual speed. In the
middle of the eighteenth century, when these first quartets
were being written, the minuet was the slow, stately court
dance with which we are familiar. But that was a recent
development, for only half a century before, in 1703, the
Abbé Brossard, in his musical dictionary, described the
minuet as 'very gay and very fast'. That this earlier tradition survived, and left its impact on Haydn, we have irrefut-
able evidence in the minuets which he wrote for various
musical clocks. In these, the relative playing-speeds are
fixed by the movement of the clock, and they show that
Haydn recognized two distinct minuet tempi – that of the
dignified dance with its beat subdivided into flowing
quavers or ornamental figures, and an altogether swifter
type moving on a crotchet beat throughout. And it was this
fast-moving minuet which Haydn, giving it a further turn

of speed, was to bring to the very boundary of the one-in-a-
bar *scherzo* which Beethoven was to claim as his heritage.
That, too, lies forty years ahead. But even in these earliest
quartets both types of minuet appear: witness the following
passages from the first and second minuets of Op. 2, No. 4.

As regards the structure of its outer movements, the
divertimento stood in the same line of development – and
at about the same stage – as the symphony of this period,
that of Haydn's immediate predecessors. The ground plan
which we know as 'first-movement form' (though applicable
also to finales or even slow movements) was already there:
that in which the movement falls into two sections of unequal length, the first moving away from its home key to a
fresh key centre, established by a fresh theme or group of
themes, the second and longer section working its way back
(through various expansions and key changes based on
existing material, and thus called the 'development') towards the home key, in which it completes the pattern by
recapitulating the first section, with such minor modifications as are needed to keep it in the home key throughout.
But that is a mere pattern. There is no drama about it. And
this was the vitalizing element that Haydn brought to the
existing inert mass. It is not for nothing that just before
these quartets were written his street serenading of an
actor-manager's wife had brought him his first stage job –
that of writing incidental music for a show which was a
cross between pantomime and music-hall. To his already
shrewd ear for dialogue this must have brought a sense of
pace, of effect, of how to build up and release a climax.
Add to this an inveterately mechanical, structural mind,
always eager to discover and try out the properties and

workings of anything, from a musical theme to Sir George Herschel's famous telescope at Windsor, and the result is a combination of qualities capable, even now, of imparting energy and movement to the most rudimentary musical shape, the most insignificant scraps of melody.

Haydn's progress thus far, both as regards structure and as regards his treatment of the string quartet as such, is summed up in the little Quartet in F, Op. 3, No. 5. Its date is uncertain but it probably belongs to the early 1760s. The famous 'Serenade' slow movement is a direct legacy from the divertimento, though the Op. 3 set as a whole has moved away from its origins by reducing the number of movements and by dropping the second minuet.* There is nothing in the F Major Quartet that could not be played by a string orchestra. Yet from the outset it shows a nice sense of texture and of fun, in the debate between the first violin and lower strings as to how the first phrase really ought to go, and the long melodious group of 'second subjects' in C

major, with its varying tone colours and groupings, gives each instrument something interesting to say. But the real test comes with the development section. What will Haydn do with his themes – merely let them wander through different keys, repeating themselves, but generating no fresh ideas, no tension? And will the return to the home key and the first subject be purely mechanical, or will it give any real sense of home-coming, of expectation first aroused, then fulfilled? The opening moves are somewhat conventional, merely continuing the debate on the first subject, first in C major, then in D minor, and ending, inconclusively but still conventionally, on a reiterated half-cadence. But the rhythm of this generates a fresh passage, new, yet

* Op. 3, No. 4, is a curious work in two movements only.

growing organically out of it, which builds up a real
moment of tension by its shifting keys and overlapping
entries, until at last it stands poised on the threshold of the
original key, F, with C, its dominant, pulsing expectantly
on the second violin. But it is F minor, not F major, that
is being suggested by the plaintive A flats of the first violin,
and it is not until the cello, with a sudden gesture of deci-
sion, plunges down on to the A natural that restores the
major, that we know that we have arrived home. Most
felicitous touch of all, the first violin has now been keyed to
such a pitch of expectancy that it strikes up before the cello
has finished – of course, with yet another suggestion as to
how the first subject ought to go. It is all very slight, and on

the smallest scale; yet everything that the classical first
movement should have – whether of symphony, sonata, or
string quartet – is there in embryo. In the 'Serenade' slow
movement, charming as it is with its muted tone and *pizzicato* accompaniment, the lower strings have a monotonous
time of it; but the minuet deftly groups and regroups all
four instruments, and the trio, in its characteristically contrasting key, B flat, makes an effective return to the style of
the Serenade. The tiny *scherzando* last movement stands
furthest from the rich and varied subtlety of Haydn's latest
finales. The tradition of the period in symphony and

divertimento was for fast-moving, feather-weight finales,
and it took another twenty years of exploration and
achievement to make possible such miracles as Mozart and
Haydn wrought in the last movements of the 'Jupiter' and
'Drumroll' Symphonies and in those of their mature quartets.

OP. 9, 17

A NEW phase in Haydn's development – one which, like
the first, comprises eighteen quartets – opens with the publication of the Op. 9 set in 1769, followed by Op. 17, of
which the autograph is dated 1771, and culminating in
1772 with the six quartets of Op. 20. Whether the gap which
separates the first phase from the second be short or long
in time, it is startlingly wide in quality and maturity. From
the opening bars of Op. 9, No. 1, we are in another world –
unmistakably the world of the solo quartet. They move at a
deliberate pace: *Moderato* is used for the first time, in the
first movement of Op. 9, No. 1, and repeatedly in its com-
panions – as against the *presto* and *allegro molto* first movements of the *divertimento*-quartets – giving room for the
parts to breathe, expand, and flower in that delicate figuration characteristic of solo stringed intruments. It is a transformation of the entire texture, as sudden as it is complete.

It is not, however, wholly unaccountable. Haydn had by
now achieved the goal of a struggling young musician's
hopes, a permanent post, and from 1761 onwards his master
was Prince Nicholas Esterházy, who, besides maintaining a
small but excellent orchestra, was himself a performer. His
instrument, the baryton, was a kind of *viola da gamba* with
metal strings at the back of the neck (in addition to the
normal bowed gut strings), which could either be plucked
or left to vibrate sympathetically; and Haydn, as part of
his duties, composed no fewer than 126 trios for baryton,
viola, and cello. We are tempted to regret that Haydn
should have been obliged to lavish on this already obsoles-
cent instrument time and energy which from our point of
view could have been more profitably spent. There could

be no greater mistake. The composition of the baryton trios gave him invaluable practice in writing free and independent parts for three solo players (no orchestral alternative was conceivable here, and no phantom double-bass), still without harpsichord (for the baryton's plucked strings supplied any chords required) and of which, now, the bass was carried by the cello. Now at last his imagination learned to release the cello from a mere foundation-bass line and let it sing in its tenor register, accompanied, guitar-wise, on the metal strings of the baryton; so that gradually the bass line itself becomes a true cello line, flexible and mobile.*

But this new-found sense of the individual potentialities of his solo stringed instruments had its dangers. With the quartets of Op. 9 and Op. 17 Haydn swings over perilously towards the *concertante* type of quartet in the florid writing for all four instruments, especially the first violin: perhaps the technique and youthful fire of young Luigi Tomasini, his leading violinist in the Esterházy orchestra, provided an additional temptation. Fortunately that powerful structural sense which was Haydn's backbone as a musician never deserted him, and we see him offsetting his new and luxuriant lyricism by a growing compactness and concentration of general design, with the recapitulation sections in both first and last movements often sharply condensed. Moreover we now find him, with ever-growing frequency, reaching out towards a contrapuntal style and texture, as if he knew – whether by instinct or reason – that in it lay an essential corrective to the expansive floridity of the individual parts: that it was, indeed, the element that would give his part-writing that unity and cohesion without which four *concertante* soloists could never become a string quartet.

* A few of the baryton trios have come down to us in arrangements for other instruments. The early F Major Trio, No. 11, of Haydn's own thematic list – in which the cello is still a pure foundation-bass – has been arranged by Walter Bergmann for recorder, violin and cello (published by Schott), and there is an arrangement by Sandberger (Collection Litolff) of a later group, Nos. 74–76, of which No. 74, with its singularly beautiful *Adagio*, has been recorded in the *Anthologie Sonore*.

The very fact that it is harder to choose a representative quartet to sum up this phase is itself the measure of the distance covered. Each work now has its own individual personality. But the F Major, Op. 17, No. 2 – especially when compared with the earlier F Major, Op. 3, No. 5 – reveals both the progress made and the possible dangers ahead. In the first movement, the ample, unfolding line of the first-violin melody, with its echoes in the lower strings (in marked contrast with the crisp repartee of the corresponding phrases in the earlier work), shows both the new spaciousness and Haydn's instinctive love of irregularity and odd phrase-lengths: here is the five-bar strain with which he answers and expands the initial four-bar sentence:

Ex.6

The music, flowing without break from the same material, moves towards C major, and here the second group of subjects as it unfolds, again spaciously and at leisure, reveals the concerto-soloist idea looming near the foreground:

Ex.6ª

(Compare the double-stopping in the first violin at the same point in the no less leisurely and spacious G Major Quartet, Op. 17, No. 5). In the development the *concertante* element spreads to the lower instruments: but, significantly, the passage is one of contrapuntal imitation which is also a very real development of the initial figure (*a*) of Ex. 6:

Ex. 7

Here we catch Haydn in the very act of disciplining his too exuberant individual parts and relating them to the organic growth of the movement. His growing urge towards terseness and concentration is also shown in the skill with which, in the recapitulation, he cuts out the previous transitional material and lets the first theme, unfolding in the shadow of its own tonic minor, flow straight into the *concertante* second-subject group. The minuet shows another aspect of his preoccupation with counterpoint: that art of combining independent melodic lines so as to make sense as harmony, which – as a living language and not as a mere training in musical gymnastics – has its roots in unaccompanied vocal music. His urge towards contrapuntal linedrawing, therefore, not merely gave cohesion to his partwriting, but counteracted its purely instrumental exuberance, bringing to it an almost vocal simplicity and purity: a tendency which will only deepen and intensify as his string quartet style reaches its full stature. Here we see the bold 'orchestral' two-part writing of his *divertimento* quartets melting imperceptibly into four 'vocal' parts:

Ex. 8

(Compare too the wonderful little E Minor Trio in the
minuet of the E Major Quartet, No. 1 of the set, which, but
for its range, might almost be sung like a motet by a four-
part choir.) The *Adagio* once more explores purely instrumental resources in the *cantabile* of the first violin and in the
deliberate exploitation of its tone-qualities by directing
certain passages to be played *sopra una corda* (on one string
only); the accompanying figuration, however, is of less
interest than that of the beautiful D minor *Siciliano* slow
movement of the E Major Quartet, with its delicate filigree
tracery.

With the Op. 9 and Op. 17 quartets Haydn begins to include in every set a work in the minor mode: a practice
which coincides with that sudden, mysterious tapping of the
underground springs of power and passion which, in the
five years between 1767 and 1772, completed the evolution
of the quiet, intelligent, competent *Kapellmeister* into the
profoundly original genius which was Haydn at forty. The
fiery unrest of the symphonies in F minor (*La Passione*), G
minor (No. 39) and E minor (No. 44) leaps out in the first
movement of the D Minor Quartet Op. 9, No. 4, and still
more in the broken phrases and minor cadences of its
Minuet. Even more characteristic of this facet of Haydn's
late but swift maturing is the C Minor Quartet, Op. 17, No.
4, for here the thinker and architect in him reinforces
passion as the initial rising phrase of the first movement is
used as a pivot to swing the music towards different keys at
crucial points in the movement:

It is again very *concertante* in style – at one point in the slow
movement the cello proclaims its emancipation in a long

florid passage; but it is significant that contrapuntal auster-
ity has the upper hand in the final movement (as also in the
D minor quartet of Op. 9), despite the upthrust of solo
technique in the double-stopping of the warm-toned
second subject.

OP. 20

BUT even such a transformation as is represented by the
quartets of Op. 9 and Op. 17 hardly prepares us for the
miracle of the next set, Op. 20, composed in the following
year (1772). It is a threefold miracle. Here at last is the
string quartet fully in being as a living entity. The *concertante* style has brought release, counterpoint has given cohesion and strength, to the individual parts; but now there
is added a sudden realization of the character and tone
quality of string quartet texture as such – coupled, paradoxically, with a far keener awareness of the essential personality of each instrument. Structurally, Haydn now
shows a far stronger grasp of general design and of the potentialities of development latent in individual themes. And, in
the last resort, it is his own musical personality which these
developments manifest, and which now stands before us in
its full stature. The sheer range of mood and temper alone
is startling: fire and grandeur in the C major, No. 2, noble
gravity succeeded by hilarious spirits in No. 4 in D major,
light-hearted grace in the A major, No. 6; even the two in
the minor differ in personality, the G minor (No. 3)
brusquer and more angular, the F minor (No. 5) touched
with profound and poignant disquiet. If, then, the Quartet
in E flat No. 1 of the set is singled out for special attention,
it is not merely that it shows to perfection yet another phase
of the evolution of the string quartet, and of Haydn's
powers of thematic development, from his earlier style. It
is also because, in its quiet and intimate warmth of melody,
harmony, and colouring, it lies nearest to the heart of his
personality. In the C Major Quartet there are touches prophetic of Beethoven; the F minor might, conceivably, have

been written by Mozart. The E Flat Quartet could have been composed by Haydn alone.

At the beginning of the first movement the part-writing is translucent, almost vocal in its smooth flow – until suddenly the cello line breaks upwards, on a little bubbling *arpeggio* phrase, to rejoin the harmony in its tenor register, and we know (as Tovey observed) that Haydn now understands the cello and its part in the string quartet with his ear and his imagination as well as with his mind:

The transition towards the new key, B flat, is no mere perfunctory 'bridge-passage', but a further unfolding of the same material, and the touch of *concertante* passage-work with which the first violin launches the second group of themes (11a) is absorbed into the flow of the melody and

caught up and shared among all four instruments in the
ensuing dialogue (11*b*):

The development makes use of a formal device which he
was later to discard: a 'false return', near the start, to the
opening key and theme, as if the recapitulation were about
to begin there and then. But from this point true development begins, and the apparently unpromising *concertante*
figure from Ex. 11 gains new point and purpose in dialogue
between cello and first violin. And in the recapitulation
Haydn shows that his 'first-movement form' is no formal
mould but a living organism, as he cuts out the repetition of
the *concertante* figure (already sufficiently stressed in the
development) and moves straight into the heart of his
second group by new and warm-toned variants of his main
theme and transition almost amounting to a fresh development.

The peculiar charm of the Minuet lies in its Trio, in
which the freshness and grace of the first violin's gentle
descent to meet the slowly ascending harmonies in second
violin and cello is enhanced by its change of key – a device
carried forward from early days but here used with heightened imagination.

With the third movement we are led beside still waters –
so still that we hardly realize their depth. Its flow – with
barely a ripple on the surface of the first violin line – is so
unbroken that we are conscious of no divisions, only of a
single unflawed and crystalline unity; yet in its motion it
traces a complete sonata-form course, subtle, and free – the
undercurrent of strength beneath its serene quietness.

Moreover, its translucency is intensified by the actual disposition of the parts, so spaced as to secure the utmost richness, depth, and clarity of sound. In the Finale, odd three-
bar phrase-lengths, persistent syncopations, a dash of
contrapuntal imitation and a haunting passage of shifting
keys just before the return to the main theme combine to
make a wholly individual movement which Haydn may
have equalled and excelled, but never repeated. It is characteristic of this most reticent of masterpieces that its Finale
ends *pianissimo*.

But if the E Flat Quartet thus embodies the essence of
Haydn, humanly and musically, the F minor, No. 5, represents a vital element in his personality, and shows no less
clearly how his new-found grasp of both texture and structure are placed at the service of emotion. It is wonderful to
watch how, in the first movement, emotion is intensified by
purely musical means: how, after his major-mode second
subject has returned in the minor in the recapitulation –
with a pathos prophetic of Mozart at his most poignant
when he uses the same resource – he further develops and
intensifies this theme, and finally adds a coda which, by
plunging it into the darkness of remote keys, adds a new
mystery to its shadowed sorrow. The same shadow falls
across the minuet, so that the tender radiance of the F major
Adagio brings a relief all the more exquisite for following
on two such sombre movements. After this lyrical flowering
the last movement brings something of a shock: for it is
headed, austerely, *Fuga a due soggetti*, and the first of these
fugue subjects is that well-worn contrapuntal formula of the
first half of the century on which Handel bases the chorus
'And with His stripes' in *Messiah*. No less than four quartets
out of the six have contrapuntal finales – three of them set
fugues – as if Haydn felt that he still needed the chastening
discipline of fugal texture to bring to his quartet-writing an
even closer unity and a still fairer distribution of interest
between the parts. But their historical importance, as Tovey
points out, transcended the immediate technical achievement, in that they 'effectively establish fugue texture from

henceforth as a normal resource of sonata style'. Indeed, the
influence of this set on the whole subsequent development
of chamber music remains unsurpassed. It is registered, as
if by a sensitive seismograph, in the sharp contrast between
the quartets written by Mozart – then aged seventeen – in
Milan in January 1773 and the set of six written in Vienna
in the late summer of the same year – not only in the two
fugal finales and the curiously powerful contrapuntal
Andante of the C Minor Quartet K. 171, but in the way in
which the part-writing throughout ceases to be orchestral
and becomes alive and individual. After the publication of
the Op. 20 quartets the string quartet, whether in Haydn's
hands or in anyone else's, could never be the same again.

Now comes the strangest thing in the whole story – that
after this achievement Haydn wrote no more string quartets
for nine years. No one knows why. It may have been sheer
pressure of routine work, the ebb-tide of creative vitality
after the great wave had broken in 1772. Possibly a sound
instinct told him that he had not even yet achieved complete mastery of string quartet texture: that such overt use
of fugal devices was too obvious, too contrived. It is perhaps
illuminating that Mozart should have turned away from
the string quartet for precisely the same period.

OP. 33, 50

IT was not, then, until 1781 that Haydn's next set of quartets appeared – those of Op. 33, dedicated to the Grand
Duke Paul of Russia, and therefore sometimes known as the
'Russian' Quartets. With this set Haydn, on the verge of
fifty, passes from the late spring to the high summer of his
powers. He himself described the set, in a circular letter to
subscribers, as being written in 'an entirely new and special
manner'. This remark – probably intended mainly as a
good selling-point – does an injustice to his earlier achievement, for there is nothing in these quartets that is not at
least implicit in those of Op. 20; even the designation
Scherzo or *Scherzando* attached to the minuets of this set,

suggestive though it is, means at this stage merely that he
has laid the emphasis on the more swift-moving of the two
distinct minuet-types found in his quartets from the outset
– though in one instance, the dark and tender *Scherzando* of
the 'Bird' Quartet in C major, No. 3 of the set, the result is
neither minuet nor *scherzo*, but a unique miracle.

Yet if there is nothing inherently 'new' about the Op. 33
quartets, there is indeed something 'special'. The unified
texture which, in the Op. 20 quartets, still involved the
deliberate concentration and struggle of the contrapuntal
finales, is now an effortless achievement. It is not merely
that the part-writing has taken on a new ease, fluency and
grace; it is rather that texture has become one with organic
structure, as the development of the themes takes possession
of the entire fabric. As Alfred Einstein sums it up, in his
great book on Mozart, 'it is no longer in the development
section that the "working-out" takes place; from now on the
smallest motive, the faintest hint of a rhythm, is significant.'

If this is true of the best known of the set, the entrancing
'Bird' Quartet, it is true to an even greater extent of the first
two – No. 1 in B minor and No. 2 in E flat. Sharply contrasting as these quartets are in personality – the B minor
summing up the pungent ironist in Haydn as the E flat
reflects the quiet, meditative gaze of its sister work, Op. 20,
No. 1 – in the first movements of both works the texture is
something to marvel at: woven with the closest consistency
from the initial theme, each instrument fully engaged, yet
of the utmost clarity and fineness. Small wonder that to
Mozart, who had come to live in Vienna that same year,
they were a fresh revelation, challenging him, too, to return
to the string quartet, and calling forth from him, over the
next four years, the six great quartets which he dedicated to
Haydn. The miraculous unity, of texture and subject-
matter alike, which Mozart achieves in the first movements
of the A major and C major quartets, K. 464 and 465, even
surpasses that achieved by Haydn in the quartets of the
Op. 33 series; yet without them it could never have been
attained.

For Haydn, from now on, texture holds no problems, and he is free to concentrate on those of structure and design. The results are immediately apparent. Whereas his instinct was formerly towards terseness, he now begins to expand. It is in the first movements of the last three quartets of Op. 33 – markedly light in temper, as if he had turned down the emotional current in order to work out a technical problem at his ease – that this new expansiveness appears; their recapitulations, instead of being sharply telescoped, grow outwards in fresh contours and with new changes of key and further developments of the main themes. From now on, the recapitulations of his sonata-form movements become increasingly varied and unconventional; the freedom shown in the symphonies from 1788 onwards (particularly the 'Oxford' Symphony and the two London sets) is already attained in the quartets. Simultaneously he becomes more keenly alive to the possibilities of the 'monothematic' movement, that is, one entirely evolved from a single theme – which, in the case of a sonata-form movement, means that the second group of subjects is either derived entirely from the first subject or at least contains a variant of it. Such a design necessarily goes in hand with freedom in recapitulation, if monotony is to be avoided. Movements of this kind are sometimes regarded as inferior in inventiveness to those with contrasting first and second subjects; yet many of Haydn's richest and most dramatic movements are monothematic, as if the act of seeing all the implications of a single basic idea called forth the best of his powers. It is no coincidence that of the Op. 50 set of quartets, dedicated to the King of Prussia, which followed close upon the 'Russian' Quartets, the finest are those which most strongly emphasize this monothematic principle, both in first movements and finales. The D Major Quartet, Op. 50, No. 6, shows Haydn at the height of this new-found freedom and mastery. The splendid monothematic unity of the first movement can best be illustrated by quotation of its main theme at successive stages of its evolution.

(*a*) shows it on its first appearance, (*b*) in the fresh variant of its rhythm into which it expands; at (*c*) it is on the threshold of A major and the second-subject group, and at (*d*) it breaks into the second group and slews it sharply round on to the remote, flat key of F. The entire development grows from these variants on a single theme: here is a passage which also shows that he can wield dissonance with a fearless hand.

So, too, does the D minor *Adagio*, in which, at the beginning of the second section, just after the double bar, he once more shows his love of dropping suddenly into a remote key (often, as here, that on the flattened sixth of the scale, F major to D flat) with an effect of vast depth and distance. This is a resource which he uses increasingly to the end of his life, and with a growing sureness of touch and vision.

The Quartet in E Flat, No. 3, is no less closely mono-thematic, in both its first and last movements, and even more subtly and allusively constructed. Its second movement, *Andante più tosto allegretto*, is a twofold achievement. Here counterpoint, no longer conscious of itself, is transmuted into an exquisite purity and definition of line, whether in the two-part harmony of its opening bars or in the delicate tracery and chromatic nuances of harmony into which it flowers as the movement progresses. But the movement is also a set of variations. Now Haydn and Mozart both wrote many movements in the form of variations, of which the majority are of the type in which the melody is embroidered with fresh decorative detail, or rescored for different instrumental groupings, without varying the general outline or the harmonic substructure; a type which, when untouched with the breath of imagination, can become merely mechanical, as Haydn's are apt to become in his more routine movements. Yet it was also in his variations that he frequently gave of his best, and his strongly creative sense of design led him to enrich the variation form with new shapes and new applications of its basic principles. Oddly enough, that most far-reaching of his inventions, the idea of double variations on alternating themes, is only represented twice among his quartets (one example is found in the F Sharp Minor Quartet, No. 4 of this series); its finest development is found in the symphonies and keyboard works. But he also evolved another type, that in which the single minor-mode variation is so free in relation to the theme that it is more like a first-movement development than a variation in the strict sense; and it is this type that is represented here, the minor variation being entirely a free development of the initial descending phrase of the theme. Ex. 14a below is the original theme on its second repetition (in the cello as at the outset, but with a fresh counter-melody in the first violin); Ex. 14b is the corresponding four bars in the minor variation:

Ex.14
Andante più tosto allegretto

(a)

Viola *fz*

Ex. 14

The tiny coda, evolved from this falling phrase, with which Haydn rounds off the movement is a final touch of sheer poetry.

He is still ready to display his contrapuntal muscles when such a demonstration will add to the strength of the movement as a whole: one such instance occurs in the recapitulation of the highly concentrated first movement of the C Major Quartet, No. 2, in which he replaces the original transition by an expansion of his first subject, in canon (Ex. 15*a*), tiptoeing upwards to encounter its own inversion, descending, and also in canon (15*b*).

And No. 4 in F Sharp Minor appears to revert to the Op. 20 manner by having a fugue for its last movement. But this tragic utterance is less rigidly contrapuntal than the earlier fugues, and yet, by a paradox, more concentrated, in that the pregnant initial figure is not only reiterated, but developed; here fugal texture and the monothematic type of sonata-form development have indeed fused and become one.

To this period belongs the isolated Quartet in D Minor (the autograph dated 1785), deceptive in its brevity and simplicity; its *Adagio*, unfolding entirely from a single lyrical curve of melody, touches that core of quietness which, in Haydn, lies 'at the still point of the turning world'.* Marion Scott has suggested that the quartet may have been written for a special group of amateurs – perhaps very young people. To the same period also belongs the arrangement for string quartet which Haydn made of *The Seven Words of Our Saviour on the Cross*, originally a series of orchestral interludes written to be performed during a Good Friday three-hour service. By arranging them for string quartet Haydn brought these beautiful and lovingly-wrought meditations within the range of a far wider circle both of players and listeners.

OP. 54, 55, 64

THE next twelve quartets are definitely 'made to measure'. They are dedicated to Johann Tost, a wealthy wholesale merchant who – there is evidence to suggest – had been a professional violinist before he turned to a more lucrative line of business. The 'Tost' Quartets – those of Op. 54 and 55, three to a set, and the six of Op. 64 – are thus characterized by the brilliance and prominence of the first violin part, sometimes even carried to excess to the detriment of true quartet-writing. It is even possible to feel, in this brilliant procession, a sameness of mood, a certain lack of mystery and shadow beneath the summer afternoon skies. But if the mood is 'set fair' there is endless variety of design, combined with the closest thematic unity. No text-book account of 'sonata form' could begin to cover the range and freedom and the inner logic of his recapitulations; nor is one movement ever a pattern for the next. The slow movements resemble each other more closely in design, and tend towards lyricism and simplicity, being for the most part either variations or built on simple ternary or even rondo lines. Yet here, too, by a momentary deepening of expression, or with one of his sudden startling uprushes of originality, Haydn repeatedly shakes himself clear of routine.

* It is unfortunate that in a recent recording, the even flow is broken by playing *acciaccaturas* instead of *appoggiaturas* throughout, with a 'Scotch Snap' effect utterly alien to the character of the movement.

There is nothing in all his quartets which remotely resembles the slow movement of the C Major, Op. 54, No. 2, in which the wild arabesques of the first violin, so far from being a mere display of virtuosity, are part of the essential nature of the passionate Hungarian lament that this movement is. And the two minor-mode works, the F Minor, Op. 55, No. 2, and the B Minor, Op. 64, No. 2, are probably neglected precisely because their pungency places them outside the range of expression regarded as representative of Haydn by our 'type-casting' habits of mind.

The last two quartets of the 'Tost' series, Op. 64, No. 5 ('The Lark') and that in E flat, No. 6, are a fitting crown to this 'high summer' phase of Haydn's creative life, for they not only represent his strength of form at its most free, spontaneous and creative, but also stand out above the others with a certain heightened radiance of sheer melodic loveliness. No one, in the 'Lark' Quartet, could begrudge the first violin his singing, soaring solo melody, and the moment when it returns at the beginning of the recapitulation brings all the delight of fulfilled expectation. But the rich new expansion of the second subject which follows is a wholly unexpected development, and its climax is succeeded by the most surprising stroke of all, as the first subject sails calmly in once more and starts a brand-new, and this time closely condensed, recapitulation. The effect of spontaneity and spaciousness combined with close unity thus achieved is unique; Haydn never wrote another movement like it. Another sort of unity is displayed by the brilliant little finale, a *perpetuum mobile* of scampering semiquavers, running into a flying *fugato* in the middle section and out again without once stopping to draw breath. The first movement of the E Flat Quartet, No. 6 – calmer and more intimate, like all Haydn's quartets in that key – unfolds in a wonderfully integrated monothematic pattern, again with a subtly free recapitulation. But the glory of this quartet is its *Andante*, unfolding serenely in upward-flowering arpeggios taken up by one instrument after another, with gentle dissonances than only heighten its poised tranquillity:

Ex.16

Yet even now, beneath the surface, there were deeper springs still awaiting release, as there had been twenty years before. This time it came about through external events. The death of Prince Nicholas Esterházy, Salomon's offer of a London concert season, and the two visits to England which resulted from it, broke the pattern on which Haydn's life had been shaped for over a quarter of a century and laid him open, at sixty, to the shock and stimulus of new impressions and new demands. The act of responding to these fresh stimuli broke open within him unspent reserves of vitality, and brought him not only the autumn harvest of his last twelve creative years – 1791 to 1802 – but also the strength to gather it in.

THE PIANO TRIOS

NONE of the fourteen string quartets of this final period was actually written in England. The six of Op. 71 and Op. 74 were composed in 1793, between the two English visits; the last eight, those of Op. 76 and Op. 77, fall between 1797 and 1799, and thus represent a later phase of his maturity than even the latest of the London symphonies, the last of which were composed in 1795. But there is an aspect of his chamber music in which England may claim her share, and which is rarely treated as it deserves: the Trios for piano, violin, and cello.

These have nothing in common with the early 'Trio-Sonatas' for two violins and string bass with harpsichord. In these, the keyboard merely supplied the *continuo* from the figured bass line; in piano trios of the period, on the other hand (definitely designed for clavichord or for the rapidly developing 'Forte Piano' rather than the harpsichord), the keyboard part is the most highly evolved. In some composers there is a real equality and interplay between piano and stringed instruments – the tradition inherited by Mozart and Beethoven. But the prevailing conception, in the latter half of the eighteenth century, was that of a kind of piano sonata with accompanying parts for violin and cello, essentially intimate and domestic in character, as the piano was pre-eminently a woman's instrument. This is the conception represented by Haydn, in whose piano trios violin and cello rarely attain more than a fleeting independence of the keyboard. They are thus neglected by string players, who find their parts insufficiently interesting; and this is a tragedy, for they contain some of the loveliest music Haydn ever wrote.

They are nearly all mature works, falling between 1780 and 1800; but of the total of thirty-one, fifteen were written after 1790, that is, in his last and greatest phase, and of these, six were composed in England – the first six of the Peters' Edition, which is not chronologically arranged. In keeping with their intimate character, even these latest works contain a higher proportion of movements – even first movements – which are not in sonata-form, but are more lyrical and more simply organized; either variations, or rondos, or simple ternary ABA form. Colour and drama are provided by his frequent choice of remote keys for his middle movements, or by sudden changes of key in the course of a movement. Thus in the G Major Trio, No. 1 * (familiar on the strength of its 'Gipsy Rondo' finale), the first movement is a curious but charming blend of double-variation and rondo, for the two minor sections are extremely free in their connexion either with the major main theme or with each other. The tender and tranquil No. 5 in E flat, likewise, has a song-like ternary first movement, with a minor variant for its middle section, in which the violin achieves some independent dialogue with the keyboard. Both works have slow movements in remote keys:

* The numerical references are to the Peters' Edition.

the gentle *Poco adagio* of No. 1 moves to E major, on the sharp, bright side of G, while that of the E flat drops to the flat sixth – though written as B major, not C flat. Another beautiful and subtly chromatic double-variation first movement is found in the G Minor Trio, No. 17, of which the *Adagio*, in E flat, is on a level with the greatest slow movements of its period. No. 18 in E flat minor, an even later work, is again a cross between rondo and double variations, in which the major *alternativo* starts as a beautifully free inversion of the minor theme:

But amid all this intimate lyricism there are some superbly organized movements of noble stature. In the C Major, No. 3 (one of the few written for a professional pianist), the outer movements, with their brilliantly free sonata-form structure, suggest the youthful Beethoven in their breadth and fiery impetus. The first movement of No. 2 in F sharp minor is hardly less brilliant, and the *Adagio cantabile* is the first version of the slow movement of the Symphony in B Flat, No. 102, and bears something of the same relation to it as one of Constable's water-colour sketches to the finished painting. And among the very finest stands No. 6 in D, for its strong and splendidly designed monothematic first movement is the continuous unfolding of a theme which in itself is one of Haydn's loveliest inspirations:

OP. 71, 74

THERE are two distinctive features about the first six quartets belonging to this final decade. In each quartet of Op. 71 and Op. 74 – and nowhere else among all Haydn's quartets – the first movement is prefaced by a short introduction ranging from a mere chord or sequence of chords establishing the key, to such extended preludes as those in the last two quartets of Op. 74, which are closely linked with the development of the ensuing movement. The other feature, and a very curious one, is that Haydn seems at times to be straining towards an almost orchestral type of sonority. This is something quite different from his primitive treatment of the string quartet as a very small orchestra; here he seems to be trying to graft his experience of a large orchestra – the richness and volume of Salomon's London team was fresh in his mind – on to his mature quartet style, with the result that at times he almost breaks its bounds. This is apparent in the leaping, angular first movement of Op. 71, No. 2 in D – rarely heard, probably because it puts a strain on the players not justified by the result. Even some of the powerful and sonorous effects of the E Flat, F Major, and G Minor Quartets (Op. 71, No. 3, and Op. 74, Nos. 2 and 3) belong almost more to the realm of the orchestra; a tiny instance is the *tremolando* with which in the G Minor Quartet, he tries to enhance the solemnity of the great E major melody of the *Largo* on its repetition:

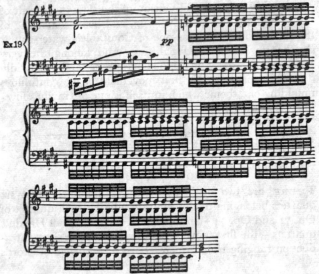

But in the C Major, Op. 74, No. 1, he has achieved what he was seeking; the scoring of the first movement, in particular, has a new and transfigured depth which finds its fulfilment in the sister movement of the great C Major Quartet, No. 3 of Op. 76, and throughout the final series.

OP. 76

WITH the eight final masterpieces composed after the second English visit, between 1797 and 1799, Haydn's creative life reaches its fulfilment. Behind them lie over forty years of deliberate hard work and slow, unconscious growth – the long patience of the husbandman who 'waiteth for the precious fruit of the earth ... until he receive the early and latter rain'. Everything is brought to fruition, both natural endowment and hard-won mastery. Here is the melodic gift that was his from the outset, with all its characteristics merely intensified: the wide span (often moving outside the octave within the first couple of bars), the purposeful sense of direction, the free and irregular phrasing, the love of folk melody so strong that – as with Vaughan Williams – it has become part of his natural language. Here his sense of key relationships, always vivid and dramatic, is used with a profounder awareness of their underlying mystery. And each work is unified by the concentration and cohesion springing from the permeation of every fibre of the texture by a living development of the themes, with the resulting freedom and organic vitality of form. In the truest and most literal sense, these quartets, both humanly and on the plane of sheer musical thought, are 'songs of experience'.

The first of the series, Op. 76, No. 1 in G, is Janus-headed; it looks back towards 1793 in its affinities with the G Minor, Op. 74, No. 3, particularly in the driving rhythm of its Finale, which also begins in the minor, but here the major tonality of the rest of the work sharpens the impact, and in the Finale of the C Major Quartet, Op. 76, No. 3, Haydn puts this discovery to more searching use. There is also a direct line of development from the *Largo* of the G minor to the no less profound and more wonderfully organized *Adagio sostenuto* of this work, and thence to the final splendours of the great slow movement of the G Major Quartet, Op. 77, No. 1. And the so-called Minuet of Op. 76, No. 1, is the first of that handful of movements in these late quartets in which the one-in-a-bar *Scherzo* – towards which the young Beethoven was also moving at this time – is virtually a *fait accompli*:

The first movement of the D Minor Quartet, Op. 76, No. 2, is perhaps the most superb feat of concentrated musical thought in all Haydn's quartets, for the entire fabric rests on the falling fifths of its opening bars. Two quotations must suffice. The first (Ex. 21a) shows the theme, in the viola, acting as bass to a new and important transitional motif leading to F major and the 'second-subject group', in which the falling fifths are still an all-pervasive presence. In the second (Ex. 21b), towards the end of the develop-

ment, we meet a resurgence of this secondary idea springing up after a shift of key from A minor into C major; this is not in itself a particularly remote modulation, but here it is given the effect of a sheer drop into fathomless depths by the long hesitation on the preceding chord (E major, dominant of A minor), by the actual 'false relation' between the viola's G sharp and the violin's G natural as the harmony changes, and by the actual spacing and scoring at the same point, with all four instruments on their lower strings.

In the recapitulation the essence of the first section is miraculously compressed into a smaller space so as to allow room for the expansion of the fiery and uncompromising coda. After such concentration some relief is needed, but the charming little *Andante* which follows has – to borrow an expressive phrase of Tovey's – a 'low specific gravity'; too low for the movements on either side of it, for the Minuet once more borders on the Beethoven *scherzo* – not so much by its speed, but by its hard-bitten humour. It is in fact the famous 'Witches' Minuet', in which Haydn's early habit of octave-doubling and his life-long preoccupation with counterpoint meet and become one, for the entire Minuet is in canon between upper and lower strings. No less gruffly startling (and Beethovenish) is the sudden jerk from re-iterated D minor chords on to D major in the Trio. The finale is in his most brilliant peasant-dance vein, with a dash of Hungarian blood in its syncopations.

The third quartet of Op. 76, in C major, is nicknamed 'The Emperor' because its slow movement is a set of variations on the 'Emperor's Hymn' – that noble melody which Haydn had given to his country as her national anthem. But there is a majesty about the whole work, springing in part from the quality of the scoring; here Haydn achieves an almost symphonic richness of sound within the true chamber idiom, using octaves, double-stopping and the lowest register of the cello with unerring effect. It also springs from the strength and poise and definition of the themes themselves, exemplified in the principal theme of the first movement; 'principal theme' rather than 'first subject', for the entire movement is evolved from its melodic and rhythmic elements. Here is the Protean theme in three successive manifestations: Ex. 22 (*a*) in the daylight clarity of its initial statement; (*b*) as it returns in the second group, the shadows of its remote key deepened by the low-lying register of all four instruments; and (*c*) in the development where, over a massive double drone in cello and viola it is suddenly transformed into a rustic dance,

> Earth feet, loam feet, lifted in country mirth,

moving with all the power of some ancestral memory.

In the variations on the 'Emperor's Hymn' which constitute the slow movement, he departs from his normal variation technique in that the actual tune is not embroidered or varied, but simply sung by each instrument in turn against a background of accompanying melody and harmony. In the third variation, in which the viola has the theme, the harmony takes on a more veiled, chromatic cast, as if for the first time, thus late in life, Haydn had realized the essential nature of the viola, as Mozart did from the outset. The last two movements hinge on major-minor contrasts. The Trio of the Minuet is in A minor, with a sudden lift into A major, which reminds us that Schubert – still a baby when this quartet was written – received a double portion of Haydn's profoundly romantic spirit. In the Finale, serious and powerful, the interplay is between C minor, which (with its attendant flat major keys) prevails over three-quarters of the movement, and the C major into which – at first with a curiously moving hesitancy, as if dazzled by unaccustomed light – it makes its final home-coming.

There could be no sharper contrast than that between the substantial, four-square strength of the C Major Quartet and the first movement of the next in the series, Op. 76, No. 4, in B Flat, ethereal in its fine-drawn lines and its lightness of texture. Yet its inner cohesion is no less wonderful, for the second subject, a dreamlike mirror-image of the first (Ex. 23*a* and *b*), returns, in the recapitulation, in a variant of Mozartian subtlety, in which once again the viola's distinctive voice is used in telling contrast with those of cello and violin. The *Adagio* springs from the same depths as the slow movements of Op. 20, No. 1, and Op. 42. Like the earlier movements, its spiritual concentration is rooted in its musical structure, for it unfolds continuously, along

Ex. 23   *Allegro con spirito*

the entire length of its subtly condensed sonata-form out-line, from its initial figure, until the moment when it reaches its climax of intensity by appearing in *stretto*, and the time-honoured contrapuntal device becomes one with inner vision:

Ex24

The last two movements, though they lower the tension, do so in a wholly satisfying way – the Minuet by its driving energy and the bold peasant-dance sonority of its Trio, the finale with a tune so English in its freshness that Haydn, forgetting his harvest of Croat and Hungarian and Austrian melodies, seems to be wandering in spirit by the side of an unborn Cecil Sharp searching for folk-songs at Strawberry Fair.

The last two works of the Op. 76 set, Nos. 5 in D and 6 in E flat, stand a little apart in that their first movements, instead of being cast in the free yet highly concentrated sonata-form of the first four quartets, are – as far as the actual structure goes – more loosely organized, one being a simple ternary movement on a lyrical melody, the other a set of variations. In both cases, however, there is a kind of extended coda in which the entire movement takes on a new momentum. It is almost as if Haydn, like Beethoven in his last phase, were moving away from the forms he had evolved and used with such mastery towards the other, un-explored potentialities still latent in music.

In the D Major Quartet the simplicity of the opening *Allegretto* is deceptive; for the D minor middle section grows out of the first phrase of the main melody as logically as any sonata-form development, and when, quickening to *Allegro*, the coda suddenly takes wing, we find that it has

caught up in its flight the entire D minor section, of which
it is a further development and transmutation.

The *Largo – cantabile e mesto –* is in F sharp major: a key
which is not only remote and bright in relation to D, but
also difficult to play in, and, for string players, hard to keep
in tune, because of the almost entire absence of open
strings. This, as Haydn well knew, not only affects the actual
tone quality, but also imparts to the players a certain tension, which heightens the emotional concentration of the
music. It achieves, indeed, an intensity of utterance all the
more penetrating for its wide time-span – the time-span not
of a small close-knit figure, but of a calm lyrical melody,
unfolding with all Haydn's characteristic spaciousness of
line. But by the time it has swung gently on its own rhythm
into C sharp major the miraculous sets in, as the initial
figures of both first and second strains of the great melody
are folded upon each other to become a single unity of
theme and counter-theme:

Ex.25

This continues as the shadows of the minor fall across the
music, until, with its emergence into the remote, luminous
region of E major, the first strain embarks alone on the
great, deep sequence of modulations leading back to the
threshold of F sharp once more. Here, and throughout the
movement, viola and cello are juxtaposed with the keenest
sensitiveness to their distinctive tone-qualities. In the Trio
of the Minuet another of the earliest types of movement is
brought to fruition – this time the ghostly minor-mode trios
of the very first sets of quartets. The Finale repeats the
achievement of the 'Drumroll' Symphony by evolving a

close-knit, free, and unorthodox sonata-form movement from a cadence and a scrap of folk-tune.

There is a touch of mystery and enigma about the E Flat Quartet, which is the sixth and last of the set; perhaps that is why it is so rarely heard. The first movement is a set of variations on a theme with a hauntingly powerful aura of Beethoven, both in its short, pregnant phrases and in the spare lines of the variations, in which Haydn adapts the technique he used with the 'Emperor's Hymn' – that of throwing fresh counter-melodies around a practically un-varied theme. In the final variation the first phrase of the theme expands into a full-sized fugue, merging into the return of the final strain, which thus has the effect of a coda. The title 'Fantasia' with which the *Adagio* is headed promises a touch of improvisatory waywardness and an absence of set form; the promise is fulfilled in its absence of key signature – though it opens in B major (the equivalent of C flat, the flat sixth of the main key) – and in its restless wanderings through a chain of distant modulations, until finally it circles back to its home key; here at last it settles down (this time complete with key signature) and calmly begins to unfold in beautiful contrapuntal lines as if it had only now, through this homecoming, realized its true self. The Minuet is on the verge of the one-in-a-bar *scherzo*, and in the wonderful Trio the scale of E flat, descending and ascending, is treated like a theme-and-variations on the same lines as the first movement – itself unvaried, but aureoled with accompanying counter-themes and har-monies. The Finale is a spirited and brilliant sonata-form movement on that free monothematic basis which, for Haydn, now constitutes normal procedure.

OP. 77

OP. 77 (1799) was also planned as a set of six, but Haydn's physical and nervous stamina were no longer equal to his still unspent creative impulse, and the two great works which we possess are all he had the strength to complete. The outer movements of both works are the crowning achievement of Haydn's sonata-form in all its freedom, concentration, and unity, and the so-called Minuets are true one-in-a-bar *scherzos*, each with a Trio dropping into the flat sixth of the home key. In character and in texture, however, they are markedly different, and sum up two distinct tendencies in Haydn's style. No. 1 in G is more chordal and harmonic, and is the culmination of all those quartets in which Haydn accords specially loving and prominent treatment to the first violin. The F Major, on the other hand, brings the final distillation of that crystalline string quartet style in which harmony and part-writing and the actual layout of the instruments are aspects of a single whole.

Not that the lower instruments are hardly treated in the G Major; in the first movement, first violin and cello carry on a running dialogue, with crisply echoing comments from second violin and viola, and the second violin takes its full share in the more lyrically soaring subsidiary theme that appears among the second-subject group and plays so important a part in the development. In the *Adagio*, the great downward curve of the main theme, given out first in unison by all four instruments, is subtly rescored and reharmonized on each reappearance, with viola and cello carrying its weight on equal terms with the first violin, whose delicate *fioriture* are no mere decoration, but a deeply expressive flowering from the parent stem. Here again, remote modulations carry the movement into regions of 'deep but dazzling darkness', both before and after the return of the main theme in the home key. In the Finale, upper and lower strings, in their discussion of the all-pervasive principal theme, bring new meaning to the *quatuor dialogué* idea, which was one strain in the string quartet's ancestry.

From one angle the first movement of the F Major Quartet, Op. 77, No. 2, may be described as 'monothematic', for the same theme serves as both first and second subject: the same, yet miraculously different. Ex. 26*a* below shows it in the clarity and definition of its first appearance, 26*b*, in its deeply-shadowed second-subject variant, veiled by the first violin's new counter-melody.

But the movement is also rich in subsidiary themes, and it is from these that the development mainly springs. The most important of them is the little rhythmic and melodic figure shown (with its counter-theme) at (*a*) below; at (*b*) a few bars are quoted from the swift-moving sequence of modulations to which this figure gives rise.

The gloriously funny *Scherzo* is a triumph of thematic concentration and rhythmic wit, for the source of it all, including the violin's cross-accents and the cello's successful attempt to imitate a pair of kettledrums, is to be found in the first four bars.

Most wonderful of all, after this brilliant instrumental fooling, is the Trio's sudden drop into D flat and serenely vocal *legato*, and the indescribable warmth and tenderness of both melody and inner parts.

If the slow movement of the sister quartet in G is the last of a great line of *Adagios*, in that of the present work all Haydn's *Andantes* and *Allegrettos* are caught up and carried on to a new plane of experience. It evolves as a wonderful blend of rondo and variation form, all growing with complete inevitability from the quiet, persistent melody, given out at first in spare two-part harmony, yet strong enough to carry the weight of development and modulation, rich figuration, and fresh counter-themes. It is only near the end that the tireless tread falls silent, and the music, floating clear of earth, rises, over slowly-shifting harmonies, to its great *cadenza*-like climax – a moment of vision on which the return of the melody in its initial simplicity sets the seal of truth.

The last movement is a 'grand finale' in every sense of the word – a polacca carried out as a monothematic sonata-form movement, with every device of close imitative counterpoint that can add intellectual zest to physical and rhythmic vitality.

Four years later, in 1803, Haydn started to compose another quartet. It would have been in D minor; but he was only able to write the two middle movements, published as his Op. 103 – a gentle *Andante* in B flat and the Minuet – a minuet this time, not a *scherzo*, but full of chromatic fire and passion to testify that it was only the physical vitality that had burnt itself out. But if he had not the strength to finish his last quartet, the glorious work to which it still bears witness was already achieved. And on that achievement, as on each manuscript as he completed it, Haydn could fitly write his *Fine – Laus Deo*.

2

Luigi Boccherini (1743–1805)*

MAURICE LINDSAY

BOCCHERINI was born at Lucca on 19 February 1743, third of the five children of Maria Santa di Donerio Prosperi and Leopoldo di Antonio Boccherini, a professional double bass player. Young Boccherini had his first lessons on the cello and the double bass from his father. By his thirteenth birthday, Luigi was already a Musician of the Chapel in Lucca, being registered as a cellist. He studied composition with a local Abbé, and in 1757 was sent to Rome to complete his studies. Four years later he was back in Lucca, this time as Director of the Chapel.

But, like Mozart later at Salzburg, Boccherini could neither be content with what was probably little better than a menial position, nor with merely local fame. So, in company with the Luccan violinist, Filippo Manfredi, he set out on a series of continental tours. The two musicians reached Paris towards the end of 1768. There, in spite of some jealous intriguing by the local musicians, Gaviniès and Gossec – a difficulty which Mozart also encountered later in the French capital! – they created a sensation; Boccherini a double one, since the critics were uncertain whether to allow him more honour for his trios and quartets, or for his virtuosic mastery of the cello.

The Spanish Ambassador in Paris persuaded Boccherini to visit Spain, assuring the composer of a warm welcome from the music-loving Prince of the Asturias and his Princess. Boccherini accepted the invitation. The Prince, however, was not on good terms with his father, Charles

* Biographical details are included in this section because of the growing interest, promoted largely by long-playing records of his chamber music, in Boccherini.

III, who ignored him completely. Soon, too, Boccherini lost patience with the Prince's musical pretensions. His Spanish patron turned out in the end to be the Infante, Don Luis. The composer married a Spanish girl and settled in Spain, composing industriously, until his patron died in 1785. For a few years thereafter, Boccherini occupied the unremunerative post of Court Composer to the King of Prussia. But when Frederick William died in 1797, he was again without a patron, and so without the means of livelihood. He returned to Spain. During his brief tenure as French Ambassador at the Court of Spain, Napoleon's brother, Lucien Bonaparte, gave Boccherini his protection; but when, in 1802, Lucien was angrily recalled to Paris, Boccherini was left to eke out a scanty living rearranging some of his music to include parts for the guitar, the instrument most fashionable among Spanish gentlemen. He died in poverty on 28 May 1805, and was buried in a pauper's grave. In 1927, his remains were exhumed, and transported back to Lucca, where they were reinterred with considerable ceremony.

Unlike Haydn and Mozart, Boccherini seldom had the opportunity, and rarely the inclination, to write for large forces. In spite of his twenty-one charming but slight symphonies, his eight sinfonias concertante, his concertos for violin, flute, and cello, his Stabat Mater, and his little *zarzuela*, *La Clementina*, he was first and foremost a chamber music composer. He wrote ninety-one string quartets and a hundred and thirteen string quintets, besides a large number of duo-sonatas, trios, and quartets and quintets for combinations which include wind instruments.

To all intents, he 'invented' the string quintet – he favoured two cellos, one of them used largely in its higher register – the piano quintet, and the string sextet, all forms richly developed by the romantic composers. But it was on his quartets and quintets that Boccherini lavished most of his gifts, and it is in their voluminous pages that we may trace the characteristics and developments of his style.

Trained as he was in the traditions of the Italian instrumental school, whose 'father' (though not founder) was Archangelo Corelli, Boccherini never outgrew his attachment to the balanced, repetitive forms which these fellow-composers used for the movements of their so-called sonatas. He was particularly attracted to lyrical slow movements of simple song-like pattern, with often an almost continuous melodic line carried by a single instrument, usually the first violin, or, in the quintets, the first cello. Such a 'song without words', bathed in the melancholy glow of fading sunshine, is the slow movement of his String Quartet in D, Op. 6, No. 1,* written during the latter part of the Paris stay. Here, the material is subjected to a certain amount of decorative variation. The two movements on either side of this *Adagio*, though couched more certainly in the cosmopolitan idiom of the sonata-form age, reveal Boccherini's reluctance to commit himself wholeheartedly to any elaborate development of his material. The first movement makes charming alternating play with two clear-cut themes; but there is virtually no development of them, though they undergo some decorative modulation when they reappear in what ought theoretically to be the recapitulation. The Finale – a minuet treated as a rondo – again avoids any serious business, though such is its charm that no one could reasonably hold that against it! All three movements reveal Boccherini's unerring sense of conciseness, as well as his feeling for rhythmic and dynamic contrast. (Two of the most obvious characteristics of his style are his fondness for short phrases repeated at sharply contrasted dynamic levels, and a lively interest in off-beat rhythmic effects; both, incidentally, characteristics which may be found in gentle guise in the well-known Minuet from the String Quintet in E, Op. 11.)

It was possibly those early quartets, charming, warmhearted, and abounding in pleasant surprises, which once led Tovey to refer, somewhat contemptuously, to 'the

* This, and the Quintet later referred to, are both available in modern editions and on L.P. recordings.

merely decorative works of the cellist Boccherini'. But as
Boccherini reacted to the influences of his adopted country,
his work deepened emotionally, and the lyrical tone-colours
in which he liked to paint grew more varied and darker.
The slow movement from the String Quintet in G, Op. 60,
No. 5, written in 1801, though still cast in the ABAB song
pattern, has a profundity of feeling and expression not to be
found in the music of his younger years. Here, there is no
mere decorative filigree-work, but a troubled, searching use
of shifting tonality, reaching out after emotional experience
of a profoundly moving kind.

The Finale of this particular quintet captures Spanish
colour by an imitative guitar effect. In some of the other
quintets from Boccherini's later output, however, the influence of Spain makes itself felt melodically, particularly
through references to Iberian folk-song. In at least one
quintet – *La musica notturna di Madrid*, in C and G, composed in 1780, but bearing no opus number – a programme
of local sound-colours is presented, the composer depicting
the arrival and departure of a serenading party, and the
street cries of the night-watchman. More fundamentally, in
all his later chamber music, there is constantly to be found
a remarkable interest in what one Italian critic has called
the 'tension of accents', a characteristic of much Spanish
folk music.

It is, indeed, this unexpected exotic flavour studding a
cosmopolitan texture, this constant sense of surprise, and
the subsequent delight at its realization, that gives Boccherini's music its distinctive savour, and is to-day resulting
in its rediscovery in many countries outside his native Italy.

3

*Wolfgang Amadeus Mozart (1756–1791)**

ERIC BLOM

INTRODUCTION

WHAT domestic music-making would be like without Mozart's chamber music is hard to imagine. Those who cultivate it would still have much to treasure, and a great deal in which perhaps to take a more passionate interest; but they would miss their most perfect felicities. Yet biographical records of Mozart show how easily we might have had to do without his chamber music. If he had not wished to dedicate six string quartets to Haydn, if the King of Prussia, Frederick William II, had not played the cello, if Mozart had not had a horn player and a clarinettist among his friends, he might have thought much of this kind of music not worth the trouble of writing. It did not easily reach private circles who could borrow or make copies, and publishers did not jump at it readily. Only about a third of it was published in the composer's lifetime, most of it late, and three works not till the last two years of his life.

If Mozart did write much chamber music – about sixty finished works, not to mention those he abandoned – it is because he loved it. This is abundantly clear, too, from its technical perfection and the grace and passion of its invention; but it is strange that, profuse and self-revealing letter-writer though he was, he should so rarely have made open confession of this love or, as he was by no means shy of doing in the case of other works of his, expressed satisfaction with what eemed especially well turned out to him – and let there be no mistake: what he felt to be good has been very much so in the world's opinion ever since. No composer has ever puzzled us more tantalizingly with the ultimate

* For index of works mentioned in text see p. 93.

mystery of inspiration, but although Mozart may not have been clearly aware of what spurred him on to do this, that, or the other, he knew very well what he had done once a work lay finished before him. And 'finished' is the word in more than one sense.

CONTRAPUNTAL DEVICES

(1) *Canon*

THE finish of his work is nowhere more evident than in his contrapuntal devices, with which we may as well start. Though no doubt he delighted in showing them off in their immaculate perfection, they are never introduced for their own sake. They are conjuring-tricks, if we like, but he had no use for them unless they produced musical magic. His superb management of canon, for instance, must do more for him than merely display itself. As it must, in the *Don Giovanni* Overture, call up mystery and awe or, in that to *The Impresario*, bubble over with wit, so in the chamber music it can weave single threads that are lovely in themselves into patterns of enhanced loveliness. The first subject of the D Major String Quartet, K. 499, is a thing of beauty and a joy for ever in its matchless shape, even when it is first presented in bare octave unison at the opening:

But Mozart cannot resist playing a heavenly game with it by developing it in canon between first violin and cello, and making it serve at this juncture for a transition to A major, by way of E major, to the second-subject group:

Canons, as Mozart must have known perfectly well, are more or less accidents; a tune, intended to overlap in two or more parts, will either fit or not, and if it does not, little can be done about it. But this was not all for him, for once he had found a theme that would go, he often saw more in it than that. He would, for example, not be content with the two-part accident, but see that a third entry could be wedged half-way in between, as in the canonic incident in the *Don Giovanni* Overture just mentioned or in his elaboration of what is at first a simple filling-up figure in the E Flat Major String Quartet, K. 428:

Sometimes, as in Ex. 2, a short canonic entry would not be enough for him, and he would carry on beyond that point with some fresh matter, still in canon.

There is something else Ex. 2 may serve to show, while we are about it, though one could find more striking instances. It is that a part apparently devised merely for the sake of amplifying the harmony or slightly enlivening the texture is not to be left by such an artist as Mozart with no better function than that of just making a casual entry and then being left hanging in mid-air. Such subsidiary phrases as those here given to the viola are always made to go to a definite destination and thus to lead a life of their own.

(2) *Fugue*

Fugue is another matter; there is no element of chance about that. Perhaps much imagination is not essential to the composer who handles it, though its product will be dull and characterless without a touch of fancy. What it does call for is the most assured gift of contrivance and the most comprehensive insight into a piece of composition as a whole. Not that Mozart went in for the writing of fugues, as distinct from fugal incidents, in his chamber music. Indeed, their construction never interested him particularly; he had to be urged by his wife, who was impressed by the Handel and Bach practices at van Swieten's house, to exercise his contrapuntal gifts in that direction, and it is significant that most of his essays in fugue – fugue as a musical form – remained unfinished, not because he was in the least incapable of completing them, but because he had little stomach for doing so. There is one fully developed fugue among the six

Quartets, K. 168–73, written in Vienna in August and September 1773, where the lad of seventeen clearly wished to impress the resident musicians with his learning. It is the finale of the most interesting work in this set, in D Minor, where the academic devices of inversion, *stretto*, pedal-points and so on, are exploited on a chromatic theme with a skill that suggests at once that if Mozart was not anxious to write fugues, it was not from any want of dexterity, but rather from a coolness of taste towards a style which no doubt he thought of as 'Gothick', in the disparaging eighteenth-century sense of the term. Let it not be forgotten that when he passed through Nuremburg he wrote home to say that it was 'a hideous town'.

Incidental fugal passages, on the other hand, he could no more resist than he could canon. The Finale of the G Major Quartet, K. 387, is full of them, and what is more, the chief theme is one of those academic tags used for generations for school exercises, but turned by Mozart to superb artistic use, here as in the Finale of the 'Jupiter' Symphony and elsewhere:

The cliché is, as will be seen here, used in the manner of a 'tonal' fugue, the parts entering in the order of ii, i, iv, iii, and see-sawing between G major and D major. The poly-phonic management is masterly in its lucidity and limpid beauty; but as though to disarm suspicion of academic display, passages are interposed which seem to go out of their way to remain purely homophonic – to be, in fact, no more than accompanied melody. However, another fugal tag soon arrives, this time by regular entries working up from the bottom part (iv, iii, ii, i):

And lo and behold! a moment later this is found to combine with perfect smoothness with the main theme (Ex. 4). Indeed it seems that anything could go with anything else in this movement, as in the 'Jupiter' Finale. There is not here the miracle of the fivefold counterpoint in the coda of that work, simply because there are not five subjects to play with, and doubtless also because the G major Papageno spirit of the Quartet Finale is intended to be more light-hearted. But the four entries of the main theme in close *stretto* very near the end are wonder enough, in all conscience.

A rather similar movement, no less complex but with freer polyphony, is the finale of the A Major Quartet, K. 464. It begins innocently with a twofold phrase that might well just shape itself into a plain-sailing first sonata-form subject:

But we begin to suspect that Mozart has something up his sleeve as soon as phrase *a* begins to indulge in imitation; and before we know where we are, we turn dizzy at a feat performed with phrase *b*, which involves itself in this sort of tangle, as though it were the easiest thing in the world to unravel:

Well, it cannot have been insuperably difficult to a born

master like Mozart, though we know that even he sometimes tried this kind of thing out in sketches; but the marvel
is that it is supremely musical and beautiful, whereas in the
hands of a mere contrapuntist of a scholastic persuasion it
would have been dry while it could have been no smoother.

This sort of thing is all quite unnecessary, strictly speaking. Good quartets have been written without it – indeed
the great bulk of them, since it takes a Mozart to do it. But
how much is added to the happiness of listeners by the for-
tunate fact that Mozart did have this facility and take the
trouble to use it! And how much more to that of players!
For it is such workmanship that makes the delight of taking
part in chamber music and spurs the performers to surpass
themselves to their own surprise, like the girl in the modern
novel who in a fit of anger finds herself saying words she
didn't even know she knew. The difference is that Mozart
players are in a much happier position.

(3) *Polyphonic texture*

Mozart is not polyphonic at all costs even in chamber music,
where such a style is on the whole as desirable as anywhere
in the secular art of his period; in fact, as much so as even
in church music, which was then not far removed from the
operatic manner, though contrapuntal writing was still
conventional in certain sections of the Mass. He would at
times content himself with a tune over or under a plain
chordal accompaniment, as in the extreme case of the
opening of the C Major String Quintet, κ. 515, a very
mature, but on the whole by no means a complex work:

Such passages, however, usually mean that he has some artful tricks in reserve. Even where there is just an accompanied melody he refuses to make things too easy for himself. The first-movement *Allegro* of the C Major Quartet, K. 465 (after that famous dissonant slow introduction) could quite easily have had its tune in the first violin supported by second violin and viola as shown in brackets on the upper stave below, to resemble Ex. 8; but what actually happens is what appears on the lower stave:

It is the difference between pedestrian and winged writing.

The last two examples may also serve to show another aspect of Mozart's use of texture: his cunning way of varying its density, by means of which alone he often obtains considerable contrast even in a medium of monochrome tone-colour. In the Quintet (Ex. 8) he reduces the five parts to four for the first fifteen bars; in the *Allegro* of the Quartet (Ex. 9) the cello does not enter until the ninth bar, where the contrast is further emphasized by a sudden change from *piano* to *forte*, the dropping of the violin tune an octave lower and the intrusion of a new, spiky phrase.

A very remarkable instance of deliberate thinning of the texture occurs in the theme for the variations which form the fourth movement (there are six altogether) in the Divertimento for String Trio, K. 563, a late and very mature and interesting work. The whole long tune – exceptionally long for Mozart – goes on for thirty-two bars of moderate time in octave unison for violin and viola, with a bass line in the cello, except for ten notes in the middle, that is to say, in two parts, so far as the ear is concerned:

One's first reaction, quite apart from the fact that the actual sound of this lay-out is rather unattractive, is to wonder why Mozart, being already restricted to an unusually slender medium, should have gone out of his way to impoverish it further, even for a moment. But of course he knew very well what he was about. The moment is not longer than the ear will bear, though long enough to tantalize it a little, and after that the three-part writing, taking up the middle phrase of the tune by way of repeat and enriching it with a particularly bewitching interplay of figures, sounds more satisfying than ever. And so, in retrospect, even the rather gawky rusticity of the tune and the sullen hollowness of its first presentation are found to have had their special artistic value. For even greater compensation there is a good deal of double-stopping in the viola part in the course of this movement, so that the Trio now and again becomes virtually a quartet.

MELODY

MENTION of what I have just called an exceptionally long tune brings us to a consideration of Mozartian melody. The melodic material of the chamber music is on the whole a matter of themes rather than tunes. It pursues the music-lover enthrallingly when he knows where to place some inescapable snatch and teases him maddeningly when he does not. Suddenly, in bed or bath, he may be confronted by such a thing as Ex. 1 or a tune like this:

He knows it is Mozart – what else could it be when it is so much the real thing as to have clung to one's memory, recognizably or not? – and he may even hear it in the particular colour of a consort of single string instruments, or perhaps of a piano with strings; but he cannot for the life of him tell where exactly it comes from. Perhaps it does not matter vastly, but it is annoying and shows how good it would be to know Mozart's chamber music well enough to identify every phrase of it, as one so much more often can, with greater help of words and concrete idea or even situation, identify a phrase in Shakespeare. It ought to be done, for here is the same kind of memorability, the same inevitable and inescapable rightness, that turns a line into a quotation.

What is it that makes so simple a thing as Ex. 1 an enchantment? It is, of course, matchlessly graceful and gracious, but not remarkable for originality or power; much less does it spread into anything like a large-spanned shape, nor is there, for the moment, any harmony to give it an atmosphere. If somebody just sang or played it in isolation, we should forget it almost immediately. Yet on only a slight acquaintance with the K. 499 Quartet, which is enough to make us fall in love with the work, we get this opening phrase indelibly printed on our mind. The reason is, I think, not so much its own felicitous nature as the fact that it recalls the first movement of the Quartet as a whole. It has no sooner sprung into our recollection than we begin to remember the wonderful things that happen to it – such things as the canonic miracle of Ex. 2. And that is why, as I ventured to assert just now, it is as themes rather than as tunes that the melodic material of Mozart's chamber music is chiefly remarkable. There are few detachable 'songs', for the bathroom or anywhere else; there are endless topics for him to discourse on and for us to listen to with delighted attention. His themes are seeds, more often than grown plants, but they are fertile and capable of flowering exquisitely.

Still, the few melodic shapes that stand by themselves are

there. They are not difficult to find, and some are dances, not songs. As to the latter, all the same, it must not be thought that the minuets are pure dance pieces, except in the earliest quartets which we do not regard as representative, since they still belong to the hybrid type of *sinfonia*, half-way between orchestral and chamber music. One minuet at least is a profoundly passionate piece of music on a large scale: that in the Clarinet, Viola, and Piano Trio, K. 498.

Sometimes a single movement contains a rich profusion of immediately singable tunes that seem to be sufficient unto themselves, such as the wonderfully gracious ideas, one after another, of the G major Finale of the Piano Quartet in G Minor, K. 478, of which these three are the best, yet by no means all that court quotation:

These, and others in this piece, are all extended themes of the rondo type, to be made to take their turn rather than to be developed, for they are fully organized already. This is broadly true of Mozart's rondo material in general, though we must remember that his rondos often, as indeed is this instance particularly, partake very largely and in all essentials of sonata-form, with one episode appearing first in the dominant and then in the tonic as a regular second subject.

First movements, in pure sonata-form, as a rule use briefer, more motivic material. The two B Flat Major Quartets, for instance, are typical in this respect. That in the King of Prussia set, κ. 589, begins thus:

that in the Haydn set, κ. 458, thus:

This last is, of course, rather like a hunting-call with its open notes of the harmonic series and its 6/8 rhythm, and equally of course, but also quite ridiculously, κ. 458 has thus acquired the nickname of the 'Hunt Quartet'. The theme is just within the upper compass of a horn in F, but much too high to sound naturally like a hunting-horn, apart from the fact that violin tone is about as far removed from that as any musical sound could be that comes normally within the proper compass. Besides, whatever Mozart may be – and he is about all we can want this side of Heaven – he is emphatically not an open-air composer. The romantic poetry of the German forest is simply not within his reach, as it is nearly enough in Haydn's in *The Seasons* and, of course, in the very blood of Weber, Schumann, and Wagner later on – to mention no others. Mozart is decidedly an indoors composer – which is by no means to say a drawing-room composer – and when he does venture outside, he stays for preference in a formal Italian garden with arbours and topiary and summer-houses. Susanna's 'Deh vieni' in *Figaro* is the perfection of summer-garden music, and so is the middle (*Allegretto*) movement of the F Major Piano Concerto, κ. 459, which closely resembles it. To think of Mozart taking part in a hunt is to strain imagination to breaking-point.

Now, all the same, this opening of the K. 458 Quartet is distinctly Germanic in character; and it is noticeable that, like his works of the serenade or *divertimento* type, the chamber music more often contains tunes striking a German note than do, for instance, his symphonies or his operas, even the operas with German words, strangely enough. The bluff, slightly uncouth squareness of Ex. 10 and 11 has a kind of backslapping friendliness Mozart can have felt only for familiars in his immediate circle. Another type of German melody is that associated with the spring song for voice and piano, *Komm, lieber Mai*, K. 596, the opening phrase of which is anticipated by the rondo theme of the last Piano Concerto, K. 595, finished only nine days earlier (January 1791). But something very similar occurs already in the Divertimento for String Trio, K. 563, of September 1788, though the resemblance here is not a note-for-note one, but lies rather in the character of these three pieces. Here are the beginnings of the tunes (all in 6/8 time and in flat keys, it will be noticed):

It is perhaps worth remarking that K. 563, which contains other tunes of a German cast (notably Ex. 10 and the trio of the rather Schubertian second minuet, in the key of A flat major which Schubert used so much more often than Mozart) is deliberately described as a *divertimento*; also that the tunes shown as Ex. 17 and 18 are said to resemble a Suabian folk-song very closely.

Where themes rather than tunes, art-music material rather than song picked up from the people, are developed in Mozart's chamber music, we more often, though not very often, find the familiar eighteenth-century opening gambit of a phrase stated in the tonic and immediately balanced on the dominant of that same key (not transposed to the dominant, which is quite a different thing). Ex. 9 is a familiar instance, and others are the openings of the G Minor Piano Quartet, κ. 478, the A Major String Quartet, κ. 464, the C Major String Quintet, κ. 515, that in E flat major, κ. 614, and the G Major Piano Trio, κ. 564 (see Ex. 27). There are exceptions where the convention is kept to, but varied by some new and arresting twist. Thus in the F Major Quartet, κ. 590, the answering phrase appears on the subdominant instead of the dominant:

and, most strikingly, in the minuet of the κ. 515 Quintet the melody of the main section begins, not on the tonic, but on the supertonic, and it is only at its close that we get the balancing phrase on the tonic chord:

The most expansive melodic lines occur, naturally enough, in the slow movements, where there is much intense lyrical beauty spreading itself at leisure. The tone is perhaps more operatic here than elsewhere in the chamber music, though it is curious that in Mozart's operas themselves slow music is rarely used. (In the whole of *Figaro* the only two really slow pieces are 'Porgi amor' and the brief episode of reconciliation near the end.) On the other hand, the variation form too attracted Mozart for slow movements: that of the A Major String Quartet, κ. 464, is a

superb example with a theme more and more freely treated
until at the end it culminates in a coda over a fascinating
drumming base, where the music becomes almost wholly
independent yet remains astonishingly relevant to what has
gone before. In the F Major Quartet, к. 590, we are reminded a little of 'Deh vieni' by the slow movement, in the
clarinet Quintet of the 'masonic' atmosphere in *The Magic
Flute* generally, in the Wind and Piano Quintet, к. 452,
very much of the second section of Leporello's 'catalogue
aria' in *Don Giovanni* ('Nella bionda egli ha l'usanza'):

and in the E flat Major Quintet, к. 614, most particularly
of the loving tenderness of Belmonte's 'Wenn der Freude
Tränen fliessen' (same key) in *Die Entführung*:

Elsewhere, in the *Andante* of the D Major Quartet, к. 575,
we hear a distinct echo of a song: Mozart's most famous –
Das Veilchen:

ORIGINALITY

IT is curious in a way that the study of Mozart's melody, of
all the ingredients of his art, should lead to a consideration
of his originality. One does not think of him as one of music's
most striking melodists, any more than one does of Bach, for

example. He is far less remarkable in that respect, not only than masters in or near his own class, like Purcell, Handel, Schubert, or Verdi, but less even – indeed in some cases considerably less – than such second-rank figures (I do not say second-rate, please note) as Brahms, Bizet, Tchaikovsky, Grieg, Dvořák, or Fauré. These six, taken more or less at random, and not here grouped together as equals, are clearly recognizable as distinctive musical characters by their melodic material, even if it is heard bare and un-harmonized. Not so Mozart, or at any rate far less easily. He must be heard, as it were, in the round; it is embedded in their surrounding harmony and texture that his melodies usually become memorable, and they live on in our recol-lection, not as isolated figures in front of an unimportant and half-remembered background, but in sharp focus with that background, which is as fascinating as they, to say the least. Even a frankly top-heavy treble line with a sub-ordinate accompaniment such as Ex. 9 is not thought of independently of its support. That is why it is not whistled about in the house – except perhaps by one fanatically devoted to chamber music – as *Fischerweise*, 'Celeste Aida', the 'Seguidilla' from *Carmen*, the love theme from the *Romeo and Juliet* fantasy-overture, or *Après un rêve* are whistled or hummed. We do not hug Mozart's tunes as if they were cherished babies; they are grown up and have a sphere of activity of their own. Yet within that sphere they are often distinctly original. Not always, and it does not matter if they are not, since it is what he makes of his material rather than its intrinsic value that is important. His invention can be easy-going; his craftsmanship is never anything but impeccable, and so is his taste. Below his best he could turn out music that is not striking for the quality of its melodic invention, but it is impossible to think of anything dating from the astoundingly early days in which he reached maturity where the least little chink in his technical armour can be pointed out, as impossible as to find an instance of any lapse in his refinement and elegance, which are quali-ties so constant that they can only be thought of as the habits of good breeding to which a person of aristocratic disposition adheres instinctively and unfailingly without so much as having to think about them. It is transgressing against taste and skill, not observing them, that would have made difficulties for Mozart.

RHYTHM

Now that we have seen that Mozart is not a highly individual melodist, we may as well note that he is not, to tell the whole truth, one of the most original composers. Yet he is unmistakable to anyone with some experience of him, for all that much of his material is the current coin of his time. There are people, even quite musical people, who say they cannot distinguish his work from Haydn's; but this is quite incomprehensible to anybody whose acquaintance with both is more than a nodding one. There are many things that distinguish them, but perhaps the most clearly evident difference, merely of atmosphere, not of a technical nature, is that already pointed out: Haydn's is outdoor and Mozart's indoor music. One would be tempted to say that this may explain why the latter's *chamber* music is so perfect, were it not that after all Haydn's too is supremely good in its own way.

What makes Mozart unique above all, perhaps, is not so much character as quality. There are composers whose music resembles his: Cimarosa's operas and John Christian Bach's symphonies, for instance, sound astonishingly Mozartian. But the others cannot go on for long before one becomes aware of a difference in stature. The coin may be the same, but theirs is copper and Mozart's is gold. What looks alike in shape is different in colour, and it has infinitely greater purchasing-power with which to acquire the world's love.

Rhythmically Mozart is not outstandingly enterprising either, though he sometimes does unexpected things, as in the G Minor Piano Quartet, к. 478, where the first movement indulges for a moment in quintuple time – a thing almost unheard of in the eighteenth century, or else used, as by Handel in *Orlando*, to suggest madness:

That Mozart was well aware of the irregularity is shown by his deliberate marking of the first and sixth beats with a *sforzando* and keeping the accompaniment in even quavers on broken octave B flats to avoid any rhythmic interference. He can also devise attractively irregular metrical schemes, especially in his minuets, though he is not as fancifully enterprising there as Haydn. The minuet in the F Major Quartet, K. 590, for example, is laid out in seven-bar phrases and its trio in five-bar phrases. There are also curious shiftings of accents on occasion, as for instance in the Finale of the Horn Quintet, K. 407 (see Ex. 11), which the ear catches as though it began on the first beat while the eye, seeing it in the score afterwards, is disconcerted to find that there is an upbeat, which seems to put the whole thing awry. Of course it all comes right eventually.

A striking originality does sometimes break through. Mozart will experiment with the unheard-of when it suits him. The famous discordant introduction of the C Major Quartet, K. 465, is too familiar as well as too long to quote as an instance, and the reader need only be reminded that, although there is nothing technically inexplicable about its false relations – which we find in older music than his: in Byrd, in Purcell, in Bach – the riddle remains why this strange incident should have suited him in this particular context, since the rest of the Quartet is quite unproblematic.

Sometimes a movement as a whole is profoundly original, simply, no doubt, because a creative artist of such fertility could not fail to strike unusual depths at times – and the better we know Mozart the more we become aware of how much passion is concealed beneath the ever wonderfully polished surfaces of his music. The trios for violin, cello, and piano are not on the whole quite so important as the string quartets and quintets, if we except the slighter King of Prussia quartets, nor do they come near the two piano quartets and the poignant Clarinet Quintet; but the Trio in E Major (from which Ex. 33–5 are quoted later) has a first movement which, with its lyrical melodies and its drastic, far-flung modulations, is one of the most characteristic things in all his chamber music. As for the marvellous, dark-coloured Trio for Clarinet, Viola, and Piano, к. 498, it is impassioned and thoughtful throughout, with a dramatic C minor episode in the apparently smooth rondo-finale and that Minuet, already mentioned, which turns the conventional dance form into an extended poem of almost hectic intensity.

HARMONY

MOZART's harmonic range is, of course, severely limited compared with that of later ages, and indeed with that of some earlier composers, notably Bach. But to judge his music by that of other periods, or even other composers of any age, is to make oneself guilty of what he was himself incapable of committing – a serious lapse in taste. A building that has the reputation of being a perfect specimen of Adam or Nash is not improved by a later architect who plasters excrescences in his own later style on it, however much one may prefer that style when it is used in its proper right. The first thing we must understand if we wish to do justice to Mozart, and thus to ourselves by taking the greatest possible pleasure in him, is that he is not diminished by his limitations, but is in fact the greatest artist in music – I do not say the greatest originator – because he never fails to work with the utmost ease, freedom, and cogency within the conventions he knew and had found valid for himself. We may feel, even while we listen to him, that we are in the mood for some other musical flavour or climate, for the idiosyncrasies of some other personality, for the atmosphere of

another century or – I was going to say country, but
Mozart as an artist has no country; he is the perfect cosmopolitan. What we must on no account do, if we want to be
players or hearers of discrimination, is to wish that he himself, as we know him, were different. For to know his music
intimately, and perhaps above all, his chamber music, as
being the most intimate, is to love it exactly as it is and to
wish for nothing else while it claims our attention for the
moment. That moment is bliss enough, and to hanker after
other delights while it lasts is to be guilty of the grossest kind
of infidelity – the fickleness at the height of felicity of the
man who does not know how happy he is and thus com-
mits treason not only against the dispenser of his good for-
tune, but at the same time against himself.

We may jib at such stereotyped tonic-and-dominant
openings as this of A Major Quartet, к. 464:

though it is worth noting that this symmetrical to-and-fro
appears very much less frequently in the chamber music
than in the orchestral works; or we may think little of such
a sequential beginning as that of the later G Major Trio,
к. 564:

But it is all a matter of context. Such preliminary remarks
about the weather may lead to the politest complimentary
exchanges, to fascinating discussions, to most graceful
epigrams or to brilliant displays of learning expressed in the
most civilized and elegant terms.

Harmony, for all its limitations in Mozart's hands, plays
a great part in making his chamber music what it is, for he
stretches and adapts his obviously economical vocabulary

to the utmost here; and such is his skill that he is often able to make a striking effect with comparatively simple means by very cunningly reducing even the basic simplicity to absolute plainness for a given time, whereupon a harmonic trick he has in reserve becomes disproportionately telling. Note, for example, the opening of the E Flat Major Quartet, K. 428, where he first eschews all harmony by stating the main theme softly in octave unison:

and after a few bars energetically restates it as follows:

The plunge on to the diminished-seventh chord at the second bar gives a tremendous thrill even nowadays, when that dissonance has long been regarded as the stalest harmonic device exploited by countless composers to produce easy dramatic effects or to serve as an ever-ready pivot for modulation (the latter because it baffles the ear's sense of tonality and thus makes a convenient short cut to various alien keys). And the chief reason why in Mozart's chamber music – not to mention his dramatic work – such common harmonic devices (the German sixth is another) retain all their original power is precisely that he not only uses them sparingly altogether, but also that he places them infallibly in contexts where they are thrown into relief by contrast. The diminished seventh is, theoretically at least, still a discord, and discords are most telling in the midst of a liberal array of concords. Placed close together without resolution, they are apt to 'kill' each other, like a quickfire succession of puns and paradoxes in an essay.

Similarly, some almost Tristanesque harmonies in the slow movement of this same Quartet (in the rare key of A flat major) are the more poignant for being surrounded by matter in which there is less dissonant tension, though suspensions (i.e. parts delaying their progressions in such a way as to produce passing discords) are a feature of this piece altogether:

Ex.30

One very important aspect of Mozart's harmonic procedures is, of course, modulation. He is not as dramatic in that respect as Beethoven, nor as surprising as Schubert, and the following startling passage in the first movement of the D Minor Quartet, K. 421, which is almost a jerk rather than a modulation, is very exceptional in his work:

Ex.31

But if he does not often do wildly unexpected things, he

modulates with great subtlety in an endless variety of ways,
and he is by no means reluctant to thrill us occasionally
with an interrupted cadence, like that in the Finale of the
G Minor Piano Quartet, K. 478, the plunge from G major
into E flat major of which by way of a concluding climax
never fails to send shivers down one's back – though shivers
of delight, not of horror (piano part only shown):

Then again he will introduce variants into the harmon-
ization of a theme, with new chromatic inflections which,
small as they are, alter the whole flavour of a passage.
Nothing could be more delicious, even in Mozart, than the
following four phrases from the middle movement of the
E Major Piano Trio, K. 542, which must be quoted at
length to show the numerous tiny changes, of part-writing
as well as harmony, with which this enchantingly graceful
theme is touched up to spring fresh surprises with a sort of
sly discretion:

Chromaticism of this beguiling kind is sometimes used, not just to add delicate new colour washes or a dash of spice, but to forward a movement by means of intricate interplay of accidentals, as in the Finale of the C Major Quartet, K. 465:

or to add interest and richness to inner parts, as in the Minuet of the D Major Quartet, K. 499:

At cadential points, where in an opera or a symphony the situation would be sufficiently saved by a plain full close, Mozart will in the chamber works sometimes land surprisingly on an interrupted cadence, as in Ex. 32, or refine upon the approach to the close with chromatic progressions, as in the Finale of the D Major String Quintet, K. 593:

TECHNIQUE

NOT much more need be said about Mozart's technical accomplishment. Still, one is anxious to expatiate upon it, not only because it is so fascinating to the professional mind, but also because, from the layman's point of view, it is so unobtrusive as to escape observation only too easily – and those whom it eludes miss endless delights. He deals with hair-raising difficulties as though they were no trouble at all, and the unfailing grace and elegance with which they are set down, without ever being paraded, makes them seem – I do not mind repeating the comparison with a gentleman's good manners – easier to observe than to offend against.

Except in the six Vienna Quartets written at the age of seventeen, K. 168–73, no doubt intended to show musicians in the capital that the young provincial from Salzburg had seen the world, met great musicians in various countries, and learnt his craft thoroughly, he never shows off technique for its own sake. Canons and fugued passages appear here and there because the musical argument throws them up and the problems they set are not to be resisted; they are not dragged in by the hair. The music flows on with sovereign ease all the time, catching itself up in little eddies and whirlpools of counterpoint, because without them the course would be dull and because it is the business of chamber music to yield delights of various kinds by turns, sometimes total effects and sometimes details for each individual player that must nevertheless contribute to the whole. Everybody must be given interesting things to do, every instrument must be congenially treated, but what is thus made to converge must above all be unceasingly beautiful and significant. A conscious exploiting of counterpoint for its own sake is to be suspected in only a single movement, and that, be it noted, in a work not at first intended as chamber music; the String Quintet in C Minor, K. 406, which was originally the Serenade for Eight Wind Instruments, K. 388. This is a minuet of the kind Haydn would amuse himself with more often than Mozart; it is in canon throughout. The first part of the main section is a canon at the octave between treble and bass. Then comes canon at the fourth between the two violins for a moment; but of course that is not enough for Mozart once he has got the bit between his teeth; presently the canon grows three-fold, at the octave again, between violas, violins, and cello (in that order). And even that will not satisfy him, for he makes the trio section go *al rovescio* – that is to say, in four parts with each pair of parts playing their strains against the answer turned upside down.

Very near the end of the E Flat Major Piano Quartet, K. 493, which is less familiar and dramatic than the G Minor, but in its way no less lovely, occurs this imitative passage, needless to say derived from one of the rondo episodes heard earlier:

It is possible that Mozart would have been happier if the violin and cello parts, which would have made a real canon but for the necessity of changing an A natural into an A flat, could have fitted without adjustment. But it was surely not beyond him to make them do so, or even to make the viola and piano parts strictly canonic too. We have already seen (see Ex. 3 and the discussion near it) how skilful he was with such close work; but he was more intent on euphony and natural flow of parts than on merely mechanical displays of skill, and here a near-canon between two parts with witty imitations in the others are as good as a feast. If we want polyphony to stagger us, we can find it too, as for instance in the Finale of the D Major String Quintet, K. 593, which combines thematic scraps fugally with the clairvoyant virtuosity we find in the Finale of the 'Jupiter' Symphony. 'Oh, and this will go too,' we seem to hear him say as he throws these bits together into a bewildering tangle which yet makes the most astonishing sense without ever sacrificing beauty. Go it does, indeed. Not Bach himself, who was much more of a polyphonist by nature, could have wrought a greater miracle.

FORM

MOZART is sometimes said to be a very 'formal' composer. If that means that he is a master of form – as he knew it – nothing could be more true; if it suggests that he used the forms current in his time in a stereotyped manner, it is utterly false. His schemes of construction are few: sonata-form for the first movements (exceptions such as the variations of the A Major Piano Sonata, K. 331, are rare) and sometimes for finales, minuets with trios, rondos for finales as a rule, and here and there variations for slow or last movements. But within these conventions he achieves astonishing variety and occasionally springs extraordinary surprises. Slow introductions may bring an element of change, but more rarely in the chamber music than in the symphonies. Even rarer are arresting, fanfare-like openings and ceremonial conclusions. There is no need in chamber music to attract the attention of an audience – indeed there often is no audience. Nor is there any sense in drawing attention to the fact that a movement is coming to a close, a device that is essentially dramatic and originated in the curtain-fall at the end of an operatic act or scene. The curtain takes a few seconds to descend, and that period is best filled in with music of no particular significance, often a mere reiteration in some rhythmic pattern of the final tonic chord. A composer who has artistic tact will know that such filling-up is not called for in chamber music, or indeed in any music not written for the stage, though it may have quite a good effect in a symphony as a reminder that the work is dramatic, if not theatrical, in character. (Beethoven actually overdid it at the end of his Fifth Symphony.) A master very different from Mozart, Verdi, was quite well aware that this kind of stagey ending is out of place away from the opera-house; there is not a single instance of it in his *Requiem*. Nor in Mozart's, for that matter, and the nearest thing to one of those empty fanfare openings in his mature chamber music is the 'hunting' call of the B Flat Major Quartet, K. 458 (Ex. 16), but even that is a tune rather than a mere flourish.

Nothing short of a detailed study of the first movements of all the mature works can show the astounding resourcefulness with which Mozart adapts a fundamentally rigid scheme. Here it must suffice to take two or three works and compare their opening movements. The two neighbouring Quartets in D Minor and E Flat Major (κ. 421 and 428) will serve as well as anything. In the former we have that startling working-out section, of which Ex. 31 shows the first few bars, with its revolutionary jerk (literally, in the sense of turning full circle) from E flat major into the very remote key of A minor, followed by a normal recapitulation, as if there had been quite enough upheaval for a time, and then a coda with the mutterings of fresh disquiet coming to an abrupt end. In the latter work we are deliberately kept quiet with subsidiary, here and there purely decorative matter, because Mozart here chooses to put some extra close work into the recapitulation, which can then stand without any sort of coda. A little filling-up figure which appeared just once in the exposition, for instance, is now worked into one of those sly little close canons mentioned once or twice before (see Ex. 3), and at the restatement of the main theme, instead of being repeated as in Ex. 29, it is now heard with a new running accompaniment for viola and cello. With his sure instinct Mozart realized that to repeat such a startling effect as the diminished-seventh chord of Ex. 29 would inevitably have meant an anticlimax, and he knew that he must find something different, but no less interesting.

A very remarkable case is the first movement of the Clarinet Quintet, κ. 581. There are quite distinctly three subjects, not the usual two, for although the third masquerades as a mere codetta in the exposition, it turns out in the recapitulation to be at first a kind of deceptive expansion into an important coda, only to show at the end, which corresponds almost precisely (except in key) to the end of the exposition, that there has been no coda at all, but an enlargement and emotional deepening of the sonata-form material. Nor is this all; the first subject is abridged at its reappearance for the recapitulation, because it had been extensively developed in the working-out section. The pathetic second subject, on the other hand, is considerably amplified and made more poignant (for this work has the same valedictory, almost morbid beauty as the Clarinet Concerto of Mozart's last year). It should be noted, too, how the clarinet phrases are turned different ways for this subject, which is now in the tonic (A major) instead of the dominant (E major), as before, to fit into the range of the instrument, and how – for this is the truly Mozartian way – this necessity at the same time produces a new blossoming of heart-seizing beauty.

The Clarinet Quintet also throws up two other formal matters of interest: Mozart's treatment of the minuet and of variations. The Minuet is here very far from being a mere dance movement, and indeed such movements do not occur in the mature chamber music, where minuets always become organized feats of composition. In this instance the Minuet is extended by the insertion of two trios instead of one, besides being highly charged emotionally: and we have already seen what great music Mozart made of the corresponding movement in the Clarinet Trio, K. 498. The final variations of the Quintet, where its mood lightens into urbane playfulness, without however for a moment becoming trifling, shares with his variations for the piano alone (both separate sets and sonata movements) the peculiarity of having a penultimate slow section which, extending to the same length *on paper* as the fast ones and being moreover repeated, becomes disproportionately long *in performance*. Against this criticism one might advance the argument that a number of quick variations mixed with a single slow one restore the balance satisfactorily; still, an uneasy feeling remains that all is not quite well, and it is certain that the concluding variations of the D Minor Quartet, K. 421, on a curiously disquieting, sadly impassioned *siciliana*, which all but the quickening final one proceed in the same moderately fast tempo, are far more highly charged with meaning. The minor key, of course, as always with Mozart, draws more intimate, personally revealing music from him. One variation here is in the tonic major, exactly as in major-key variation movements one is invariably in the tonic minor; and there again it is that section which is usually the most significant and often the most elaborately worked.

MAJOR AND MINOR

THERE can be no doubt that Mozart was well aware of the confessions the use of minor keys drew from him – confessions of hidden passion and anguish that lay beneath his normally placid and sunny nature – and this must be the reason why throughout his catalogue, works in minor keys are very much fewer than those in major tonalities. They are in fact in a striking 'minority' in more senses than one. His three main minor keys are those of C, D, and G. Others occur, but rarely. There is only one separate piece in B minor, a short but very fine *Adagio* for piano, and only one instance of F sharp minor altogether, the slow movement of the A Major Piano Concerto, K. 488; in E minor not much more than a very daring early Violin Sonata, K. 304. He does not go to four sharps for C sharp minor at all, but rather surprisingly frequently to four flats for F minor. In A minor there is a Sonata, K. 310, and an important Rondo for Piano, K. 511, but no orchestral or chamber music and no concerto at all. Beyond that nothing, but we must remember that he did not use the extreme sharp and flat major keys either.

Now even his three principal minor keys appear very rarely in the chamber music: D minor for two string Quartets and part of an unfinished Piano Trio, K. 442, which ends in D major and was completed by the Abbé Maximilian Stadler. The two important G minor works, Piano Quartet and String Quintet, also both end in the major. C minor takes a peculiar position; apart from the Adagio and Rondo for Glass Harmonica, Flute, Oboe,

Viola, and Cello, K. 617, of which the former alone is in the minor, there are only two arrangements, though both make very imposing works in their second versions; the Wind Serenade, K. 388, arranged as a string Quintet, K. 406, and the Adagio and Fugue for String Quartet, K. 546, of which the Fugue is that for two pianos, K. 426.

Keys, and especially minor keys, clearly had very distinctive 'colours' and emotional implications for Mozart, and these are found in the chamber music, as elsewhere. D minor is passionately dramatic, G minor pathetic, C minor sombre, solemn, and elevated – Mozart's masonic key, it has been said. But the major tonalities too have special connotations, though they are not always so clearly revealed. Thus E major often has a kind of loving seriousness, as in the only chamber work in that key, the Piano Trio, K. 542, not to mention the characteristic arias of Ilia in *Idomeneo*, Fiordiligi in *Così fan tutte*, and Sarastro in *The Magic Flute*, which all have something of that quality. B flat major is often sedately gay, E flat major as often very profound and C major ceremonious. F major, not frequently used in the chamber music * (nor is there an important symphony in that key) is rather nondescript in mood. G major is gay and carefree; it is Papageno's principal key in *The Magic Flute*, and it is curious to note that both finales of the two big G minor chamber works just mentioned, in going into the major, bring forth some distinctly Papageno-like music, as does also the Finale of the G Major Quartet, K. 387, and that of the G Major Piano Concerto, K. 453.

TREATMENT OF INSTRUMENTS

SPACE allowing, it would be possible to go on expatiating on various aspects of Mozart's chamber music; but there are other composers, as one is apt to forget while he occupies

---

* But the magnificent Piano Duet Sonata in F, K. 497, is really a chamber work on a grand scale and has been arranged for the instruments used by Schubert for his Octet.

one's mind or one's ears. Just a brief mention must be made, however, of his treatment of instruments, not in combination – for that has been the subject of more or less the whole of this essay – but in isolation, as separate strands in the fabric of his chamber works. We know that he loved playing the viola in string quartets, and indeed that instrument in these works, not to mention his use of two in the quintets, where they make such rich middle parts, is given enticing things, of the kind that appear much more rarely elsewhere (as, for instance, its angry gestures in Figaro's aria 'Aprite un po'' or its fascinating fill-up figures at the beginning of the fugal music for the armed men in *The Magic Flute*). The cello parts too are much more detailed and interesting than those which as a rule merely double the basses in the orchestral music (though we must not forget the little concerto for 'Batti, batti' in *Don Giovanni*). They are indeed almost over-exuberant in the King of Prussia quartets; but when a royal cellist commissions music in which he wishes to take part, a composer had better write accordingly. The wonder is that these bits of virtuoso display are fitted in with such discretion, and we may perhaps allow ourselves a chuckle over the difficulties with which Mozart may have slyly taxed his exalted patron to the utmost of his skill, if not beyond. For it is not easy to imagine anyone dealing with these parts who has other things to do in life than to practise an instrument.

The early quartets with flute or oboe parts in place of the first violin were also works written to order, the former carried out with some reluctance, since Mozart did not greatly care for the flute some thirteen years before it became 'magic' for him. Even so, these are works of great youthful charm. The horn and the clarinet, however, were treated with greater personal concern, not only because they were instruments Mozart particularly loved, but also because the parts were written for his friends Ignaz Leutgeb and Anton Stadler respectively. The oddly scored Horn Quintet, K. 407, is not very important, but shows the delight Mozart took in writing for Leutgeb. The works with clarinet parts,

on the other hand, show great personal affection and, as we
have already seen, unusual profundity.

Index to works mentioned in this essay

4

Ludwig van Beethoven (1770–1827)

ROGER FISKE

INTRODUCTION

A MAJORITY of musicians would probably agree in regarding Beethoven's string quartets as the highest peak in the
whole range of chamber music. This opinion is not, perhaps,
held with the certainty and unanimity evinced forty or fifty
years ago and more, when men still believed in progress.
The history of the arts seemed then a tale of steady improvement from the primitive to the civilized; there might
be valleys between the peaks, but each peak was a little
higher than its predecessor. Thus Beethoven's quartets were
better than Haydn's and Mozart's because, being able to
profit by their example, he made of this form of music
something more highly developed, both technically and
emotionally. Such phrases do not seem quite so watertight
as formerly, and some would deny that technical and emotional development necessarily produces greater art. Nevertheless, we can agree both that Beethoven's chamber music
is different from that of his predecessors and that it is one
of the great wonders of music.

Beethoven himself believed passionately that the world
was getting better and better, and he welcomed the French
Revolution, which was raging as he wrote his first mature
works. He is essentially a post-Revolutionary figure, whereas
Haydn and Mozart belong to the previous age, and to some
extent the reason that Beethoven's music was different is
that his Europe was different. Haydn and Mozart normally
preserve an Augustan restraint, and their most emotional
moments are within, though sometimes only just within, the
bounds allowed by the kind of society for which they wrote.

Beethoven, despising the aristocracy on principle (though condescending to accept a livelihood from individual members of it), allowed his passions full scope, and was able to do so because he was writing for largely new audiences, which, whatever their social class, were alike in enjoying good music; whereas Haydn wrote his early works for 'socialites' who might not have any liking for music whatever. But there are more important reasons for Beethoven's apparently greater depths. For instance, social upheavals tend to beget more extreme emotions than does a settled age, and these are likely to be reflected in both literature and music. But the chief reason for what is new in Beethoven's music is, of course, Beethoven himself; he thought more deeply than most men, and, by some wonderful chance, had the technique with which to express what he thought. His music burns, rages, laughs, and laments so intensely that his audiences were at times both puzzled and embarrassed by it, much as we are by 'modern' music.

Unfortunately it is beyond the power of words to describe this intensity, this kernel of Beethoven's muse. It is much easier to write of his methods than of his substance; and methods, however interesting to the more enquiring type of musician, may have nothing whatever to do with a composer's greatness. Readers who hope that what follows will illuminate this greatness for them will find, at best, reflections of light rather than the great light itself; for that they must listen to the music. All Beethoven's trios, quartets, and quintets (without wind instruments) are mentioned below (in order of composition) and some will touch off digressions about Beethoven's chamber works generally.

PIANO TRIOS AND QUARTETS

Early Piano Quartets. Three three-movement works written in 1785 (Beethoven's fifteenth year) and first published shortly after his death. They have not the astonishing competence of the piano quartets Mendelssohn wrote in his early 'teens, their part-writing being rather clumsy; yet they are not without interest. It is, indeed, very surprising that Beethoven should have written at all for this combination of instruments which at that time was scarcely known. These works must be even earlier – by a few months – than Mozart's two piano quartets, usually considered among the first of their kind, and Beethoven may well have had no models at all. He thought well enough of No. 3 in C to borrow two tunes from it for his first set of piano sonatas; the second subject of the first movement is used at the same point in Op. 2, No. 3 (bars 27–32; also 39–41), while the opening of the slow movement is used at the same point in Op. 2, No. 1.

Piano Trio in E Flat, ('No. 8'). Written about 1791, but not published until 1830. All three movements are in the same key, the middle one being a minuet and trio. This rather unsatisfactory scheme is found in Haydn's Trio in F (No. 26 in Peters' Edition) which had been published in 1785, and also in some string quartets by Rosetti. For some reason composers never wrote a minuet in any key but that of the work. In the first movement we again find hints of later and better music:

Change the rhythm of (*a*) in the example above, and fill but bars 1 and 3 of (*b*) with scales (as Beethoven himself does at the end of the movement), and we have two of the three elements that make the cheerful finale theme of the First Piano Concerto. The cello part has the freedom it enjoys in Mozart's trios (and is denied in all of Haydn's), but by and large this is a dull work.

Piano Trio 'No. 9', Op. 44 : fourteen variations in E flat. Written about 1792 and published in 1804. Beethoven's opus numbers are a guide to the date of publication, but not of composition; he often dug up an old work to make a little money out of an unsuspecting publisher, and on this occasion he dug up something that might better have been left buried. It would be hard to devise a less distinguished theme. The String Trio in E Flat (Op. 3), written about the same time, is almost equally unsuccessful, but from now on there are to be no more failures. Beethoven was a surprisingly uneven composer, but when, as in his chamber works, he was writing to please his connoisseur friends, not to mention himself, there was little fear of his falling below his best. We may note in passing his great liking at this time (1791–6) for the key of E flat. Besides the last three works I have mentioned, Op. 1, No. 1 (piano trio), Op. 4 (string quintet; *alias* Op. 103 wind octet), Op. 7 (piano sonata), and Op. 16 (quintet for piano and wind) are all in this key; according to the dates given in *Grove*, that makes seven out of the first fifteen works, or eight out of eighteen if the early piano quartets are included. There is, I think, an affinity of mood between the better of these E flat works; they have a serenity that can also be found in Mozart's instrumental works in this key.

Piano Trios, Op. 1, in E Flat, G, and C Minor. Written 1793–5 and published in 1795. Haydn, back in Vienna after his first visit to England, gave Beethoven lessons from December 1792 until January 1794, when he left to spend another year in London.* He must have watched and perhaps assisted at the birth of at least one of these trios, and it is significant that he himself was writing piano trios at this time, throwing off ten or so† (and much other music besides) in the time Beethoven took to write his three.

When Haydn returned from his second trip in 1795, he heard a play-through of his pupil's trios and was so unwise as to advise him not to publish the C minor. Beethoven, well

* Beethoven immediately started lessons with Albrechtsberger; these went on for fourteen months, in fact until Haydn's return.

† Nos. 1–7, 13–14, and 18–20 (in Peters' Edition) were all published about 1795; nearly all Haydn's piano trios are late works.

aware that it was the best, was indignant, and for some time relations between them were strained.

With no other combination of instruments could Beethoven have so disturbed Haydn. His symphonies, string quartets and choral works were not to outstrip those of his master for several years, but these piano trios must have made Haydn's dozen seem embarassingly old-fashioned. For some reason Haydn usually made his piano trios playable as violin sonatas, the cello parts following the piano bass note for note and thus being quite redundant. Did his publishers think that music equally playable by two or by three would for that reason sell the better, or is this doubling a relic of the *continuo* convention of Bach's day? And yet Mozart's trios have independent and essential cello parts, although they are earlier than most of Haydn's. If Haydn approved of Beethoven's free cello parts (and Mozart's), why did he not write some himself? Perhaps he did not approve. But at least he agreed with Mozart that chamber works with a piano should have a maximum of three movements, whereas chamber music without piano should have four. I know of no explanation for this, unless it be a relic of the early eighteenth-century fast-slow-fast design, a convention preserved in works with continuo instruments, but ignored in those without. Whatever the reason, Beethoven thought little of it, and in his Op. 1 (and also in his Op. 2 Piano Sonatas) added a *scherzo* or minuet to make each of them a four-movement work. So far as I can discover, these were the first chamber works with piano to have four movements. Thus these trios were bigger than Haydn's, more 'modern' in texture, and, as far as the C minor was concerned, altogether more 'modern' in feeling. Probably Haydn was unfamiliar with the C minor, which was composed during his absence in England, and accordingly was both surprised and embarrassed by its display of emotion. He probably thought it blatant and lacking in refinement.

That opening is neither innocent nor urbane; it is restless and questioning, and in no time the music rages, with angry *sforzandi* in every part; which makes the lyrical second

subject all the more welcome.

The contrasts in this music must have seemed electrifying in their day. Not that the piano could then make the great clatter we all expect of it nowadays. Indeed, it was precisely because the forte-piano had only a limited range of dynamics that composers wrote so many piano trios; violin and cello versus one forte-piano was an evenly-matched contest. It is not so now; the two strings have no chance against the modern grand, as Tchaikovsky inadvertently demonstrated in his own piano trio. In the last hundred years composers have generally preferred the piano quartet or piano quintet as providing a better balance.

Amongst other things, Beethoven must surely have learnt from Haydn, during those lessons, a sense of adventure where keys are concerned. Mozart was not adventurous over keys; he nearly always put his slow movements in the subdominant. Beethoven put the slow movement of his G Major Piano Trio (Op. 1, No. 2) in the unexpected key of E, which is precisely what Haydn was doing that same year in his 'Gypsy Rondo' Trio, also in G. We may guess that Beethoven did this on his master's advice, or as a compliment to his taste. Perhaps he also learnt from Haydn how to disguise the start of his recapitulation:

At the very start of the finale of this G Major Trio that violin tune was accompanied by rather unenterprising chords on the piano, one or two to the bar; this return slips in so quietly that one scarcely notices it. Haydn himself had a liking for that particular trick. But it must have been Beethoven's own idea to write *scherzi* instead of minuets for the E Flat and G Major Trios. The minuet had long been out of fashion as a dance, and after the revolution it must have seemed as dead as the dodo. The six quartets Haydn wrote in 1781 (Op. 33) have *scherzi* (not very characteristic examples), but elsewhere he does not use the title and it did not strike him as absurd that, in his last eight string quartets, four of the minuets are marked *allegro* and four *presto*. To Beethoven the minuet was never a reality, and he seldom used the title except when he was writing a consciously old-fashioned dance movement. In other words, he wrote a quick dance at this point much as Haydn did, but used the more up-to-date title.

It is curious that the slow movement of the C Minor Trio should end with a surprisingly prolonged anticipation of the C Major Bagatelle for Piano, Op. 119, No. 2. Was Beethoven aware that he had almost written this piece in his Op. 1?

Piano Trios, Op. 70, in D and E flat. Written in 1808 and published in 1809. The previous three trios were dedicated to Count Lichnowsky, no doubt in return for patronage; these two are dedicated to Countess Marie von Erdödy, a young Hungarian who, being partly paralysed in the legs, could only walk with difficulty. Beethoven was at this time already more than half deaf, and their tragic disabilities probably drew them together. The Countess even let Beethoven live in her house for a time, and it was there that he wrote these trios; he always had remarkable powers of attracting the attention of young women socially his superiors, despite the fact that he was far from handsome and altogther lacking in social graces. Years later Beethoven was still writing to the Countess, notably about the many ailments which afflicted him, even though, as he told her, he was drinking seventy-five bottles of medicine a month. The violinist and composer Spohr gives a pathetic account in his autobiography of a rehearsal of the D Major Trio which he heard in Beethoven's house. 'It was not an enjoyable experience. To begin with, the piano was terribly out of tune, a fact which troubled Beethoven not at all, as he could not hear it. Furthermore, little or nothing remained of the brilliant technique which used to be so admired. In loud passages the poor deaf man hammered away at the notes smudging whole groups of them, and one lost all sense of the melody unless one could follow the score. I felt deeply moved at the tragedy of it all. Beethoven's almost continual melancholy was no longer a riddle to me.'

The D Major has only three movements, of which the middle one is magnificent and the last rather trifling. The first two movements are highly original in that their two contrasted themes are not well separated from each other, but announced almost together right at the start of each movement. The first movement begins with a vigorous theme for all three instruments in bare octaves, and this is followed almost at once by a smooth lyrical tune on the cello:

There is indeed another tune later on, but it is unobtrusive and accompanied by octave scales deriving from Ex. 4 (a). In the development, bar 2 of (b) is combined with bar 1 of (a). The slow movement begins:

Ex. 5

That is almost the sum of the thematic material. This must be one of the slowest slow movements ever written. Crochets last about five seconds each, a duration hard to parallel in music. To get even a moderate amount of movement into his music, Beethoven has to resort to large numbers of hemi-demi-semiquavers which give the pages a forbidding appearance. This need not deter the listener, who can here enjoy one of Beethoven's darkest movements; he is aiming at Gothic gloom on the grandest possible scale and achieving it with tremendous dramatic power. The frequent low rumblings in the piano part help to suggest the ghostly atmosphere which in Germany has caused this work to be shown as the 'Geister' Trio. It is curious that Beethoven's sketches for this movement occur on the same page in his notebook as a sketch for a projected opera about Macbeth; this too is in D minor, and it is not impossible that Beethoven had the three weird sisters in mind when he first conceived this music.

The E Flat Trio has nothing so fine as the slow movement of the 'Geister' Trio, but it is much more even as a whole. It has the now regulation four movements; the first has a slow introduction, a most unusual feature in piano trios, and the second may be conveniently described as double variations; two themes (one major and one minor in this case), are varied alternately. Beethoven tried this in the same year in his Fifth Symphony; he must have long forgotten his old animosity towards Haydn, for, although this is one of the commonest of all slow movement forms in Haydn's string quartets and symphonies, Beethoven had never previously attempted it. (So far as I know, there are no 'double variations' in Mozart.) The third movement is not labelled either minuet or *scherzo*; it is really more of a waltz, with a trio in which strings and piano are used antiphonally, and by copious use of double stopping Beethoven makes his two stringed instruments sound like three. The Finale is remarkable for having a second subject in G. Beethoven, in his last quartets, usually preferred to have his second subject a third up or down rather than at the dominant, but it was unusual at the time he wrote this trio. (But for a yet earlier example see the String Quintet in C below.)*

Piano Trio, Op. 97, in B flat, 'The Archduke'. Written in 1811 (but not published till 1816) and dedicated to Archduke Rudolph, younger brother of the Emperor of Austria, and a keen amateur musician. It is hard to know why this particular work should have become known as the 'Archduke', for Beethoven also dedicated to the same person his Fourth and Fifth Piano Concertos, the Piano Sonata *Les Adieux et le Retour* (written when the Archduke was forced to fly from Vienna as Napoleon's army besieged and captured the city), two of the late piano sonatas, the *Grosse Fuge* for string quartet, and the Mass in D (written for the Archduke's installation as Archbishop of Olmütz, but finished three years too late for the ceremony). The Archduke was a portly, unattractive young man who took lessons from Beethoven from 1803 to 1806, composed a little, and played the piano well enough to tackle some of Beethoven's concertos. Nearly all the Hapsburgs were musical, a fact which did much to establish Vienna's position as the chief music centre of Europe. The Archduke was fully capable of distinguishing between Beethoven's greater and lesser

---

* Haydn delighted in the wildest key contrasts between one movement and another, notably in his last string quartets (Op. 76 and 77) and in his last piano sonata. But I do not think he ever put a second subject in an unconventional key, nor, it need hardly be said, did Mozart.

works, and was observed to show displeasure on those occasions when a masterpiece was dedicated to someone else. He should be remembered with gratitude for having organized an annuity for Beethoven in 1809 which kept him from want, the only condition being that the composer should not accept employment outside Vienna.

The Trio opens with a theme of sufficient breadth and spaciousness to establish the mood of the whole work:

Beethoven's alchemy is such that he scarcely needs any more material than this. However, as a brief interlude, he gives us a gently descending second subject in the unexpected key of G; this too comes first as a piano solo, to be immediately repeated by strings. After a solid, rather pompous climax the composer turns to what must have been for him the most pleasurable of tasks: the development of his opening theme. He draws a broad sustained paragraph from each phrase of it. The cello introduces bar 1, and this is taken up as a suitable subject for conversation by all three instruments. Eventually the cello switches the conversation to the phrase starting at the end of bar 2, trying it out first *arco* and later *pizzicato* against curious trills on the piano. Soon the rising scale of bar 3 is speeded up into quavers, and discussion of this leads to a climax, after which Beethoven returns to his opening music, restating his themes and adding a short coda of suitable grandeur.

The *Scherzo* is innocently impish. The piano is silent until the strings have picked out the main tune. The Trio or middle section has two tunes, the first a mysterious *fugato*, the second by way of contrast a *bravura* affair with all the dash of a Weber waltz. Beethoven asks for more repetition than usual; *scherzo* – trio – *scherzo* – trio – *scherzo* – coda (based on the mysterious *fugato*). Often in performance this is reduced to the more conventional *scherzo* – trio – *scherzo* – coda.

The slow movement, which is very long, has one of those broad sustained tunes only Beethoven could write. Note the Haydnesque choice of key:

Then follows a set of variations in which the harmonic structure of the theme is more carefully preserved than the melodic outline.

Var. I. The piano decorates the theme in triplets.

Var. II. For a few bars the piano picks out the theme against a new semiquaver figure on the strings, but soon the semiquaver figure takes command and the theme appears only intermittently.

Var. III. The violin has a version of the theme as a background to decorative music in demi-semiquavers on the piano.

Var. IV. So far each variation has had more movement than its predecessor. Beethoven now returns to the simple crochets and quavers of his opening; in fact, the theme is scarcely varied at all, except for some fascinating short-lived modulations. The music leads into a warm romantic coda with something of the feeling of a nocturne. Violin and cello alternate with rhapsodic snatches of the original melody.

There is no break between the third and fourth movements. The finale, which is in rondo form, is something of
an oddity, different in mood from any other music. The
main tune trips along with a gaiety that is somehow not
quite real, while the principal episode is definitely uncouth:
perhaps it is one of Beethoven's jokes. The music has an
indefinable quality that is continuously fascinating. The
fourth and last appearance of the rondo theme is in a new
rhythm, six-eight, and marked *presto*; and here the music
is more obviously light-hearted. Throughout this movement
the piano writing is noticeably more difficult than that for
the strings. The violin part is kept unusually low, the
player scarcely using the top string at all. On the other
hand, much of the cello writing is extremely high.

It is perhaps worth adding that this trio has not been left
free from the ministrations of arrangers. Soon after Beethoven's death the slow movement theme was made into a
hymn with words by Goethe, and later it was orchestrated
by Liszt as an introduction to his cantata for the Beethoven
centenary celebrations of 1870.

This trio is Beethoven's supreme achievement for piano
and strings.

Piano Trio Movement in B Flat ('*No. 8*'). Written in 1812
and published in 1830. Beethoven only finished one short
movement and perhaps wrote no more because he realized
that it was not very good. It passes comprehension why he
chose the same key as he had used for the 'Archduke'. Or
could it be that this was the original finale to that work and
that Beethoven wisely discarded it?

The 'Kakadu' Variations, Op. 121a. Written before 1816
and published in 1824. Many of Beethoven's works are
overplayed; this one is unduly neglected, a masterwork
known to very few. It begins with the same joke that
Dohnanyi later used in his *Variations on a Nursery Theme* – a
long tragic slow introduction leading up to a comically futile
little tune, 'I am the tailor Kakadu', from a long-forgotten
opera by a contemporary Viennese composer of light music
called W. Müller. Beethoven must have known him.

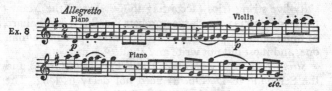

There is another anticipation of Dohnanyi in the final variation, where the last four bars of the above quotation are made to skid into a most unexpected key:

Before that there has been a variation for piano alone, one showing off the violin, one showing off the cello, and even one for violin and cello without any piano at all. A delightful and inventive work, not at all easy to play.

WORKS WITHOUT PIANO

BEETHOVEN wrote five string trios before he attempted a string quartet; after his first batch of quartets he wrote no more string trios. It has often been said that the trios were written as a preparation for the quartets, the implication being that trios are easier to write, but the argument does not hold water. It is, in fact, harder to achieve either richness of tone or variety of texture with three instruments than it is with four. The truth seems to be that, around the turn of the century, the string trio went out of fashion because it was not such a suitable medium for the new music as it had been for *style galant* works. Haydn had written sixty-five string trios (according to *Grove*), and the Mann-heim composers wrote large numbers too. But it is very hard to think of any composers after 1800 who wrote more than one, and most did not write any at all.

String Trios in Serenade Style. The E Flat Trio (Op. 3) and the Serenade in D (Op. 8) need not delay us long. The former dates from about 1792, has two slow and two minuet movements (which, with the first and last, makes six in all) and is a dull work, redeemed in part by a goodish finale. One of the Minuets is marked *allegretto* and the other *moderato*; it is tacitly assumed by musicians that in Haydn and Mozart these words as applied to minuets are synony-mous, but this trio suggests that they were not synonymous for Beethoven.* Which was the quicker? Or was the differ-ence one of style rather than speed?

The Serenade (*c.* 1796) is charming, but such a light-weight work that it seems absurd to listen to it with solemn attention. The opening French march is repeated at the end and there are five short movements in between.

String Trios (Op. 9) in G, D, and C minor. Written 1797–8 and published 1798. Beethoven is wonderfully clever at making three instruments sound like four, and technically these trios are a triumphant success. The C Minor is the best – Beethoven was invariably on the top of his form in this key – but the Finale of the G Major is a splendid achievement for a young man. Just when, in the middle of the development, the *moto perpetuo* is in danger of outstaying its welcome Beethoven introduces a new unison *misterioso* theme in falling thirds with wonderful effect. Earlier in this movement, Beethoven discovered the pleasant effect of starting a tune in the wrong key and only slipping into the right key at the end of it; the dominant key of D is expected here:

---

* It is however quite certain that a minuet marked *allegro* goes dis-tinctly faster than one marked *allegretto*, *moderato*, or nothing at all. Conductors and string quartets frequently ignore this distinction. Mozart nearly always compensates for the greater speed of an *allegro* minuet by writing a much longer movement.

Another similar example occurs at the same point in the Finale of the String Quintet, Op. 29. Beethoven was showing at this stage his liking for immediately repeating a short tune a tone or a semi-tone higher (a liking incidentally that is shared by Michael Tippett). For instance, the Trio of the *Scherzo* in this G Major Trio* (and the surprisingly similar Bagatelle in C, Op. 33).

The C Minor Trio opens with a theme the essence of which came to obsess Beethoven in his last years:

His striving for new dramatic tension is exemplified by the very large number of *sforzandi* in this movement and by such sudden contrasts as this (immediately after a string of *fortissimo* chords):

* See also the start of the String Quartets, Op. 59, No. 2 (Ex. 30), and Op. 95, and Ex. 2 above (Piano Trio in C Minor).

Ex.12

This is of course based on the opening theme (Ex. 11). The slow movement has nobility, the *Scherzo* (Beethoven's only example in six-eight?) has some remarkable loud and rough syncopated effects near the end of the main section. The Finale easily triumphs over the handicap of tunes reminiscent of other works, the first of the Finale to the String Quartet in F, Op. 18, and the second (in E flat minor!) of the opening to the C Minor Piano Trio (Ex. 2). This movement may represent Beethoven's second thoughts, for the Finale of the *Pathétique* Sonata, Op. 13 (also in C minor) is said to have been first sketched for string trio, and it can hardly have been intended for any other work but this. I wish I had space to illustrate the freshness and indeed opulence of the scoring in these three trios. It is a pity that there are so few ensembles to play them.

STRING QUARTETS, OP. 18

THE Op. 18 String Quartets in F, G, D, C minor, A, and B flat, were written in 1798–1800 and published in 1801. My advice (which after all, no one need take) is that anyone contemplating the purchase of an early Beethoven quartet on records should start with No. 4 in C Minor; it is the most passionate, the most easily enjoyed, and very nearly the best. Those with quieter tastes might try the G Major, the most feminine, a charming work. And the aim of both parties should be to graduate up to No. 1 in F, the biggest and, in my view, the best, though perhaps not the most likeable at first. For reasons of space, I shall discuss these three works to the virtual exclusion of the others.

The F Major starts with a dull looking little tune:

Bach would (very nearly) have written it ♩. It is a measure of the new thinking that Beethoven brings to string quartet writing that he should find a fragment of melody just over a bar long sufficient material for the greater part of a long movement. Haydn and Mozart began their *allegros* with something altogether more melodic and less disjointed. This is not a song, lyrical or tragic, such as opens all Mozart's 'Haydn' Quartets, but a discussion of a philosophical point among equals. Changing the metaphor, Beethoven has found half a dozen dusty-looking notes in an attic and he is going to polish them up till they shine like the gold that they are:

For a brief period Beethoven digresses from his main topic to enchant us with a gentle contrasted tune starting on the solo violin. But long before the double bar this main topic is being touched on once again. Mozart in his later works (e.g. the G Minor Symphony) usually develops his opening tune just *before* the double bar (as well as after) and Beethoven probably learned to do so from him. In the development he adds a corollary to the little turn of bar 1, and tries it both ways up with most exciting results:

When the opening section returns, the music to a large extent is rewritten so that, already in Beethoven's very first quartet, there is a hint of that sense of continuous development from the first bar to the last that characterizes so many movements in the later quartets.

The slow movement is said to have been inspired by the tomb scene in *Romeo and Juliet*. Its great tragic intensity was a remarkable achievement for so young a man. The main theme, over a throbbing bass, contains the little turn that peppers the pages of the first movement:

Beethoven later 'orchestrates' this with wonderful effect, his two inner parts in octaves. This was a common device in the late quartets, but a novelty in 1800:

Every time this melody appears it is given an accompaniment of increasingly tragic intensity, culminating in the version near the end high on the cello.

The *Scherzo* and Finale are less remarkable, but very good movements all the same. It is perhaps worth pointing out that the Finale is extremely difficult, notably (at the end) for the viola player, who in the eighteenth century expected to enjoy a quiet time, both in orchestral and chamber music. For whom a quartet such as this was written is in fact quite a question. Could the many amateur quartet groups in Vienna cope with its difficulties, or was it *only* played by Beethoven's friends in the professional orchestras? Apply this question to a Bartók quartet and the answer is obvious. Nowadays this question does not need asking. No one writes quartets for amateur groups any longer, and composers intend their chamber works for ensembles of the highest skill, with all day and every day in which to practise. This quartet is symptomatic of this change of direction in its early stages. Fortunately for the few amateur groups that still survive to-day, the other quartets in the Op. 18 group are a good deal easier, Nos. 4 and 5 being probably the least difficult.

The second quartet in G is very different from its predecessor, light and gracious and altogether charming. Beethoven shows his desire to say three things (almost) at once in the very first bars:

We noted this tendency in the Piano Trio in D (Op. 70, No. 1). The second subject, as Ernest Newman has pointed out, begins with one of Beethoven's commonest harmonic 'fingerprints':

The slow movement of the *Pathétique* Sonata, written a
year or two earlier, begins with this same harmonic progression, and it is not difficult to find other examples. The
slow movement has a *scherzo* episode in the middle, and
when the slow music returns the cello has the main tune,
previously the property of the first violin. Unlike Mozart,
or for that matter Schubert, Beethoven nearly always continues cerebrating during his recapitulations, and so main-
tains or even heightens our interest in his music at just that
point where attention so often flags in Schubert's sonatas
and symphonies, in which recapitulation follows exposition
practically note for note.

The fourth quartet in this set is a work of great strength
in Beethoven's C minor vein. It begins:

The cello part prompts a digression on what might be called
the repeated-quaver-accompaniment opening. This had a
considerable vogue from about 1780 to 1800. For instance,
a majority of Dussek's piano sonatas of this period begin
very much like the above quartet (Dussek anticipated a
surprising number of Beethoven's more dramatic effects),
as do several of Rosetti's string quartets, which probably
date from the late 1780s. The *locus classicus* for this sort of
opening is the Mozart C Major String Quintet (K. 515),
in which the three middle parts have repeated quavers for

the first thirty-seven bars, with one six-bar intermission. The five string quartets and quintets by Förster published in one of the Denkmaler volumes *all* begin in this way. When, in 1794, Haydn left Vienna on his second trip to London, Beethoven took lessons from Albrechtsberger in counterpoint, and from Förster in quartet writing, and could have learned this effect from him. The opening of the first Rasoumovsky (Ex. 22) *looks* like Förster, though its emotional undertones make it sound very different. There seems no doubt that Haydn, Mozart, and Beethoven affected this device far less frequently than their contemporaries; it does after all make composition rather easy.

To return to the C Minor Quartet, the second theme is interesting as having affinities with the first (see bar 3 of Ex. 10). This is a commonplace in Haydn, but rare in Beethoven and Mozart.

Ex. 21

On the other hand, the extreme lyricism of the above example is something Beethoven probably learnt from Mozart. Haydn, before Mozart's death, was little interested in contrasted lyrical second subjects. When he does attempt them, as in the 'London' Symphonies, the result is a little unconvincing; they are never the memorable part of a movement, and one feels he is glad when they are over. Mozart, on the other hand, is usually at his most romantic in his second subjects, and indeed they proved the moment in sonata-form for which nineteenth century romantic music was best fitted. Beethoven likes the second subject of this quartet so well that he uses it in the development, a comparatively rare feature in classical music up to that time.

Instead of a slow movement, he wrote a moderate-paced graceful *scherzo* which opens with a *fugato*; it resembles in form and mood the slow movement of the First Symphony, written about the same time. No doubt he felt that so intense a first movement needed something light-weight to follow. The Minuet shows Beethoven's dawning impatience with minuet-and-trio form and its rather too numerous exact repetitions. He omits the second repeat in the Trio and directs that the Minuet itself is to be played *più allegro* the second time. (He had already slightly varied the repeat of the *Scherzo* in the String Trio in G, and in the third of these Op. 18 quartets.) This Minuet has something of the intensity of the first movement, and no trace whatever of the urbane charm of a real minuet.

Incidentally it is curious that Albrechtsberger also wrote a string quartet with both a minuet and a *scherzo*; it would be interesting to know whether he did so before or after Beethoven wrote the C Minor Quartet; one presumably caused the other.

The Finale has a desperate gaiety and makes a splendid end to this very fine quartet. A friend pointed out to Beethoven that in bars 9 and 10 there are concealed consecutive fifths between viola and cello, and asked how he justified the use of these forbidden intervals. Beethoven at first denied their presence and then, confronted with overwhelming evidence, said grandly, 'I allow them.' Actually there is a far worse pair in bars 25–6 of the preceding minuet.

As regards the remaining quartets of the Op. 18 group, I must content myself with pointing out the interesting experiments in 'doubling' in the Trio of the Minuet of the fifth quartet; the fact that the second subject of the Finale of this same work is identical with one in the Finale of the *Pathétique* piano sonata; the quite astonishing syncopation in the *Scherzo* of No. 6 (very hard to play); and the wonderful slow introduction to the Finale of this same work. Beethoven headed the introduction *La Malinconia* and directed that it should be played with the greatest delicacy. What a pity the Finale itself proves such an anticlimax!

STRING QUINTETS

THE only string quintet worth serious consideration is Op. 29 in C, written in 1801 and published the following year. I feel great affection for this work, even though I realize that parts of it are not very good. The opening makes me think of the start of Schubert's B Flat Piano Sonata; it has something of the same nobility. But this promising mood is cut off in its prime and replaced by a trivial short-breathed triplet figure, effective enough combined with the 'noble' theme in the development, but sadly out of place here. The second subject is one of the first for which Beethoven chose the 'wrong' key – A major – and he keeps in this key right to the end of the development. In his last quartets he constantly puts his second subject a third above or below the first. The long slow movement needs no qualifications; it is a lovely sustained piece of writing. I think Beethoven had been looking at the slow movement of Mozart's G Minor Quintet, but he could not have had a better model. The *Scherzo* is good (doubling at *four* octaves in parts of the trio!), but the Finale rather less satisfying though a highly original piece of 'orchestration'. At the start the four lower strings play a shimmer of very quickly repeated notes, while above these are scurrying wisps of phrases on the first violin. The second subject starts a semitone higher than expected (A flat instead of G) with good effect. Towards the end of the development, Beethoven suddenly abandons tempo, time signature, and key, and introduces a brand new minuet-type tune in A major. Mozart brings this off in at least one of his violin concerto finales, but it somehow does not quite answer here. In fact, this movement never 'comes together' into an entity. Frankly, this endearing work is not one-tenth as well written as Mozart's String Quintet in the same key.

There is also a very short sprightly fugue for string quintet which Beethoven wrote in 1817, when the problems of a new kind of fugal writing were beginning to fascinate him. It was published as Op. 137. His Op. 4 needs no more than

a mention here, as it is a string quintet version of the previously written wind octet, confusingly published later as
Op. 103. No doubt Beethoven (or his publisher) thought it
would have more chances of performance in the string
version. Of rather more interest is the string quartet version
(in F) of the E Major Piano Sonata, Op. 14, which Beethoven made in 1802. Much of the first movement transfers
to the new medium easily and effectively, but nothing could
look less like string quartet writing than the Finale of this
sonata, and Beethoven shows wonderful ingenuity in the
face of frightful odds. But even he is beaten by the G major
section, producing admirable string music at this point, but
only by altering the original out of all recognition. In my
view, this quartet is an improvement on its piano sonata
original.

STRING QUARTETS, OP. 59

THE 'Rasoumovsky' Quartets, Op. 59, in F, E Minor, and
C, were written about 1806 and published in 1808. These
three quartets were commissioned by Count Rasoumovsky,
who had come to Vienna as Russian Ambassador in 1792.
The Count was a violinist and had his own quartet, led at
one time by Schuppanzigh, he himself playing second violin. Förster was his musical instructor and librarian. The
Count asked that each of the commissioned quartets should
contain a Russian folk-tune, but Beethoven only remembered this in the F Major and the E Minor.

These quartets are in some ways the most wholly successful in existence. It has been argued (not by me) that in the
wonderful late quartets Beethoven overstrained the medium
and attempted the impossible. But no one could deny the
complete success of these three works; Beethoven found
heights never before scaled by man and reached the top
with triumphant ease. His technique in these middle years
was equal to demands that would have floored all his contemporaries; at about the same date he was writing the
Fourth and Fifth Symphonies, the Fourth Piano Concerto,

and the Violin Concerto, his titan's vigour as yet unimpaired by the fact that even at this date he could hear very little of what he wrote.

The first of these three quartets is the largest and I think greatest. It begins:

All seems diatonic and on the surface. But almost at once there are vague undercurrents:

This music slowly broadens like a great river. There is much writing in thirds, the two violins being paired together, and the viola and cello, and later some of the curious knees-bending-and-stretching music –

– to which Beethoven was addicted all his life; for instance, in the first movement of the Fifth Symphony (bar 196) and in the finale of the Eighth (bar 458).* There is no double bar, which enables Beethoven to pretend to repeat his opening section and then surprise his listeners by doing no such thing. Soon the little quaver-phase in bar 3 of the opening cello tune is spotting the paper like a rash; the development ends with a *fugato* on what is to all intents and purposes new material.

It is comparatively rare in Beethoven for the *scherzo* (or minuet) to precede the slow movement, but it happens in this quartet, also in the Ninth Symphony and the 'Archduke' Trio. Haydn chooses this order in four of his six 'Russian' Quartets (Op. 33), but thereafter only four times in thirty-three works. Mozart chooses this order in three of the six quartets avowedly influenced by Haydn's 'Russian' set, and only once after that. There is seldom any apparent reason for the choice. It would seem that Beethoven, in this first 'Rasoumovsky', was reverting to an order that had been unfashionable for twenty years. But much the most remarkable fact about this *Scherzo* is that it is in sonata form; from now on he was to write no more conventionally constructed *scherzi* in his string quartets. This is also, so far as I know, the first *scherzo* that is not in the key of the work (or in its major or minor equivalent); in Haydn and Mozart it is always the slow movement that is in the contrasted key, never the minuet. It may seem pedantic to mention these points, as they will not help the listener to a greater appreciation of the music, but they are given here as examples of Beethoven's attempts to shake himself free from the conventions of classical music. This is certainly quite unlike any other *scherzo*. It is a completely unified piece of music, and yet the tiny phrases on which it is built cover an astonishing range of emotions: idyllic happiness:

---

* Brahms was also addicted to these 'exercises on the spot', e.g. in his Third Symphony, slow movement (bar 57), and Fourth Symphony, first movement (bar 227). But he was stiffer in his joints than Beethoven.

jauntiness:

deep melancholy:

The slow movement is one of Beethoven's most sublime:

This opening melody is immediately repeated by the cello, and Beethoven sustains and intensifies the tragic feeling of the opening with absolute mastery throughout this long movement. Just as the slow movement of the early F Major seems to me the greatest achievement in the Op. 18 group, so this similar but more mature movement is surely the greatest achievement in the 'Rasoumovsky' group. The music leads without a break into the finale, which is based on a Russian folk-song given out on the cello. As with most of the Scots, Irish, and Welsh tunes he later arranged, Beethoven mistook the character of this folk-song, being under the impression that it was a much faster and more cheerful tune than it really is.

In this respect he was no more successful in the E Minor Quartet, where the Russian tune is used for the 'trio' section of the unnamed third movement:

Ex.29

This is the well-known 'Slava' (Glory) that comes in the coronation scene of *Boris Godunov*, in the orchestral *entr'acte* representing the battle of Poltava in Tchaikovsky's *Mazeppa*, and in several works by Rimsky-Korsakov.* It is, of course, a great soul-stirring patriotic hymn, not at all the delicate little flower Beethoven made of it. Fortunately, it is perfectly easy for non-Russians to adopt Beethoven's ignorant attitude towards these tunes and we shall then enjoy what he makes of them very much indeed.

This E Minor Quartet is much the most elusive of the three. It begins, as does the 'Eroica', with two chords that have no purpose other than to attract our attention. No previous composer could have written what follows:

Ex.30

---

* Both these Russian tunes are given in Rimsky-Korsakov's collection of Russian folk-songs (Nos. 13 and 45); 'Slava' is also given in the *Oxford Book of Carols*, No. 107.

This music has a romantic melancholy in marked contrast with the virility of the C Major Quartet. The first movement, like that of the D Major Trio (Op. 70) has two repeats, and I hope the reader will bear with me while I digress on what is, to me, a puzzling subject.

Under the heading 'Repeats' *Grove* propounds the old adage that the first section in a sonata-form movement was repeated to allow the listener a second chance to grasp the thematic material before it was developed. Late in the nineteenth century this may well have been the excuse given for this practice, but it can hardly have been the reason in classical times. We tell students that sonata-form means 'Tunes – Development – Tunes', because this is the simplest way of explaining it, besides which it is true if there are no repeats. But, apart from the last five quartets (which date from about 1799), Haydn, with only two exceptions, repeats *both* sections of *all* his string quartet first movements, and Mozart does the same in nine out of ten of *his* 'famous' quartets. Thus, the scheme is: ‖: Tunes :‖: Development – Tunes :‖, and the repeats are due not to a desire to plant the themes, but to the conventions of binary form dating from the time of Bach and Handel; perhaps due also to the natural desire of amateurs to play everything a second time and get it a little better.* This last theory is borne out by the fact that the second repeat survived much longer in chamber works than in symphonies. In Mozart's last ten symphonies he either has no repeats at all in the first movement (e.g. Nos. 33–5) or only the first repeat (e.g. Nos. 38–41). But all his string quartets have the second repeat except K. 575. Haydn started to abandon the second repeat in his symphonic first movements in the late 1780s.† But in piano sonatas and chamber works it was not

* Repeats must also have been welcomed because they allowed the first violin to show his skill in extemporising decorations. Spohr heard a Haydn quartet in Hamburg in 1817 and complained that the leader 'introduced so many irrelevent and tasteless ornaments that it was impossible for me to feel any pleasure in it'; the practice lingered on until quite late in the century.

† There is no second repeat in Nos. 84, 86, or 92. All the other pre-London symphonies repeat both halves.

generally abandoned until some ten years later, when Haydn, Beethoven, Clementi, and Dussek all chose to do without it at about the same time. All Haydn's quartets up to the 'Emperor' (*c.* 1797) have the second repeat (with one exception) but none thereafter; two of Beethoven's Op. 9 trios and Nos. 5 and 6 of the Op. 18 quartets have this second repeat, but none of the early piano trios have it. Did composers lead the way in dropping it, or were they merely bowing to circumstances, performers having in practice been leaving it out for years? And just *what* made Beethoven revert to the second repeat in this E minor 'Rasoumovsky'?

The third 'Rasoumovsky' is the most straightforward and perhaps the most immediately attractive of the three. It has a slow introduction, a common enough feature in classical symphonies, but a rarity in string quartets, there being only one example in Haydn's and only one in Mozart's. Unlike Beethoven's later slow introduction this one has no thematic connexion with what follows, and its veiled keyless indecision throws into strong relief the forthright *allegro* tune that follows. I find the slow movement a shade monotonous, but the Minuet is graceful charm itself. As in the Fifth Symphony, the 'dance' movement has a coda leading without a break into the Finale. This is a bustling fugue (with a good many homophonic episodes). I quote from half-way through, where the main theme (in quavers) is joined by a new counter-subject (in minims):

This movement has that muscular energy that was one of Beethoven's most original contributions to music; other examples can be found in the first movement of the Fifth and the last movement of the Seventh Symphonies.

OP. 74, 95

Two more quartets, Op. 74 in E Flat and Op. 95 in F Minor, were written in 1809 and 1810 respectively. Like the Op. 18 set, Op. 74 is dedicated to Count Lobkowitz, one of the three guarantors of Beethoven's annuity, which began in the year of its composition. Again the first movement has a slow introduction, and it is worth noting that both the first theme of this and that of the *Allegro* move immediately into the subdominant. This was always a favourite trick of Beethoven's, and it actually occurs at the start of his First Trio, Op. 1 No. 1, as well as of his First Symphony. The frequent *pizzicato* accompaniments in this opening movement have led to the work being known as the 'Harp' Quartet. The *Scherzo* is one of those in which the trio comes twice, and it leads straight into the Finale which is a set of variations. Two of Haydn's 'Russian' Quartets end with variations and so does Mozart's D Minor; the only other example in Beethoven's chamber works comes in the Clarinet Trio. The extremely fast speed of the *Scherzo* probably caused Beethoven to choose a form which could start comparatively slowly for contrast.

The F Minor is the shortest of all the quartets, not because Beethoven has less to say, but because he says it more concisely. This fascinating work is really much more akin to the late quartets than to those of the composer's middle period. The music constantly avoids the obvious with that touch of perversity that is so enthralling in Beethoven's later works. The second subject starts on the viola:

Ex. 32

This is repeated immediately by cello and second violin, but never in the whole movement quite rises to the surface on the first violin.* It is indicative of Beethoven's new terseness that there are no repeats, and that in the recapitulation this second subject comes a mere seven bars after the first.

The slow movement is refined and a little impersonal, and demonstrates Beethoven's increasing interest in *fugato*. It leads straight into the *Scherzo*, another of those in which the trio section comes round twice, though by now Beethoven is fully composing his dance movements; each 'recapitulation' is in fact a new development of the previous version. When the trio section first appears, Beethoven slips up a semitone from F to G flat; this has happened more than once in the first movement (and see p. 117). The Finale, which has a tiny slow introduction, has rather more romantic warmth than the other movements.

Already in this quartet we feel that deafness is causing Beethoven to turn in on himself and that the outside world is ceasing to interest him.

THE LATE QUARTETS

IN the list below the works are given in order of composition:

Key	Composed	Published	No. of movements
E Flat, Op. 127	1824	1826	4
A Minor, Op. 132	1825	1827	5
B Flat, Op. 130	1825	1827	6
	(Finale 1826)		
Grosse Fuge, Op. 133	1825	1827	
C Sharp Minor, Op. 131	1826	1827	7
F Major, Op. 135	1826	1827	4

* Did Elgar have this tune in mind when writing the first movement of his Second Symphony?

These were the last works Beethoven wrote, and he wrote no other music at this time. It will be noticed that, the F Major apart, each quartet has one movement more than its predecessor. The *Grosse Fuge* was originally the finale of the B Flat Quartet, but the publisher, Artaria, complained that it made an already very long work of quite intolerable length. Beethoven, with unexpected meekness, wrote a new finale which was in fact the last music he completed. The fugue was published separately, both in its original form and in a piano duet version, apparently made by Beethoven himself. At the time these quartets were written, Beethoven was to all intents and purposes cut off from his fellow-men by total deafness, and his life was made yet more miserable by constant stomach disorders and headaches. It is to be remembered that by our standards he would be judged no more than middle-aged at his death.

It has always seemed to musicians that these quartets were the expression of a man who was spiritually no longer as other men, and their technical and emotional difficulty for long prevented their being either played or understood. I was myself brought up to believe that, wonderful though they might be, they imposed more strain on the listener than any other music; perhaps more strain than any composer had a right to inflict. But there seems to have been a great change in our attitude to these quartets since the war. The Third Programme has brought to light (if that is the word) music which, by comparison, makes Beethoven's most abstruse movements seem almost naïve, and those who hear these quartets now find no great difficulty in appreciating them. To-day it is Bartók's quartets that are regarded with the respectful apprehension accorded to Beethoven before the war. I do not wish to overstate this point of view. These quartets are unlike any other works of their century, and they do need many hearings before they fully reveal themselves, but each has at least one movement that makes an immediate appeal. These are arguably the finest quartets yet written, and so worth some trouble.

The E Flat is a smiling contented piece, reaching

sublimity in the slow movement. In the first movement, few of the classical conventions are left. The short slow introduction is integrated with the movement (it recurs twice later on); the various sections of sonata-form, so carefully isolated by Mozart, here merge one into the other so that the second subject appears without warning; we scarcely notice when the development begins or ends because the music in fact develops continuously from first bar to last. Much of it derives from the first *allegro* tune, each of the phrases marked below being developed later on:

There follows a set of variations on a long sustained theme, whose second half starts melodically and harmonically just like the second half of the slow movement theme in the 'Archduke'. It is hard to see the connexion between some of the variations and the theme; failure to do so need not diminish anyone's enjoyment of this lovely music. The *Scherzo* begins with a device much loved by Bartók: the inversion of the main theme.

This dotted rhythm reminds one of the *Scherzo* of Op. 95. Beethoven's sketch books reveal that the uneven rhythm was an afterthought. The Finale is a pleasantly ambling piece with a curious coda in which, most unusually at this point, the speed slackens, so that good playing is needed to prevent a sense of anticlimax. The first tune in this coda appears to be new, but is in fact the opening tune of the movement in a new rhythm.

The A Minor and B Flat Quartets and the *Grosse Fuge* were conceived at the same time and themes for all three are inextricably muddled in the sketch books. Beethoven was obsessed by the top four notes of the minor scale, their attraction being that one of the intervals is a tone and a half.

Ex. 35

That is *not*, as it stands, a theme in one of these quartets (though it *is* the opening of the C Minor String Trio; see p. 109). But let us now examine the beginning of the A minor:

Ex. 36

(only essential notes shown)

It will be seen that there are two versions of the four notes: the cello's (immediately repeated a fifth higher by the first violin) and the viola's, in which bar 2 comes before bar 1. Beethoven spent much time searching for an *allegro* countersubject before he hit on this:

Ex. 37

(only essential notes shown)

Notice that viola and cello divide the slow tune between them; some ten bars later the two violins are dividing it, while viola and cello have the countersubject. There is the most heart-warmingly lyrical second subject and then the music comes to a standstill as the development begins; a low cello note all on its own is in fact the start of our slow tune in canon:

There is a barely noticable alteration here; the leap-up is in fact a semi-tone greater than before, and Beethoven has unwittingly tumbled on the main theme of the *Grosse Fuge*:

But if we isolate bars 4–7 of this we are back in the A Minor Quartet (see Ex. 37).

In the sketch books there are numerous tunes using both the larger and the smaller leap in all manner of rhythms; the majority had to be discarded.

In the C Sharp Minor Quartet Beethoven is still working on his *idée fixe*. The fugue with which it opens has for subject:

While the last movement has two contrasted themes, both announced near the start:

Clearly these three great works have a very special unity.

QUARTET, A MINOR, OP. 132

LET me now take these late quartets individually, the **A**
minor first. This, it will be remembered, has five movements. In the first movement the dual first subject and the
lyrical second subject described above come round three
times and defy analysis in terms of Mozartean first movement form. The scoring of this second subject is miraculously varied each time, the omission of the first three notes
on its last appearance having, for some inexplicable reason,
a quite breathtaking effect. The *scherzo* (not so called) is
rather a dry piece, but not for that reason lacking in
interest. Its two themes are announced together in the
fifth and sixth bars, the one in crotchets having started the
movement off:

The whole of the *scherzo* section derives from these two
phrases, or parts of them. I suspect Beethoven to have had
in mind, consciously or unconsciously, the equally dry
minuet of Mozart's A Major Quartet, also based on two
two-bar phrases, the one rising, the other falling. According
to Daniel Mason, the trio section derives from a tune
Beethoven wrote in extreme youth for a court ball; what his
evidence is I do not know. The music suggests that they had

bagpipes at the ball. Discerning students will notice the theme of the C sharp minor fugue (Ex. 40) on the lower strings in unison octaves towards the end of this trio section.

The slow movement is headed 'Song of thanksgiving to the Deity on recovering from an illness, written in the Lydian mode'. Poor Beethoven, his recovery was all too imperfect. Bartók, in his Third Piano Concerto, wrote a similar slow movement (so similar that coincidence can be ruled out) when he too had just recovered from an illness; but as with Beethoven, his life was almost over. The frequency with which Bartók comes to mind as one studies these late quartets is a measure of the tremendous influence this music had on him. The slow movement of the A Minor Quartet is in double-variation form like the slow movement of the Ninth Symphony. The first theme is like a very slow chorale, the lines separated by two or three bars of close imitation; the second is vigorous and is in fact marked 'Vitality regained'. The chorale has two variations and the 'vitality' theme one, so that the form is A B A B A.

This is a very slow and very long movement, for me the most difficult listening in all Beethoven's music. Someone has irreverently described the piece as like a man seeing how slowly he can ride a bicycle without falling off. The end can be overwhelmingly beautiful, but it is a very long time before you get there.

There follows a short intentionally trivial little march in binary form, providing listeners with welcome relief from the higher thought. This leads straight into the finale with its warm romantic 'valse triste' theme. It is hard to credit that this essentially intimate tune was originally intended for the finale of the Ninth Symphony.

QUARTET, B FLAT, OP. 130, AND GROSSE FUGE, OP. 133

THE B Flat Quartet starts with the biggest of all Beethoven's quartet first movements, yet this, alone of the late quartets, has a repeated exposition. There are three short themes:

Notice that both the slow introduction tune and the second *allegro* tune are characterized by a rising sixth; in fact, both are distant cousins of the *Grosse Fuge* subject. Beethoven as in Op. 132, wisely places a very short movement (in *scherzo*-and-trio form) after this very long one, and then comes the first of the two slow movements, entrancing music with something of the grace and charm of eighteenth-century court life reinterpreted in terms of music as Beethoven knew it in 1825. The fourth movement, too, is immediately appealing. It is headed *Alla danza tedesca* (in the style of a German dance) and has this ingenuous little tune:

Notice the lavish expression marks, and the favourite device of a crescendo followed by a sudden drop to *piano*. The sketch books show that this movement was originally to have been in A. Perhaps it was to have followed the 'Song of Thanksgiving' in Op. 132. Next comes the intensely tragic and very slow *Cavatina*, of which Beethoven said, 'Never have I written a melody that affected me so much', and lastly the rather superficial finale Beethoven wrote at the request of Artaria. The second subject is pretty, and somehow got into Borodin's subconscious; when he found that the first movement of his A Major Quartet was based on an all-too-similar theme, he saved the situation by adding the words 'inspired by a theme of Beethoven's' under the title.

By this time Beethoven's key contrasts are normally based on the interval of the third, major or minor. The finale of the B Flat Quartet begins in G, a third above the key of the *Cavatina*, and a third below the real key of the movement, which is reached at the end of the first subject. This key relationship must have been very carefully considered, for the *Grosse Fuge*, the original finale of this quartet, also starts in G before arriving in its true key of B flat. Here is a brief analysis of the tremendous fugue:

Introduction. The theme in unison octaves, as given on p. 130; I shall call it A for brevity; next, three transformations of A, as they will occur in the three main sections of the fugue (fast, fairly slow, *scherzo*), but in the reverse order. All this takes less time to play than to describe.

First Fugue. A double fugue, A being the counter subject; the main subject has wide leaps and a dotted rhythm. The energy generated in this section is overwhelming; the music is cruelly difficult to play and usually sounds a bit of a scrape. Very loud all through.

Second Fugue. Fairly slow. A is again the countersubject and does not appear for some bars. Very soft all through.

Third Fugue. Scherzo. A, here the principal subject, sounds very jaunty in 6/8 rhythm. This is a long section with reminiscences of what has gone before.

Coda. Based largely on the dotted-rhythm subject in the First Fugue.

Grove, in the first edition of his *Dictionary* (1889), wrote: 'Of the fugue one has no means of judging, as it is never played' Fortunately instrumental technique has more or less caught up with its difficulties and performances are now fairly frequent, some of them by string orchestras. These, I feel, make the music sound too smooth and playable; to make its full effect this fugue needs a certain roughness, as though it were only by a hair's breadth within the players' capabilities. Whether it succeeds as a composition will probably remain a matter of opinion; it is certainly one of Beethoven's most ambitious undertakings. If it fails, it fails magnificently.

QUARTET, C SHARP MINOR, OP. 131

THE C sharp minor is the most original and the most consistently sublime of these quartets. This music floods the mind with its beauty. In the B Flat Quartet the six movements, wonderful as they all are individually, do not perhaps quite coalesce to make a unified work. In the C Sharp Minor Beethoven solves with complete success the problem of equating variety with unity. The seven movements all run into each other.

The quartet starts with a slow quiet fugue whose theme has been given on p. 130. In this music Beethoven seems to have escaped from the world of men and to have achieved utter spirituality. It seems almost irrelevant to mention technical details, but the three phrases marked on p. 130 are all used in sequence; the one beginning on the second note of bar three can also be found in diminution (twice as fast) against the theme itself:

Immediately after this the cello enters with the theme in augmentation, that is, twice as slow. The fugue ends on a bare C sharp, which turns out to be the leading note of the next movement, which is in D. We have already noticed Beethoven's fondness for sidestepping up a semitone. This second movement has, for contrast, a rather uncertain gaiety with a hint of pathos under the surface. The third is no more than a short introduction to the set of variations that follows. As so often in Beethoven, it is not helpful to search for the tune in the variations; frequently it isn't there. The harmonic scheme rather than the melody above it is his basis for this music. The first four bars can be reduced to:

and this progression can be found (more or less) at the start of each variation.

There follows a very fast bucolic *Scherzo*, introduced with a false start on the cello, to show that Beethoven is in good humour. The sudden explosion and the sudden *adagio* bars (wait for it!), though not actually funny, are decidedly humorous. The naïve second tune comes in a variety of doublings; for instance, on the two violins, and very uncouth on the two lower strings. The sixth movement is a wonderful little *Adagio* in G sharp minor; a mere twenty-eight bars are enough for Beethoven to express a world of sadness. The finale is a robust piece in sonata form, and the themes have already been given on p. 131.

QUARTET, F MAJOR, OP. 135

FOR the little F Major Quartet I have all too little space. It is half the length of the others, and Beethoven clearly wrote it as a relaxation after the tremendous strain of committing the others to paper. It does not attempt to plumb the depths of human experience, yet achieves something very near perfection in its own humorous epigrammatic way. It is not inappropriate that Beethoven should have taken leave of music in this unobtrusive way, like Samson 'calm of mind, all passion spent'.

As might be expected, Beethoven's chamber music, in particular his string quartets, had a profound effect on composers, performers, and listeners, and I shall end this chapter by trying to show just what this effect was.

First, Beethoven's effect on the composer. Haydn wrote eighty-three string quartets, Brahms three, and it is very hard to think of any composer after Beethoven who reached double figures. In our own century this falling off might have been ascribed to a decline in demand, but this can hardly have been the reason in the nineteenth century. It was in fact Beethoven himself who did more than anyone to dam the flood of chamber works tossed off in sets of six or more by his predecessors. As we have seen, he greatly increased the emotional range of the string quartet, enriched its texture, and overthrew the structural conventions that for long had made composition a comparatively simple business, posing and solving fresh problems of form with each work that he wrote. Later composers could hardly ignore this one-man expedition into the unknown; nor indeed did the better of them wish to do so, for they were aware of at least some of the wonders of the new world he had opened up. But it must have seemed idle to explore exactly the same ground as Beethoven, and indeed they must have been aware that they lacked the necessary equipment to venture so far; and yet it was hard to find an alternative direction in which to strike out. The one certainty was that exploration of some kind was now obligatory; it was no longer sufficient, as it had been in the eighteenth century, to stay quietly at home amid familiar surroundings. In other words, Beethoven made his successors almost self-consciously aware that great things were expected of the composer, and as a result writing music became an increasingly tortuous business, a struggle against odds, a waiting for inspiration followed by a hammering of inspiration into shape. Anyone who wrote quickly would from now on be suspected of having little of worth to say, and perhaps find himself criticized for 'lack of significance' or 'failure to integrate his ideas', or any of the other evils on which the modern critic pounces so assiduously. Brahms destroyed a dozen quartets before he allowed one to be published; to an eighteenth-century composer it would have been incomprehensible that a man should destroy a quartet he had just written.

In the orchestral field composers could take refuge in the tone poem or in lush Wagnerian harmonies, but there were few prospects in such directions for anyone who wanted to write quartets. It would perhaps be reasonable to acclaim Bartók as the first worthy successor to Beethoven in this form of composition.

Beethoven also made things difficult for the player. The quartets of Haydn and Mozart, not to mention those of their many inferior contemporaries, were welcomed in countless homes and played for the fun of it by people who would never have dreamed of turning so pleasurable an activity into a drudgery with hours of hard practice. But Beethoven's later quartets were much too difficult for the average amateur, and only after hours of hard practice could they be made effective by professionals. That people were not used to practising such music is implied by a passage in Spohr's autobiography.

I selected for the occasion ... one of the finest of Beethoven's six new Quartets (Op. 18) ... But already after a few bars I remarked that those who accompanied me were as yet unacquainted with this music, and therefore unable to enter into the spirit of it. If this really annoyed me, my dissatisfaction was much more increased when I remarked that the company soon paid no more attention to my play. For by degrees, a conversation began, that soon became so general and so loud that it almost overpowered the music. I therefore rose up in the midst of my playing ... (but later) willingly resumed my violin and played *Rode's* Quartett in Es, which the Musicians knew and therefore well accompanied. A breathless silence now reigned, and the interest shewn in my play increased with every passage ...

One hopes that Spohr learnt from this experience that Beethoven quartets without rehearsal do not succeed; there seems much less hope of his learning that they are not violin solos. It was this very difficulty of Beethoven's quartets that helped to bring about the innovation of professional chamber music groups playing at public concerts for profit, and until such groups appeared (and generally speaking they did not do so until the latter half of the nineteenth century) his late quartets were scarcely ever played anywhere. The eventual result of writing music which could only be played by professionals with all day in which to rehearse was, of course, a decline in amateur music-making, for which Beethoven must share responsibility with Signor Marconi.

Before Beethoven, a chamber music audience can scarcely be said to have existed. Such music was invariably written for the performers, and on those occasions when a few friends happened to be in the same room, they mostly listened out of politeness and with only half an ear. The performer tends to be much more indulgent towards a thin composition than the listener, for he has something to occupy his mind other than the musical content of the work in question. In the eighteenth century this indulgence gave the facile composer a certain security. But to-day the man who writes chamber music within amateur capabilities can hardly hope to be taken seriously; in fact, it is tacitly assumed that the good composer writes for the discerning listener rather than the moderate performer. Such a change in attitude would probably have occurred if Beethoven had never written a note, but there can be little doubt that he was a prime initiator of this change and that he caused it to happen very much more rapidly than it would have done without him. It was, of course, his isolation in deafness that made him increasingly ignore the musical needs of the world around him and write as it were in a personal vacuum from which all outside influences had been extracted. We would not wish it otherwise, for it would seem that deafness, so far from having been a handicap to Beethoven, became a positive asset, hastening his own development as a composer and making possible the wonderful music of his last years. But we should be thankful to belong to a generation that has learned to deal with the difficulties Beethoven put in the way of his contemporaries. On record and on radio we can hear, and hear again, the inventions of a titan among composers, until the sounds that rampaged round his soundless head become part of our very lives.

5

Franz Schubert (1797–1828)

WILLIAM MANN

INTRODUCTION

SOME of the most wonderful and widely loved chamber works in all music were written by Schubert. But it would be too much to postulate him as primarily a chamber composer. The case is weakened by at least three symphonies, by much stage music whose greatness is only unrecognized because the premises of its composition belong to the dead past of history, by some church music which is adored by those who know it. If the solo and duo piano works and the songs are excluded from the category of chamber music, then the scales must tip substantially.

The concerted chamber works with which this chapter is concerned bask in spheres beyond odious comparison; even considerations of greatness seem quite unimportant to the merits of the quintets, quartets, trios, and the octet. They are music to be loved, and they inspire an affection that in human affairs we accord to our closest relations and to those friends from whose company we are never long absent.

Schubert wrote something over thirty concerted chamber works. It is astonishing to realize that the intense love and tenderness with which posterity regards them is wholly inspired by the last nine that he completed. The others are, expectedly, not negligible; the gramophone is beginning to make some of them available, and one or two of them will be dealt with here in more than general terms. The spirit of Schubert dwells in them; they pave the way to the works that we know. But they do not begin to match the nine masterpieces which will be separately treated at the end of this survey.

Relaxation and easily found magic melody are the

characteristic qualities of Schubert's music, and this applies
to his chamber music. But there is more to it than discursive
eloquence and a widow's cruse of tunes. The boy who could
write *Der Erlkönig* and *Gretchen am Spinnrade* turned into the
man who wrote *Die Winterreise*; and this poet of melancholy
also composed the G Major String Quartet, and its fellows
in A minor and D minor (not more tragic for all their
minority of mode), and the trio of the C Major Quintet.
What is more, if Schubert was the greatest melodic genius
who ever lived, and although he is averred to have been an
unlearned composer, he was a master of harmony, and an
adventurer in key climates so audacious that it is possible to
declare harmony as the most striking element of these
chamber works; I shall therefore touch almost more on
harmony than on melody in this survey. And whether in the
breezy holiday atmosphere of the B Flat Piano Trio and the
'Trout' Quintet and the Octet, or in the inward contempla-
tion of the C Major Quintet, or in the pathos of the three
great string quartets and the C Minor Quartet movement,
there is a naturalness that recalls Jean Paul's phrase about
miracles in broad daylight. Formally, even these masterpieces are not flawless -- for example, to begin your recapitulation in the subdominant, so that the movement may
automatically end in the tonic, looks very like cheating --
but their forms arrive with such innocent spontaneity that
we generally accept them, even forget to notice their idiosyncrasies. This music seems to have happened of its own
accord and so, like the wise sayings of our children, we are
strengthened in our love for the mouthpiece of such inevitability. Schubert had good opportunity to play chamber
music (like Mozart, he preferred the viola, while his
brothers were the violinists and his father the cellist), and
so every incentive to compose it. From the age of thirteen
he wrote, or at any rate started, two or more chamber
works every year until 1817, when he achieved full mastery
of the medium. The early works are more compact than
their successors were to be, with terse, sometimes perfunctory development sections; as may be expected, they lean

heavily on the best models. Yet they foretell the later master in their habits and their experiments.

A fragmentary Introduction and Allegro in G Major for String Quartet is the first work in the list (D. 2,* 1810); even the fragments show us an inquiring mind, for the theme of the *Allegro* borrows its contours from the Introduction. Three movements for quartet (D. 3, 1811) were re-shaped later, an *Andante* into a piano piece (D. 29), another *Andante* and an *Allegro* as part of a string quartet (D. 32).

The first whole work is a string quartet (D. 18, 1812) which begins in C and ends in B flat major; it is one of three quartets that explore the idea of progressive tonality; the other two are lost. As in D. 2, the opening *Andante* supplies the thematic shape of the following *Presto* in G minor; adventures in tonality distract Schubert from his home climate in the final *Presto* and, not for the last time, in his career, he has to regain B flat at the eleventh hour. The C Major Quartet, which borrowed two earlier movements (D. 32), begins with a 6/8 *Presto* indebted to *opera buffa*, and it too gives its melodic contour to the minuet which follows; it is strange that Schubert did not pursue this device into his maturity – links between movements in his last chamber works are so tenuous and subtle as to seem unintentional. To the same year belongs a single *Allegro* movement for piano trio. Here and in the B Flat Major Quartet, finished in the following year (D. 36), Schubert is still the careful student; the Finale of the quartet has a likeable Haydnesque theme. 1813 was more prolific in chamber music for Schubert: the C Major Quartet (D. 46) begins with a heart-felt chromatic *Adagio* introduction, recapitulates the first subject of the subsequent *Allegro* in the dominant, and has its Minuet in the unorthodox key of B Flat major. The same dominant recapitulation turns up in the finale of the D Major Quartet (D. 74); Schubert was to learn, as I have hinted, that a subdominant recapitulation makes the homecoming less arduous, sometimes positively attractive. Also

* Numbers with prefix D refer to the thematic catalogue compiled by Otto Erich Deutsch (Dent).

belonging to 1813 are two *Allegro* movements of a String Quartet in B Flat (D. 68), two movements of a wind octet, and some dance movements for quartet. But the most important, if only because it has been accorded an opus number and so qualified for wide circulation, is the E Flat String Quartet, Op. 125, No. 1 (D. 87); it is a pleasant, here and there a characteristic work. The second subject of the first *Allegro* borrows its rhythm (long-long-short-long) from the first subject group. The *Scherzo* involves the *acciaccatura* followed by a downward plunge which, since Mendelssohn and Saint-Saëns, have had asinine connotations. The *Adagio* is melodiously Beethovenish; the finale brings forward triplets in 2/4 time with the relaxing effect that we find in almost all of Schubert's mature masterpieces. None of the movements venture far from their home key and, perhaps because Schubert is not inclined to much experimenting, the work is superficially polished and so gratifying. It has been recorded.

Two published string quartets belong to 1814: the D Major Quartet starts with a perplexing *Allegro* – perplexing because the exposition never really reaches the dominant until just before the double bar, because in the flood of tunes (at least four of them attractive) the ear can find no 'subsidiary group of ideas' to point the shape (all the tunes are in D major, though there is the semblance of a fifth in F sharp minor), and most of all because after a development section which characteristically reaches the Neapolitan warmth of E flat major, the recapitulation begins in C major and then gets lost, resulting in some new ideas but not much recapitulation. The melody of the *Andante* falls into uneven groups of phrases and is only too thankful when it can break into running quavers. The Minuet takes its Trio, effectively, in B flat. The *presto* Finale is the most successful movement, with a laughing theme in three-bar phrases, and some telling excursions into E and B flat major.

The B Flat Major Quartet, Op. 168 (D. 112) is more sure of itself and of its author's personality. It begins as though for a fugue, thinks better of it, and modulates into G minor before reaching the dominant. The exposition is long and involves much preliminary extension of themes, so that a comparatively short development (typically it starts in D flat major) is not to be censured; Schubert finished the movement in four and a half hours, which was quick work even for him, when we consider how elaborate it is. The *Andante* is in G minor, rather Beethovenish; the best part about it is the heavy emphasis on A flat (the Neapolitan second) in the coda. The Minuet is Haydnish, in E flat, and the rhythm of the Trio (its *pizzicato* bars too) recalls the Trio of Beethoven's Ninth Symphony. The *Rondo* is sparkling and very diatonic for Schubert and part of the theme looks forward to the *Scherzo* of the Great C Major Symphony.

There is a charming Guitar Quartet in the record catalogue wrongly ascribed to Schubert, who only provided it with a trio and a cello part. The rest is the work of one Matiegka. Schubert's adaptation of this dates from 1814.

The G Minor Quartet of 1815 (D. 173) is attractive, but not as significant as the key might have suggested to a composer who loved Mozart. The melodies are not yet fully characteristic though they stay in the head; Schubert begins the recapitulation of the first movement in the relative major, in such a way as to suggest that the development is still in progress. The E Major Quartet (D. 353), composed in the following year, was posthumously dignified as Op. 125, No. 2. The shade of Mozart falls across its first and last movements: the second subject of the opening movement has the same rhythm as the melody which opens Mozart's G Minor Symphony, K. 550, and is even developed by antiphony and inversion in the manner of the bridge to the recapitulation of Mozart's movement; the Rondeau takes its tune, lock and stock, if not barrel, from the Finale of Mozart's Thirty-ninth Symphony, K. 543. Schubert's key sense is seen at its most percipient when, in the first movement, he reaches the dominant and then quits it for C major, the better to establish B major when the music returns thither. The *Andante* has a typical dotted rhythmical gait; again the recapitulation brings an experiment, for

Schubert returns to A major by way of D flat, in which key he starts his reprise.

And at this point Schubert, the chamber musician, passes out of his apprenticeship, for the String Trio in B Flat Major (D. 581, 1817) though concise and unpretentious, is certainly a masterpiece; searching in tonality, utterly characteristic and poised in its themes, and blessed with felicitous texture – a work to cherish. Two years later, no complete chamber work intervening, he wrote the 'Trout' Quintet which must be discussed at length.

QUINTET IN A MAJOR FOR PIANO AND STRINGS, OP. 114, D.667 ('THE TROUT')

IN the summer of 1819, Schubert and his friend Vogl (the singer of so many of his songs) went on a walking tour together in Upper Austria. One of the places they visited was Steyr, where Vogl had been born. There was a flourishing musical community there, presided over by Sylvester Paumgartner, a wealthy musical amateur who played the cello. Schubert was happy at Steyr (there were plenty of pretty girls about the place); we can hear as much in this piano quintet which Herr Paumgartner commissioned from him. It seems that he and his musical friends had been playing, or were going to play, Hummel's Piano Quintet, and wanted another work for the same unusual combination. For the strings who collaborate with the piano are not a regular string quartet; instead of a second violin, Hummel used a double bass and Schubert obediently did the same. The greater weight of string sonority makes a fuller contrast to the resources of the piano, and is particularly suited to antiphony between piano and strings. Schubert's ear nevertheless told him that, with a growling double bass in the company, he must be cautious with the bass register of the piano, and so we find a large proportion of the piano part written in the treble clef, and often in octaves between left and right hand (a habit that he did not trouble to overcome in his later piano trios). Thus, baldly described, the piano part seems tediously simple, but it is exceedingly grateful to play, and is not without its tricky passages. The double bass part is the dull one; only one moment of glory comes to gratify its exponent, in the variation movement. The cello part, on the other hand, is full of rewarding melodious writing, though we gather that it was too difficult for Paumgartner's modest accomplishment.

(No autograph score of the 'Trout' Quintet exists; it is supposed that Schubert wrote out the parts in his head, but it seems more probable that a rough score, which may perfectly well have been his only draft, was lost or thrown away. In 1829, very soon after Schubert's death, Joseph Czerny acquired the parts of the 'Trout' Quintet as part of a Schubert bequest, and only after this was a score published.)

The nickname of the quintet comes from the song *Die Forelle* (D. 550, 1817) which Schubert uses, slightly altered, as the theme of the variation movement in the quintet.

First movement: *Allegro vivace*. The exposition is dominated by an uprushing *arpeggio* that acts as a refrain, rounding off statements here and there, and opening proceedings by declaring the key. The double bass, glued firmly to his lowest A, further emphasizes the key, as the other strings propose the principal subject in its simplest form. The key-declaring *arpeggio* is important for, as already shown, Schubert habitually jumps in and out of more or less foreign keys all the time. Two phrases of the first idea have been expounded, both firmly in A, when the music jumps, magically because without any fuss, into F major, and the piano gives out an extension to the subject in high octaves which are to be so characteristic of this work. The carefree blandness of the music is partly due to a passion for triplet movement; the quaver pulse of the accompaniment is constantly being varied by the triplets of the refrain, or of some new antithesis or afterthought suggested by the refrain. The journey to the dominant, E major, for the second subject involves visits to C major (the mediant C, and the submediant, F, are as natural allies of Schubert's home keys as the conventional dominant, E, or sub-dominant D, in A major). By the time that E major is reached, triplet movement is well established, and the piano ripples easily along in triplets under the second subject which is, roughly speaking, a love duet for cello and violin (Ex. 1). The rhythmic pattern is extremely characteristic of Schubert, the longer note values of the thesis being shortened in the antithesis. The gentle flow of the love duet

Ex. 1

is interrupted by the refrain and a cadence; but it is resumed and rounded off by a pendant for piano solo. C major is still a favourite goal for excursions (it was the mediant of A, and is also the submediant of E major, the dominant which has now become an assumed tonic). There is a miraculous switch into C major, when all the instruments suddenly hush, while the right hand of the piano plays high octaves. We are back in E for the codetta, which divides its energies between semiquaver runs and an athletic dotted figure; the piano part is rarely out of the treble clef during this section. A final affirmation of E major having heralded the double bar and the end of the exposition, the development begins by plunging straight into C major, *pianissimo*, for strings alone. The first subject is discussed in its original form. When the piano (octaves in the treble clef, as usual) joins in, the music moves away towards E flat, which is as far away from A major as you can get, and pretty far from E. Nevertheless, for Schubert it is no distance, since the dominant, B flat, is the Neapolitan second in A major, and this in Schubert's affections takes second place only to the mediant. Having arrived at this impossible key, Schubert and his instruments stay there, playing happily with their triplet runs and dotted figures; they have gone halfway round the tonal world, and therefore any further modulation is a step to-wards home. Such steps have eventually to be taken, and at length Schubert rises by step to C flat = B natural, which is of course the dominant of the dominant. We are still listening to those triplet runs, and continue to do so until we return to the recapitulation. But this does not begin in A major. Schubert innocently begins his recapitulation in D, the subdominant, so that his second subject and coda may drop effortlessly into A, the home key. But this means that B major is one door further down the street than we thought.

The recapitulation starts with the later, and more attractive form of the first subject (the original form was fully discussed in the development). Thereafter it is perfectly strict. With this music, the lazy man's recapitulation is everybody's delight; nothing is more welcome than a second bite at these irresistible cherries.

Second movement: *Andante*. There is no need to observe in such detail the remaining movements; the characteristics of a balanced masterpiece persist throughout the length of the work.

This *Andante* falls into three sections, which are thereafter repeated in different keys. The first section beginning in F major has the principal tune in octaves on the piano; the third bar proposes a dotted rhythm, and the ninth a triplet pattern, both of which are features of the whole work. The second strain (at bar 24) moves into F sharp minor (the Neapolitan second of F, as alluded to above); the tune for viola and cello may recall part of the Serenade *Leise flehen meine Lieder*. The third strain is reached with bar 36 in D major; here the dotted rhythm takes a new turn, one that is only perfectly to be formulated when the music reaches G major, in a typical Schubertian jogtrot. with the tune in soft treble octaves on the piano. Note the Lydian fourth (C sharp) and the flattened sixth (E flat) as standard fingerprints of the composer. The double bar is reached in G major (the dominant of the dominant), and the music plunges quickly up a step into A flat major (Neapolitan second!) for a literal restatement of these three sections, the last of which remains in its incipient key instead of reaching

for the subdominant, so that the whole thing ends properly
in the home tonic of the movement. The naïve rambling of
the movement hides a harmonic scheme worthy of a cross-
word expert.

Third movement: *Scherzo, Presto*. The tune of the *Scherzo*
seems straightforward enough when it starts, but its four-
bar phrases have an extra pair added on at the end. The
music reaches C major, an old friend, before we have time
to turn round, and stays there at the half-time bar. The
second strain moves into the dominant of F major, and is
much concerned with imitative counterpoint. The trio is in
D major and antiphonal by nature, the two hands of the
piano being pitted against the two upper or two lower
strings. At the end the four string parts are answered by
four parts in the piano. There is a marvellous journey into
B flat major in the second half of the trio.

Fourth movement: *Theme and Variations. Andantino –
Allegretto*. Schubert's setting of *Die Forelle* exists in five versions, whose pace markings vary from *Mässig* (*Moderato*) to
Etwas lebhaft (*Poco allegro*). The pace of the variation movement here is a compromise, but we may note that the tune
has been refined down and made more demure, with new
rhythmic values and a flowing harmonious texture, as a
theme for variations in D major (the song was in D flat).
First of all, it is played by strings alone. At *Variation* 1 the
piano decorates the tune (octaves in the treble clef!) against
a limpid triplet accompaniment carbonized (so to speak) by
a *pizzicato* bass. In *Variation* 2 the triplets move to the violin
part; viola and cello take the tune, whose phrases the piano
echoes romantically. The piano babbles happily away in
semi-demiquavers in *Variation* 3. At last, in *Variation* 4, the
double bass is allowed a tune to play, though doubled by
the cello – double bass players find Schubert a cowardly
writer for their instrument. The other two instruments have
a dummy accompaniment to play, but it is a model of tact
and felicity with touches of counterpoint or comment, every
now and then, to bring all the parts into relief. *Variation* 5
launches noisily into D minor, and for the first time makes

an attempt at metamorphosing the tune; the double bass
again has a hand in this. It is not an inspired metamorphosis, but the change to F major makes more than sufficient amends, and the second half is exuberantly contrapuntal. *Variation* 6 is serene with dotted and double dotted
rhythms, and a doubt whether it is in B flat major or minor.
Later it reaches D flat major (the mediant again; that is why
B flat minor was suggested) on the way to F. Seven extra
bars plunge into D flat minor, in order to modulate enhar-
monically, and in unusually respectable order, into the
dominant of D major for the last variation, which is marked
Allegretto, and which gradually reveals the distinctive accompaniment figure of the original song. At the third repeat of
the second half, the piano excels itself in lovely leaping
figuration. The movement dies away to nothing, as in the
prelude to the song.

Fifth movement: *Finale, Allegro giusto*. A held E calls attention; compare it with the held note similarly placed in
Schubert's late B Flat Piano Sonata (D. 960). The difference
is that here it stands at the front door of A major, the home
key, but there it misleads the way into C minor instead of
B flat. The jogtrot theme here is firmly in A, in spite of a
gratuitous swerve into G major (Ex. 2). The theme is
rounded off by a repeat of its first strain. The drooping
curve of the first phrase is exploited in a bridge passage

Ex. 2

that reaches D major, for the second subject, via C and D
minor, and much antiphony. The second subject is twofold:
the strings have a swinging tune, shared between them,
while the piano has a rocking-horse figure that ends with a
nonchalant chromatic descent. The whole thing reaches a
cadence in F sharp minor, from which the music turns con-
templatively, and for once in even quaver movement, back

towards the first subject, reshaped by the piano as follows:

When this musing reaches what sounds like a codetta, we are still in D; Ex. 2 is reset into small, repeated phrases, beneath garrulous triplets for piano, which are discussed briefly at the start of a new section in B flat major. Ex. 3 is also involved, and the small repeated phrases return in the treble clef on the piano. D major is reached again in a serene section based on the bare bones of Ex. 2. There is a brief outburst in D minor and then D major is confidently established. What has this to do with a development section? Nothing; for the cadence in D heralds a double bar and an optional repeat mark. The rest of the movement is simply a literal recapitulation of what has been already heard, starting in E major and finishing up at home. There is no official development section; but unofficially all the material has been discussed. If the thrushes of Steyr choose to sing this song twice over, with only a change of key, no one has yet complained. If Schubert takes the lazy way out, we may remember that he was on holiday, and that the holiday relaxation of the 'Trout' Quintet has always been its most engaging feature, the inspiration of some of Schubert's most generously captivating melodies.

OCTET IN F MAJOR FOR CLARINET, HORN, BASSOON, AND STRING QUINTET, OP. 166, D. 803

ON 6 March 1824, Moritz von Schwind wrote to his friend Schober: 'Schubert has now long been at work on an octet, with the greatest zeal. If you go to see him during the day, he says, "Hullo, how are you? – Good!" and goes on working, whereupon you depart.' The octet had been commissioned by Count Ferdinand Troyer, an amateur clarinettist at the court of the Archduke Rudolph (dedicatee

of Beethoven's Trio, Op. 97). He wanted something like
Beethoven's Septet; the resemblances were much com-
mented upon, then and later. Troyer took part in the first
performance, sometime in March 1824; the Octet had been
completed on 1 March, before Schwind wrote his letter.
The public first performance did not take place until April
1827. Contemporary criticism found it too long; it is certainly long, with six movements, but not lengthy; indeed,
form and content seem masterfully matched for such an
informal composer as Schubert.

First movement: *Adagio – Allegro*. The first idea of all
forecasts the dotted rhythm and rising contour of the later
Allegro.

F major is quickly forsaken for A flat major, the minor
mediant, and here the clarinet proposes a faster dotted
rhythm, highly characteristic of Schubert. At a shift into
B flat minor, the clarinet prophesies the octave leap and
dotted rhythm of the second subject (Ex. 5). Schubert's
command of form is sometimes decried, but this introduction shows the extent of his skill as the tool of genius. The
first subject of the *Allegro* has hardly been announced when
the first violin moves almost automatically into triplets, and

the other instruments catch the habit. The music takes a
firm but unconventional turn into D minor (or rather it is
a looking-glass convention, for in minor keys it is perfectly
acceptable to take your second subject in the relative
major) for the second subject (Ex. 5 above). The rhythm
is close to that of the first subject and vestiges of that idea
continue to be heard underneath. The clarinet tune draws

an added effect of yearning from the dominant thirteenth at the end of its first line, and this is reinforced when the horn repeats the tune in F major (it proves to be a perfect invention for the natural horn, entirely devoid of accidentals, for once in Schubert's way). Despite this invasion of D minor, Schubert is destined to end his exposition in the proper key of C major, and thither the music moves, halting at E flat major on the way. The dotted rhythm accompanies the even semiquavers of the codetta theme, and reaches its climax in a dramatic jump of two octaves for the horn. A reversion to D flat for a reminiscence of the second subject is designed only to emphasize the stability of the dominant C major. (It is, or should be, misleading, incidentally, to refer to the key in which an exposition ends as the dominant, for the composer has been at pains to establish it as a new tonic; conventional theory prescribes dominant as its name, but in this circumstance 'half-tonic' or some such name would designate its function more accurately.) Schubert marks the exposition to be repeated, and leads back to it via the octave jump that forecast the second subject. At the second-time bar he switches simply and magically up a semi-tone to land in F sharp major (his favourite key of the Neapolitan second). The point of the switch is to whisk us away into B minor where the second subject is dealt with, acquiring a haunting new transformation played by the clarinet and, later, the second violin. A flat major has been reached when the wind trio finds a new chorale-like idea (one might sing *Nur wer die Sehnsucht kennt* to it) and this proves to be akin to the opening phrase of the slow introduction which is now briefly alluded to before the recapitulation breaks in. The coda is marked *più allegro*; it flaunts the first subject and at the end is suddenly hushed to a steady rhythmic pulse as the horn takes up the second subject, and mulls it over at a comfortable tempo, rising to a *fortissimo* before the final cadence which involves a tricky turn.

Second movement: *Andante un poco mosso*. The tune in B flat major is another gift for Count Troyer, effortlessly melodious, as the whole movement is, supported by the accompaniment figure that the whole world knows from Schubert's *Ave Maria* (though it is differently stressed here). A repetition glides in without a perceptible pause and now the clarinet adds an upper part. The later extensions of the tune bring back the rising dotted figure of Ex. 2, by a surely unintentional act of cyclicism. There is no reason why this melodious improvisation should reach an end, but eventually formal instincts assert themselves and a sort of cadenza for violin, clarinet, and viola leads to a recapitulation. The coda begins with strings alone, dealing imitatively with the tune. They collapse on to an accompaniment which pulsates like an anxious heart, and over them the clarinet takes wing in D flat major. In the closing bars echoes of the main tune drift about over a tonic pedal. So shackled, Schubert cannot avoid ending in the right key.

Third movement: *Allegro vivace.* The tune of the *Scherzo* has a habit of gliding into irrelevant keys; the first line feints into D minor and then behaves as if it had never moved. Very shortly (at bar 17) it jumps directly from F major into the dominant of its own dominant. After these alarming escapades nothing could be more poised than the jaunty clarinet solo which ends the first strain. The second strain, in which the clarinet duets with bassoon, settles in D flat major, and is only shifted by the return of the main tune, now enhanced by a finely flying coda, surmounted not for the first time by an octave leap for the horn in a dotted rhythm. The Trio is staid, with a slower moving melody in C major over a plodding staccato bass in regular crotchets; the modulation to the dominant seems unconvincing probably because it is made at the last moment. The *Scherzo* is repeated note for note but this time, with no trio to follow immediately, the two final chords make an oddly brusque, almost comic effect, as though someone had left the room in mid-sentence, slamming the door on his interlocutors.

Fourth movement: *Andante.* This is a theme with variations, as was the corresponding movement of Beethoven's Septet. The theme is the first part of a duet from Schubert's earlier opera *Die Freunde von Salamanka.* Schubert sets it, here

as there, in C major. A theme chosen for variation has to
have a prominent distinguishing mark: in this theme it is
the sudden lift to the sixth degree of the scale, in the last
line of the tune, thus:

These variations have been peppered with scorn by commentators, partly because they are decorative, not developing variations. Yet their place in this work is a relaxing one;
fun and games are needed at this juncture, not an intellectual exercise. *Variation 1* varies the theme in babbling triplets with some airy counterpoint. *Variation 2* is busy, its triplets spread out through the strings, with a double dotted
figure for wind and cello; the characteristic rise to A is
ignored. For all the blackness of the semi-demiquaver accompaniment, *Variation 3* is more serene; the accompaniment
is translucent and colourful with *pizzicato* viola and skitter-
ing *arpeggio* punctuation for the first violin. The tune is
shared between horn and woodwind. *Variation 4* features
triplets again, and gives the cello a chance to shine. C major
is at last exchanged, in *Variation 5*, for C minor; clarinet and
bassoon in octaves give the tune a long face. At the rise to A
(now flat), the harmony takes a heady turn into D flat.
Musicians are all agreed that *Variation 6*, in A flat major, is
the pick of the set, with its luminous texture, exquisite
counterpoint, and peaceful *arpeggio* figuration which leads
in an epilogue back towards C major for *Variation 7* (*Un
poco più mosso*) which Maurice J. E. Brown chastises as a
'distasteful episode'. It is frankly comical, with its town-
bandish dummy accompaniment and frenzied violin
bravura. At the end, the brakes are applied and we are
returned wistfully to the tune, now refracted and meta-
morphosed. Echoes of it linger in the air and die away to
nothing.

Fifth movement: *Menuetto, Allegretto*. The tune is passed
between strings and wind As with many other themes in

the octet, the anacrusis is dotted both here and in the Trio. A triplet or two adds a carefree touch to the music, and these become important in the second strain, most of all in the lovely clarinet solo over a swaggering accompaniment in A flat major. The return to the main tune is very free with much echoing of single phrases. The Trio is delightfully expansive, with a cello part that recalls the accompaniment to Schubert's *An Sylvia*.

Sixth movement: *Andante molto – Allegro*. The slow introduction, veiled in mists and strong drama, explores the jungles of tonality; the sun is hardly glimpsed until the dominant of F minor and major materializes at the end, though there is the always familiar dotted rhythm to point the relevance of events. Then the *Allegro* arrives, and home territory is reached. The main theme sounds like a fugue subject, but its course turns out to be a march with an exhilarating tail to its tune. The march is exposed at length, first by strings, then by the whole consort, then extended in phrases of uneven length. An old and successful gambit, disjunct phrases that collide at the distance of a tone or semitone, seems like a second subject; but the real one only arrives when C major is established. There is a pause, a dominant middle pedal is set in motion (compare this whole process with the parallel passage in the Great C Major Symphony), and the wind breaks into a garrulous tune, straight out of a comic opera overture. After a further glance at the march, now blessed with a counterpoint in triplets, the exposition comes to a full stop in C major for the second time, and we turn directly into A flat for the middle section: the march is set in imitation, and new colliding patterns, as above, are produced; C sharp minor, which has only Schubertian relevance to prevailing tonalities, somehow arrives, and the second subject has a new innings in A major. The march tune is inverted, but Schubert does not press this head-hopper's view, and a firm pedal C, with cello trills buzzing above it, leads back to the march and a recapitulation. The end of it dives without warning into G flat major and the slow introduction (which had no relevance to the main *Allegro*) returns with added *bravura* for the first violin, even more mystifying. Again the sun breaks through, and *Allegro molto* is breathlessly adopted for the coda, which turns the march into something like a dervish dance. Schubert tries a canon on the march theme, but the impetus of the moment is too much for his learning. There is a close season for counterpoint as for other pursuits.

The first of the four mature string quartets is a single movement, the so-called *Quartettsatz* in C minor (D. 703, 1820); but it stands by itself, like the Unfinished Symphony, to complete satisfaction. It is an *Allegro assai* of hectic, dramatic power, wide-ranging in its ideas, at times almost Wagnerian. The design is audacious and, in effect thrilling, for although the Wagnerian storm opening influences the transition subject in A flat and the second subject in G major, it is not recapitulated exactly until after those melodies, in what proves to be the coda; so that the recapitulation seems to start with the transition subject and in B flat major (the dominant of the relative major). Schubert left an incomplete *Andante*; it was to be in A flat major.

The only one of these four great quartets to be published in Schubert's lifetime was the A minor work, Op. 29 (D. 804, 1824). The very first bars are enough to promise an unforgettable experience: over a pulsating bass whose rhythm pushes the music forward irresistibly, the second violin describes a bleak accompaniment figure (reminiscent of *Gretchen am Spinnrade*, which Schubert had set some years previously). And then the first violin enters with a tune whose forlorn aspect is to colour the whole work. Merely to look at the small changes with which the melody expands and becomes more expressive, in this first group of ideas, is to realize how completely genius had found itself. And the lead-back to the recapitulation, with the pulsating bass now spread through the three lower parts as a diminished seventh, is the most moving of all its transformations, even more moving than the turn into A major which paradoxically gives the melody an even more melancholy tone of voice.

The second movement is a contemplative, serene tune in C major, known from Schubert's music for *Rosamunde*; but in its context it too seems tinged with wistfulness as it reaches for E major, pauses, and returns via the dominant of B flat to C major. The Minuet would cast gloom on any ballroom; its octaves with a third below them cry out in pain, and it is significant that Schubert had used them before to the words *Schöne Welt, wo bist du?* The Finale starts gaily enough in A major and seems almost irrelevant until the sad second subject in C sharp minor pulls it in perspective. The quartet ends happily; but did not Schubert write the B flat Piano Trio at the same time as *Die Winterreise*? – it was part of his nature.

The D Minor Quartet, known as *Death and the Maiden*, opens with a sharp call to attention, not a harmonic surprise, but a boldly rhythmic one, with a prominent triplet element that pushes the first group of ideas remorselessly forward, and underlies the melting, rather Brahmsian, second subject in thirds and sixths. The triplets turn into running semiquavers before this subject is fully exposed. Both subject groups are fervently discussed, and the return is so disguised and enhanced as to sound like more development, though the arresting rhythm of the first statement cannot be mistaken. The music moves into the minor for a strenuous quasi-fugal interpolation. At the end of the recapitulation the rhythm of the opening returns in a grey, frightening transformation, before a quick coda.

The slow movement consists of five variations on a tune from Schubert's song *Der Tod und das Mädchen*, whence the nickname of the work. The fourth is in the major and the fifth returns to G minor and includes a coda with a very soft reminiscence of the theme.

The *Scherzo* has a theme astonishingly prophetic of the one Wagner used to portray his *Nibelungen* (the theme played by all the anvils in *Rheingold*); the trio is in D major with a more tranquil tune, but the *Nibelung* rhythm remains in the minor parts.

The Finale is an uneasy *Presto* with a jogging main subject. The second subject, in longer notes, is heard after a pause and, in later stages, comes near to the song of the Erl King in Schubert's song. There is a *Prestissimo* coda.

STRING QUARTET IN G MAJOR, OP. 161 (D. 887, 1826)

IF only one of these three last quartets is to be described in detail, then on grounds of style it must be the last of the three, the one in G major. It is by far the most impressive (which is not necessarily to imply the most moving) and original – perhaps the most original in language that Schubert wrote – yet entirely characteristic, and entirely self-assured; the audacities arise spontaneously, without the conscious experimenting that the younger Schubert had indulged in when he wanted to express his feelings.

First movement: *Allegro molto moderato*. This is not progressive but perplexed tonality:

The conflict of minor and major is to persist, not quite to the end of the work. The jerky rhythm of bars 3 and 4 later induces transports of rhythmical counterpoint that looks more like Bartók than it sounds. The rhythm of bar 5 is carried forward into the second movement. This opening section is like an introduction or a text, though it is repeated in the recapitulation, but *vice versa*, minor moving to major, and in the closing bars both adventures are combined, with G major the eventual victor. The second part of the first group of ideas begins with a shudder of G major and above it, like the beginning of a symphony by Bruckner, the first violin breathes a gentle tune in short phrases (still a hint of G minor), which are later repeated by the cello.

There is an even more Brucknerian passage at the start of
the development when the passage is recalled in E flat
major with a rising counter-subject for viola. The expanding
chords of Ex. 7 are extended, with other less drastic implications, and presently, after the Bartókish passage, F sharp
major is reached. This is the mediant of D major, but the
second subject, which has Schubert's favourite conga
rhythm (strong accent on the second quaver of the bar),
only reaches D from the springboard of F sharp, and this
gives a touch of disquiet to what is otherwise a mild, not
very melodious idea – the harmony and rhythm are everything to it. Schubert takes care that the theme is well fixed
in our minds as he moves with firm deliberation via B flat
major to D. There is a good deal of *tremolo*, reminiscent of
the *Quartettsatz*. The climax of the development is reached,
during elaboration of a second counterpoint to the Brucknerian tune, with a grinding tonic seventh on C, and in the
reprise it is the theme itself which is ornamented. The movement ends with a curiously mild and formal procession of
tonic chords, as though to say 'That is that, for the present
at any rate'.

Second movement: *Andante un poco moto*. The melodious
cello solo in E minor has a pathetic ring for all its diatoni-
cism; perhaps the swaying octave Bs in the accompaniment
are responsible. The tune reaches in vain, towards its close,
for the sunlight of C major, but is driven back to E minor.
The subsidiary section is bold and firmly G minorish,
recalling the first movement with its dotted rhythms. In the
middle of its frenzy there occurs the following surprise:

It looks bitonal and it sounds bitonal – very like a passage
in Bartók's Fifth Quartet; J. A. Westrup has shown that
the persistent figure is, in each case, a harmonic anticipation of the subsequent diminished-seventh chord, but his

explanation does not banish the ear's surprise, and Schubert
had no intention that it should. The first melody reappears
in B minor, set as a free canon, and canon is retained for a
third, more cheerful tune in G which interrupts this reprise;
at a later repeat the tune is made to sound less cheerful,
almost saturnine, by being shared between first violin and
cello. The E minor tune eventually gains E major and,
rather unconvincingly, the movement ends in this Picardian
key.

Third movement: *Scherzo, Allegro vivace*. Here is another
anticipation of the *Scherzo* from the Great C Major Symphony, in B minor this time. The second strain includes a
masterly lightning modulation from C sharp minor back
to B minor; and a beautiful quasi-Neapolitan cadence
reaching from E flat major back to B minor. The Trio in
G major has a *Ländler* tune and a bagpipe drone, so irrelevant to the rest of the quartet as to sound cynical.

Fourth movement: *Allegro assai*. The Finale is a long and
marvellously inventive *rondo*, of almost diabolical energy.
True to the spirit of the whole quartet its theme veers
between the minor and major modes of G; and true to
Schubert it pays homage to the minor submediant, E flat
major. The first time bar promises B flat major and breaks
its word, only to keep it after the repeat of the *rondo* theme
(for which reason the repeat should always be observed).
The second subject, or first episode, proposes and elaborates
a garrulous tune in G major, reminiscent of Rossini's
Figaro, and his catalogue of 'Rasori e pettini, lancetti e
forbici'. After a change to D major, a third idea, imitatively
inclined, stresses the rhythm we all associate with Beethoven's Fifth Symphony, though here the effect is of a
tarantella. A fourth tune, having apparently exhausted the
rhythmic possibilities of quavers in 6/8 metre, collapses into
dotted minims; but quickly resumes the tarantella. These
four ideas are exchanged and elaborated, without perceptible pause for thought, but with consummate inventiveness. At last, loud chords with D at top and bottom seem to
proclaim G minor; and then Schubert drops the basket

that contained all his eggs; he ends with the Haydnesque tune and in cloudless G major. He has the best possible precedent in Mozart's G Minor String Quintet, and we have already remarked his ability to be cheerful in adversity. But on this momentous occasion it is difficult not to be disappointed.

TRIO IN B FLAT MAJOR FOR VIOLIN, CELLO AND PIANO, OP. 99, D. 898

IT is one of the miracles of the world that Schubert was able to compose this trio at the time when he was conceiving *Die Winterreise*. There is no trace of melancholy, let alone the black despair that is ascribed to Schubert at this period, and O. E. Deutsch has questioned its ascription to the year 1827.

It is a blissfully happy work, rich in cheerful melody, unusually diatonic for Schubert, although full of characteristic modulations and key switches.

First movement: *Allegro moderato*. The principal tune sails in at once, all sunshine and swagger:

The punctuating figure in the left-hand piano part enhances the *élan* of the tune, and will be further used later. Schubert's favourite triplets, as well as the dotted rhythm of the figure, are at once in evidence. At first the tune only lasts four bars and then, as if to show that it is less strenuous than it seems, stops and starts again, a tone higher, in C minor. This time it spreads out to its full length, which admittedly is only two bars longer. Triplets and the dotted figure are interchanged and, as the music moves carefully into D major, the feeling is of transition to the second subject. But D turns back to B flat and we hear the first

subject again, this time in octaves on the piano, modulating
to F. Once arrived at the correct key for the rest of the
exposition, Schubert strengthens it by roaming a little
towards the dominant of D, in order that, when he returns
to F major, the key will seem like home and not a temporary
lodging (for all his love of foreign keys, Schubert had a
masterly grasp of tonality). The cello halts on A, the
dominant of D, and converts it into the mediant of F for the
start of the second subject which swoops up and down.
The postface is concerned with octave jumps, borrowed
from the bass of Ex. 9, and answered by seventh iumps from
the second bar of the second subject. The key is now firmly
fixed as F, and to make certainty more sure, a pause of a
bar is taken at a cadence, and the codetta then resumed,
with an identification of the second subject and the octave
leaps. The exposition is not enclosed by a cadence: it ends
on the verge of B flat, so that the music either leads back
to the major of the opening or straight on to the development which plunges into B flat minor, and deals straight-
forwardly, first with the first subject, then with the second
combined with a figure from the transition group. Firmly
the key centre shifts as far away as possible to E major, in
order to move back, remarkably early, to the dominant of
B flat. But the development is not yet over; the first subject
has a new innings in G flat and then D flat, returning by
stealth and just when we least expect it, to B flat for the
recapitulation. Everything happens in good order, including
the bar's rest. But at the moment when the first subject is
brought back, a plunging coda is launched. It takes a
pause in A flat, at a *molto fortissimo*. The piano resumes
quietly and wistfully, only to make an about face into B flat
for a coda to the coda on the transition figuration.

Second movement: *Andante un poco mosso*. The key is E flat
major. Over a rocking 6/8 accompaniment, the cello de-
lineates a suave melody in its alto register:

Ex.10

The third and fourth bars exemplify a Schubertian finger-print; the same phrase is repeated and altered rhythmically, its dotted rhythm being opened out. At the end of the tune the cello proceeds with a new strain that acts as a counter-subject to the repetition by the violin of the tune itself (see the slow movement of the Octet). The piano has its share of the melody after a modulation to B flat, and this time the intervals of the tune begin to alter and enhance expressiveness. The minor third has been insinuating itself into this major mode tune, and before long E flat major has returned, become minor, and led to the inevitable mediant, G flat major. The middle section begins in E flat, then drifts into C minor for a more anxious episode with much off-the-beat pedal accompaniment (comparable with the slow movement of the 'Unfinished' Symphony). The piano has the tune which breaks, also inevitably, into octaves in the treble clef: such inevitabilities bring nothing but delight in Schubert. Scales and *arpeggios* ripple through the texture, and we are still in C (major) when the suave melody floats back, into A flat. E major and C major are traversed and suddenly, without a thought of preparation, the music jumps into E flat major and the end, with a coda of lingering echoes, is in sight. This is the most chromatic of the four movements, a haven of evening scents and quiet companionship.

One of Schubert's compositions ascribed to the same period is an *Adagio* in E Flat for piano trio. There is no evidence to suggest that it was intended for this trio except the key and the supposed date of composition, but they amount to a very strong coincidence indeed. The *Adagio* (originally listed as a Nocturne) has a long, floating tune that recalls the *Adagio* of the C Major Quintet in its leisurely pace; but the middle section is an empty affair, cluttered up with schoolroom *arpeggios*. One can see why Schubert would not choose to include it in Op. 99. It may, of course, have been a study in piano trio writing, as a preparation for Op. 99.

Third movement: *Scherzo, Allegro.* The *Scherzo* is over in a flash, although it progresses in units of two bars; rhythmically Schubert is almost chained to a pattern of three crotchets followed by six quavers, as in bars 3 and 4:

but in fact this pattern gives the movement the impetus that makes it seem so fleeting and full of charm. There is an endearing moment of hesitation at the double bar, before the music settles in A flat; the first strain has a penchant for C minor (comparable with the second start of the principal theme in the first movement).

The Trio in E flat moves more leisurely; enthusiasts for organic unity may like to trace a back reference to the *Andante*. The double bar here finds the music anchored by the most insecure of granny knots to G minor; but Schubert casts off at once back to E flat major, so no harm is done.

Fourth movement: *Rondo, Allegro vivace*. The theme of the *rondo* is muscular but utterly amiable, The first episode begins more pugnaciously:

It is disarmed by a new cheerful tune, but retaliates with a two-part invention for strings, set against heavy pianoforte trills – the passage has a Beethovenian effect. It ends in A flat (how often this trio has visited that key). The disarming tune and Ex. 12 alternate and we expect a return to the *rondo* theme, when the time signature switches to 3/2, the key to D flat, and Ex. 12 is combined with a strange version of the *rondo* theme. The theme itself is not brought back until this is over. It now appears in E flat, and its first four notes are then taken apart. The 3/2 episode returns in B flat and is rounded off by Ex. 12 followed by the disarming tune, the two-part invention and their exchanges, all in B flat major. The 3/2 episode is recapitulated in G flat major now. What we then expect is a third repeat of the *rondo* theme, but what we get is a *Presto* coda based on Ex. 12 and the first four notes of the *rondo* tune. The tune itself is lost for ever, but in the excitement there is not time to regret it.

Schubert followed the B flat trio with another in E flat major, Op. 100 (D. 929, 1827). It is longer, more thorough-going, less endearing than its predecessor. The *Andante* in C minor is the most satisfying movement, beginning with a suggestion of the parallel movement in the Great C Major Symphony, and continuing with a poignant cello tune (believed to be a Swedish folk-song) that is later raised to a passionate climax in C sharp minor. The opening *Allegro* is serious, thematically not very felicitous, and long-winded, as is the Finale which has better tunes, a quasi-Turkish episode, and a welcome return of the cello *cantilena* from the *Andante*. The *Scherzo* proceeds cautiously in canon, and has a Trio that goes through the correct motions without once rousing its composer's inspiration. It is fair to add that some musicians think highly of this Trio.

QUINTET IN C MAJOR, FOR 2 VIOLINS, VIOLA AND 2 CELLOS, OP. 163, D. 956

ALL Schubert's chamber music was like a preparation for this quintet, his masterpiece, and perhaps the greatest of all his works in range of emotion, quality of material, and formal perfection. If the first two movements and the Trio of the *Scherzo* are finer and more profoundly moving than the rest, the whole is ideally balanced, and the medium (that of Boccherini's, not Mozart's string quintets) gives a richness and luminosity of texture that Schubert nourished with all the power at his command. When one listens to the masterly counterpoint, spontaneous and everywhere polished, it seems incredible that Schubert could have applied for lessons in counterpoint with Simon Sechter. In eloquence and originality of language the quintet at least equals the Great C Major Symphony, the greatest songs, and the late B Flat Piano Sonata which he wrote shortly afterwards.

Schubert had completed the C Major Quintet by 2 October 1828, so he states in a letter of that date. He refers also to a forthcoming private rehearsal of it; no public performance took place until 1850.

First movement: *Allegro ma non troppo*. We think of C major as a muscular, triumphant key: the 'Jupiter' Symphony, the Finale of Beethoven's Fifth Symphony, and the overture to *Die Meistersinger* have nourished the idea, but no confirmation is to be found in the opening of this quintet:

Intense, in its movement from the shadowy tonic to the heart-searching diminished-seventh which leaves its mark in a minor third on the upper line, and back to the tonic now touched with the poignancy of an *appoggiatura* added sixth – intense, yes, but a more profoundly pessimistic aspect of C major is not quickly to be found.

The first sentence becomes more tender, though still anxious, still overshadowed with the diminished-seventh chord, and ends evanescently on high and on the dominant. Schubert is able to use his ensemble as two antiphonal choirs and now assigns the second sentence to the lower four parts, with the first cello taking the upper line – throughout the work the first cello's upper register is favoured, and this it is which gives the texture its luminous quality. The second sentence begins in D minor – the supertonic minor, as in the B flat Trio – and ends in the depths of C major. By raising the fifth degree gradually, while the other two notes remain constant, the music stirs itself, antiphonally, into the dominant of E minor. Now a silver lining begins to gleam through the clouds, as the dominant moves towards the tonic major, with more *appoggiature* to increase tension. C major arrives *fortissimo* and, with polyphonic flashes of lightning above, the tune of Ex. 13 is thundered out by the two cellos, and again lumbers towards the dominant. Now, between beating triplets, viola and first cello softly exhale a new transitional idea; it is quoted as an example of the chromatic Schubert:

So, fixed on the dominant (not in it), a firm cadence is reached and, by one of the wonders of the world (the more miraculous because he had used the device before, but never to such shattering effect), Schubert arrives in E flat major for the second subject, a serene, evening tune that floats in and out of G major and, at one memorable moment, is transfigured by a sudden shaft of C major sunlight. It floats, as other tunes in this work are destined to float, on a cushion of rhythm and harmony too evocative in atmosphere to be called a dummy accompaniment.

The rhythm of the tune should be marked and learned in view of what follows. When the violins repeat Ex. 15 the accompaniment acquires triplets in place of ordinary quavers, and a more comfortable gait. It ends in G and is further extended in pseudo-imitation, with a penchant for the dominant of E minor. The prolonged cadence of this extension leans firmly on A flat (the Neapolitan second of G major) and includes uplifting octaves for first violin and cello. The coda in E minor and G major must also be quoted because, like Ex. 15, its rhythm, but not its exact contour, is much elaborated later:

The rhythm of Ex. 15 is also referred to against a new counter-rhythm. The exposition closes with a big chord of G major which looks back to C major the first time and forward, when the exposition has been repeated, to the soft E major seventh chord which begins an astonishingly rich development section, at first concerned in A major with Ex. 15 and its new rhythmic countersubject, then Ex. 16, which is also connected with the same counter-rhythm. F sharp major leads to the brink of its subdominant, D flat, where Ex. 16 grows more lyrical and acquires a soaring counter-subject for violins. The process is repeated in B instead of D flat major (each a semi-tone away from the home tonic). Ex. 16 is treated imitatively with sturdy effect and with a triplet countersubject also in two-part imitation; we have reached D minor and move up by minor (mediant) modulations, to A flat minor, then by a switch to E minor, and up to G as the dominant of C. This last is the most carefully stressed tonality; C minor is firmly implied in precipitous scales of A flat major. The bridge to the recapitulation, with its new detached violin countersubject and its allusion to the turn in Ex. 13, is wonderfully consoling; and the recapitulation itself (beginning *vice versa* with the tune in the first cello part, and retaining the detached figuration) is no longer apprehensive, but merely instinct with a mystical ethereality. When the modulation to E minor is reached, the characteristic octave plunge is extended so as to reach F major; you may regard this as the lazy man's way of re-capitulating the second subject in the home tonic; or you may look back through Schubert's works, realize his omnipotence in the dominions of modulation and key change, and understand that F major is here to heighten the tension of the passage. When the second subject is reached, now in A flat major, its second note is altered at the repeat by violins, from B flat to B natural, quite gratuitously but, for this once, most poetically. The extension of the second subject is now further lengthened. The codetta comes quietly to rest in C major, and now Ex. 13 returns for the coda proper, with new flashes of lightning on the diminished-seventh. The closing bars, on a tonic pedal, apotheosize Ex. 15 and then sink to rest, not without clouding their serenity.

Second movement: *Adagio* (E major). The long, flowing tune of this *Adagio* is surrounded by a *pizzicato* bass and a punctuating descant in such a way that, with its three-part harmony, it sounds airborne. The metrical counterpoint is inevitable in Schubert. The part writing of the three inner parts in the melodic corpus is superbly managed with just enough independence to maintain metrical equilibrium in a melody that proceeds with the barest perceptible rhythm. These comments will be better understood by reference to the first four bars:

The example ends in F sharp major, and the music drifts, as if fascinated, to and from this key; but the three quavers at the end of almost every bar (though not the second and third of Ex. 17) push the harmony, like waves on a flowing tide, towards new and magical harmonic climes. Half-way through, the violin countersubject begins to vary, first with *pizzicato* then with alternating *pizzicato* and *arco*. A touch of melancholy creeps in at the codetta with references to A minor (the subdominant minor of a major key). When the melody comes to rest, a semitone trill introduces F natural which is to be the home tonic of the middle section, and the *locus classicus* of Schubert's lifelong fondness for the Neapolitan second. This is a stormy dramatic section, with a long passionate tune for first violin and cello. The tune itself leans gratefully on the Neapolitan second, G flat: and, when it shifts towards F minor, on D flat as the Neapolitan second of the dominant in a scale that favours the Lydian fourth of F minor – we had better have an example, with L for Lydian and N for Neapolitan on the appropriate notes:

Ex. 18

Eventually the middle section ends in C major and a series of magical modulations leads through the dominant of B minor (with a back-reference to the echo effect in the first subject of I) to A major, and so to E for a reprise with new florid work for the outer parts. At the half-way mark a more involved form of the old *pizz* and *arco* punctuation is resumed. The codetta has a more hectic violin part, and the true coda flashes menacing into F minor, recalling, in a single chord, the fevers of the middle section. It then sinks back serenely into E major. It was no more than a ripple on a tranquil sea.

Third movement: *Scherzo, Presto*. After calm succeeds the storm, after the hushed *Adagio* this imperious, daemonic *Scherzo*, propelled by its own one-in-a-bar 3/4 metre. Half-way through the first strain we are in A flat major, from which the dominant G is no great distance to Schubert, so that when established it is no dominant but, as explained above, a new tonic. From it Schubert plunges straight away into E flat at the start of the second strain, and punctuates his developments with thunder and lightning. When he sets a *cantilena* going, it is still daemonic, though heard alone it might come from a placid impromptu with rippling *arpeggio* accompaniment. B major and more claps of thunder lead back to C and the reprise with its purely gratuitous voyage into E flat major. The *Scherzo* ends with a C major whack; and now the Trio, *Andante sostenuto*, enters and once again the sky is overcast. It is the gloomiest, most perplexing Trio ever attached to a *scherzo*. Viola and second cello suggest F minor in their gaunt procession down the scale (one cannot help thinking of Wotan's spear). But it is in D flat that the string quintet meets together with grave faces and implications of G flat minor. The German poet Gellert wrote (in a song set by Beethoven)

> *Denk', O Mensch, an deinen Tod;*
> *Säume nicht, denn Eins ist Not!*
> (On thy death, O Man, reflect
> Woe untold awaits neglect.)

And the music here muses on lines that can be associated with *Der Tod und das Mädchen*. In the second strain the melody reaches up, in B flat minor, to the ninth degree, with despairing effect, then shrinks back into D flat. It circles about A major and its dominant, again only to return. The coda of the Trio sinks twice more to uncover the dominant of C major, at which second violin and viola swell, on repeated Gs, into the tempests of the *Scherzo* again.

Fourth movement: *Allegretto*. It is time for the release of tension, but too many clouds have loomed for complete peace of mind. And so the Finale begins with a rough but not anxious tune in C minor. It passes through E minor before the sun of C major breaks through. The second subject is Viennese café music raised to a state of glory; even this moment of relaxation is laid out elaborately, especially in its later stages where the second violin has the melody, the first violin a nonchalant running descant, the viola a harmonic middle part, while the two cellos share a rhythmic bass. The episode ends in D, whence it proceeds back to G; musical detectives may be minded to link one phrase of this *Nachgesang* with the tune of Ex. 13 for both share the turn and the span of a minor third. If G major is a new tonic, it is a kingdom poised on a feather; Schubert does his best to upset its equilibrium with prods towards G minor, and

D major, B flat major, or C minor, for he spreads himself in transparent undulating harmonies over a leisurely cello melody, the whole looking forward in flow and texture to Mendelssohn's *Hebrides* Overture and even part of the development in the Finale of Brahms's First Symphony. The harmonies swell into the C minor tune. Instead of falling upon the second subject, the first is treated to imitative counterpoint which takes it into B major and B flat major, and acts as a postponed development section. It returns to a cadence in C major and, after a breathing space, the second subject is able to be recapitulated. The Mendelssohnian seascape follows and then, *più allegro*, the C minor tune begins to race. It reaches a *più presto* and a state of joyous exhilaration. Suddenly the daemon clutches hold of the coda, drives it into F minor, with a tread like the Commendatore's statue, upsets the dominant-seventh at the last cadence with a whole tone trill on D flat in the bass, and interposes a grim Neapolitan second on the final octave C; across C major, and across Schubert's amiable Neapolitan finger-print, there has fallen the chill shadow of eternity.

6

Felix Mendelssohn (1809–1847)

ANDREW PORTER

'As a composer of chamber music,' says the new *Grove*, 'Mendelssohn claims greatness almost without qualification.' The chief work singled out for praise is the A Major String Quintet, Op. 18, which is indeed a delightful piece. But the two works the reader is most likely to encounter are the String Octet, Op. 20, and the Piano Trio in D Minor, Op. 49, and it is these which will be considered in this chapter. The former is one of Mendelssohn's best pieces, the latter perhaps one of the more trivial on which virtuosi have lavished their skill (though there will be found many people to disagree with this verdict).

In Mendelssohn's early manuscript volumes we find him trying out his hand in various chamber combinations as in almost all other mediums. Among the 1821 compositions are five three-movement pieces for string quartet. Op. 1, the C Minor Piano Quartet, was begun in September 1822; Op. 1, 2, and 3 are all piano quartets. These were originally performed at the Mendelssohns' Sunday morning concerts; two programmes for 1824 noted by Moscheles begin respectively: 'Felix's C Minor Quartet', and 'Felix's F Minor Quartet'. From this year dates the Septet for Violin, Two Violas, Cello, Double Bass, and Piano, later published as Op. 110; and in 1825 came the String Octet – the earliest of Mendelssohn's works in the international repertory.

OCTET FOR STRINGS IN E FLAT MAJOR, OP. 20

THE distribution is for double string quartet – though never treated as such, but always as a single body. As one might expect, there is a good deal of doubling, and a good deal of inner parts 'filling in', especially with *tremolos*. But the last movement, which is predominantly contra-puntal, often presents eight real parts; and throughout, Mendelssohn shows a skill in his treatment of texture and string-colour which we might find incredible in a boy of sixteen, did we not know that his next opus would be the Overture to *A Midsummer Night's Dream*.

The first movement is marked *Allegro moderato, ma con fuoco*, and there is certainly fire in the wide-flung principal theme:

In its extension it climbs even higher, and impetuously tumbles still further, to the violin's lowest note. All this is given to the first violin, supported over an orchestral sounding *tremolo*, while what might have been simple E flat *arpeggios* are enriched by having the bass, in the third bar, descend to a dissonant D, a passing-note to the C minor harmony of the first half of the fourth bar. It is instructive to reduce these opening bars to the clean, strongly-written four-part harmony which underlies them; comparison of this with the pulsing, urgent score affords some measure of Mendelssohn's skill in handling the medium.

The theme passes to the cellos, and is punctuated now by a distinctive signal on the violins: (*a*) ♩. ♫♫ . A new motif prepares us for the arrival of the second subject (Ex. 2, below), by reversing its first bar. But before this subject arrives there is much development of the original theme. Eventually, and in company, almost all the while, with the main theme, this smooth conjunct melody sails in on fourth violin and first viola:

The section closes with Ex. 1 in further presentations.

The first part of the development consists largely of modulatory gestures so brilliantly laid-out that there is no hint of 'padding'. But then a very beautiful, quiet passage leads (letter D) to Ex. 2, in F minor now, and soon with its note-values augmented in the second and third bars. The motif formed by reversal of the first bar leads back to the main key, and the recapitulation is heralded by brilliant *fortissimi* across four octaves. When Ex. 2 reappears it has gained an expressive counter-melody on first violin; and before the brilliant close, a quiet modulatory passage, a moment of reflection, recalls the central episode of the development.

As a construction, the *Andante*, in C minor, is a little less shapely. It opens in a *siciliano* rhythm, such as we often find in corresponding movements by Mozart, and the Mozartian clichés, the characteristic shapes and figures, are used extensively. The themes are hardly worth quoting on their own account. The first is in this rhythm: ♪ ♪ ♫♫ | ♪ ♪♫♫ ; and the second, this: ♪ ♪♫♪ ♪♫♪ . Starting in E flat minor, this second theme mounts to a climax, and leads to a very beautiful central episode in E flat major (letter B), with smooth conjunct melodies. The original themes, elaborately worked, return in the opposite order, giving to the movement an approximation to *Bogen*, or arch, form (the arch leans to one side). It is worth noting that the individual entries of the instruments are always telling, and the range of tone-colour remarkable.

Mendelssohn's motto for the *Scherzo* (so he confided to his sister) was the following stanza from Goethe's *Faust*:

> *Wolkenzug und Nebelflor*
> *Erhellen sich von oben;*
> *Luft im Laub, und Wind im Rohr,*
> *– Und alles ist zerstoben.*

('Trails of cloud and mist brighten from above; breeze in the foliage and wind in the reeds – and everything is scattered.')

The connection between the music and the first two lines

seems a little tenuous, unless we think of trailing wisps of cloud being rapidly blown across the sky; certainly the music is all rustle and activity, and the movement blows away and scatters in the final page. This *Scherzo*, *Allegro leggierissimo*, 'must be played *pianissimo* and *staccato* throughout' – so Mendelssohn noted in the score. It is in sonataform, over in a few minutes but delicately worked and developed. The first subject establishes G minor in light but definite gestures:

The interplay between the instruments is bewitchingly deft. A few touches, and we are in B flat for this elfin melody, whose piquancy is considerably enhanced by a bass descending by steps from B flat, and gently touched in (as are all the accompanying chords) in the same rhythm as the tune:

The section closes with a series of detached chords, which, varied by their inversion, open the development. This has less to do with the themes than with the figures which accompanied them; they are broken up, inverted, and linked by suggestions of the two main themes. In the recapitulation Ex. 4 returns in E flat, and the detached chords are extended for nineteen bars, growing ever fainter until they whisk out of sight.

Any description of this *Scherzo* – as of the *Midsummer Night's Dream* one – must seem unbearably cumbersome when one hears the music. To quote Tovey: 'eight string players might easily practise it for a lifetime without coming to an end of their delight in producing its marvels of tone-colour'. When Mendelssohn conducted his Thirteenth Symphony (now known as No. 1) at a Philharmonic Society

concert in London in 1829, he substituted for its Minuet
an orchestral arrangement of this *Scherzo*; this version was
published in 1911.

The Finale was written, possibly, in emulation of the last
movement of Mozart's 'Jupiter' Symphony. Emulation is
perhaps not the right word; there is no pretentious attempt
to create something on the same plane, but rather a boyish
glee in playing about with themes and combining them in
unexpected ways. The movement is a *perpetuum mobile* which
contains some fugal expositions. First we have an eight-part
exposition of Ex. 5, with the last three entries piled in a
stretto:

Then a new theme, which with its regular counterpoint is
shown below (the example is quoted an octave lower):

A series of modulatory gestures in Mozartian vein (letter A)
appears to be leading us to new keys, but in fact lands us
straight back in E flat, and Ex. 5 as a violin solo over
tremolo accompaniment. In a long, inventive passage the
material we have had so far is broken up between the instruments, each player adding to the jigsaw puzzle in turn,
darting in as if he suddenly saw where the piece he has in
his hand fitted. The first violin, solo for ten bars, leads to
the next idea, which is also exposed as a fugue, together
with the original subject:

Ex.7

Three entries are reckoned enough, and then it is the turn of Ex. 6, so far heard only as a melody, to be handled as a fugal exposition. But first it must drop its frivolous ending and acquire, instead of the quavers, the close shown as Ex. 6*b*. Then we start ranging in keys (up to this point E flat has prevailed almost continuously) and when we reach F minor (at letter G) the composer has another surprise for us, in the shape of the *Scherzo* theme, Ex. 3 (quoted here in E flat, from a few bars later):

Ex.8

This theme inverts to form a useful bass.

It remains only for the composer to combine as many of these melodies as he possibly can in counterpoint; and although Mendelssohn never quite succeeds, like Mozart, in bringing all his themes together, he sometimes tricks the unwary listener into believing that he has brought it off!

PIANO TRIO IN D MINOR, OP. 49

BETWEEN 1827 and 1839 Mendelssohn wrote five string quartets, the first two (Op. 13 in A major and Op. 12 in E flat) dating from 1827 and 1829, the others (Op. 44, Nos. 1 to 3) coming, after a break of nearly ten years, in 1837–8. These are beautifully worked, and contain some thoughtful movements which deserve an occasional hearing. In 1839 the first of his two piano trios appeared, Op. 49 in D minor. A team such as Cortot, Thibaud, and Casals could achieve elegance in this work by way of a gentle approach, and they made the music sound worth-while. On paper, or when performed for brilliance, it seems vapid. What was deft in the Octet has become glib; what was romantic has turned sentimental. Invention sparks freely, but at a low voltage.

For example, here are the two main subjects of the first movement, *Molto allegro ed agitato*, of this D Minor Trio:

Each is introduced by the cello. In the first, the enhancing of a basically tonic-and-dominant tune by dissonant passing notes in a descending bass (so effective in the Octet) has become a facile trick; and the lurching harmony in bars 2 and 3 of the second subject fails to raise a smile to-day only because the instrumental touch is so light. The airy grace of the lay-out, indeed, does something to redeem the banal material. Most of the movement is concerned with these tunes and sugar-icing from the piano. Structurally, we may note that the recapitulation is interrupted by a second 'development', if that be not too grand a word for some conventionally achieved modulations.

The slow movement, *Andante con moto tranquillo*, in B flat major, is like one of the sweeter *Songs without Words*. The theme has two sentences, each introduced as a piano solo and then echoed by the violin. There succeeds a variant, in B flat minor, and then the tune returns tricked out in new finery. On the last page there is a short duet between violin and cello, of as little musical significance as those interchanges between coloratura soprano and flute which close Sir Henry Bishop's songs.

The *Scherzo*, as we would expect, is more palatable, though the material is still by Mendelssohn's own standards second-rate. The movement is monothematic, without Trio, and skitters away quite attractively.

The Finale, *Allegro assai appassionato*, opens with a slightly gipsy-sounding strain, which soon collapses hopelessly on to the tonic:

The movement is a *rondo*, the second theme, in F, showing the same dactyllic rhythm as the first. The third theme, in B flat, is first cousin to that of the E Major Song with Words, Op. 33, No. 3, and although the tempo is faster, the melody is underlain by similar *religioso* harmonies. Throughout, Mendelssohn uses the two deflatory phrases of Ex. 10 with deplorable readiness.

The C Minor Piano Trio, Op. 66, which came six years later, has more interesting ideas in it, though the working is still superficial. The String Quintet in B Flat, Op. 87, of the same year, and the Sixth String Quartet, Op. 80, of 1847, are better pieces altogether – indeed the latter is perhaps Mendelssohn's finest quartet. His facility in superficially effective piano writing seemed to vitiate much of his work for that instrument, whether in the solo pieces, the concertos, or the trios. When writing for strings, Mendelssohn was generally less fluent, and more self-critical.

7
Robert Schumann (1810–1856)

JOAN CHISSELL

THOUGH Schumann had once or twice dabbled in chamber music as a young man, it was not till 1842, when he was thirty-two, that he seriously turned his attention to this medium. As a pianist himself, in love with one of the finest young pianists of his day, he had little thought for anything but piano music for the first ten years of his composing life. That was until 1840, when, with the deep happiness of his marriage to Clara Wieck, his feelings overflowed in a great outpouring of song. But a great change took place in him from that time onwards. The recognition which had come to him as a miniaturist no longer seemed to satisfy him; accordingly, his goal now became the conquest of larger designs, first in the orchestral sphere in 1841, and then the following year in the sphere of chamber music. His three string quartets, Op. 41, appeared in the early summer of 1842, and the Piano Quintet, Op. 44, and Piano Quartet, Op. 47, towards the end of the year. His enthusiasm for this new medium spread over into 1843, which saw the completion of the Andante and Variations for two pianos, two cellos, and horn, Op. 46 (subsequently recorded for two pianos and therefore outside the scope of this chapter), also the Fantasiestücke for Piano, Violin, and Cello, Op, 88 (revised in 1850). Three more piano trios (Opp. 63, 80, and 110) followed, but the first two not till 1847 and the last not till 1851.

When composing miniatures as an exuberantly romantic young man, Schumann had never suffered from his lack of a sound academic training in harmony and counterpoint. His intensely susceptible imagination responded to the stimulus of the world about him as spontaneously as the strings of an Aeolian harp to the wind; every sensation was

immediately translated into a brief character-piece epito-
mizing the mood of the moment and then terminating. It
was not until he became filled with the desire to spread his
wings that he grew aware of his technical shortcomings, in
particular his difficulty in prolonging and unifying an argument by an orderly development of his material. Thus it
was that in the early 1840s he deliberately began to turn his
back on extra-musical stimulus – the 'literature, people, and
politics', responsible for so many of the delightful romantic
miniatures of his youth – in an earnest attempt to improve
his capacity for reasoning in terms of pure notes. He was
particularly concerned to improve his counterpoint, previously pushed into the background by his delight in unexpected harmonic adventure, and also to see how much
unity he could impart to his music by making a little go a
long way, in other words, by thematic metamorphosis in
place of prodigality of new material.

In his three string quartets, composed after close study of
the quartets of Mozart, Beethoven, and Haydn, this change
of style won golden opinions from hitherto dubious friends
and critics, including Mendelssohn and Hauptmann. The
latter was even moved to write 'At David's I heard three
quartets of Schumann's: his first, which pleased me greatly
indeed, made me marvel at his talent, which I thought by
no means so remarkable, judging from his previous pianoforte pieces that were so aphoristic and fragmentary, sheer
revellings in strangeness. Here, too, there is no lack of the
unusual in content and form, but it is cleverly conceived
and held together, and a great deal of it very lovely.' To-
day, however, these works are rarely played, and in the first
two of the three the explanation would seem to lie in the
composer's calculated preoccupation with craftsmanship at
the expense of those spontaneous 'revellings in strangeness'
which to twentieth-century ears are amongst the youthful
Schumann's most endearing characteristics. In the A minor
quartet the slow introduction to the first movement and the
development section in the Finale are fine examples of
Schumann's ability to write good counterpoint when he

really put his mind to it, and both first and last movements derive a great deal of inner unity from the close relationship of first and second subjects – the second grows out of the first in each case. But the material itself is strangely impersonal for Schumann. He is more his old imaginative self in the fleet, ternary-form *Scherzo* (with its echoes of Mendelssohnian elves and sprites), and in the introspective slow movement (with a main theme uncommonly akin to the opening of the *Adagio* in Beethoven's Choral Symphony), though the scoring of this latter movement shows that he was still thinking too much in terms of keyboard texture. The Second Quartet in F begins with great promise. The all-important first theme which dominates the opening *Allegro* has more impulse to its flow than its equivalent in the earlier quartet, and Schumann explores its contrapuntal possibilities to the full in a well-reasoned argument which is markedly in advance over the earlier A minor first movement in the development section. The second movement is cast in variation form, always Schumann's happiest solution of long-term planning; the scoring reveals a true understanding of the string medium, and some of the harmonic progressions are as refreshingly venturesome as his youthful ones while possessing a new, mature logic of their own:

This quartet is, however, let down by its two concluding movements, the one a *Scherzo* and the other in sonata-form. The subject matter is not very distinguished in either, and Schumann flogs it like a dead horse with excessive repetition (but no real development) in varying keys.

By far the most memorable of the three works is the last

in A major, for here Schumann's heart is as much involved as his head. Both first and second subjects in the first movement are endearingly lyrical, independent melodies, and even in the very brief development section, concerned only with the first subject (notably its appealing falling fifth in the chord of the added sixth) Schumann relaxes from his earlier contrapuntal rigours. Formally, the second movement is among music's most unconventional *scherzi*, since its main F sharp minor *Assai agitato* theme is followed by four variations and an F sharp major coda. The two deeply expressive themes of the introspective slow movement are briefly developed and recapitulated in the pattern of a sonata-form argument, and the Finale is an invigorating, free *rondo*. The connecting link between all four movements is the interval of the falling fifth and its inversion, the rising fourth.

Having been parted from his own instrument for the space of three quartets, Schumann could do without it no longer – all his remaining chamber works include the piano. His first step was the bold one of combining it with the four strings whose medium he had just begun to master, in the Piano Quintet in E Flat Major, Op. 44, the first work ever written for this particular combination of instruments. And in the first happiness of reunion with the piano, his creative imagination took on a new lease of life. Not only do the themes of the Quintet glow with all his old, irresistible charm and spontaneity, but there is also inspired craftsmanship behind their 'working-out' and scoring – that is why the work is one of the supreme achievements of his entire output. In the exposition of the first movement, the way in which the resolute first subject,

dissolves into gracious lyricism,

Ex.3

never fails to delight, while in the compact development
section (the only instance where the piano takes too much
on its own shoulders) it undergoes a further cunning transformation. The second subject, another radiantly romantic
melody, is expanded so persuasively by the intertwining
strings, to the accompaniment of the piano, in the exposition, that it is wisely omitted from the development section
altogether. From E flat major Schumann moves to C minor
for the slow movement, in form a sonata-rondo, and in
character rather like a funeral march, though the music's
predominating sombreness is effectively relieved by the
major tonality of the second subject on both its appearances.
As a craftsman, Schumann shows outstanding skill in the
way in which he imparts continuity to the argument by
allowing figuration from the agitated, central episode in
F minor to persist while the viola recapitulates the main,
march theme – not to mention his borrowing of a brief
linking phrase from the first movement as a means of
approach to this central F minor section. In the virile
Scherzo miracles are worked with ascending and descending
scales, an idea Schumann may have imitated from the Trio
in the *Scherzo* of Haydn's E Flat String Quartet, Op. 76,
No. 6. The movement is extended by a second trio; the
close resemblance of the main theme of the first trio to the
opening subject of the first movement in inversion is a
further source of unity in the work as a whole. In this
respect, however, the coda to the Finale is his *pièce de résis-
tance*; after an extended sonata-form argument, daringly
unorthodox in its key-scheme and extended by a new idea
in the development section, the main theme of the first
movement is brought back in augmentation as the subject
of a *fugato*, with the first theme of the Finale as the counter-

subject. Never again did Schumann rise to such masterly contrapuntal heights.

The strain of so much extended, abstract thinking was beginning to tell on Schumann's health when he plunged into the E Flat Major Piano Quartet towards the end of 1842, so that while the work aims at greater profundity of thought and feeling than the Quintet, it lacks the effortless spontaneity of the earlier work, and in comparison suffers from thickness of texture – largely owing to the piano's apparent determination to be 'in on everything'. Nevertheless it has many fine points. The sonata-form argument of the first movement is spaciously conceived, and is marked by powerful climaxes, notably at the junction of the masterly development section and recapitulation. The G minor *Scherzo*, again extended by a second trio, derives a great deal of charm from a recurrent *staccato* phrase used to link each section:

Ex.4

and the ternary form slow movement brings a nostalgically romantic main theme of rising and falling sevenths as well as an arresting key-change from B flat to G flat for its middle section. The Finale's main theme is anticipated at the end of the slow movement in a link for which the cellist has to lower his bottom string to B flat. Structurally, the last movement is the least satisfactory owing to Schumann's reversion to a tiresome habit (formed in his early piano sonatas) of repeating the development section after the normal recapitulation of the exposition before proceeding to the coda.

From four and five instruments, Schumann's attention ultimately turned to just three – piano, violin, and cello. He was very tired when he began the first of his four trios (later revised as the *Phantasiestücke*, Op. 88), hence, perhaps,

his deliberate reversion to short, sectional, fanciful movements called *Romanze*, *Humoreske*, *Duett*, and *Finale*, reminiscent of his brief, youthful miniatures for piano. In fact, the
pieces would seem to have been composed at the piano, so
redundant do the string parts seem in all but the third *Duett*.
His notebooks reveal that he lavished very much more
thought on the three extended trios which followed several
years later; the first two, dating from 1847, can take their
place alongside any in the repertory, but the last does give
forewarning of the composer's approaching mental collapse.
Scoring still remained a major problem in the D Minor
Trio, Op. 63. Sometimes the violin merely seems borne along
on the surface of the rich keyboard texture while the cello
doubles the bass line, yet on the credit side there is an episode in the development section of the first movement,
with the strings playing *sul ponticello* and the piano *una corda*
and *staccato* high in the treble, which shows a keener appreciation of tone colour *per se* than anything else in Schumann's
entire chamber output:

Since its material is new, this episode is also Schumann's chief formal innovation in an otherwise orthodoxly constructed work with first and last movements in sonata-form, the *Scherzo* with only one trio, and the slow movement in ternary form. The harmonic idiom, however, is richly and expressively chromatic, particularly in the first and third movements, and when the bright D major of the Finale is reached after much earlier groping in dark, minor tonalities, the imaginative listener can be forgiven for thinking Schumann to be reaffirming Beethoven's 'I shall take Fate by the trhoat; it shall not wholly overcome me.'

The F Major Trio, Op. 80, in comparison, is an extravert and wholly happy work, and its scoring is much less thick, its texture much better ventilated. There are three subjects instead of two in the sonata-form plan of the first movement, all of them of beguiling charm. The nobility of the expressive slow movement is in no way disturbed by its enharmonic plunges from flats to sharps and back again, and the *Scherzo* is attractively winsome. The Finale shows Schumann in tip-top contrapuntal form in the development section. The last Trio in G Minor, Op. 110, has some fine ideas in all four movements, particularly the dark, impassioned opening subject of the first, but they tend to become mere formulae, somewhat wearily manipulated, as each movement progresses. Chief evidence of the composer's declining powers comes in the loose construction of the Finale.

In conclusion it must be admitted that with the exception of the magnificent piano quintet, Schumann's chamber music is not as immediately endearing as his miniatures for piano and voice composed in the full flood of his youthful romanticism. But even if extended, abstract thinking did not come easily to him, there are too many deep and and searching beauties as well as ingenuities of construction in his chamber works to justify their present-day neglect.

8

Johannes Brahms (1833–1897)

PETER LATHAM

NOBODY knows how much chamber music Brahms actually composed. He said himself that he wrote twenty string quartets before producing one good enough to publish, and though he was not on oath he may have been telling the truth. Sir Donald Tovey asserts that the work we know as the First Sonata for Violin and Piano was actually the fifth, and guesses that the published chamber music probably is scarcely a quarter of what he wrote. Certainly no composer was a sterner critic of his own works than Brahms. Even as a boy he would make periodic bonfires of his compositions, and the habit of destruction remained with him through life. At the end, when he knew death was approaching, he spent much time in his study tearing up old manuscripts so that they should not be published after he was gone. One piece eluded him, an early *Scherzo* for violin and piano. This was in the hands of Joachim, who sanctioned its posthumous publication under the title *Sonatensatz*. But it is the only posthumous chamber work we have; in his task of destruction, as in so much else, Brahms was very thorough.

Such compositions as were allowed to survive underwent a ruthless process of pruning and revision. Sometimes they lay on his desk for years, and the final product might turn out to be something quite different from the first draft. Thus the C Minor Piano Quartet started life in C sharp minor and had to wait twenty years before it was given to the world; the F Minor Quintet was a string quintet and then a two-piano sonata before it emerged as a piano quintet.

With all this destruction, deliberation, and painstaking modification the bulk of music that has reached us appears surprisingly large. There are twenty-four works in all (not counting the *Sonatensatz*), and each is a full-scale piece with three or four movements. Not all of them concern me here; the seven duet sonatas and the works with horn and clarinet are examined elsewhere in this volume. My business is with the compositions for strings (two sextets, two quintets, three quartets), and those for strings and piano (a quintet, three quartets and three trios).

They are, as will be seen, a mixed lot. Unlike Mozart, Haydn, and Beethoven, Brahms lays no special stress on the string quartet, and he published no string quartet at all till he was forty; the earlier pieces are for string sextet or for various combinations with piano. But then, in 1875, come the two String Quartets in C Minor and A Minor, and these are followed after a two-year interval by the B Flat. That is all; after the B Flat he abandons the form for ever. I suspect it was the very excellence of the classical master-pieces that made him shy of the string quartet. Above all he feared the Beethoven comparison: 'You don't know,' he said, 'what it means to the likes of us when we hear *his* footsteps behind us.' He was perfectly well aware that he lacked Beethoven's heroic stature. And yet, being what he was, he could escape neither the footsteps nor the compari-son. His character, his gifts, his very limitations guided him to the classical forms as inevitably as Wagner's nature guided him to opera. No one since Beethoven has been so unmistakably, so obviously a classic as Brahms. He was not Beethoven's equal, but he *was* his successor. As early as 1862 Hellmesberger, leader of the best Quartet in Vienna, ex-claimed after trying over the G Minor Piano Quartet, 'This is Beethoven's heir!' – and before long all Vienna agreed with him. The thing was patent.

Not that we find many actual echoes of Beethoven. In the B Flat Sextet, at the end of the first section of the Trio, we get an emphatic reiteration of the tag

Ex.1

in a context that is bound to recall the corresponding pass-age in the Trio of Beethoven's Fifth Symphony; and the

middle section of the *Romanze* in the C Minor String
Quartet opens with the sudden introduction of repeated
notes in a triplet rhythm, an effect that inevitably reminds
us of the *Cavatina* in Beethoven's Quartet, Op. 130, the
resemblance becoming still more obvious when Brahms
continues with sobbing phrases separated by rests:

But it would be strange if a man so soaked in Beethoven as
was Brahms should not occasionally quote his hero by sheer
accident, and these two fragments in twenty-four major
works do not amount to much. What is much more significant is that all but one of these twenty-four pieces begins
with a movement in sonata-form,* and that the succeeding
movements all conform to classical patterns. Now and again
too this punctilious reverence for Beethoven's designs in
general is accompanied by some more particular influence
of the Beethoven spirit. The fine, vigorous fugue that concludes the String Quintet in F Major is Brahms all through,
yet one wonders if it would ever have been written had not
Beethoven composed the fugal Finale of his Third Ras-
soumovsky Quartet. Even more Beethovenish is the C
Minor String Quartet. As we have seen, he knew the comparison that would be made and delayed publishing a string

---

* The exception is the Horn Trio. Here the nature and limitations
of the natural horn account for the abandonment of sonata-form and
the adoption of another of Beethoven's patterns — the one he used for
his Piano Sonata in F, Op. 54.

quartet till he was sure he could offer the best that was in him. But when the time came there was no evasion of the issue. The passionate striving of the first and last movements, their conciseness, their strength, their logic, reveal his kinship with Beethoven far more convincingly than the little echo of Beethoven's *Cavatina* in the slow movement.

It is in his ability to develop an idea, to find new continuations to it, to build a logical and shapely movement, to see the wood in spite of the trees that Brahms proves himself Beethoven's heir. Other elements in his style derive from different sources. Melodically he is proud to learn from Schubert. Compare the theme of the Finale to the B Flat Sextet with that of the Finale to Schubert's B Flat Piano Trio; compare the opening of the slow movement of the Piano Quintet with Schubert's song 'Pause' (from *Die Schöne Müllerin*). Between the second of these pairs there is some thematic resemblance – which matters very little. What does matter is that he has been able to assimilate something of Schubert's magic, to assimilate it so completely that it becomes pure Brahms – but Brahms writing with Schubert looking over his shoulder, as one commentator has expressed it. In the same sort of way the first, third, and fourth movements of the B Flat String Quartet breathe the spirit of Haydn. Look at the opening:

Again, Schubert and Schumann are full of unexpected felicities in the realms of harmony and modulation, sudden twists of genius that give the impression of inspired impromptu. Brahms takes them, welds them into the fabric of classical harmony and produces a well-ordered system of his own, rooted in tradition, but fertile in new resources. What he made of them may be seen in the *Poco adagio* of the G Major Sextet, or the first page of the Piano Quartet in C Minor.

But the composer to whom (after Beethoven) he owed

most was J. S. Bach. All through his life the rediscovery of Bach was going on, and the effect of that progressive revelation on Brahms was profound. It so happens that among the works falling within the scope of this essay there is only one full-dress fugue, the finale of the F Major String Quintet. But there is a rich crop of *fugatos*, some of them elaborate. With his supreme mastery of counterpoint he moved easily and naturally in the fugal medium, and such a movement as the Finale of the G Major Sextet shows how skilfully he could blend fugal style with sonata form, thus invoking the spirits of Bach and Beethoven by a single incantation. Canon is one of his favourite devices. The canonic trio to the *Scherzo* of the A Major Piano Quartet is perhaps a trifle stiff, but the Trio in the G Major String Quintet is beautifully easy and musical, even when in the coda it becomes a double canon four in two by inversion. Such formidable technical problems as this – or the canon four in one by inversion after the double bar in the first movement of the G Major Sextet – slip by so smoothly that one may hear the passage several times before one appreciates its consummate skill. The A Minor String Quartet was dedicated to Dr Billroth, but it was written for Joachim, another canon 'addict'. Canons therefore are to be expected, and things are further complicated in the first movement by a pair of cryptograms. Joachim's motto, F.A.E. (*frei aber einsam*) must be combined somewhere with Brahms's motto, F.A.F. (*frei aber froh*). My quotations give the first subject of the movement and some of the things that happen afterwards:

Having thus disported himself in his first movement Brahms

introduces a dramatic canonic episode into his lyrical slow movement, interrupts the Trio of his *quasi Minuetto* with another canonic episode, four in two this time, and cannot refrain from slipping in yet another canon near the end of his finale. Yet with all this technical accomplishment there is little of the dry-as-dust in the Quartet; Brahms makes real music all the time.

But there was more to be learnt from Bach than the way to make fugues and canons. One of his most characteristic qualities is his ability to write, like Bach, long stretches of easily-flowing lyrical music wherein the interest is sustained by the converse of several well-contrasted melodic lines. Examples of this kind of treatment are so numerous that it is difficult to select, but perhaps the *Scherzo* of the G Major Sextet may be taken as a specimen.

Brahms loved to sit at the feet of Bach, and always with the happiest results. Yet at the same time he took full advantage of the emancipation from the strict *obbligato* style achieved by the earlier Viennese masters. A string quartet is not necessarily written in four real parts throughout, still less is a sextet written in six. Not only will Brahms lighten his texture when he wants to by giving rests to one or more instruments (as Bach does), but he will vary it by giving a melody to two instruments simultaneously playing in octaves, he will write passages that are not strictly contrapuntal at all, with chords across the strings wherein twelve or more notes may well be sounded together, or with harmonic figures of accompaniment. In this way he entirely avoids the thick and monotonous effect of continuous six-part writing. In his whole output there is no work more transparent than the G Major Sextet; in all the length of it I doubt whether there are fifty bars of strict six-part writing. Yet it is inevitably a sextet, requiring no more and no less than six instruments. Brahms never heard Stanford's advice, 'Let the light into your music', but no one knew better than he how to apply it.

It is noteworthy, however, that he enjoyed rich effects, and that on the whole he liked dark colours better than light; he preferred the contralto voice to the soprano, and in his writing he avoided the string trio, that most tenuous of media. His earliest works for strings only were sextets, his latest quintets. Now when you turn a quartet into a quintet by adding a second viola it is the middle of the harmony that you thicken, and when a second cello is brought in to make it a sextet the texture is still further darkened. The beginning and end of the *Grave* from the F Major Quintet reveal Brahms's love of these deep, warm colours. Yet he knows how to avoid muddiness. The G Major Sextet has already been adduced as an example of transparency (especially the first movement), but I might just as well have cited the *Un poco allegretto* of the G Major Quintet.

Brahms has been accused of insensitiveness to colour. An adequate answer to that charge would take me beyond my terms of reference in this essay. Chamber music, especially chamber music for strings only, is notoriously more a matter of line than of colour. Even so we need not let the case go by default. Listen to the *Poco adagio* of the G Major Sextet and hear Brahms rejoicing in the opportunities for varied richness that six stringed instruments provide for the skilful composer; turn to the *Scherzo* of the same work and feel the charm of those *arco* chords with *pizzicato* accompaniment. Are these the products of musical colour-blindness? Again, what could be more effective and dramatic than the bowed *tremolos* accompanying the canon in the *Andante moderato* of the A Minor String Quartet? Even the dour C Minor String Quartet contains a passage at the end of the *Romanze* in which, as Tovey says, 'The viola sounds like a pair of deep-sea horns and the violoncello like all the harps of the sirens.' When one comes to the works with piano examples of colour are so widespread that one does not know where to begin. I will content myself with alluding to the superb sonority of the *Scherzo* from the F Minor Quintet, and the mysterious, low-pitched piano arpeggios in the *Poco adagio* of the A Major Quartet.

Here and there, however, Brahms employs a special sort of colouring that requires a further word of explanation.

One of the features of life in the Central Europe of his day was the gypsy band. These gypsies came reputedly from Hungary, and their music had a peculiar style of its own. Many composers, Brahms among them, were fascinated by the '*Zigeuner*' tunes and rhythms and used them for their own purposes. None of them seems to have enquired very carefully into the origin of these tunes, and in describing them they use the titles 'gypsy' and 'Hungarian' as if they were interchangeable. Nowadays, thanks to the researches of Bartók and others, we are aware that gypsy music is one thing and Hungarian music quite another. In failing to make that distinction Brahms (like the rest of them) was in error. It doesn't matter much so long as we realize that when he says 'Hungarian' he generally means 'gypsy' (*Zigeuner*). He excels in writing music of the gypsy type, and the movements in which he employs the idiom have a distinctive flavour of their own. The chamber music affords several examples: the last movement of the G Minor Piano Quartet is a *Rondo alla Zingarese*, the last movement of the G Major String Quintet is in the rhythm of a Czárdas, and there are gypsy elements in the Finale of the F Minor Piano Quintet and the slow movement of the C Major Trio. Most remarkable of all is the slow movement of the Clarinet Quintet, but that I must leave to be discussed by another writer.

In the domain of form Brahms found the classical models so well suited to his cast of thought that he needed to make few changes. Only in the *Scherzo* does he evolve something new of his own. His starting point is the impetuous '*presto*' *scherzo* that we associate with Beethoven. The three early piano sonatas, as well as the B Major Trio have *scherzos* of this type, and examples can also be found later, in the Piano Quintet, for instance, or the C Minor Piano Quartet. These are full-blooded affairs. Quite different in mood, though not in *tempo*, is the *Scherzo* of the C Major Trio, *pianissimo* almost throughout, an eerie rustling at twilight, and a similar effect is created by the *Scherzo* of the C Minor Trio which, as Tovey says, 'hurries by like a frightened child'. These crepuscular *scherzi* are not to be found in the early works, they are a discovery of the mature Brahms.

But the general tendency of the mature *scherzi* is to be slower. The G Minor Piano Quartet of 1861 has a gentle movement in 9/8 time, marked *Allegro, ma non troppo*. It sounds like a Nocturne, and Brahms fights shy of calling it '*Scherzo*', using instead the title '*Intermezzo*', which here makes an early appearance in his music. But by the time he reaches the G Major Sextet (1865) he has overcome his scruples and writes '*Scherzo*' above his very steady-paced second movement in 2/4 time. In the Trio, however, he surprises us with a 3/4 *presto giocoso*, vigorous and somewhat bucolic. This and other examples wherein *scherzo* and trio are strongly contrasted in rhythm, speed, and mood, culminate in the very beautiful and elaborate middle movement of the F Major String Quintet (1882) – almost the only movement by Brahms that won the approval of Hugo Wolf. It is a combination of slow movement and *scherzo* in a single design, and its shape resembles that of a *scherzo* with two trios. Brahms begins *Grave ed appassionato* in 3/4 time. The cello, pitched well above the other four instruments, sings an expressive melody in C sharp major, but the first viola answers in C sharp minor, and this turns out to be the main key of the section, which extends to some thirty bars and ends with a full close. Next comes an *Allegretto vivace*, light and graceful, in A major. In the formal scheme the *Grave* takes the place of the *Scherzo* and the *Allegretto* of the first Trio. It runs to about the length of a normal trio, but at the end it veers away from A major and prepares for C sharp minor. The recovery of this tonality brings back the *grave* tempo and the *grave* theme, but Brahms writes a new, more impassioned continuation, though he closes as before in C sharp minor. The next section, a *Presto* in ₵ time, constitutes the second Trio. There was nothing revolutionary about writing a second trio; Beethoven had done it in his Fourth and Seventh Symphonies, and elsewhere. But with Beethoven the second trio is a repetition of the first; Brahms's second trio appears at first sight to have nothing

in common with the first save its A major tonality. But then
we look more closely and discover that it is in fact an ingenious variation of the first trio, the 6/8 theme being modified to fit the ₵ rhythm :

Rhythmic metamorphoses of this sort are common enough
in Wagner and Liszt, but Brahms is often supposed to have
avoided them; in fact he uses them quite frequently.

The *Presto* over, the music returns to the *Grave* for the last
time, though what we get is less a *da capo* than an extended
coda based on the *grave* theme. But after coming to rest in
C sharp major nine bars from the end of the movement the
music oscillates between chords of C sharp and A major
and unexpectedly decides to close in A, the key of the two
trios. The whole piece is an imaginative masterpiece of the
first order, completely original, full of surprises, yet a
wholly legitimate descendant of the classical *scherzo*.

How should we listen to Brahms's chamber music? In-
telligently, of course – but is that all? Ilona Eibenschütz,
who knew him, said to me, 'You English make Brahms so
cold! In reality he was such a human person.' Let us enjoy
his tunes, kindle to his rhythms, rejoice with him, grieve
with him, dream with him. But let us also remember that
he was a very reserved man. He tells us his thoughts, but
leaves us to guess at his feelings, though the feelings are
surely there. In speech he was often obscure, saying things
that were susceptible of more than one meaning, and his
music often presents the same ambiguity. Richard Specht
tells us that the Piano Quintet contains some of 'the gloomiest music Brahms has written', and Tovey calls the first
movement 'powerfully tragic'. Yet Clara Schumann was
'charmed' by the music – a word that hardly suggests

tragedy – and Karl Geiringer describes the first movement as 'lively'. When the pundits disagree to this extent we lesser folk had better be careful. Let us dream our dreams, by all means, but let us also be reticent about them. Our neighbour may have dreamt quite a different dream, and who is to say whether either of us is right?

9

Bedřich Smetana (1824–1884) and
Antonín Dvořák (1841–1904)

JOHN CLAPHAM

INTRODUCTION

SMETANA'S father, we have been told, danced a polka in the inn courtyard at Litomyšl when his third wife at last presented him with a son. It is unlikely the dance was in fact a polka, as this popular modern Czech dance was not adopted by the people of Prague until eleven years later. But by the time Smetana and Dvořák reached maturity the polka, together with the *furiant, sousedská, skočná,* and other Czech dances, formed an important part of the musical personalities of the two composers. The national dance rhythms were in their blood.

The polka first appeared in chamber music in Smetana's String Quartet in E minor, *From My Life,* and later in Dvořák's String Quartet in D minor and his String Sextet. The *furiant,* or swaggerers' dance, was found by Dvořák to make an excellent *scherzo.* In several of his best examples this dance's attractive cross accents are a prominent feature, and these can be seen clearly in the *Scherzo* of his *Terzetto*:

This theme can be re-barred satisfactorily in slower triple time with two bars becoming one and sounds as if it should be – until the last four bars give indications of quick 3/4 time. Sometimes Dvořák increased the rhythmic excitement by the simultaneous use of the apparent duple rhythm and real triple rhythm in melody and accompaniment, as in the *vivace* section in the *dumka* movement of his String Quartet in E Flat (Ex. 4*b*), and at the beginning of the *furiant* of his String Quartet in A Flat.

Dvořák borrowed the *dumka* or elegy from Ukraine, and made it into a personal possession. His most characteristic *dumky* (the plural form of *dumka*) consist of alternations of melancholy laments and wild dances, and demonstrate the rapid changes of mood from one extreme to another which are natural to the Slav temperament. There are fine examples in the second movements of the String Quartet in E Flat and the Piano Quintet, and throughout the *Dumky* Trio.

Czech folk-songs were hardly every used directly by Smetana and Dvořák, and only Dvořák occasionally betrays their indirect influence to any appreciable extent. Smetana, in creating for the first time a national Czech style, consciously aimed to express the spirit of his people in general terms. His choice of national subjects for opera and for symphonic poems found favour, but the influence of Liszt and Wagner on his music was frowned on by the more extreme nationalists. Dvořák, a more impressionable man, was a pan-Slav as well as a follower of Smetana along the paths of Czech nationalism; and having chosen to write chamber music and symphonies he turned towards Vienna, to learn from the classicism of Beethoven and Brahms and the uninhibited romanticism of Schubert, a composer to whom he was temperamentally akin. Influences from outside, however, could seldom subdue for long the instinctive spontaneity of Dvořák's Czech peasant soul.

Both Dvořák and Smetana had a deep love for their country. It was a tactless remark of Herbeck to the effect that Czechs, although excellent performers, did not seem capable of creating music of their own, which made Smetana swear to found a Czech national style. Dvořák, profoundly hurt that Simrock, the publisher, despite representations, persisted in printing his Christian name in the German form, wrote: 'Forgive me for this digression: I was only trying to explain that an artist also has a homeland in which he must have firm faith and to which his heart must always warm.'

SMETANA

SMETANA only wrote three chamber works during his years of maturity. The first of these, the Pianoforte Trio in G Minor, Op. 15, was written prior to embracing nationalism in its strongest form, and 'composed in memory of my exceptionally gifted child Bedřiška who died early in her fifth year as the result of scarlet fever'. Smetana's grief for his daughter colours most of the work, and is epitomized in the chromatic descent through a fifth which occurs prominently in the first two movements and somewhat disguised in the Finale.

His two String Quartets, although autobiographical, were not quite the first of their kind to enter the realm of programme music, for Haydn had already arranged his orchestral *Seven Last Words* for string quartet nearly ninety years earlier, but Smetana's works were the first important programmatic works conceived for that medium. They have had no progeny of significance except Schönberg's *Verklärte Nacht* and a Tolstoy inspired string quartet by Janáček. In Smetana's case his departure from custom was a perfectly natural step, because most of his creative thought, whether in the sphere of opera or the symphonic poem, was concerned with the expression of non-musical ideas in terms of musical sound.

The Quartet in E Minor, *From My Life*, is perfectly satisfactory apart from its programme, but an understanding of the basis of its inspiration throws light on the course of events in the last movement. The first movement, which is in sonata-form, represents Smetana's youth, his love of art, his romanticism and his inexpressible yearning for something intangible, and it has suggestions of a warning of his future deafness. The long declamatory main theme given to the viola represents Fate, and the initial falling fifth gives the hint of tragedy to come:

There is a wistful second theme, suggesting romantic yearning, which appears in G major and passes to minor keys. The stormy development leads back directly to the second subject. The second movement – a sturdy polka, with a reminder at the beginning of Schumann's Piano Quartet – recalls the happy days of his youth when he composed much dance music and adored dancing. The slow movement expresses the bliss of his love for the girl who became his first wife, and here Liszt's influence may not be a coincidence, for it was he who gave Smetana the financial security he needed in order to marry Kateřina Kolář. The Finale describes his joy at the discovery that he could express national sentiments in music, but towards the end a high sustained note is heard, the fatal whistling in his ears that heralded his deafness, and this is followed by the tragic falling fifth from Ex. 2. The second theme from the first movement returns with a ray of hope and a reminder of former happiness, but the work ends with painful regrets that the promise of his early career has been terminated.

Smetana's lesser-known String Quartet in D Minor, No. 2, is an attempt, the composer stated, to put on paper 'the whirlwind of music in the head of one who has lost his hearing'. The first two themes (a) and (b) represent the mental disorder and depression resulting from his deafness:

A new beginning is made in which the musical germ that is the basis of these themes becomes transformed into (*c*) by the faith reborn in Smetana at the thought of returning to creative work. After a new expressive theme has been heard the themes return in a different order without development; (*b*) comes last and is made more poignant by means of chromatic harmony. In the two middle movements Smetana finds joy once again in the creation of national music. The second movement, the most immediately appealing of the four, is a syncopated polka which changes to a gracious lullaby in 3/8 time. The Finale represents the victory Smetana had gained for the time being over Fate. This confessional work is brief, unpredictable in form, and was probably influenced by the music of Beethoven's last period.

DVOŘÁK — THE STRING WORKS

UNLIKE Smetana, who avoided writing oratorios and church music, who was not attracted by symphony and concerto writing and rarely wrote chamber music, Dvořák wrote freely in all available forms. Chamber music was one of his principal and most successful means of expression. It is surprising that only three or four of his chamber works are at all well known, for several of the neglected works are just as fine and fully representative. He is known to have written fourteen string quartets, apart from his arrangement of twelve songs for string quartet, but as he matured late the earlier ones can be passed over here.

A convenient starting point for us is the String Quintet in G with double bass written in 1875, the same year as the Symphony in F; the Quintet is a cheerful yet somewhat inconsequential work with an attractive *Scherzo*. The String Quartet in E by frequently veering towards minor keys reflects his sorrow for his daughter who had died, but this work is excelled by the melancholy String Quartet in D Minor of 1877 referred to earlier. Dvořák's increasing skill is shown here by his economy of thematic material and successful grafting of a first movement theme on to the coda of the slow movement. Besides showing further mastery, the String Sextet in A and the String Quartet in E Flat make a more generous use of national colouring, just at the time when the composer's Slavonic Dances were taking parts of Europe by storm. The Sextet has a lyrical first movement, a fascinating *dumka* in polka rhythm, a *furiant*, and a theme with variations that emphasizes B minor delightfully in preference to the tonic, A major.

The striking thing about the opening of the E Flat Quartet is the beauty and freshness of its *arpeggio* texture. The principal theme unfolds itself in leisurely fashion, moves to A flat, becomes more animated while passing to other keys, and then gives way to the second theme which is presented quietly in polka rhythm. The development springs almost entirely from the principle theme, but when this is heard solemnly in augmentation the cello intrudes with a reminder of the polka. The recapitulation is much shortened and there is an extended coda. An appealing *dumka* follows with an elegiac theme (*a*) that is soon transformed into a typical *furiant* (*b*):

A Romance and a *skočna* follow, the latter being a lively reel in 2/4 time.

The next work, the String Quartet in C, is less unified in style than the one in E flat, but national elements are conspicuous in the first and last movements and in the trio. The opening theme makes us expect drama and we are not disappointed; Dvořák's use of key and modulation is remarkable. The work was written for Vienna, the home of Beethoven, and in the *Scherzo* we can detect the latter's guiding hand. 'Why don't you all kneel?' Dvořák used to cry to his class of students whenever a sonata by his idol was being played. After an interval appeared a slighter and more intimate work, the *Terzetto* for two violins and viola. The delightful *furiant*, which has a waltz as a trio, has already been quoted in Ex. 1.

Six years later, while in the United States, Dvořák wrote the String Quartet in F and the String Quintet in E Flat. It is rather misleading to call the Quartet 'The Nigger', for it contains no negro melodies. Both works use themes on pentatonic scales, that is, scales that have only five different notes and lack semitone intervals. Negro tunes are often pentatonic, but so are those of Scotland, Russia, China, and elsewhere. Dvořák had written pentatonic themes and syncopated Slovak rhythms similar to those found in negro melodies long before going to America. His American works are in general thoroughly Czech, but the inclination towards pentatonicism in them was undoubtedly stimulated by his interest in negro spirituals.

The layout of the beginning of the Quartet in F – *tremolo* violins, pedal note in bass, viola theme – is similar to that at the beginning of Smetana's First Quartet, but Dvořák's opening has more refinements, and his theme is not declamatory like Smetana's (Ex. 2) but is pentatonic and pithy. How far removed in spirit Dvořák could be from negro song while writing pentatonically is well illustrated by the second of his two second subject themes (only the last bar of which infringes pentatonicism):

The beautiful long nostalgic slow movement melody, exquisitely accompanied, is the crown of the quartet. The main *scherzo* theme reappears augmented in the tonic minor in the trio; the second *scherzo* theme was derived from the song of the scarlet tanager. The finale is wholly frivolous except for a brief chorale-like episode.

The first movement of the rather more exotic companion work, the Quintet in E Flat, may show by its frequent trochaic 'drum rhythm' on repeated notes signs of the influence of Central Algonkin music, which Dvořák heard in Iowa, but the 'drum rhythm' heard at the beginning of the *Scherzo* bears no resemblance to the rhythms of the Algonkins or of their Sioux neighbours. In the *Larghetto* we are strongly reminded of Beethoven in the second half of the minor-major theme used for variations; the original sketch of this portion of the theme was intended for a new American National Anthem, probably with the words, 'My country, 'tis of thee'.

On returning to Czechoslovakia, Dvořák wrote two splendid works, the String Quartets in G Major and A Flat, the second of which had been begun in America. It is clear in these, his last chamber works, that he was overjoyed at being home, and was prepared to offer fresh solutions to problems of form. In the G Major Quartet the highly original and brilliant first theme (Ex. 6), a quiet theme first heard in E minor, and the second subject theme in triplet rhythm which appears in B flat major (and B major), are all combined in the unusually highly wrought development of the first movement.

The *Adagio*, in the form of free variations on two closely related themes, one minor and the other major, is outstanding for its depth of feeling. A lightweight *Scherzo* and a cheerful *Allegro* follow. In the latter the third theme from the first movement plays a leading part.

The Quartet in A Flat, without aiming as high at the one in G, achieves a better balance of its movements and has a magnificent *furiant*. The first movement has two themes in A flat, the first being essentially a decoration of the notes of the tonic chord and having an important tailpiece of three notes, and the second theme an expressive melody with characteristic drops of a seventh and a sixth, the latter descent accompanied by a chromatic chord of the ninth; a hunting call serves for the second subject. Most of the first subject is short-circuited on recapitulation. In the *furiant* the athletic theme carries this dance's cross accents to extremes:

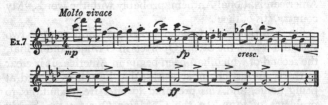

The four *ff* bars prove to be important; they provide a counter-theme when the second violin takes over the main theme, and later they are inverted to form the beginning of the trio melody. Dvořák's ability to write long melodies is again amply demonstrated in the *Lento*. The finale is rich in ideas and departs from orthodox sonata form by having two distinct second subjects in contrasting keys (E flat and G flat), but Dvořák's instinct was right when he made only the first of these return in the tonic.

DVOŘÁK – STRINGS WITH PIANO

THE Piano Trio in B Flat, the Piano Quartet in D, and the Piano Trio in G Minor belong to the period of the F Major Symphony and were the first of Dvořák's published chamber works to include piano. In the first of these the themes are treated with some imagination and a movement in polka rhythm is included. The Piano Quartet is pleasant music, but rather diffuse, and not as yet highly characteristic of the composer. The Second Piano Trio was the first work to be written after the death of the composer's daughter.

An enormous gulf separates these works from the Piano Trio in F Minor written seven years later during a time of personal crisis. It offers pianists music which is written in a mature style at last, and those who admire the D Minor Symphony, Op. 70, must appreciate the Trio's powerful and almost symphonic first movement and notice an anticipation of the Symphony's finale in the poignant coda of the Trio's slow movement. Dvořák seldom hit upon so fine a theme as this for the beginning of a work:

Its potentialities begin to show at once as it flares up dramatically in the next few bars. The development grows entirely out of the first subject themes, and this process of growth or re-creation continues strikingly in the recapitulation. Although the influence of Brahms is noticeable in this Trio, the fascinating colouring of the plaintive C sharp minor dance, which comes second, is pure Dvořák. After a contemplative slow movement with a martial middle section there is a *rondo* in *furiant* rhythm with a waltz as second subject. At the end of this movement the change from the minor to the major mode is brought about by the return of Ex. 8.

Dvořák composed the three remaining works during the five years prior to his stay in U.S.A. All are strongly national in feeling. The first of these, the deservedly popular Piano Quintet in A, shows not a trace of the mood of the F Minor Trio, and intoxicates hearers with its melody, vital rhythm, colourful scoring, and contrasts of mood. The first movement is rich in themes, hovers between major and minor in its opening section, and is peculiar in having more bars in the submediant key than in the tonic in recapitulation and coda combined. The slow movement, a *dumka*, is 'framed' with four bars for piano alone. In the fifth bar the viola plays the principal theme on its lowest string while the piano has a counter-melody high in the treble – a felicitous example of contrasted tone colours:

Two contrasted sections, the second of which is a wild dance, break in on the elegiac mood. The brilliant *Scherzo*, although labelled *furiant*, lacks the customary displaced accents. The Quintet ends with a radiant *rondo*.

The Piano Quartet in E Flat has unluckily been overshadowed by the Quintet. The principal theme of the first movement consists of a challenge from the strings, which subdivides into two parts, and an evasive and playful response from the piano:

Both development and coda are built on these ideas. Following a false reprise in the development, the first subject and transition are omitted entirely from the recapitulation. A wide range of emotion is expressed in the *Lento* and a charming *ländler* follows. During the Finale, which is a good-humoured sonata-form movement in the unusual key of E flat minor, an *arpeggio* figure for the viola, accompanying a piano solo, blossoms out delightfully at the cadence.

The Dumky Trio is a set of six typical *dumky* in the keys of E minor, C sharp minor, A major, D minor, E flat major, and C minor, united by similarities of emotional feeling. The forms are simple and the first three *dumky* are played without a break. In the first *dumka* there is a thematic link between *Lento maestoso* and *Allegro*. A plaintive character is maintained in the first part of the third *dumka* despite the major key. The fourth *dumka* starts with a halting accompanying figure for the piano and in the third bar the violin adds a monotonous quaver figure; two bars later the cello enters with the melody. This beginning is perhaps even more effective than the striking call to attention over an added sixth chord at the commencement of the work. The Trio as a whole is outstanding for its wealth of themes, its colourful scoring and its varied treatment of the idea of melancholy.

10

Ernest Bloch (b. 1880)

ANDREW PORTER

FOR chamber music, written by a Swiss, that we can live with, study, and hear again and again with increasing satisfaction, we must turn to the works of Ernest Bloch. The chamber pieces of Frank Martin (born in Geneva, 1890) are early, and not characteristic; his Piano Quintet (1920) is French-influenced, suggesting something between César Franck and Fauré, while the String Trio (1935) and Quartet (1936) are again French in manner, with an admixture of dodecaphony. Honegger's *Petite Suite* is an airy trifle composed for his niece and nephew; while his three String Quartets (the first of them a very early work) are relatively unimportant.

But Bloch's chamber music is both available for our study, and rewarding of it. Principally, there are four String Quartets and a Piano Quintet (in addition his catalogue shows several descriptive pieces for piano trio and for string quartet, two violin sonatas, and a suite for viola and piano). All four String Quartets and the Piano Quintet are recorded. Bloch, born in Geneva in 1880, in 1897 a student at the Jaques Dalcroze Institute, and by turns resident in Switzerland and in America, is a figure defiant of classification. He is an individualist. One of the elements in his style is a certain Jewish plangency, which finds specific expression in the two Jewish works, the 'Sacred Service' and *Schelomo*. In England, before the war, he was ranked in importance with Bartók and Hindemith; a Bloch Society was founded in 1937 and his music was often heard. One can safely say that to-day he no longer stands so high in general acclaim.

Bloch's String Quartet, No. 1, in B minor, dates from 1916, and is a rich, violent, somewhat indigestible work, written partly in Geneva and partly in America. In the second movement we find that one short section carries the indications *frenetico, martellato, marcato, furioso, feroce*, and *strepitoso*. The *pastorale* movement which succeeds it is serene and contemplative; the finale returns us to agitation. Bloch in his younger days was trained as a violinist under Ysaye, and his writing for strings is masterly. In this First Quartet, as in his later chamber works, we can appreciate his command of the medium: three effects particularly favoured are harsh ejaculations, a floating wisp of rather tentative melody high on the strings, and a rich, saturated texture.

All three are found in his next chamber work, the Piano Quintet completed in Cleveland in 1923, one of his most approachable and colourful compositions. The three movements – as in all five of Bloch's principal chamber works – are interrelated. The 'motto' theme here is that announced by the piano; the principal theme of the first movement follows on the strings. In the second subject we hear the quarter-tones which have won for the Quintet a certain notoriety; but here, as elsewhere in the work, quarter-tones are used for their colouring and evocative power, not so much for any structural significance.

The *Andante mistico* opens with a theme on the viola which is developed from the first subject of the first movement. The indication of *mistico*, and the later one *misterioso*, describe this gentle, searching movement. The finale progresses from *Allegro energico* to a theme marked *barbarico*. The intention of the movement is apparently to build order and calm from chaos and trouble; and a final long ascent on the piano leads to an untroubled chord of C major.

Bloch's Second String Quartet, of 1945, follows roughly the scheme of the first; but it is atonal, and far more terse (some thirty-three minutes, against the fifty minutes of No. 1.) A motto theme drives through the four movements; again there are harsh passages, and again a firm control (which guides a *passacaglia* and fugue in the Finale) prevents emotion from overspilling its banks. This Quartet was first performed by the Griller String Quartet. The Third String Quartet also is dedicated to this ensemble. It is particularly well worth study by anyone interested in contemporary music; and we shall examine it a little more closely.

Here, in the shortest, most concise, and perhaps most enjoyable of his major chamber compositions, the seventy-six-year-old composer breaks new ground. The tone is positive and optimistic from the start, not only after violent struggle and tentative exploration. And, perhaps for the first time, there are gleams of humour.

The scheme of the Quartet is as follows:

1. *Allegro deciso*, 2/2, A minor. About four minutes. Dated 7 December 1951.

2. *Adagio non troppo*, 3/4, D minor. About five and a half minutes. Dated 4 January 1952.

3. *Allegro molto*, 3/8, E minor. About six and a half minutes. Dated 11 February 1952.

4. *Allegro*, 2/2, A major. About seven minutes. Dated Agate Beach, Oregon, 25 March 1952.

The first performance was given by the Griller String Quartet in New York, in January 1953; the first London performance was on June 21 of the same year, in a Festival Hall recital which marked the twenty-fifth birthday of the Griller Quartet.

As in the two earlier Quartets and the Piano Quintet, the movements are thematically connected. All four grow from the figure propounded in the second and third bars – the 'germ' of the work, the point for discussion. The figure itself is a chain of interlocked descending fifths: D–G, B–E, A–D (C):

These fifths recur in each movement, and in one form or another permeate the entire texture. It is for this reason that the Quartet, like its predecessors, makes a tight, close-knit impression. But, more than them, it is varied in its parts, affecting in its content, and grateful to the ear in its care for pleasing sound.

The first movement, whose opening is illustrated above, is a rhythmical one. The fifths are propounded three-deep in octaves, and the rhythm throughout has a healthy squareness. Minims, quavers, and trills provide relief, but the basic motion is of crotchet chords slashed out with masculine certainty. The second subject, companion to first, moves at the same basic crotchet speed, but more smoothly. All four parts are shown in the example below:

The impression the whole movement leaves is of strength and enterprise.

The *Adagio* opens with a lulling figure on the viola, soon taken over by the cello, and then the first violin enters with:

where the first two bars seem to be concealing E–A, D–G, B flat–E. A few bars later this decoration of the basic idea (or what Schönberg would have called the *Grundgestalt*) gives way to the original form, unadorned, in unmistakable even quavers: F–B flat, D–G, C–F (D). This generates counter-melodies which are in turn developed, while the theme itself is never wholly absent. In this movement we see the *Grundgestalt* trace its way through the most beautiful figurations and sonorities.

The third movement is a *Scherzo* with its own main theme,

and only a hint now and again, though a very definite one,

of the basic idea. Several things are charming, among them
a bell-like effect in which the first violin leaps up and down
over octaves, and a sudden and unexpected transformation
of Ex. 4 into something very like a popular song! Immediately after this, as if in reproof, we shade into mysterious
harmonies, *moderato*, and soon afterwards hear, first high
cello foreshadowings of the basic theme, and then on the
first violin the theme itself in the form it will have for much
the last movement – with the first fifth diminished, and the
tempo augmented:

The tempo soon picks up again; the theme moves from
crotchets back to quavers, and at the close is heard in conjunction with Ex. 4.

In the Finale Bloch gets down to discussing the theme in
many aspects and rhythms, with *passacaglia*-like passages,
and eventually a proper fugue (this use of *passacaglia* and
fugue recalls the Second String Quartet). The opening bars
present the upper part of Ex. 5, in minims now, and three
octaves lower. The inversion of the basic theme, with rising
fourths instead of falling fifths, is readily perceptible by the
ear; and if this note has left any impression that the
Quartet is in any sense a mere 'paper' composition, a single
hearing will suffice to dispel it. To the attentive listener the
structure, so cumbersome to explain, will make itself clear
without a score. The Quartet ends in a resolute A major,
and seems to sum up in its last section the many statements
about interlocking fifths which we have listened to while it
has run its course. (The score of Bloch's Fourth String
Quartet was not available when this chapter was written.
The work was first performed by the Griller Quartet at a
B.B.C. concert broadcast from the Wigmore Hall, London,
in January 1954. It continues the line of serenity found in
its predecessor, with vigorous contrasting sections, and also
employs the 'cyclic' principle.)

I I

Béla Bartók (1881–1945)

MOSCO CARNER

INTRODUCTION

BARTÓK's first essay in string quartet writing (later suppressed) is said to date from 1899, when he was a youth of eighteen; his last, from December 1944 (nine months before his death), when he sketched out a few brief ideas for a planned Seventh Quartet. Between lie the six published quartets the dates of which are as follows (the figures in brackets indicate the composer's age at the time of composition):

No. 1, Op. 7	1908	(27)
No. 2, Op. 17	1915–17	(34–6)
No. 3	1927	(46)
No. 4	1928	(47)
No. 5	1934	(53)
No. 6	1939	(58)

A glance at this table and consultation of the complete list of Bartók's works elicit the significant fact that, along with the piano, the string quartet was the solo medium that held the composer's undiminished interest, from his student days up to almost the very end of his life. The six quartets occupy a central position in Bartók's creative career, they form its very backbone. Or to change the metaphor, they may be likened to the pages of a diary to which a great artist confided the most private experiences and adventures of his heart and mind. In point of style they contain the quintessence of Bartók's musical personality and as a series they afford a fascinating study in creative development. Each may be said to stand at the culmination of the respective phases of his artistic growth and each, with the possible exception of No. 1, is a masterpiece in its own right.

Certainly, we may declare our preference for this or that quartet, we may find the one more immediately accessible than the other, yet this is irrelevant to the objective recognition that within its terms of reference, each of the quartets from Nos. 2–6 is a rounded whole and sums up the essential problems, tendencies, and aspirations peculiar to the successive stages of Bartók's maturity.

Beethoven comes to mind, with whom the string quartet possessed the same significance in his creative career; and it can be said without fear of contradiction that not since the Viennese master has an outstanding composer made this medium so intimately his own as Bartók has. The parallel can be extended. Just as the series of seventeen Beethoven quartets constitute the apogee of the classical form, so do the series of six Bartók quartets mark the consummation of the modern genre. For profundity of thought, imaginative power, logic of structure, diversity of formal details, and enlargement of the technical scope, they stand unrivalled in the field of modern chamber music.

The quality of uniqueness that attaches to these quartets is enhanced by the following fact. One of the mainsprings of Bartók's creative life was to achieve a synthesis of East and West. In the quartets this synthesis may be said to reach its most sublimated form, and we realize the full measure of Bartók's achievement when we bear in mind that this consummate fusion of two such very different musical cultures is effected in a medium which we regard as at once the purest and most subtle manifestation of Western musical thinking. To have harnessed so fruitfully the instinctual forces residing in Eastern (Magyar) music to the most intellectual of our musical forms – therein lies, to my mind, the historic significance of the Bartók of the quartets.

This synthesis, however, was achieved at a price. A criticism that must be levelled against Bartók's quartet style (as, indeed, it must be brought against Beethoven's too, from the Rasoumovsky Quartets onward) is, that sometimes it bursts the framework of the medium with explosive vehemence. Responsible for it in Bartók's case was not (as it was in Beethoven's) a powerful symphonic urge, but the percussiveness of his harmony, rhythm, and dynamics. Bartók does not aim at orchestral effects, though occasionally he writes passages of a quasi-orchestral texture and sonority (second movement of No. 2, First Part and coda of No. 3, Finale of No. 4): it is the complex of features we connote with the 'barbaric' quality of his general style that militates against the intimacy and inwardness of the string quartet medium. However, if seen in the whole context of Bartók's achievement, this aspect moves into proper perspective and must be accepted as an integral part of his conception of string-quartet writing. Without it, the quartets would not be what they are.

Before dealing with the six works individually, let us first attempt a general outline of their style and see in which way they reflect Bartók's development over the years. Broadly speaking, five stages may be discerned:

1. The early period when Bartók was under the influence of the late German romantics: First Quartet.

2. The period during which a purer, more individual kind of romanticism fuses with elements of Magyar folk music: Second Quartet.

3. A phase of technical experimentation and intellectual abstraction, the period of the 'difficult', expressionist Bartók: Third Quartet.

4. A gradual relaxation of the expressionist tension and a return to a more lyrical expression: Fourth and Fifth Quartets.

5. The 'classical' phase, characterized by a comparative simplicity in form, texture, and tonal relations and by a newly gained equilibrium between the intellectual and emotional aspects of Bartók's personality: Sixth Quartet.

The series thus shows, in respect of aesthetic and technical difficulties, a crescendo and diminuendo – a kind of arch, if you like, in which the 'keystone' is represented by the Third Quartet. (Yet supposing one wished to study the quartets in their order of progressive difficulty, the best method, I suggest, would be to begin with the first two, then tackle No. 6, and work one's way back through Nos. 5 and 4 to the Third Quartet.)

One of the most striking aspects of the quartets lies in Bartók's varied and highly individual treatment of the classical form. He never abandons it but he introduces a number of significant modifications and novel features, most of which serve the purpose of achieving a greater organic coherence, both in the single movement and the quartet as a whole. His chief device for obtaining unity between movements is the romantic one of the cyclic idea which in the mature quartets he develops and applies in an original manner. In No. 1 the young Bartók is still content with deriving the first subject of the Finale from an *ostinato* figure in the preceding *Scherzo*, while in No. 2 first and last movements are thematically linked. But in Nos. 4 and 5 the cyclic idea is extended to four of the five movements and applied in a manner at once more intellectual and intrinsic, by means of the so-called arch-forms A–B–C–B–A. This enables the composer to establish between the movements not only thematic but also formal and emotional correspondences. In No. 6 we find him resorting to the cyclic idea in the form of a motto-theme, but here too its application shows individual modifications. No. 3 stands apart, in that overall unity is achieved by its one-movement form, in which the four sections relate to one another in the pattern A–B–A–B (coda), the last two sections constituting greatly modified recapitulations of the first two.

In the form of the individual movements, however, Bartók closely adheres to classical models: sonata, *rondo*, and a simple A–B–A in the fast movements, while the slow ones are always three-sectional. The one exception is provided by the *Lento* of No. 2, in which Bartók appears to be reproducing the serial, chain-like arrangement characteristic of a certain kind of Magyar folk music: four thematically unrelated sections, but held together by the typically Western devices of a recurrent cadential motive and a coda of reminiscences.

Yet with so searching a mind as Bartók's it is not

surprising that the detailed structure of the traditional forms should undergo significant alterations. This is particularly true of the recapitulation of a sonata movement and, more generally, of any repeat of previous material. Bartók carries the conception of the classical reprise to the point where it sometimes takes on the character of a complete reorganization and radical 'rethinking' of the exposition, with the result that in certain movements the correspondence between exposition and recapitulation becomes so vague and tenuous that one is tempted to speak of an ideal reprise rather than a real one, a return in the spirit rather than in the letter. The most remarkable instance of this will be found in the *Ricapitulazione della prima parte* of the Third Quartet and in the slow movements of the Fourth and Fifth Quartets. Again, in the opening *Allegro* of No. 5, the recapitulation partly reverses the order in which the themes follow each other in the exposition; in addition, the themes themselves reappear in their inverted form. Occasionally, however, the recapitulation will represent a simplified, more straightforward version of the expositions as in the first movement of No. 2 and the *Prima parte* of No. 3 (p. 7, 11).* In short, Bartók knows no mere formal repeat but revitalizes it by an organic regeneration of the expository material.

Organic regeneration is also the secret of Bartók's motive development (as it is of Beethoven's). It accounts for that compelling logic and cohesion which are felt even in his most complex and difficult works; and the immense subtlety and pliability of this process is perhaps nowhere shown to more remarkable effect than in the mature quartets. Like the Beethoven of the late quartets and piano sonatas, Bartók concentrates on a few and often insignificant motives, and by a variety of devices he evolves from these germ-cells the ever-changing tissues of his fabric: stretching and contracting of intervals, diatonic and chromatic versions

* Page nos. refer to miniature scores. No. 1 is published by Rózsavölgyi, No. 4 by the Wiener Philharmonischer Verlag, and the rest by Boosey and Hawkes, who now have publication rights of all Bartók's music.

of the same figure, fragmentation, inverted and retrograde forms, and rhythmic variation. In certain movements the music seems to stem from a single protoplasmic cell which proliferates into the most unexpected and multifarious shapes. It would take a large number of pages to show how in, say, the first *Allegro* of No. 4 the texture of the whole movement has grown out of a simple six-note chromatic motive. Such movements are not merely monothematic but, to coin an appropriate word, *monocystic* (one-cellular), the theme, or themes, being offshoots of the cell, and the whole movement showing *continuous* growth.

In an interview given in 1939 Bartók named Bach, Beethoven, and Debussy as the three masters from whom he had learned most.* Beethoven's influence we have noted in Bartók's motive development and the close attention he paid to matters of form. As for Debussy, it is true he had shown Bartók one of the ways by which to emancipate himself from the classical concept of major-minor tonality, and he also coloured (to some extent) the Hungarian master's harmonic style, yet there is little direct influence of the French composer to be felt in the quartets – one or two Debussyian fingerprints occur in the first two quartets. And although Bartók's impressionism, as exemplified in the 'night music' of the slow movements of Nos. 4 and 5, can be traced back to Debussy, it is so personal as to *appear* to have grown on his own soil. Bach, however, who revealed to Bartók 'the transcendent significance' of counterpoint is, like Beethoven, more in evidence, and for the patent reason that the four individual parts of the string quartet medium offer an especially wide scope for polyphonic writing. In his later quartets Bartók cultivates a predominantly linear (non-harmonic) counterpoint in which harmonies are mostly the logical result of the part-writing. This largely accounts for the marked harshness of the harmonic idiom of Nos. 3–5. In addition, the scholastic, 'automatic' devices of inversion, retrograde motion, canon,

---

* See *Béla Bartók*, by Serge Moreux. London, 1953.

imitation, and *stretto* are used in profusion, and on several occasions subjects are stated in canon, as in the opening movements of Nos. 1, 3, and 5. At times, however, the impression cannot be resisted of a *de trop*, a feeling that Bartók is straining these devices and making too self-conscious a use of them, as witness the contrapuntal *tour de force* of the Finale of No. 5. On the other hand, he handles them with remarkable freedom and rarely sacrifices the shapeliness and equipoise of his melodic lines to the demands of strict logic. Another characteristic is his habit of making a fugue the centre of a development section, and it is worth noting that all these fugues share a common feature, in that they are fast scurrying pieces in subdued dynamics and in *leggiero* style. Unlike the fugues of the late Beethoven, Bartók's are not dramatic but (like some of Bach's) of a 'motoric' kind and greatly intensify the rhythmic drive of the movement in which they occur.

If we once more cast a comprehensive glance at the melodic and harmonic style of the quartets, we observe a characteristic change as the series progresses. In the melody a gradual process of fragmentation takes place. Themes are replaced by motive-generated configurations, which change their shapes in kaleidoscopic fashion; and there is a preponderance of small (mostly) chromatic intervals over wider diatonic ones. (It is largely in what has aptly been called 'imaginary folk tunes' (Moreux), melodies invented in the style of Magyar music, that Bartók keeps closer to themes in the accepted sense, as witness the *Seconda parte* of No. 3, the fourth movement of No. 4, and the slow movements of Nos. 4 and 5.) From the Fifth Quartet onward, however, Bartók's melodic writing gains in consistency and sweep: for example, the singularly beautiful motto-theme of No. 6.

To turn to the harmonic aspect. The quartets clearly reflect Bartók's emancipation from romantic (Wagnerian) chromaticism and the traditional major-minor tonality of his early period to the individual style of his maturity. Partly under the influence of his native folk music, partly of Debussy and Stravinsky, Bartók turns to a 'diatonicized' chromatic writing in which the five chromatic notes stand in their own right, equal in status to the seven diatonic notes (their former 'parents') and often replace them, thus becoming an integral part of diatonic major-minor. This in turn leads to a very considerable extension of Bartók's tonal orbit. In Nos. 3 and 4 the tonal perspective recedes to a point where the tonic becomes scarcely perceptible, and where a note or a chord may serve merely as the point of departure and return at the end. Providing, however, that we discard the traditional notion of tonality, we may say that No. 3 is 'on' C sharp, No. 4 'on' C, and No. 5 'on' B flat. Here again the Sixth Quartet marks a return to a more clearly defined key, the first and last movements being in what is a much expanded D major-minor. Hand in hand with the composer's free handling of chromaticism and tonality goes an increase in the dissonant character of his harmonic texture. To the classical principle of chord-building by superimposed thirds, is now added that of superimposed seconds, tritones (augmented fourths), and perfect fourths, the latter (in descending form) being a characteristic feature of the melodic style of Magyar folk music. And to heighten their pungency, Bartók will often present the discords in an exposed, naked form. It is significant of his harmonic development that while in the Second Quartet he would still mollify the harshness of certain harmonies by a special layout and scoring (see, for example, the bitonal passage on p. 17, Tempo I), in the Third Quartet he would intensify it by percussive triple and quadruple stops, played 'at the heel' and *martellato* (pp. 6–7).

Lastly, a word or two on Bartók's special sound effects. Up to the Third Quartet he confined them to the traditional *arco-pizzicato*, *con sordino*, and an occasional *sul ponticello*. In the subsequent works other devices are introduced, some for the purpose of increasing harmonic and rhythmic percussiveness. We already mentioned *martellato*, 'at the heel', and difficult triple and quadruple stops (sometimes with the use of open strings). To these must now be added *col legno*; extended and simultaneous *glissandi* on all four instruments, sometimes in double-stops; 'brush' *pizzicato* in which plucked chords are linked by *glissandi*; up-and-down arpeggio of a guitar-like effect; a new kind of percussive *pizzicato* in which the string is plucked with such force that it rebounds off the fingerboard producing a snapping sound; and lastly, quarter-tones in the *Burletta* of No. 6, employed with the (apparently) satirical intention of suggesting 'out of tune' playing.* But we must add that Bartók shows himself fully aware of the fact that the effect of such special contrivances is in inverse ratio to the frequency of their use, and, on the whole, he resorts to them with circumspection and a fine ear for their fitness in the context.

In the following pages no elaborate analysis is attempted (which would be impossible in the space at my disposal) but merely a more detailed description of salient points of the form and other aspects of each quartet. If my personal experience be any guide to the student who is making his first acquaintance with these quartets, he should pause to reflect that even the most detailed analysis will fulfil its purpose only if that which is first grasped by the intellect, eventually becomes an imaginative experience. To reach this point, close study must go hand in hand with a realization of the actual sound: and the inner ear ought to be assisted by frequent hearings of this great yet certainly difficult and in some respects esoteric music, in live and recorded performance. Only then will it gradually yield its full meaning, scope, and wonderful inner coherence.

FIRST QUARTET, OP. 7

Lento – Allegretto – Allegro vivace

THE First Quartet bears eloquent witness to a young mind at once powerful and ardent in expression and resourceful in form and technique. Yet in the light of the composer's

---

* Characteristic passages in which these devices occur will be cited in the more detailed discussion of the quartets.

later development it is only natural that we should find it
uncharacteristic and immature in several respects. The texture is thick, often overcrowded with thematic tissues, there
is insufficient 'air' in it; and in the second and third movements one cannot help the impression that Bartók's youthful
impulses ran away with his formal discipline. (In later
years he criticized this quartet for its lack of economy.) It is
a romantic work – intensely so. Curiously enough, while in
the immediately preceding Fourteen Bagatelles, Op. 6, and
the Ten Easy Piano Pieces the composer had cast off the
spell of the German romantics, in the First Quartet the
influence of Wagner and Brahms is still potent. Both melody
and harmony are saturated in Wagnerian chromaticism
(which must be distinguished from Bartók's later 'diatonicized' chromaticism), as may be seen from the opening
theme of the *Lento*. It bears an almost twelve-note appearance and its un-Bartókian, expansive tortuous line recalls
Brahms:

Ex. 1 is stated in the form of a double canon, and it may well
be that the opening *Adagio* fugue of Beethoven's Quartet
in C Sharp Minor, Op. 131, was at the back of Bartók's
mind when he conceived this beginning. Here and there
also Debussy's influence makes itself felt, viz. the whole-tone
passages in the *Allegretto*, p. 11, after ⑨, and at the end of
the Finale; and the *Lento* contains a passage (p. 6, at ⑨)
which bears a strong textural resemblance to a passage
occurring in the first movement of Debussy's Quartet (p. 2,
bar 17 *et seq*.), in both an expressive cello theme being set
against fast-moving chords in parallel progression.

In point of style No. 1 cannot be said to be fully integrated. There is, indeed, a marked cleavage to be noted

between the first two movements on the one hand, and the last on the other. The Finale is undoubtedly the most Bartókian of the three, for here we hear the first unmistakable echoes from his growing absorption in Magyar folk music. (His researches in this field began in 1905, three years before the composition of the First Quartet.) Already the Introduction shows characteristic features: a division into *tempo giusto* (upper strings) and *rubato-parlando* (cello recitative), a stamping percussive rhythm, and in the melody an emphasis on the Magyar fourth. The *Allegro* proper opens with those obstinate note-repetitions in grating seconds which Bartók later often uses as a kind of ritornel to set off the various sections of his dance-like movements. Similarly, the chief thematic material of the movement proclaims a native flavour: the first theme, in its marked rhythm and syncopations (Ex. 2*a*); the lyrical second, in its pentatonic steps (Ex. 2*b*),* and the fugue subject (derived from Ex. 2*a*), in the ornamental triplet 'kink'(2*c*):

Although we are still far from the 'barbaric' quality of Bartók's later style, the rhythmic drive of this movement is considerable and here and there we already find those

---

* It has a family likeness to the beautiful cantabile theme in the first movement of No. 6, composed thirty-one years later (see Ex. 20).

percussive triple and quadruple stops which will increasingly occur, as we progress in the quartet series (pp. 32, 33, and at the very end).

The form of the First Quartet is uncommon. Instead of the traditional *Allegro* in sonata form, the opening movement is a rhapsodic *Lento* in a simple A–B–A. With the two succeeding movements, which are both sonata movements, the tempo quickens progressively from *Allegretto* to *Allegro vivace* and thus the whole quartet is given a firm sense of direction toward an agogic (tempo) climax. Overall unity is achieved by the ubiquitous presence of a semitonal *appoggiatura* motive while the main subject of the Finale (Ex. 2*a*) stems from an accompanying *ostinato* in the preceding *Scherzo*:

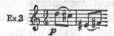

The first and second movements are also linked by a short transitional figure in thirds, which leads, without a break, from the end of the *Lento* (viola and cello) into the somewhat Brahmsian *Scherzo* introduction. The recapitulation of both these movements already shows the young Bartók's concern with a greatly varied repeat, notably in the remarkable compression and modification of the *Scherzo* reprise. The key of the First Quartet is A minor, though its opening suggests something like F minor.

SECOND QUARTET, OP. 17

Moderato – Allegro molto capriccioso – Lento

DURING the period of nine years, which lie between the completion of the First and the Second Quartets, Bartók reached his first maturity. He became increasingly engrossed in the collection and study of folk music, the direct fruit of which were various settings of Magyar and Rumanian songs and dances; he had composed such large-scale works as the opera *Duke Bluebeard's Castle* and the ballet *The Wooden Prince*, and written the famous *Allegro Barbaro* which marked, so far as his piano music was concerned, his first wholly individual and characteristic work. The Second Quartet occupies the same position in his chamber music. It may be said to contain the essential features of his subsequent quartet style – partly fully developed, partly in embryonic form. If it looks backwards at all, it is in the romantic feeling of the first and last movements, but Bartók's romanticism has now shed the strong emotional colour of the First Quartet. It is restrained, subdued, more inward, though moments of impassioned outbursts are not absent.

In point of style the Second Quartet is a fully integrated work. True, in the first movement we still hear a Debussyian echo in the organum-like progressions of perfect fifth (p. 8 at ⑨), and occasionally Bartók's harmonic experiments are too obviously contrived, as witness, in the Finale, the too-frequent use of 'false relations' and fourth-chords. But these, if anything, are very minor blemishes in a work otherwise so homogeneous, rounded, and poetic in utterance. Moreover, the assimilation of features of Magyar folk music is here complete. And although Bartók's harmonic idiom has considerably gained in pungency since the First Quartet – the opening of the Finale, for example, constitutes a little study in clashing major and minor seconds – on the whole the composer appears anxious to tone down such harshnesses by a careful choice of layout, dynamics, and scoring. Thus, in the bitonal passage of the first movement (p. 17, Tempo I) the clash between C in the treble and C sharp in the bass is hardly perceptible, owing to the *pp pizzicato* of the cello; and in the Finale the *con sordino* serves to mollify the grating effect of the opening seconds, apart from lending the whole movement a veiled, mysterious colour. Altogether, the relative euphony and marked melodiousness of No. 2 makes it, perhaps, the most immediately attractive of the series.

Again, the form shows a departure from the norm: three

movements, of which the last is a *Lento*, the order of the
First Quartet being here almost reversed. And again
thematic cross-references are established, the first and last
movement being linked by the figure *x*, which opens the
first subject of the *Moderato* and in rhythmic augmentation
pervades the *Lento*:

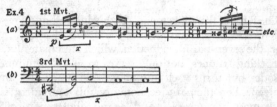

The *Moderato* is a movement of great lyrical beauty proclaiming its marked *cantabile* character in such themes as
the expansive second subject Beginning with an expressive
viola theme (p. 5, ④) it proliferates into passionate, truly
Bartókian phrases which are marked by Magyar triplets.
(This ornamental figure is anticipated in the first subject.)
And the nostalgic coda (p. 17, Tempo I), which establishes
a clear A major-minor, is sheer poetry.

The ensuing movement fully bears out its title *Allegro
molto capriccioso*. It may best be described as a series of
capricious Magyar-inspired dances, written in a vein of
which the *Allegro Barbaro* is so characteristic an example.
In all such movements an almost savage rhythmic drive
sweeps everything before it. The music derives a further
impetus from the conflict between a major and minor third,
D–F sharp–F natural, a conflict which ends with the
assertion of the minor interval. The seed of this struggle lies
in one of Bartók's *Ur*-motives or basic motives (figure *x*)
which generates the movement's main theme, a rocking
dance-like phrase, with augmented seconds and Magyar
ornamentation in its tail:

Technically speaking, the whole movement may be said to be 'about' the critical interval which for our Western ears decides the fundamental difference between major and minor. It is worth noting that in one of the pieces of his later *Microcosmos* (Vol. IV, No. 108) Bartók dealt with the same problem, giving this study the significant title *Wrestling*.

The form of this movement is highly interesting: a *rondo* in which most of the episodes are variations of Ex. 5; moreover, the seven-bar introduction, which anticipates Ex. 5 in its rocking tritones, not only serves to set off a number of episodes but turns itself into an episode (p. 24, |11|, and p. 30, |22|). The thematic economy of this movement is indeed most remarkable, and as an illustration of the immense plasticity of Bartók's variation technique the passage on p. 25, |11|, may be cited in which the introduction is so transformed as to be almost unrecognizable.

The muted coda is a brilliant piece of string writing, tearing along in *Prestissimo* and producing a strange effect in its heterophonic character.*

If the *Allegro* is a dynamic, extrovert piece, the following *Lento* is static and highly introspective in the bleakness of its opening, which almost conjures up the desolation of a lunar landscape. In mood it seems to be prophetic of the melancholy Finale of the Sixth Quartet of twenty-two years later. Except for brief impassioned moments, the music is subdued to the point of almost motionless tranquillity. Impressionist and Magyar elements commingle in a highly original manner. Note, for example, the alternative 'high' and 'low' in the scoring of the opening, and the etiolated colour produced by the muted strings. At first there is no theme but merely wisps of a melody, and not until p. 48, |4|, does the music really crystallize into a sustained coherent phrase, a broad folksong-like theme moving in (chiefly) pentatonic steps and harmonized in fourth-chords. Mention has already

---

* Heterophony denotes a primitive kind of counterpoint characteristic of Eastern music, in which all instruments play simultaneously slight variations of the same melody.

been made of the fact that this movement seems to reproduce the chain-like sequence of unrelated sections peculiar to a kind of Magyar music: there are four parts with their own material: *Lento – Un poco più andante – Lento assai – Tempo I*. These sections are held together by the cadential figure Ex. 4*b*, while the coda (p. 50, *Lento assai*) briefly reviews the whole movement at the same time reorganizing the thematic material.

THIRD QUARTET

Prima parte – Seconda parte – Ricapitulazione della prima parte – Coda

DURING the ten years which separate the Second from the Third Quartet, Bartók's development moved toward a *ne plus ultra* of concentration and subtilization. It is Bartók's expressionist period represented by such works as the two Violin Sonatas, the Piano Sonata, and the First Piano Concerto – works that show him at the height of his intellectual modernism. This is the 'difficult' Bartók of whom all his commentators speak – elliptic, elusive, enigmatic, uncompromising, and harsh to the point of aggressiveness. Like the expressionist Schönberg, the Bartók of the years between 1922–7 appears almost exclusively concerned with the projection of an inner world in which the frontier dividing the conscious and rational from the unconscious and irrational is practically non-existent. The music of this period takes on a significance at once private, symbolic, and arcane. Not unlike the Beethoven of the late quartets and piano sonatas, Bartók here seems to be communing with himself rather than attempting communication with the outside world. It is for this reason that the Third Quartet is the least accessible of the six, making extraordinary demands on our perceptive and imaginative powers. Yet it is no less a masterpiece than the others and differs from them only in that its aesthetic and intellectual premises are more difficult to apprehend.

With a composer of Bartók's type concentration of form goes hand in hand with an intensification of expression. The Third Quartet is, thus, the most concentrated and intense of the series. It is in one movement yet divided into four sections which follow each other in the simple pattern Slow–Fast–Slow–Fast. Thematically they are related in a manner which may be illustrated by two interlocking spans:

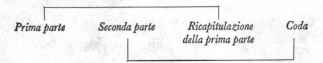

| Prima parte | Seconda parte | Ricapitulazione della prima parte | Coda |

In the following analysis the sections will be taken according to their thematic correspondences and not their actual order of sequence. The First Part constitutes a supreme example of Bartók's technique of developing virtually the whole of a movement from a single germ-cell. Here the *Ur*-motive is a simple pentatonic figure consisting of a rising fourth and a falling minor third. We first hear it at the beginning of the opening theme (after five curtain-like introductory bars):

(This theme, incidentally, is stated in the form of a free canon.) The immense power of regeneration which lies in figure *x* can be seen from these examples:

The First Part is in three sections, the middle one of which recalls, in its fragmentary texture and subdued dynamics, Bartók's 'night music' style. Although it introduces new material, not derived from the basic motive, the bitonal bass reiterates figure *x* in *ostinato* fashion. The development (starting pp. 5, 6) is punctuated by savagely percussive double and triple stops for all four strings which by their simple homophony achieve a dramatic contrast with the surrounding contrapuntal texture. In the repeat of the first section (p. 7, 11) Bartók introduces the 'real' theme of the movement, a broad swaying tune of Magyar flavour which grows out of the first three Notes of Ex. 8.

The suggestion may be ventured that the theme, or at any rate its first three bars, was perhaps Bartók's initial idea, and that instead of stating it at the very beginning (as most composers might have done) he seized upon its most characteristic motive and evolved from it the best part of the movement before showing us in Ex. 8 the purest and at once most beautiful manifestation of the *Ur*-motive's generative power.*

The recapitulation of the First Part compresses the material to such an extent that sometimes a few bars have to do duty for perhaps a dozen bars of the 'exposition'. This last section has seventy bars, as against 122 of the first section. Moreover, by means of most subtle transformations, Bartók achieves the effect of a psychological rather than physical return to the First Part. He has perhaps never written music more fascinating in its elliptic and recondite allusions than this *Ricapitulazione*.

---

* There is a certain parallel here with Sibelius's method of gradually assembling a symphonic theme from previous particles.

The Second Part yields to our understanding more readily. With its relentless forward-driving rhythm, its percussive chords, syncopations, and *glissandi*, it clearly springs
from the soil of native dances. The form is that of Varia-
tion-cum-Sonata-form. Here is the variation theme, a folk-
dance-like tune harmonized in 'primitive' parallel triads:

No sooner has it been stated than it throws off a brief semiquaver motive, Ex. 9*b*, which is already a kind of variation
retracing the theme's characteristic double-backing outline in rhythmic diminution. It is actually this motive which
provides the basis for the ensuing variations, to which Ex.
9*a*, also varied, furnishes the bass. While the melodic pattern undergoes relatively minor changes, there are frequent
alterations of the rhythmic units (2/4, 3/4, 6/8, 5/8, and 3/8).
On p. 13, a bar before 10 cello and viola introduce the
'second subject' in the form of another variation, characterized by syncopations, whole-tone progressions, and descending fourths:

The treatment of this theme is largely in imitation and
stretto. The development (beginning p. 17, Tempo I) deals
with both 'subjects', contains such special sound effects as
col legno and *sulla tastiera*, and finally culminates in a light-
fingered fugue whose subject derives from Ex. 4*b* (p. 20, 31).
Imperceptibly, the fugue leads into the recapitulation,
when the variation theme is at once stated in canon while
the second subject appears both in diatonic and chromatic
versions (p. 24, at 38 and 40). There is a short reference

to the *martellato* passage of the First Part which presently returns in the much altered version of which we have already spoken.

The Coda is nothing else but the transformed reprise of the Second Part. The pace is increased from *Allegro* to *Allegro molto*, the basic metre changed from 2/4 to 3/8, the contrapuntal texture becomes denser, canon and inversions in *stretto* predominate, and towards the end the aggressive character of the music is greatly heightened by obstinate note-reiterations, incessant motive repetitions, double-stop *glissandi* and up-and-down arpeggios. The movement concludes on a chord of three superimposed fifths based on C sharp, which represents the 'key' of the Third Quartet. Bartók's free conception of tonality during his expressionist period may be seen from the fact that, apart from the very opening and a brief passage in the First Part, C sharp is not in evidence again until the last few bars.

FOURTH QUARTET

Allegro – Prestissimo con sordino – Non troppe lento –
Allegretto pizzicato – Allegro molto

In the Third Quartet Bartók advanced furthest in the direction of intellectual severity, uncompromising harshness of emotional expression, and formal experimentation. The Fourth, written a year later, marks a certain retreat from the 'exposed position' taken up in the preceding work though the first movement still has some hard things to say. Not that his style shows an intrinsic change. We still find a (predominantly) linear counterpoint, a predilection for scholastic devices, pungent discords, ferocious rhythmic drive (Finale), and special sound effects. Yet the new gains acquired in the Third Quartet are now seen to be in the process of consolidation on a broader formal basis, and such movements as the wonderful elegy of the third and the delightful serenade of the fourth suggest a mind of more mellow humanity and more accessible to gentler, more relaxed moods.

Nevertheless, the quest for creating overall unity and correspondences between movements by novel means continues. Thus the five movements, of which the Fourth Quartet consists, are conceived in the so-called arch form A–B–C–B–A, in which the two outward and the two inner movements, respectively, mirror each other, while the central piece C stands by itself. In a sense, the music progresses from A to C and then retraces its step.* Correspondences between the four movements are not merely thematic but are also felt in the form and character of the music:

Allegro – Prestissimo – Non troppo lento – Allegretto – Allegro molto

As in the Third Quartet, it will be more expedient for our purpose not to follow the actual order of the movements, but to take the corresponding pairs together. The first and last movements – in sonata and ternary form, respectively – derive their complete material from a single germ-cell of six notes which is concealed in the seventh bar of the *Allegro's* opening subject (Ex. 11*a*):

Ex.11

* Gerald Abraham has made the interesting suggestion that the arch form may have been suggested to Bartók by Alfred Lorenz's book, *Geheimnis der Form bei Richard Wagner*, which appeared in 1924. (See 'The Bartók of the Quartets', *Music and Letters*, October 1945). Yet it is also possible that Bartók derived it from Alban Berg who employed the arch form on a smaller scale in the second movement of his *Chamber Concerto* (1925) and in the third movement of the *Lyric Suite* (1926). Bartók may well have heard both these works before the composition of the Fourth Quartet (1928).

What an unpromising idea it looks! It is the measure of Bartók's organic thinking that from it he evolves a well-nigh inexhaustible fund of seemingly new motives of which I quote some important ones from both movements (see above). Yet it would, I believe, be extremely hard to detect the relation between Ex. 11*a* and *f*, without hearing the intervening stages of this metamorphosis. As one of Bartók's recent biographers aptly remarked, it is because the composer allows us to share his thought-processes rather than leaping from the basic motive to its furthest transformation, that his music carries such logic with it.*

The first movement is an abstract piece of music wholly concerned with problems of form, design, and texture. It provides a most rewarding study of Bartók's monocystic motive-development. Not a single phrase is to be found which has not grown, in one way or another, from the simple six-note motive. And as though the composer wanted to press home its fundamental importance, he closes the movement with Ex. 11*a*, *pesante* and doubled in three octaves. Although this *Allegro* represents one long and continuous development, the traditional four 'sonata form' sections can be clearly discerned: exposition, up to bar 49, development proper to bar 92, recapitulation to bar 126 (but slightly reversed, with the basic motive now preceding the opening theme Ex. 11*a*), and coda.

The corresponding fifth movement evokes the atmosphere of a ferocious Magyar dance. The introduction with its stamping triple and quadruple stops, widely spaced and using open strings, completely breaks the framework of the string quartet medium and produces a most resonant orchestral sonority. Again, the main theme (Ex. 11*d*) is set against a throbbing percussive accompaniment punctuated by *sf* chords which create an exciting cross-rhythm (3/8 and 2/8 versus the basic 2/4 (or 4/8)). By contrast, the middle section (beginning p. 52, bar 152) is deliciously airy and graceful, with crisp mordents and guitar-like arpeggios on all

* *The Life and Music of Béla Bartók*, by Halsey Stevens. New York, 1953.

four open strings (second violin and cello). As in the first movement, the recapitulation (beginning p. 57, bar 238) opens with a slight reversion of the material, the main theme now preceding the introduction. In order to fashion the link between first and last movements still firmer, Bartók reintroduces, in the coda of the Finale, the few final bars of the *Allegro*, and again closes with the *pesante* version of the germ cell. Both movements are 'on' C, though tonality here is more clearly defined in the Third Quartet.

The correspondence between the second and fourth movements is on several levels. Both are light-weight *scherzi*, both are played throughout in a special manner, *con sordino* the *Prestissimo*, *pizzicato* the *Allegretto*, and both share the same thematic material:

Ex. 12*c* represents the diatonic extension of the involuted chromatic Ex. 12*a*, while the identical changing-note motives Ex. 12*b* and *d* are inversions of a figure in the tail of Ex. 12*a*. Yet this is not all. One is tempted to assume that Ex. 12*a* is itself a variant of the chromatic *Ur*-motive Ex. 11*a*, so that in the last analysis not only the two outward movements but also the two inner ones appear to have sprung from the same germinal idea.

Though the *Prestissimo* and the *Allegretto* are, as has been said, *scherzo* movements, there is a marked contrast of mood between them. The one may be described as a *perpetuo mobile* to which the muted strings lend a strange shimmer, not unlike that of the *Allegro misterioso* of Berg's *Lyric Suite*; while the delicate guitar-like accompaniment of the other conjures up the intimate atmosphere of a serenade. It is here that Bartók first uses the 'snap' *pizzicato*.

In this dynamic quartet the only point of repose is provided by the expressive lyricism of the slow central movement. Its form is a simple A–B–A plus coda. Section A is introduced by a sustained chord, *pp*, first *non vibrato*, then *vibrato*. This forms a most delicate harmonic background for a wistful cello recitative of Magyar character: melismatic embellishments, syncopations, and drooping fourths and fifths. There are three 'verses' of it, each beginning a third higher than the previous one (D–F–A).* This kind of grave melody is said to be pecular to the music of the *tárogató*, a woodwind instrument of ancient (Eastern) origin, whose dark colour is somewhat akin to that of our clarinet.†

The middle section (beginning p. 33, bar 34) is an exquisite atmospheric study evoking the mysterious sounds of nocturnal nature. The extent to which Bartók developed a personal impressionist style, may be seen from an instructive comparison of this and other examples of his 'night music', with Debussy's *Les sons et les parfums tournant dans l'air du soir*, the fourth piece in Book I of the Piano Preludes.

FIFTH QUARTET

*Allegro – Adagio molto – Scherzo – Andante – Finale:
Allegro vivace*

THE Fifth Quartet followed the Fourth after an interval of six years, yet in general style and form it stands far closer to its immediate predecessor than the latter stands to the

---

* The opening theme of the *Allegretto* is stated in a similar manner: four entries in successively rising fifths (A flat–E flat–B flat–F).

† Originally it possessed a double reed, but Bartók must have heard its more modern, single-reed version.

Third Quartet, from which, we recall, it is separated by one year only. Intrinsically, the Fourth and Fifth Quartets are sister works, they form a pair, the chief difference between them lying in the fact that the later work carries the process of intellectual relaxation and lyrical expansion another stage further. Significantly enough, we now have two slow movements (while No. 4 had only one), the melodic lines have become ampler and the harmonies on the whole less astringent.

But the formal organization is the same as in No. 4: again the arch form A–B–C–B–A, yet C is now a *Scherzo* flanked by two slow movements, in which Bartók reaches a new height of evocative lyrical poetry.

Let us again consider the related movements in conjunction. The opening *Allegro* and the Finale are both in sonata form, both are 'on' B flat, and both share some of the material. Their thematic correspondence may be seen from a comparison of their first subjects. That of the *Allegro* consists of three distinct ideas, while that of the Finale is essentially a simple scale figure within the range of a tritone:

The connection between the two subjects is a remarkably subtle one: the repeated B flat of *a* corresponds to the repeated E of *d* (with Bartók tritone relations often assume the function of the classical tonic-dominant); similarly, the ascent in *b*, from B flat to E, is mirrored in *d* in the descent

from E to B flat, and the chromatic 'kink' *x* of *b* appears
inverted in *d*. In other words, the main subject of the
Finale represents a free inversion of part of the first movement's opening theme.

As for the second subjects of the two movements, they
too derive from the *Allegro*'s main theme:

Ex.14

a is mainly a diatonic step-wise version of Ex. 13*c*, while *b*
suggests a variant of the chromatic 'kink' *x*.

In the first movement such subtle relations extend also
to seemingly unconnected ideas as at A and B, which
contain tissues stemming from the opening theme, in
particular figure *x*. Essentially, it is the same monocystic
development as we noted in the first movement of No. 4;
but as a sign of Bartók's advance toward a more clear-cut
melodic articulation, we find here the thematic material so
moulded as to produce more differentiated, readily recognizable shapes. Thus we can speak again of themes in the
more established sense of the term, themes whose contrasting
character clearly sets them off from each other: there is the
percussive first subject (stated in canon); there is the dance-
like transitional theme at B, with its wide leaping intervals, and changing cross-rhythms which produce a rhythmic 'canon' between treble and bass; and there is the gently
undulating lyrical line of the second subject, at C. Moreover, a clear sense of tonality is felt in the individual themes
as well as in movement as a whole, and the beginnings of
the three sonata sections show a simple quasi-classical
patter: tonic: B flat – 'dominant': E (tritone again!) – tonic:
B flat. The recapitulation (beginning at F) represents a
clearly recognizable return of the exposition yet with a
characteristic modification. The order in which the themes

appear in the exposition is now largely reversed and, in addition, all are reintroduced in their inverted versions. In other words the recapitulation represents the 'mirror' of the exposition.

The Finale is, broadly speaking, similarly organized. In character it belongs to Bartók's 'motoric' or *perpetuo mobile* movements. Of a predominantly polyphonic texture it abounds in inversions, canons, *stretti*, and passages in reversible counterpoint. The development centres on a fugue (beginning p. 75, bar 369) whose subject derives from the first movement's opening theme:

Ex.15

It is a most uncommon fugue. The subject has the marking *oscuro* and is at once stated against a purely harmonic (colouristic) background: percussive note-reiteration on the two violins, *col legno*, and a drone-like ostinato on the cello. The whole fugue constitutes an illuminating example of the meeting of East and West in Bartók's music.

Uncommon in a different sense is a brief episode, marked *Allegretto con indifferenza*, in the coda, p. 88: a trivial tune in a clear A major and harmonized in *cliché* fashion with alternating tonic and dominant, to be played *meccanico*. The whole passage produces the effect of barrel-organ music. One is here strongly reminded of Mahler's deliberate use, in his symphonies, of trite tunes, in order to suggest commonplace aspects of life. Bartók's strange episode is like a sudden grimace, an ironic sneer – an impression heightened by the strident dissonances produced by the bitonal passage (A major against B flat major, bars 711–720).*

Like the first and last movements, the *Adagio* and the *Andante* share the same ground plan, A–B–A plus coda, and some of the material. Both open in an atmospheric manner, the fragmentary motives and trills of the one corresponding to the repeated *pizzicato* notes, slurs and *gruppetti* of the other. Then the music gains substance leading to a middle section based on a Magyar-inspired theme of serene lyrical expression (Ex. 16*a*), which the *Andante* presents in a beautifully expanded version (Ex. 16*b*). Note the perfect balance between the two halves of this theme, the second half representing a free and embellished inversion of the first:

Ex.16

Both movements contain a chorale, the *Adagio* at [A] and the *Andante* at [D] – a feature almost invariably associated with Bartók's 'night music' (see, for example, the respective slow movements of the Second and Third Piano Concertos).

The *Andante*, which is the more extended piece, develops Ex. 16*b* in an impassioned ecstatic section (p. 53, *Più mosso, agitato*) to which the 'cry' of a leaping minor third adds a poignant accent.† This remarkable movement ends mysteriously on a cello passage of plucked triple-stops linked by *glissandi*.

The central movement is a most engaging *Scherzo* in *alla Bulgarese* rhythm, for which Bartók evinced a predilection

* The Finale of the Viola Concerto contains a passage of similar triviality, also in A major and extended over more than fifty bars.

† The same motive occurs in the slow movement of the Viola Concerto where it is marked *piangendo*.

in his later period (see the last six pieces of his *Microcosmos* and the Trio of the third movement of his *Contrasts*). The asymmetrical pattern of the *Scherzo* proper is $\frac{4+2+3}{8}$. There are three sections of which the first is marked by fleeting figures (mostly in up-and-down arpeggio). In the second section they form the delicate background for a sprightly theme of folk dance character (Ex. 17*a*, below).

The Trio is cast in a more complex 'Bulgarian' rhythm, the initial pattern $\frac{3+2+2+3}{8}$ alternating with $\frac{2+3+2+3}{8}$ and $\frac{2+3+3+2}{8}$. The string writing here represent a real *trouvaille*. The first violin, *pp* and muted, traces out a delicate arabesque consisting of a ten-note ostinato which is repeated (in several transpositions) no less than sixty times. This lends the movement a sense of feverish excitement which reaches its highest pitch on p. 38, *accelerando*, when the second violin adds the 'mirror' version of the *ostinato*, and the viola, a few bars later, doubles the treble and ninth an octave lower, *ff*. Before and after this climax the string texture is of a shimmering diaphanous quality and into it Bartók weaves an enchanting melody which seems in the vein of a (Magyar?) children's song (Ex. 17*b*):

Ex.17

SIXTH QUARTET

Vivace – Marcia – Burletta – Mesto

WITH the Sixth Quartet, written five years after the Fifth, we reach the 'classical' Bartók, the Bartók of such works as

the Music for Strings, Piano and Percussion, the Violin
Concerto, and the Divertimento for Strings. The chief
characteristics of this period are: a relatively greater simplicity of form and technical devices, themes of a more
sustained, broader nature, harmonies of lesser harshness, a
sharper tonal perspective, and greater transparency of texture. So far as the quartets are concerned, these changes,
which first began to show in No. 4, reached their culmination point in No. 6. It is significant that in No. 6 Bartók
reverts to the classical scheme of four contrasting movements and uses a simpler, less intellectual device than the
arch form, in order to achieve an overall formal unity – the
motto-theme. This theme is a sad, mournful viola melody
with a marked drooping tendency, most beautifully shaped
and balanced and, like the variation theme of the Violin
Concerto, an exquisite example of the perfect fusion of the
melodic and rhythmic inflexions of Magyar music with
Bartók's personal manner:

As already intimated, the motto as such was a favourite
device of the romantics but Bartók applies it in a novel
manner. Ex. 18 prefaces each of the first three movements
but, on each occasion, in a slightly different and texturally
richer manner, until in the Finale it becomes the actual
material of that movement. Instead of serving as a device
for the mere 'rubber-stamping' of the various movements
(as we often find it used in Tchaikovsky and Liszt), Bartók
achieves an organic integration of the motto-theme. For in
a sense the Finale *is* the motto. Besides, the codetta of the
first movement (p. 4, *Vivacissimo, agitato*) appears to derive
from the opening motive of Ex. 18, while the theme of the
Marcia stems from a figure contained in the fifth bar of the
motto.

The opening of the first movement proper echoes the beginning of Beethoven's *Grosse Fuge*, Op. 133, in that the first subject is stated by the four strings, in a ten-bar long *pesante* introduction, in rhythmic augmentation, before appearing in its 'true' form:

The remarkable transformations which this theme undergoes in the course of the movement is yet another illustration of Bartók's art of continuous progressive development. And for a most instructive example of his variation technique, I refer the student to the passage (p. 4, bars 81–99) where Bartók follows up the statement of the lovely Magyar-inspired second subject with two successive variations (second violin – viola) (Ex. 20). Two other features worth

noting are the almost classical manner with which the three main sections of this sonata movement are set off from each other, and the clear sense of tonality which is a Bartókian D major-minor. If the general mood of the music is exuberant, even gay, this suffers a complete reversal in the following three movements.

The ensuing *Marcia* is harsh, aggressive music through which a fanfare (p. 21, beginning at bar 59) cuts like a sharp knife. (The march theme shows a family likeness to the *Verbunkos* of Contrasts, written a year before the Sixth Quartet.)

The Trio is in *rubato* style, with agitated *tremoli* on the violins and strummed, guitar-like chords on the viola. Against this nervously excited accompaniment is set a high-lying passionate cello recitative, marked by a restless alternation of major and minor thirds and *glissandi*. A

polytonal (four-key) *cadenza* for all four instruments leads
to the recapitulation of the March which is now greatly
changed, some of its material being inverted.

Somewhat related to the mood of the *Marcia* is the grim,
sardonic humour of the *Burletta*. Its harmonic, rhythmic,
and dynamic ferocity recalls the Bartók of the expressionist
period. Grating discords, fiercely percussive chords 'at the
heel', much down-bow playing, *glissandi*, and slurs lend
this movement its 'barbaric' quality. Moreover, the quarter-
notes of the first violin played against the 'true 'notes of the
second violin (bars 26 *et seq.*) create a deliberate 'out of tune'
effect.

Relief is introduced by the wistful lyrical middle section,
an *Andantino*, whose two ideas are freely derived from the
first movement's two subjects: both are free inversions of
Ex. 19 and 20, respectively, and are themselves linked by
almost identical cadential figures (*x*) in the tail end:

Ex. 21

The repeat of the first section shows interesting modifications: the opening in *pizzicato* (some of it of Bartók's 'snap'
variety), the addition of a new triplet motive with a skipping fourth in its tail, and a singularly dramatic effect
in the coda (p. 40, bar 135 *et seq.*) where Ex. 21*b* makes
three vain attempts to break the mood of this savage
burlesque.

So far, the motto has played an all but preludial part in
the work. In the Finale it becomes the generating theme of
the whole movement revealing its full emotional significance in the poignant sadness of this *Mesto*. And when on
p. 44, bar 46 *et seq.*, the two subjects from the gay first
movement are recalled *p*, *molto tranquillo*, the second of

which is to be played *più dolce*, *lontano*, one's thoughts inevitably turn to Dante's *Nessun maggior dolore che ricordarsi del tempo felice nella miseria* ('There is no greater sorrow than to recall a time of happiness in misery'). There is a sinister shudder in the *tremolo* chords, *sul ponticello*, on the last page, and after a last heartrending cry, the movement closes in darkness, on the dying motto.

Considering the extraordinary nature of what was to be Bartók's swan-song as a quartet writer, one cannot resist the feeling that the work possesses a poetic, extra-musical significance – perhaps even a 'programme'. There is the peculiar use of the motto – an *idée fixe*, three times rejected until at last it is accepted,* there is the melancholy character of the motto itself, there is the brief dramatic interlude in the *Burletta*, there are those wistful reminiscences from 'a time of happiness' in the Finale, and there is the bitter irony of the two middle movements and the sombre introspection of the *Mesto*. A sense of profound personal tragedy seems to emanate from it all. Perhaps a clue to it is to be sought in the fact that Bartók completed the quartet when the conflagration in Europe had already broken out. He was then in Budapest and may well have experienced a feeling of despair and spiritual isolation, if not frustration. We do not know. Yet the work suggests with an almost aching poignancy some such state of mind which the composer may well have consciously depicted in the music. At any rate, No. 6 is the only one among his mature quartets in which we have the clear impression that strong subjective emotions press to the surface with uncommon insistence.

* This has already been pointed out by Professor Abraham (op. cit.).

PART TWO

—

12

Duet Sonatas without Wind Instruments (from 1700)

DENIS STEVENS

INTRODUCTION

THE duet sonata as we know it to-day has a history of only three and a half centuries, although the basic idea of the duo from which it sprang can hardly be far removed from the very fountain-head of human culture and behaviour. Although I make no claim to be a musico-ethnologist, I am constantly being reminded of the primeval power of the duo by an eighteenth-century engraving which looks down from my study wall. It is called 'Harmony before Matrimony', and it depicts a delightful salon scene, with a much-engaged young couple singing together from a book clearly entitled *Duets de l'Amour*. The lady, besides singing her part, is also playing an accompaniment on the harp, apparently quite oblivious of the two small, squabbling cats in the background. It echoes, as well as caricatures, those well-known lines from Herrick's *Hesperides*:

> Rare is the voice it self, but when we sing
> To th'lute or violl, then 'tis ravishing.

The so-called *bicinia*, or duets for two voices, which were so popular during the late Renaissance, were probably performed quite often in the manner praised by Herrick: the singer would dispense with the necessity for a second voice by playing its music on a bowed or plucked string instrument. From this method of performance it was but a short step to the omission of the words altogether, and the duet for two instrumentalists was the logical result.

The first flowering of the duet sonata occurred at about the same time as the first flush of interest in the violin, that queen of stringed instruments whose Italian home was equally and naturally the home of the very earliest duet sonatas. Fortunately many early printed editions of these sonatas have been preserved for us, so that we can savour the freshness and originality of works by Giovanni Battista Fontana and Biagio Marini, both of whom lived when the fame of the Amati family of violin makers was at its height. An English composer who visited Italy in search of new ideas and fresh inspiration was so overcome by what he heard that he changed his name from plain John Cooper to its colourful and Italianate form, Giovanni Cooperario: he, too, has left a number of violin sonatas, and they not only possess a unique charm of their own – they have, in addition, influenced a great many English composers of the seventeenth century.

It will be seen that the violin was in certain ways responsible for the formative early years, if not the actual birth, of the duet sonata; and that position of pre-eminence has remained until to-day, when the great majority of duet sonatas heard in concert-halls, on records, and over the air, involve the violin and the piano. The violoncello has a smaller though highly interesting repertoire of its own, while the viola, making a late start as a solo instrument, has nevertheless brought into being a number of beautiful and often remarkable works. Thus, in spite of the early vogue for the trio-sonata, and the emergence of first the harpsichord, later the pianoforte, as a self-sufficient medium for the satisfying tonal design which we know as sonata form (in its broadest sense), the duet sonata has really had the longest and most continuous history; and present-day developments indicate that this history is by no means a closed book.

Before the time of Bach and Handel, the duet sonata was often played by either less or more people than its title implies. It was, in fact, a sonata for solo violin and *continuo*, and the music was printed in separate books – one containing the violin part, and the other the bass. This bass part-book, which usually assisted the harpsichordist by indicating chords numerically as well as giving the actual left-hand part, was often played by a viola da gamba or cello in addition to the harpsichord. The cellist, as we know from many baroque paintings, sat slightly to the left or right of the harpsichordist, and shared the same music. It is easy to see why this idea of reinforcing the bass part came about, for very few harpsichords built during the seventeenth century possessed a 16-ft register, and their lower range lacked depth although it probably had plenty of power. The cellist supplied just that extra touch of stability to the ensemble.

A duet therefore became what was virtually a trio; but the opposite began to happen when – during the last few decades of the century – publishers began to print the violin part above the bass part, just as it is in the piano scores printed to-day. The difference between our scores and their *partiture*, as they were called, was that the baroque editions had only to print the figured bass part with the violin stave above it, whereas nowadays three staves are needed. The two-stave editions of such composers as Uccellini, Pietro degli Antonii, and Francesco Lelli rapidly became popular with keyboard players, who found that they could conveniently dispense with the violinist, if they so wished, by regarding the treble and bass staves of the *partitura* as if it were a solo keyboard sonata! In fact, there is little doubt that the true origin of the keyboard sonata was the baroque duet sonata for violin and keyboard.

BACH

BACH's six sonatas for violin and harpsichord were among the first to contain a carefully written out keyboard part rather than a figured bass. It was quite probable that the composer filled out the keyboard part here and there when he himself played them, and it is not improbable that he tolerated an overlooking cellist if there happened to be one in the household; yet one can fairly say that these sonatas are, for most players' purposes, sufficient in themselves. Their predominant texture is that of the trio-sonata: the violinist plays one part, and the harpsichordist two. Very occasionally the strictness of the part-writing is relaxed in order to allow for a few full chords in the harpsichord part, and sometimes added sonority is achieved not only by keeping up a consistent three-part texture for the keyboard, but also (as in the B Minor Sonata, the first of the set) by giving the violinist extensive passages in double-stops. The Third Sonata (E major) is also something of an exception, for while the fast movements – 2 and 4 – adhere to three-part polyphonic writing in Bach's most agile and supple vein, the slow movements – 1 and 3 – are much more free in their outlook on the number of notes that may appear simultaneously in a right-hand chord. In the opening *Adagio*, the violin weaves arabesques of splendid beauty over a short, curling motive in thirds, with a pedal E in the bass. It is not until the eighth bar is reached that the pedal is replaced by a slowly-moving harmonic rhythm:

The *Allegro* is gay and bustling, full of double counter-point yet equally alive with memorable melodic ideas, one

of which seems almost to have been inspired by the shape of
the violin's opening phrase in the first movement:

In the *Adagio ma non tanto* there is all the poetry and mystery that the key of C sharp minor suggests; the two instruments are in as close and harmonious a communion as ever
Bach achieved. The bass moves quietly, regularly, and
nobly on its way through countless harmonic regions, and
it is here perhaps that one wishes for the cello's help in
sustaining the melodic line. The final *Allegro* gives the
impression at first of perpetual motion, so dexterously and
rapidly do the two instruments exchange their brilliant
figuration. A middle section brings with it contrast to the
semiquavers by introducing new material in triplet quavers,
but the unquenchable *perpetuum mobile* returns and reigns
supreme until the close.

Bach wrote other duet works for violin and keyboard, and
though they are less frequently heard than the sonatas, they
are full of interest for players and listeners. There is a most
attractive Suite, a Sonata in G, a Partita in E Minor, and
an isolated but extremely fine Fugue in G Minor for
Violin and Continuo. There are also three sonatas for
gamba and harpsichord, and they deserve to be heard
more frequently than they are, even if the gamba's place
is taken by the cello, to which most listeners would ascribe
greater expressive powers. That great Bach scholar, Johann
Nicolaus Forkel, found them to be 'all admirably composed, so that even in our day most of them would be heard
with pleasure by connoisseurs'. If this remark seems slightly
patronizing, we must remember that Forkel was writing
over a century and a half ago, when tastes in music were
somewhat less wide and less developed than they are
now.

HANDEL

HANDEL, when aged about twenty, wrote a Sonata for

Gamba and Harpsichord, the latter instrument having a fully written out part in *concertato* style. The gamba was much cultivated in north Germany at that time (about 1705) but less so in England as far as solo performance was concerned. By the middle of the century this work was being copied with instructions for performing it on the violin or *viola da braccio*. Handel's sonatas for violin and continuo are excellent works in their own right, and the six that come from Op. 1 show that he had a first-rate understanding of violin technique. This he learnt in his younger days as a violinist in the opera orchestra at Hamburg, and it is pleasant to think that he may often have sought to improve his resources as a violinist by studying not only the works of the then famous Bolognese school, at whose head Corelli stood, but also the music of his fellow-countrymen – Johann Jakob Walther and Heinrich Biber.

Handel was certainly not unmindful of the possibilities of polyphonic suggestion in violin writing, since both of the A major sonatas exploit it in the course of their second movements. Yet his heart must have been pledged to the arioso, for it is exactly this type of lyrical melodic line that gives the sonatas their winning charm and their rich variety of emotional content. The opening movement of each sonata shows the breadth and extent of the musical paragraphs that Handel loved to write. Most of them are melodies so well-knit and finely constructed that it would be a pity to quote no more than a fragment; yet the opening bars of the last sonata of the set (in E major) gives us the principles of construction in a nutshell:

Ex.3
Violin

The third movement of each sonata is usually a short *arioso*, sometimes forming a complete movement, binary in structure; at other times a mere link – though an expressive one – as, for example, in the First Sonata in A Major. This particular *Adagio* affords some insight into the manner in which Handel expected his slow movements to be ornamented, and there is an almost equally good example in the corresponding movement of the Third Sonata (F major). One of the finest of the slow movements is undoubtedly the *Larghetto* of the D Major Sonata, whose opening phrase announces the pathetic vein of the whole movement:

The final movements often show their indebtedness to dance forms, and they also exhibit virtuosic tendencies in at least two cases (sonatas 4 and 5) although we have no way of knowing whether they were designed to be played by any particularly gifted violinist among Handel's large circle of acquaintances.

MOZART

THE second half of the eighteenth century saw the temporary eclipse of the violin as a solo instrument in duet forms. Composers other than those whose primary interest in the violin was that of a travelling virtuoso thought of it as an instrument which could effectively *accompany* a solo sonata on the harpsichord. Thus Mozart refers to his earlier sonatas for violin and keyboard as 'Clavierduetti with Violin' or – as on the title-page of his six sonatas published in 1781 – 'for Harpsichord or Pianoforte, with Violin accompaniment'. This was certainly true of his sixteen juvenile sonatas, where the violin part is often unimportant to the point of being redundant; yet this very set published in 1781 (in spite of its title-page) caused a reviewer to comment that 'both instruments are kept constantly on the alert, so that these sonatas require just as skilful a player on the violin as on the harpsichord'.

The first sonatas in which Mozart treated both instruments on equal terms were the so-called Mannheim Sonatas; of these, the E Minor (K. 304) is one of the most frequently heard. There are only two movements, yet there is a feeling of unseen strength in the unison phrases and contrapuntal writing of the *Allegro*, and the dance-measure of the *Tempo di Menuetto* is overclouded by passionate grief:

Mozart's greatest achievement in the realm of the duet sonata was in the three works composed between 1784 and 1787; the Sonata in B Flat (K. 454) written for Strinasacchi, the E Flat Major (K. 481), and the A Major (K. 526) which dates from the same time as *Don Giovanni*. The first of these three is in many ways typical of the wonderfully balanced duet-writing which was without equal in the last two decades of the eighteenth century. Mozart was full of enthusiasm for the work, and wrote to his father in April 1784: 'The famous Strinasacchi from Mantua is here, a very good violinist; she plays with much taste and expression. Just now I am composing a new sonata for her, and we have to play it together next Thursday.' Regina

Strinasacchi was then about twenty years old, and was busily touring Europe after a brilliant musical education at the *Ospedale della Pietà* in Venice. Her arrival in Vienna was the occasion for a very special concert at the Imperial Court, and possibly because her fame had preceded her by several weeks at least, Mozart was anxious that his part in the proceedings should not be thrust too far into the background.

Accordingly, whilst giving her a hearty welcome and a hastily-written violin part, he did no more than sketch his own part, so that the Emperor Joseph himself noticed from his box that the composer was (or appeared to be) extemporizing an accompaniment. An imperial inspection, conducted after the concert, revealed that the piano part was, in fact, almost devoid of notes. The present condition of the autograph manuscript confirms this remarkable state of affairs, which nicely set off the virtuoso composer against the virtuoso violinist.

The *Largo* is neither a long introduction nor a short movement: it is, as Einstein says, in the nature of a triumphal arch through which one passes to reach the *Allegro*. But the essence of equality is there from the very beginning. For every keyboard phrase there comes a corresponding contour in the violin part, and when the violin gives free rein to its cantilena the piano replies with proud and decorative brilliance.

The *Allegro* begins with a simple motive in similar motion, the counterbalance coming with the second subject, in which the violin's *arpeggio* ascent is perfectly matched by the falling figure in the piano part. Further on still, the harmonic structure is of the slightest when the violin does for a few bars achieve personal prominence in a gay dotted rhythm:

In the *Andante* the two instruments find a more than adequate musical vehicle for their expressive powers.

Although the essential feature is implicit in the broad melody which opens the movement, there is time for brilliance within that broadness, and for subtlety within apparent simplicity. A modulation between minor keys a semitone apart is one of many arresting touches:

The theme of the *Rondo* is sinuous though fundamentally straightforward, and once more the partnership of violin and piano seems even and equal. The episodes, garrulous and expressive by turns, throw the theme into relief without in any way distracting attention from its tender optimism.

BEETHOVEN

It is tempting to pause and discuss Mozart's splendid piano duet sonatas, and his two beautifully written duets for violin and viola, since all of these works are a boon to musical partnerships. Beethoven's ten sonatas for violin and piano, however, and his five for cello and piano, are so well embedded in the repertory that they claim immediate discussion. In the realm of duet sonatas, these fifteen by Beethoven will always maintain a high and honoured place. That they should vary in quality is inevitable: but their variety of form and style has nothing haphazard about it. If they were to be played in succession over a period of only a few days, the sympathetic listener could not fail to perceive a powerful sense of structural development, for the works span the greater part of Beethoven's creative life. He had no blueprint for sonatas of this type. He took the form as he found it – a duet sonata in which the stringed instrument was, at least in theory, the accompanying instrument – and rebellious as he was, he saw to it that the first three for violin and the first two for cello embodied nothing capable of upsetting the normal relationship.

The Three Sonatas for Violin and Piano, Op. 12, were dedicated to Salieri, whom Beethoven admired and respected enough to call himself his pupil. They were written during the last few years of the eighteenth century, and were published in 1799. One of the most memorable movements is the *Rondo* from the First Sonata (D major) which has a theme of infectious, almost irresponsible gaiety:

The A Minor Sonata (Op. 23) and the F Major (Op. 24) were both dedicated to Count Moritz von Fries, and they were in all probability composed during 1801, the year of their publication. The first of the two has an opening *Presto* in tarantella rhythm, whose grip on the composer seems to have lasted beyond the final bar-line and well into the second movement, an *Andante scherzoso, più allegretto* where syncopations and dotted rhythms abound. The whole mood of the sonata is too urgent to allow a real slow movement to enter into the scheme of things; soon the *Allegro molto*, with its foretaste of the type of violin writing in the Kreutzer Sonata, lets loose an eight-bar theme of Beethovenian build:

Ex. 9

The F Major ('Spring' Sonata) is altogether more relaxed, and a perfect foil to Op. 23. It took Beethoven some time to hammer out the famous opening melody from what was, in its first stages, a very four-square sketchbook tune. Here it is in its final form:

Ex. 10
Violin

The pastoral vistas of the *Adagio*, the brilliant *Scherzo* with its deliberately unaligned staccato chords, and the peaceful and poetical nature of the *Rondo* have a fresh quality which almost certainly inspired the anonymous musician who gave the work its nickname.

Beethoven's three sonatas published in 1802 as Op. 30 were dedicated to Alexander I of Russia. The longest and most powerful of the three is the second, in C minor, which has four movements as opposed to the three movements of the sonatas which flank it. In the opening movement of the C Minor Sonata, equality between the violin and piano soon shows itself in the *fortissimo* chords which are hurled from one instrument to the other. It seems hardly possible that such music could have appeared under the conventional title of 'Pianoforte Sonatas with Violin Accompaniment'. The A Major Sonata is notable for a delightful set of variations, which constitute the last movement of this generally cheerful and optismistic work. If, however, a movement of especial significance had to be quoted from the G Major Sonata, it would not be the sturdy, swinging 6/8 which begins the work, nor yet the garrulous and amusing finale. The duet sonata is seen at its best in the slow movement, here marked *Tempo di Minuetto, ma molto moderato e grazioso.* From the very first, both instruments share the good things that Beethoven provides:

If the popularity of the Kreutzer Sonata (A major, Op. 47) as a recital piece has not waned, it is due not only to the tremendous musical qualities of the work as a whole, but also to the perennial challenge which it issues forth to all violin and piano virtuosos, no matter how skilled or how self-sufficient. There are practical considerations, too, for the travelling virtuoso wants a work of concerto stature to play with his pianist, and a real concerto obviously will not do. Critics do not like hearing violin concertos with the orchestral part played on a piano. But the Kreutzer Sonata is, in Beethoven's own words, 'written in a highly concerted style, just like a concerto', and the work is thus ideal for the virtuoso recital. Its strength lies in its originality, apparent from the bold and unprecedented entry of the unaccompanied violin at the very beginning, and right throughout the entire work. The variations are among the

finest ever written by Beethoven, and the Finale, with its
dominant-coloured theme, brings the *concertante* element to
the fore even more markedly than the first movement.

Like the Kreutzer Sonata, the last sonata (G major,
Op. 96) allows the violin alone to say the first word. But
there the resemblance ends, as far as style and mood are
concerned. The partnership of the two instruments is here
more intimate, if less flamboyant and vigorous, than in the
Kreutzer. Beethoven has passed beyond the bounds of
revolution and invention for their own sakes: what he has
to say is more original than ever before, simply because it is
said in a quiet and unassuming way. Could there be any
closer communion than that of the first movement's opening bars?

The *Adagio*, although short in comparison with some in this
series of sonatas, is intensely expressive, combining beauty
and fullness of decoration with a total lack of fuss and of
display. The *Scherzo* begins in the tonic minor, and soon
proves itself more playful than powerful: its coda brings
home the key of G major once more, and so prepares us
for the friendly atmosphere of the *Poco allegretto* with which
the sonata ends. An air of rustic simplicity cannot, however,
banish the spell of peaceful reminiscence which acts as a
middle section, and (at one and the same time) as a written-
out cadenza for the violin and the piano. To play and to
strive together is one thing: to think together is another.
Thus we see in these ten sonatas the true transition from
music *per se* to musical thought; and we can only regret
that after 1812 Beethoven wrote no more sonatas for violin
and piano.

In the cello sonatas a similar phenomenon may be witnessed. The early sonatas of Op. 5 (F major; G minor) are excellent works of their kind, perhaps even remarkable for the year 1796, when Beethoven himself played the piano part at a court performance in Berlin and was duly rewarded by a box of *louis d'or* from the dedicatee, King Frederick William II of Prussia.

The best known of the cello sonatas is the one in A major (Op. 69) which appeared in 1809 and was dedicated to the Baron von Gleichenstein. As in the last violin sonata, the *Scherzo* is in the tonic minor; but here it is more extended in form and matter, the main theme setting the mood for the greater part of the movement:

A short *Adagio* leads to a joyous *Allegro* in first-movement form, the five-note phrase heard at the commencement acting as a generative and inspiring factor in the irresistible flow of music.

There are two more sonatas for cello and piano which are occasionally given a hearing: they date from 1815, and were published four years later. The Sonata in C (Op. 102, No. 1) has no printed dedication; but it is said that the composer, on being visited by the English pianist Charles Neate, inscribed the work to him in his own hand. The slow introduction presents the cello in cantilena mood, the theme being simple in shape, moving first down, then up. The opposite happens with the theme of the *Allegro vivace*, thus heightening the contrast between C major and A minor:

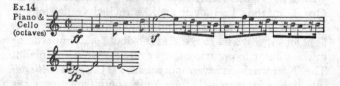

There is a coquettish corollary to this theme, and the second group is dominated by an insistent triplet-figure. The jerky rhythm of the opening bars plays a large part in the development, and when the return proper comes there is a hint of canon. An *Adagio* follows, with filigree figuration linking the two instruments. Then the melody of the first *Andante* returns, decorated and enhanced by its own recollections. But the tranquil mood soon passes, the end of a trill turning itself into the germ of the final *Allegro*. Here, a number of bright and bustling themes are heard, the rhythm of the first being well to the fore. The great moments, however, are in the dramatic pauses, ended each time by a low note on the cello: the fifth is added, and the piano comments pointedly. The coda brings with it a reluctant farewell to the staid beauty of a C major close.

Beethoven dedicated the D Major Sonata, Op. 102, No. 2, to the Countess Maria von Erdödy. It is a strong, terse work, typical in many ways of the composer's mature style; and significantly enough the last movement is a three-part fugue. This may well have been Beethoven's answer to the prevailing problem of texture in sonatas for cello and piano. The piano was then undergoing modifications which increased its tonal and dynamic range, and there was consequently a very real danger that the cello would eventually be pushed completely into the background. Beethoven avoids this by his skilful internal balance between the two instruments, and by his concentration on line and counterpoint, which he was wont to call *Arbeit*.

In his solitary work for viola and piano, we find a completely different vein of composition, for the 'Notturno', as it is called, really dates from 1797. It was published in that year in its original form as a string trio – the Serenade in D, Op. 8. In 1804 Beethoven made a revised version of the work for viola and piano, and although the substance is light for so great a master, there is no doubt of its importance in the still far too restricted repertoire for viola and piano. The 'Notturno' has seven movements: (1) *Marcia: Allegro*, in which jerky march-rhythms and smooth triplet passages alternate and combine; (2) *Adagio*, a lyrical and easily-flowing movement; (3) *Menuetto: Allegretto*, a slight and amusing little structure built on a six-bar theme, with trio in the sub-dominant; (4) *Adagio*, alternating with *Scherzo*; (5) *Allegretto alla Polacca*, with a dashing theme whose pace is only once slackened, when the coda brings an envoi highly typical of the composer; (6) *Andante quasi allegretto*, a theme and six variations leading straight into (7) *Marcia*.

SCHUBERT

Schubert's contribution to the domain of the duet sonata was less in bulk than that of Beethoven, for there are only six works for violin and piano, and one for arpeggione and piano, this last-mentioned work being played usually on the cello. The arpeggione was a hybrid instrument, a cross between guitar and cello, invented in 1823 by a Viennese instrument-maker. Its popularity was short-lived, although at least one instruction-book was published – the work of one Vincent Schuster, to whom Schubert dedicated the Sonata in A Minor. It is very much the kind of work one imagines would have shown off the new instrument to advantage, for the piano part is relatively unimportant, and remains so even when the modern cello takes the place of the arpeggione.

The *Allegro moderato* is graced by a long first theme, with pendant passage-work of the greatest brilliance. There is much play on short repeated figures, in Schubert's most garrulous vein, and it is these that make up the greater part of the movement. The *Adagio*, which is in E major, was doubtless intended to display the cantilena rather than the range of the instrument. There is no break between this and the *Allegretto*, which begins optimistically in A major with a pleasant tune in duple rhythm. A brilliant episode follows, then a return of the first theme. A change to E major introduces a melody of folk-tune flavour, but the former brilliant episode (now in A minor) again intervenes before the main theme returns for the last time.

The three sonatas, or sonatinas, of Op. 137 were composed in 1816, and such is the quality of their charm that
they have never gone out of favour, although they are perhaps more frequently heard nowadays in private musical
gatherings than in public concerts. Violinists tend to choose
the A Major Sonata or the C Major Fantasy, since there is
nothing in these earlier works which can be described as
virtuosic. The first has three movements only; the second
and third each have a minuet and trio, thus making a
four-movement scheme. In both the First and Third
Sonata, the opening *Allegro* theme is given out in unison by
the two instruments, in concordance with the classical
method of establishing tonality by an arpeggio theme of
some kind. Quite separate in this respect is the A Minor
Sonata, in which the piano alone has the opening theme.
When the violin enters, the theme is hardly echoed, let
alone repeated:

Similar touches of originality and invention are heard
throughout this sonata, which is probably the best of the
three.

The A Major Sonata, Op. 162, dates from 1817, and its
sunny, warm-hearted melodies are among Schubert's
finest. Less frequently heard than this is the *Rondo brillant* in
B Minor, Op. 70, which was written in 1826, only a year
before Schubert's last work for violin and piano – the
Fantasy in C Major, Op. 159. The *Rondo* is a show-piece,
without doubt, but it is far from being superficial, and there
is a subtle and buoyant contrast between what Willi Kahl
refers to as 'the rigidity of the march and the lightness of

the dance'. Schubert's last work in the form of a violin and
piano duo has even greater strength and originality than
the *Rondo*, and the fact that it is couched in the style of a
Fantasy gives it its remarkable structure and length. In
the lyrical flow of its melodies, the range of its harmonic
effects, and the difficulty of execution and ensemble, it is
far ahead of anything written before, and may be fairly
set at the peak of Schubert's achievement in the field of
chamber music.

SCHUMANN

ALTHOUGH the duet literature for viola and piano has
been enhanced by Schumann's *Märchenbilder* as notably as
that for cello and piano has been by the *Fünf Stücke im
Volkston*, it is once again the medium of violin and piano
that has profited most from Schumann's small list of works
in duet form. Only two violin sonatas are known and
played, yet there is in effect a third sonata, two of whose
movements originally formed part of that composite work
written for Joachim and based on his motto (F.A.E. = *frei
aber einsam*). The other movements were written by Schumann's pupil, Albert Dietrich, who contributed the first
movement; and Brahms, who wrote the *Scherzo*. Schumann's
replacement of these two movements remains unpublished.

His Sonatas in A Minor and D Minor were both written
in 1851, when he was forty-one years of age. They contain
music which is typical of his varied and complex personality,
now powerful and energetic, now wistful and dreaming.
There is a feeling of true chamber music in the way in
which violin and piano exchange their musical thoughts
and actions, and whilst the classical conception of form and
design is always present, there are certain romantic tendencies in both works; notably the *Romanze*-type of slow
movement and the use of cyclic form, albeit in a primitive
state. In the A Minor Sonata, the main theme of the first
movement returns in the Finale, in combination with the

busy semiquaver motive and pedal:

Similarly, the third movement of the D Minor Sonata quotes the theme of the *Scherzo* (second movement), using it to build a middle section to the tripartite formal scheme. The great length of the first movement of this sonata probably accounts for its frequent listing as *Zweite grosse Sonate* in nineteenth-century editions; nevertheless, in spite of its length it contains much fine music.

BRAHMS

BRAHMS's contribution to the F.A.E. Sonata has already been mentioned; and although this *Scherzo* is rarely heard, the three sonatas for violin and piano have become an established triptych in duet literature of the romantic age. In the G Major Sonata, Op. 78, there is a pastoral atmosphere from the very outset. The gently undulating rhythms of the first movement, rich in supple and subtle accents, throw into strong relief the noble and dignified melody of the *Adagio*, where fullness of texture is aided by the violin's statement of the melody in self-contained two-part harmony. The Finale, which draws on the theme of the *Regenlied*, Op. 59, exhales a peaceful though slightly melancholy mood, the two instruments seemingly in communion with themselves and with nature.

Sometimes known as the Meistersinger Sonata (because of the momentary similarity of its first three notes with the theme of the Prize Song) or the Thun Sonata (because of Brahms's trip to the Lake of Thun in Switzerland, where he began the work), the second of the group shows the composer in a happy, optimistic frame of mind. The slow movement is especially interesting, as it contains a lively, *scherzo*-like section which appears twice by way of contrast and colour, and once again as a short coda.

The D Minor Sonata, Op. 108, was written between the years 1886 and 1888, and was published in the following year with a dedication to the pianist and conductor, Hans von Bülow. It is longer than either of the previous sonatas, and is cast in a more sombre mood and broader design than they are. The combination of slow movement and *scherzo* in the A Major Sonata here gives way to a separate movement for each. The powerful and expressive first movement has an altogether remarkable development section, whose bass is a continuous dominant pedal. Over this there glide mystic *arpeggios*, changing and crossing with an occasional reference to the main theme of the movement, which, however, is not heard in its entirety until the recapitulation. The *Adagio* is a splendidly sonorous movement, with a broad theme for the G string and an unobtrusive but important figure in the piano part. The ensuing *Poco presto e con sentimento* is an admirable foil to this, and gives both instruments an opportunity to display their coquettish and dramatic talents. There is no light-hearted humour here; an undercurrent of seriousness is felt throughout the movement, in spite of the chattering theme and the brisk arpeggios. The fury of the final *Presto agitato* derives its outline from the tender counter-subject heard in the slow movement:

Ex.17
Piano

Brahms arranged his two clarinet sonatas (Op. 120) as violin and piano sonatas, but they are rarely heard in this form. On the other hand, the alternative versions with viola instead of clarinet are well-known items in the repertory of the viola and piano duo, and are well suited to this combination.

The second of the two is perhaps the most frequently played, and its opening movement, with the marking *Allegro amabile*, inevitably recalls the mood of the A Major Violin Sonata written eight years previously. There is indeed something lovable about the contour of the first theme. A variant of it, with gently falling cadence, leads without ceremony to a quiet second melody, in typically Brahmsian canonic rhythm. The development section contains some of Brahms's most exquisite harmonic inventions. The viola begins the second movement, *Allegro appassionato*, in E flat minor, with the piano replying no less insistently. Both instruments indulge in brusque modulatory excursions, until the theme is elongated by the viola in a bridge passage which leads to a song-like *sostenuto* in B major. After this change of mood and colour there is a sudden return to the opening theme by way of its second phrase. The *Andante con moto* which ends the work is a theme and variations: the homely flavour due to the swinging, repetitive rhythm gives the theme its naïve charm and quiet mood. The first two variations are placid; then follows a gracious movement full of conversation. The tempo changes to *Allegro*, and the mood becomes minor, but as the tempo slackens the major key returns, and the theme brings with it a cheerful ending.

There is a gap of over twenty years between the composition of the two cello sonatas, both of which are highly prized by players and listeners alike. The E Minor Sonata, dedicated to Josef Gänsbacher, was written between 1862 and 1865. Most of the themes allotted to the cello are in the minor key, and the lower range of the instrument is exploited somewhat too thoroughly at the expense of the rich upper registers of the A string. There is no denying the sombre lyricism of the opening theme of the work, however; and the *fugato* finale, in spite of its gruff utterances, has much to commend it. In the F Major Sonata, Op. 99, written in 1886 – the same year as the Violin Sonata in A and the Trio in C Minor – Brahms has given us a work of great beauty and splendid design. The four movements all bear the stamp of the composer's maturity, but they are widely contrasted and reflect a real mastery of style.

The agitated quasi-tremolo of the piano has a marked effect on the cello part at a later stage of the opening *Allegro vivace*, for it is more than a mere accompaniment to the bold assertions of the first theme. In similar manner the second subject prompts the rhythmic pattern of the chords which accompany the cross-string tremolos of the cello, as they appear in the development. For the *Adagio affettuoso*, Brahms chooses the key of F sharp, and introduces two motives which interchange between the two instruments with great charm and subtlety. A subsequent theme in F minor keeps up the dotted rhythm, but in diminution.

An *Allegro passionato*, in F minor, brings the piano into the foreground, until a heavy duplet figure heard in the cello part paves the way for a second strain. The opening bar of the movement is never lost sight of, but the middle section comes as a pleasant relief in the major key, with a suave and delightful cello melody. The last *Allegro molto* is in *rondo* form, with a *mezza voce* theme which has an amusing difference of opinion over the notes E and E flat:

The episodes are cunningly varied, both as to key and mood.

Many sonatas for cello and piano were written in the latter part of the nineteenth century, and although those by Grieg and Saint-Saëns are still occasionally to be heard, there is nothing that can be rated as high as the Brahms F Major in quality of workmanship and melodic appeal. Similarly, in the earlier part of the century, the sonatas by Mendelssohn will never rival the reputation of the Beethoven A Major Sonata, or even that of Schubert's solitary work, although it is not really a cello sonata at all. The second of the Mendelssohn sonatas (D major, Op. 58) is nevertheless a work of great charm and amiable fluency.

FRANCK

THE French school produced two perennially fresh sonatas within ten years of each other: the first sonata of Fauré, Op. 13, and the sonata by César Franck. Both are in the key of A major, and their dates are 1876 and 1886 respectively. Fauré's sonata was the work of a young man, of a man whose outlook on composition was relatively untrammelled by the greater influences of his age. Franck's sonata, on the other hand, was one of the crowning achievements of a long and arduous career, and it undoubtedly shows its creator in a more favourable light than some of the organ works and orchestral pieces. There, Franck is often the victim of a self-imposed mysticism which now seems charged with sentimentality; but he rises above this in the sonata, achieving a rare fusion of poetical and dramatic elements, and making the maximum use of the duet's capabilities in order to enhance these elements. The first movement is pure poetry, from the questioning tone of the first few bars to the wistful *envoi* at the close. There are two main themes, and they are so disposed that the violin occupies itself with the first, and the piano with the second. They rarely exchange thematic material: each instrument keeps carefully to its own theme. This is in complete opposition to the normal scheme of the classical sonata, and it tallies with very few of the typical sonatas of the romantic school. Franck remained an individualist to the end of his days, and nowhere is this individualism better perceived than in the opening movement of the Violin Sonata.

The second movement is rich in dramatic qualities and passionate utterances of a kind rarely resorted to by Franck. A lyrical turn occurs at the first subsidence of the frenzied opening mood, and the flowing theme of the violin is soon

countered by an expressive figure, falling steadily as indeed
the bass of the theme itself tends to:

Changes of tempo and temper intervene, now in tranquil
fashion, now with fiery grandiloquence, before the main
theme (once again in D minor) returns to dominate the
structure. The movement ends in a tempestuous but successful assertion of the major key.

Franck called his third movement *Recitativo-Fantasia* and
it is perhaps best understood as a growing, improvisatory
structure which links the poetic elements of the first movement with the dramatic touches of the second. The theme
marked *drammatico* is the one chosen for reappearance in the
last movement:

There are brief reminiscences of the sonata's opening theme
when the tempo gradually quickens, and the violin sings

dolcissimo of pastoral serenities until Ex. 20 returns, with a slow and sorrowful coda ending on the unexpected chord of F sharp minor.

Far too well known to need quotation, the melody in canon which begins the *Allegretto poco mosso* is one of Franck's loveliest. The episodes, instead of giving us new material, remind us of the old; and just as Franck at the age of sixty-four (when this fresh and radiant work was written), may have looked back on the faith and strife of his earlier years, so in this Finale we are allowed to review the music of previous movements in a new light. The end is joyous and triumphant – a reminder to us of what Franck may have achieved had he not been the victim of an accident that proved fatal.

GRIEG

IN Norway, Grieg produced four sonatas (three for violin and piano, one for cello and piano) between the years 1865 and 1887, and they are still prized for their distinctive melodies and northern charm although the rich chromatic harmony that Grieg uses so extensively may eventually cause the works to be dated though never, one hopes, completely abandoned. The Cello Sonata in A Minor and the third of the violin sonatas are both works of considerable stature, and they prove their composer to have a sympathetic and individual attitude towards chamber music, in spite of his output being so small.

FAURÉ

FAURÉ, like Grieg, produced four sonatas, these being equally divided between violin and cello. The two sonatas for violin and piano differ tremendously due to the years that separate them: Fauré in the twentieth century was a different man from the Fauré of 1876, when the first violin sonata was written. The later of the two works dates from

1917, and is dedicated to Queen Elizabeth of the Belgians. Although it is not frequently heard, it is a work of great elegance and is highly typical of the composer's mature style. There is a lingering and long-drawn-out sweetness which reflects the spacious days that were to vanish for ever at the end of the 1914–18 war. Yet Fauré was urged on, as it were, by this new interest in the duet-sonata, and composed the two cello and piano sonatas very soon afterwards. The D Minor (1918) was dedicated to Louis Hasselmans, and the G Minor (1922) to the Alsatian composer Charles-Martin Loeffler, who had then settled in America. Both sonatas are eloquent and elegiac, and sympathetically written for the two instruments.

DEBUSSY

Two of the most important of the French war-time sonatas were those by Claude Debussy. His Cello Sonata was the first to be completed, in the summer of 1915, and although a set of six was intended, only three were eventually written. Returning to chamber music at the end of his life, Debussy found a medium of unsuspected resource and restraint. Though he is said to have wished, in this Cello Sonata, to evoke the spirit of old Italian comedy, there is something witty and fantastic that can only be the work of one who signed himself 'Claude Debussy – Musicien Français'. The sonata has its own very especial organization, with a decided leaning towards cyclic rather than classical sonata form, and a cunning display of exquisite effects in the realm of pure sound.

The third of the set, for violin and piano, is perhaps the best known. When the violin established the G minor tonality of the first and last movements, there is a suggestion of the cardinal principles of both classical and romantic sonatas, as if Debussy were intent on getting the best out of both, whilst yet retaining his own personal stamp and his own inimitable mannerisms. The first movement in particular brings out unsuspected sonorities of both piano and violin by means of expressive and colourful arpeggio figures:

The second movement consists of *chinoiserie* of the most delicious kind – *fantasque et léger* is the composer's marking, and throughout the most subtle and spontaneous effects are cajoled from the duo. The Finale, after a cloudy opening, bursts into an assertive G major with a trail of joyous semi-quavers, which are soon interrupted by a slightly sinister interlude:

When the fervour abates, there comes a languid, almost soporific theme, reminiscent of *Ibéria*; but the first tempo returns, and the shimmering *tremolando* of the violin leads suddenly to a new and expressive version of the helter-skelter semiquavers. This theme is retarded even more significantly, beneath a staccato succession of triplet-figures, before the time comes for a final return to the *très animé* of the opening, and a rapid version, in the major key, of the G minor melody that began the work.

RAVEL

RAVEL's Sonata for Violin and Cello, composed between 1920 and 1922, is dedicated to the memory of Debussy, whose music it seeks rather to honour than to evoke. It is a work of elaborate genius, making the most out of a seemingly unhelpful combination, and achieving a truly artistic expression of the possibilities of this rarely exploited duet-form. The Sonata for Violin and Piano, which occupied the composer for the five years immediately following the first sonata, has never proved immensely popular, although the *Blues* of the slow movement and the breathtaking *perpetuum mobile* of the Finale lend themselves extraordinarily well to virtuoso performances.

THE TWENTIETH CENTURY

AMONG the more modern of French sonatas, Poulenc's (in memory of Garcia Lorca) deserves to be placed in the front rank not only through its fine craftsmanship, but because of its immediate and striking appeal.

Italy has given the violin and piano duo a number of important and interesting works, chief among them being the sonatas by Pick-Mangiagalli and Respighi (both in B minor), the two sonatas of Busoni, which contain much of his finest music, and the powerful and impressive Sonata in A by Pizzetti. Malipiero's D Minor Sonata for Cello and Piano, although a comparatively early work (1907) is highly typical of its author's elegant yet impassioned style.

There is understandably more for the piano than for the cello in Rachmaninoff's G Minor Sonata, though it is still highly regarded as being one of the few successful works in this genre by Russian composers. The sonata for the same pair of instruments by Dmitri Shostakovitch, written in 1934, is a work of great brilliance, and shows an uncommon knowledge of the technique and capabilities of the cello. Violinists in search of Russian music usually turn to Prokofief, whose two sonatas give ample scope to his peculiar genius; or to Stravinsky, whose *Duo Concertant* is one of the established pieces in the modern repertoire.

The stimulus for the *Duo Concertant* came from Samuel Dushkin, the violinist whose close artistic collaboration with

Stravinsky had brought about numerous transcriptions from stage works. The score of the *Duo* was completed in 1932, shortly after Stravinsky's fiftieth birthday, and received its first performance later in the same year. In his autobiography the composer says, 'It is my love for the bucolic poets of antiquity and for the *savant* art of their technique that determined the spirit and form of my *Duo Concertant*. The theme evolves through the five movements of my piece, which form an integral whole, and, so to say, a musical parallel to ancient pastoral poetry.' There is a similar marriage of music and poetry in the title of his lectures given at Harvard University, when he held the Charles Eliot Norton chair of poetry. It is as if he wished to mingle musical and poetical terms in equal numbers, even in the title chosen for the *Duo* – 'Cantilène' and 'Gigue' posing as song and dance, while the rustic flavour of both varieties of 'Eglogue' joins with the Bacchic 'Dithyrambe' in a purely poetical outburst of feeling.

The toccata-like opening of the 'Cantilène' soon makes way for an ecstatic and richly-scored theme played by the violin, but the keyboard part never loses touch with the toccata. A similar principle is found in the first 'Eglogue', where ingenious canonic phrases are soon thrust aside by a vigorous and harmonic violin part, the supporting material retaining a persistently linear outlook in tenths. The second 'Eglogue' is quieter in mood, graceful yet angular, and not without a hint of lyrical or pastoral dialogue:

The violin, leaving aside polyphony, contributes to the restrained texture in purely melodic vein. In the 'Gigue', all is excitement and dash, with a bass recalling the slight but haunting contour of an earlier theme. Abundant thirds and tenths, in a short middle section, create a new atmosphere consistent in both rhythm and function. The 'Dithyrambe' exploits a fresh and powerful declamatory style, with both instruments taking equal shares in a finely-developed drive towards the climax. The ending is serene and mysterious.

Of the Hungarians, Kodály has given us a sonata each for violin and piano, violin and cello, and cello and piano. All three date from the first two decades of the present century, and they display undistilled nationalistic trends functioning within the boundaries of an essentially classical conception of form. The Sonata for Cello and Piano, perhaps the most frequently played of the three, was given in the first concert to consist entirely of the composer's works, during the year 1910, and may therefore be said to mark an important stage in his career.

Bartók also wrote a duo sonata when in his early twenties, though the stringed instrument was the violin: in fact he never wrote an extended piece for cello and piano, the *Rhapsody* being a transcription of an orchestral work. It was not until the years 1921–3 that Bartók again returned to the duo, and then he completed two full-scale works entirely different in thought and structure, yet complementary in many other ways. Both were written for the violinist Jelly d'Aranyi. The first sonata was performed on August 7 in Salzburg, at the 1922 Festival of Modern Music, the precursor of the I.S.C.M. In the course of its by no means inconsiderable length, the composer gives free rein to his melodic imagination, his fantastic command of rhythmical subtlety, and his strong feeling for contrasts in timbre and register. The *Trois Études* of 1918 and the *Improvisations* of 1920, both for piano, had placed him in the forefront of advanced technico-musical idiom, and in the two violin sonatas the surplus of this transcendental energy obliges the violin also to conquer new heights in means and ends of expression.

The first movement is imbued with a fiery intensity
which welds together the ever-changing pulse of the music.
There is a constant ebb and flow of harmonic and rhythmical tension, although lyricism (admittedly of a highly
chromatic type) is by no means rejected as a factor of contrast. There is plentiful evidence of economy in melodic
material, and a fine grasp of the possibilities of classical
form; for, like Beethoven, Bartók knew how and by how
much to shorten a re-statement.

To the violin's improvisatory beginning of the *Adagio*,
the piano responds in a stately sequence of minor chords,
rising stepwise. Apparent clashes of tonality show the
brightness of Bartók's inner ear, for there is sound logic
behind such asperities as these. Even the close, with its
feeling of irreconcilability, is a logical extension of chord-
progressions heard previously.

A breathless violence, coloured by the percussive piano
writing and a G-string exposition for the violin, proves the
finale to be no weakling, no musical afterthought. As in the
first movement, there are moments of near-lyricism, when
melodies from Hungary's remoter parts, or even from
Arabia, emerge to lend their own powers of persuasion to
halt the breakneck race. The final *Presto* is the most brilliant
passage in the entire work:

yet the last cadence of all is still uncompromising, and still
unerringly logical.

Although a few of the German *fin de siècle* duos are still
occasionally heard (notably the sonatas by Strauss) it is to
Reger and Hindemith that we have to go for sheer bulk of
output and variety of medium. Reger's seven sonatas for
violin and piano, and his four splendid works for cello and

piano, deserve to be heard from time to time, for they show
a mind of progressive cast choosing – as Brahms did before
him – the forms and formulas of the classical era, and bringing from them new meaning and new life. Hindemith, on
the other hand, has produced works for a greater variety
of instruments: three sonatas for violin, three for viola, one
for viola d'amore, and one each for cello and double-bass,
the duo partner in all being the piano.

His Sonata for Viola and Piano, Op. 11, No. 4, though
dating from 1923, gives us an entirely characteristic combination of those cerebral and lyrical qualities which
Hindemith has brought to the craft of musical composition.
He asks that the three movements be played without a
break, and that the join between the second and third
movements shall be so cunningly concealed that the
audience will not realize that the Finale has begun. In any
case, this movement is really a continuation of the variations
that go to make up the second movement.

The sonata begins with a kind of fantasia, full of cadenza-
like passages for the viola, the initial theme of peaceful
nature reappearing in a fine *fortissimo* climax. When the
peaceful mood returns, the viola states in simple and unaffected style the folk-song-like theme used as a basis of the
variations, seven in number. The Finale has a theme of its
own:

Ex.25
Viola

but this is cunningly interlaced into the last three variations.
A brilliant coda built on the main variation theme keeps
its melodic share in the foreground right up to the last note.

Switzerland has produced at least two composers whose
duos hold a firm place in the modern repertory: Arthur
Honegger and Frank Martin. Of the former, there are two
powerful and highly individual violin sonatas dating from
1916–19, and works for viola and cello written in 1920. As
early as 1915, Martin had written his first Sonata for Violin

and Piano, and the second was not to follow until 1931. A few years later came an interesting essay in a new medium: a *sonata da chiesa* for viola d'amore and organ.

The most important of the American sonata duos are undoubtedly works of the calibre of Aaron Copland's Sonata for Violin and Piano, written in 1943, and Quincy Porter's Second Sonata (1929). Barber's Sonata for Cello and Piano has become an established work in the cellists' repertory since 1932, when it was first published. Its freshness and lyricism, allied to traditional forms and design, place it firmly among the finest cello sonatas of the century. Bloch's magnificent Viola Suite (1918), as well as his two sonatas for violin and piano (1920 and 1924) were composed in America, and they demonstrate to perfection the intense feeling of which Bloch was capable, even in the most intimate of chamber music *media*.

The English scene has traditional and quasi-exotic schools of composition; and these lines of demarcation, however clumsily drawn, help to visualize the position of the duo sonata in twentieth-century England. It is to be regretted that Elgar's chamber music, a late flowering of his genius, plays so small a part in modern concert programmes. The Sonata for Violin and Piano, with its Aeolian harp effects, is a particularly delightful work. The three sonatas for violin and piano by Herbert Howells are sturdy and individual contributions to the modern repertory, and likewise deserve to be heard more often. Rubbra's two for the same combination show lyrical gifts that are never cramped by lack of understanding for either instrument, and the three by Bax, similarly imbued with lyricism and poetry, are to be reckoned among his best chamber music compositions. The two cello sonatas and the sonatina by Bax, and the sonata by Moeran, are all works prized by cellists who treasure the particular melodic vein of these composers. Ireland's two violin sonatas, and his striking and highly typical Cello Sonata, are conceived in true chamber music idiom, and it is characteristic of Ireland's continual seeking after perfection that he revised the D Minor Violin Sonata on two occasions. Violists rejoice in Bliss's vigorous and yet highly sympathetic sonata, written in 1932 when the composer had already embarked on a successful group of chamber works. Violin and piano sonatas by Walton and Vaughan Williams (1950 and 1954 respectively) are both lively and significant essays in a by no means outworn form, as their thoughtful structure and refined lyricism proves.

Of the less insular composers, Delius (with three violin sonatas and one for cello) has considerable appeal, although the string parts seem awkward at first. Britten has never followed up his early Suite (1935) for Violin and Piano, yet there are three fine works by Berkeley – a sonata and a sonatina for violin, and a Sonata in D Minor for Viola. More recently, Reizenstein (Violin Sonata, 1945; Cello Sonata, 1947) and Racine Fricker (Violin Sonata, 1950) have given evidence of their considerable gifts in the field of the duo sonata, and it is to be hoped that more works of the same quality and interest will follow in the fullness of time.

13

Chamber Works with Wind Instruments
(from 1700)

JOHN WARRACK

INTRODUCTION

NEARLY every great composer has written chamber works in which wind instruments feature largely, even exclusively. Some of these are uncharacteristic early pieces, written as a student exercise; some are the fruit of requests from groups of players; some are independently conceived works in which the music requires the special quality of concerted wind for its expression. Few of them reach the loftiest level of musical achievement; and wonderful though many of them are, their composers have in every case more than one string chamber work with a stronger claim to greatness. Even the many beautiful works that combine a single wind instrument with strings do not offer themselves for comparison with the greatest music written for string quartet or quintet. We should be inexpressibly the poorer for the loss of Mozart's Oboe Quartet or his Clarinet Quintet, or of Brahms's Clarinet Quintet. But it would be a smaller loss than that of, say, Schubert's C Major Quintet, or of Beethoven's last quartets.

It must be allowed that there is a serious practical disadvantage to their appreciation. For economic reasons no wind player can devote his life to performing in one chamber ensemble, as can the member of a string quartet, and there are therefore no full-time wind groups to prompt the public taste. The rare examples of a wind ensemble (Dennis Brain's quintet, for instance) consist of free lance players who have to fit in rehearsal and performance times with the other chamber or orchestral engagements that provide their living. Yet were there a demand it could easily be met; most orchestral wind players, no matter how soured or how hard-bitten, are glad of the chance of an evening's chamber music. The conclusion is inescapable; there is something basically unsatisfying in wind tone unrelieved by string tone, something that makes a whole concert of it wearisome and that makes the medium unsatisfactory as a vehicle of the highest in art.

The reason is to be found in the extreme individuality and limited expressive range of wind instruments. The composer who writes a wind quintet (which consists normally of flute, oboe, clarinet, bassoon, and horn) has at his disposal five striking colours, but they are so striking that they will always catch the ear, and never blend into the pure unanimity that the string family achieves. To take a particular example, if a violin plays a tune to the accompaniment of second violin, viola, and cello, the subsidiary instruments blend happily into an accompanying role. But if an oboe plays a solo over clarinet, bassoon, and horn, the tones of these accompanying instruments will always be obtruding themselves, though the composer score never so wisely.

The best wind works are those which exploit the timbres of the instruments and blend them and contrast them the most tellingly. The greatest music is concerned with higher matters than these; it uses instruments literally, as instruments to its purpose, not as objects of study and delight. Even in the works for a solo wind instrument and string ensemble, works which are generally on a higher artistic plane than wind quintets, the balance is still tilted towards the display of the solo instrument's beauties. The music is at the service of the instrument, becoming in a sense programme music.

There are also incidental problems which, though perhaps not the composer's most immediate concern, make effective performance more difficult. There is the question of 'bad notes'. Certain registers, even certain notes, are commonly weak on every instrument: with the clarinet, which overblows at the twelfth, it is the patch between the top end of the lower octave and the twelfth, the so-called 'throat notes' (which are also awkward to finger); on the oboe the C sharp will tend to be flat, the lower G difficult to sustain quietly; and so on. The fact that certain chords in works always sound thin or out of tune is due to an unwitting piece of mis-scoring of this kind. And this is to say nothing of the individual weaknesses that beset every wind instrument ever built, which are far more pronounced than those of string instruments. A distinguished orchestral player has said that it takes at least a year for a newly-formed wind section of an orchestra to discover all each others' problems and so begin to play properly in tune.

These technical problems are incidental, and it is the concern of the player to overcome them, not of the composer to avoid them. But when a certain strength or weakness is very pronounced on every flute or clarinet it also begins to assume the status of a natural characteristic, and it must have an influence on the music written for those instruments. The most obvious example, the basic problem common to every wind instrument, is the question of breathing. Because we know that the players must breathe we subconsciously expect the music to fall into phrases of reasonable length, and it will only sound natural when it does. It is always useful for a player to have well-developed staying power, but this can defeat its own ends, and impose a sense of strain on the listener. There is an old glassblowers' trick usually known as 'double-breathing' whereby the blower uses the reservoir of air in his mouth to keep the outward stream flowing whilst re-filling his lungs through his nose. This sounds impossible; it is in fact quite simple to do, and with practice can easily be applied to the oboe, which uses very little air. However, a famous oboist once played the cor anglais solo in Act III of *Tristan und Isolde* in this manner without seeming to breathe at all, with the result that the audience was gasping for breath on his behalf and unable to listen properly. For these reasons a device known as Samuel's Aerophor, which runs a constant supply of air into the player's mouth from a small foot bellows, has never been needed, though Strauss suggests it for the horns in his *Alpine Symphony* and *Festliches Präludium*.

The technique of wind instruments makes unusually complicated and arduous demands upon the composer. The test upon his craftsmanship is severe; and it is noticeable that the composers with an interest in the craft of instrumentation write the most effective wind music whereas their more romantically minded colleagues often avoid the constricting medium altogether. The truly great composer makes and breaks what rules he pleases, as usual.

BACH

IN his great study of Bach's music, Dr Schweitzer writes: '. . . for him there was really only one style – that suggested by the phrasing of the stringed instrument – and . . . all other styles are for him only modifications of this basic style'. For a man with such a deep knowledge and understanding of all instruments Bach was extraordinarily unthinking in the matter of his wind writing. There is no evidence for supposing the existence of a lost technique, as with his high trumpet parts, yet in his works there is a complete disregard for wind players' need to breathe, let alone for their need to rest the lips for longer periods.

Glancing at the six sonatas for flute which are his most important wind chamber works, one might well believe them to be for some stringed instrument. A closer inspection shows a remarkable understanding of flute sonorities. Loeillet gave the instrument no more than simple tunes, Quantz's five hundred works extended the range, but Bach was the first to explore the instrument's emotional powers and to write as a matter of course beautiful and effective passages that remain difficult even with the modern Boehm fingering. The higher notes (up to G) and the lower notes (down to D) are used freely, and the player's tone must be strong and true throughout this whole register if he is to achieve a proper balance with the accompaniment.

These six sonatas are in two sets, three with clavier accompaniment, three with figured bass only. They were written during Bach's six years at Cöthen between 1717 and 1723, as was the G Major Sonata for Two Flutes and Bass which he later revised into a sonata for viola da gamba and cembalo. This work, incidentally, gives a further clue to Bach's careful interest in flute timbre, for in the original the bass is meticulously figured, with full, rich harmonies to balance the soloists exactly at every point, and in the viola da gamba version the cembalo player is allowed a free (unfigured) hand.*

The three sonatas for flute with clavier are of greater musical importance than their companion works, and of them the first, in B minor, is the largest in every sense. The opening *Andante* is a superb piece of writing: the accompaniment is almost exclusively in two parts, so that there is never any question of the flute being swamped by harpsichord tone, yet the florid melodic lines create the feeling of a wonderfully rich texture.

In the ensuing *Largo* a reverse procedure is used: the harpsichord accompanies the flute with rhythmic chords, only breaking into rapid runs to introduce the elaborately ornamented flute part. The final *Presto* is again different, an ingenious three-part fugue leading to a gigue based, in the Buxtehude style, on material in the fugue.

The remaining sonatas of the two sets are lighter in spirit than this fine work, though no less masterly in construction. A particularly attractive touch of tone colour is in the *Allegro* of the E Flat Sonata where the right hand of the harpsichord becomes almost a soloist in its own right in a delightful silvery contrast with the flute.

Friedemann Bach wrote little for wind (his three sonatas for flute and cembalo are, characteristically, lost), and

* The most wonderful example of Bach's understanding of wind timbre is not in a chamber work at all, though it is 'chamber' in scale – the aria 'Aus Liebe will mein Heiland' from the *St Matthew Passion*, a contralto aria with a flute obbligato accompanied only by mournful notes on two *oboi da caccia* (cors anglais).

Philip Emanuel Bach wrote nothing, but Christian Bach left a considerable quantity, including a sextet for oboe, two horns, violin, cello, and piano. Few of his wind works are played to-day, though a very pleasing little quartet in two movements for flute and strings (Op. 8, No. 1) is sometimes heard. Léon Goossens has on occasions performed it on the oboe, which suits it well.

Haydn's contribution to wind music, and the larger part of Mozart's, consist of divertimenti and serenades for wind band. The eighteenth century brought its serenades indoors from below ladies' balconies, its brassy tower music down from the heights, its cassations in from the alleyways, and set them round the tables or in the musicians' galleries of the nobles who paid to be diverted. Being played indoors, they are chamber music in the literal sense, but in style and atmosphere they remain out-of-doors music. Even with the more refined tone of modern instruments they make their best effect in the open air, and the trios, quintets, and sextets are in feeling miniatures of the larger outdoor works for full wind band. They are therefore not treated here.

MOZART

MOZART learnt much about instrumental timbre from his *divertimenti*, and this knowledge is nowhere more skilfully applied than in his Quintet for Piano, Oboe, Clarinet, Horn, and Bassoon (K. 452). It is well known that he considered it his finest work to date (he wrote so to his father after the first performance), and it remains one of the most remarkable and original works for wind instruments ever to be composed. The musical material is perfectly suited to the unusual demands of the combination, the formal organization is of an astonishing originality within a conventional framework, and the writing for the instruments allows each a part of almost equal importance with ample opportunity for rests. Yet this work is perhaps the most difficult in the entire wind repertory, not from the technical point of view (that dubious distinction is probably reserved for Villa-Lobos's Trio for Oboe, Clarinet, and Bassoon), but in the way of successful performance. It is a work that gets no easier with rehearsal after a certain point, one in which the players can never relax. One reason lies in the very skill of the thematic organization. The tunes are all in short phrases, depending as much upon the varied tone colour of the answering phrase as upon the line of the melody. This not only binds the five instruments together in the very bones of the music, but it allows them plenty of breathing space. From it there arise two problems, however: the necessity of unremitting concentration from the players on the point of the next entry, which may be on a different and unexpected beat of the bar each time the phrase occurs, and the fact that a complete tune must often be phrased through several players, one answering or blending into the next with impeccably smooth style. Added to this there is the fact that unless the pianist sets the curiously evasive speeds of the *Allegro* in the first movement and the *Allegretto rondo* exactly right the music will sound much too fast or too slow when it comes on the wind. Most works can be played several degrees faster or slower without harm; the E Flat Quintet has but one tempo, and that discoverable only by trial and error.

A natural device for a work of this construction is the sequence, and Mozart's *Largo* introduction builds up its mass of tone and deploys the instruments on three sequences:

The *Allegro moderato* is in sonata form, with the first subject announced by the piano and answered by all the wind:

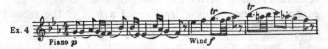

The second subject is similarly split up:

So far the exchanges have been closely reasoned almost to the point of terseness; a greater freedom now enters into the argument, with some brilliant solo displays from the piano, and after a brief working out of these the exposition ends with a little cadence figure that is repeated twice to introduce the development. This is surprisingly short (only sixteen bars in all) and is based closely on the first two bars of Ex. 4. The recapitulation treats the first subject more freely while repeating the second subject with few embellishments. The brilliant piano figures from the exposition are repeated, the material previously heard is delightfully rearranged about the instruments, and the movement ends with the same cadence figure that closed the exposition, separated here by cheerful arpeggios on piano and horn.

The *Larghetto* is again in sonata form, of a kind, but it is much simpler and much more free in construction. The first subject is again in short phrases, with a sequential answer:

After a slightly elaborated repeat of this there follows a brief dialogue between the wind, each with a different remark to make in its two bars, over an *arpeggio* piano accompaniment, leading by way of a *tutti* to the second subject on the piano over repeated wind chords.

Some free imitation on this leads to the close of the exposition.

The development is not strictly speaking a development at all in that it leaves these two subjects on one side and introduces fresh material in the shape of a broad tune first heard on the horn. A fascinating eight-bar chordal progression on the wind leads back to the first subject, slightly decorated. The wind dialogue of the exposition is repeated, and, with the second subject broken up in imitatory fragments and scattered to the wind instruments, this beautiful and extraordinary movement ends.

The last movement is the simplest of the three, a cheerful sonata-rondo on two themes:

The most striking feature of the movement is the *cadenza*, an elaborate quasi-extemporization, heaping sequence upon sequence with no reference to Ex. 8 and 9, that eventually emerges unconcernedly into the first subject. With a completely fresh tune thrown in for good measure by the piano this most wonderful work comes to a close.

Outstanding among Mozart's works for solo wind instrument and strings is his Clarinet Quintet (K. 581). Written in 1789 for the famous player Anton Stadler, a close friend of the composer and a member of the same Masonic Lodge in Vienna, it explores the range of the instrument in some of his most serene and lovely music. The clarinet fascinated him increasingly in his later years – its capacity for smooth phrasing and fluent leaps and its lugubrious chalumeau register were in keeping with his more reflective moods – and in this work he has captured the essential spirit of the instrument more successfully than in the elusive concerto (K. 622). The frequent use of the chalumeau register also reflects a liking for that quality in the instrument on the part of Stadler, who extended the compass of his clarinets downwards from E to C, and was also well known as a basset-hornist. As a technical example of clarinet writing, this work and the concerto set a style which has been developed with improving key systems but never basically altered, certainly not surpassed. And as an example of sensibility towards texture the *Larghetto* of this quintet is a miracle.

The delightful Oboe Quartet (K. 370) is more extravert in character, and shows less interest in the instrument's particular qualities. The *tessitura* is unusually high by modern standards: the soloist is consistently kept in the upper half of the treble stave and well above it, and the work even ends with a top F, a note which causes the finest player some anxiety. Mozart avoids the ripe, sonorous low notes, except very fleetingly and emphasized only in deliberate contrast to a high, singing phrase. Presumably this was either because Friedrich Ramm (for whom it was written) was more skilful in his use of the high register, or, more probably, because the lower notes were then coarser in quality than they are to-day. It is a captivating piece, by no means easy to play well, but irresistible in its sparkle. An original touch is the passage in the perky *Rondo* where the oboe suddenly breaks out of the rhythm into common time while the strings doggedly insist on the movement's proper 6/8.

On 10 December, 1777, Mozart wrote to his father from Mannheim that a certain Dutchman (one de Jean) had offered him 200 gulden to compose 'three short, simple concertos and a couple of quartets for the flute', for which Mozart later describes him as 'that true friend of humanity'. There resulted the two concertos (K. 313 and 314), composed at Mannheim at the beginning of 1778, and the two flute quartets (K. 285 and 298) and an opening *Allegro* in C major of a third quartet (K. Anh. 171). By 18 December Mozart was writing to his father to say that one of the quartets was nearly finished, and the date it eventually bore was Christmas Day. It is in D major, simple, attractive, and straightforward in style. There is an *Allegro*, followed by an *Adagio* (with the strings accompanying the flute melody *pizzicato*) that leads to a *Rondo*.

K. 298, in A major, was perhaps written in Paris. It is no less light and easy. The first movement is a set of variations on a simple theme; each instrument answers in turn. Following a minuet the work ends with a *rondo*, over which Mozart's individual sense of humour has caused to be set the lucid indication: '*Allegretto grazioso, ma non troppo presto, però non troppo adagio, così, così, con molto garbo ed espressione.*'

This sort of thing was generally reserved for the discomfiture of the long-suffering Ignaz Leitgeb, Mozart's hornplaying cheese-merchant friend for whom the four concertos and the quintet (K. 407) were written. The latter was styled by the composer *das Leitgebische*, and by its technical difficulty reflects much credit on its dedicatee, especially as it must have been played on a valveless handhorn. The first movement is in fairly conventional sonata form; the *Andante* is a calm, relaxed song; the Finale is an irrepressible *rondo*. The whole work is concerto-like in spirit while remaining one of Mozart's most attractive and wellwritten chamber works.

An unusual set of pieces, long neglected but now available on a gramophone record, is the group of six *Notturni* for soprano, mezzo-soprano, and baritone, two of which are accompanied by two clarinets and one basset horn, and the

other four by three basset horns. Five of them were written
in 1783 for evening entertainments in the house of Gottfried
von Jacquin, an accomplished amateur singer; the sixth
dates from 1788. The texts are mostly by Metastasio, and
are in the masochistic, near-adulterous conventions of
courtly love. One of the most attractive of them, *Due
pupille amabili* (K. 439) echoes uncannily the exquisite
Roundel attributed to Chaucer known as *Merciles Beaute* –
'Your yën two wol slee me sodenly'. The virtue of the pieces
lies in the amazing variety of texture Mozart works with the
accompaniment, and their very stiffness and formality has
a certain charm of its own.

Even more of a curiosity is the *Adagio and Rondo* in C
(K. 617) for glass harmonica, flute, oboe, viola, and cello,
written in 1791 for a blind girl named Marianne Kirch-
gessner. The poet Gray described the glass harmonica as 'a
cherubim in a box', which is not at all a bad image. There
is a remote, ethereal singing quality in it that is at first
enchanting, but one quickly becomes bored and then mad-
dened by an instrument with so little earthly character. Its
bad effect on the nerves even led to it being banned by the
police in parts of Germany. There is no blend whatever
with the accompanying instruments, not even with pure
sound of the flute (also poor in overtones), and in spite of
the efforts of Bruno Hoffman, the only modern virtuoso,
there is small chance of Mozart's very attractive music ever
becoming well known.

BEETHOVEN

IN the direct line of descent from Mozart's piano and wind
quintet is Beethoven's work for the same combination, also
in E flat (as is most of his wind music). It is an inferior work
to its begetter, but its neglect is certainly not justified. Like
the more enterprising septet, it dates from his first period,
treading carefully though with ambition the paths of classical form. There is no feeling that the music calls for these
five instruments and these only, as there is in Mozart's

work; indeed, a quartet version by the composer for piano, violin, viola, and cello appeared simultaneously, with the same opus number (16) in 1796. It tends in style much more towards a solo piano work with wind accompaniment, especially as the themes are invariably stated in full by the piano and answered by concerted wind. This opposition of forces persists, though to a lesser degree in the *Andante*, throughout the work. Mozart solved the problem of texture by knitting his instruments together in the themes; Beethoven sets them in contrast to each other, piano against wind, with the piano *primus inter pares*. This is basically a less satisfactory plot, and there is evidence that Beethoven himself felt this, for his string version includes passages accompanying the piano that do not appear in the original.

The work opens with a fanfare in unison on the notes of the tonic chord for all instruments, answered gracefully by the piano, and then repeated with a wind reply. Thereafter the instruments are each given a hearing; the forces are displayed, the wind weaving patterns over accompanying figures on the piano. The contrast of wind versus strings is then re-emphasized, and over a dominant pedal on the piano the introduction pauses, and plunges into the first subject of the *Allegro*:

Ex. 10

(The first half only is quoted.) The wind, led by the clarinet, answer literally, over a skeleton piano accompaniment which turns to triplets as the wind one by one declare a three-bar phrase based on the opening of the first subject. They then relapse into chords, and the piano leads into the *cantabile* second subject:

Ex. 11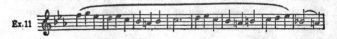

As before, the clarinet leads the wind answer, and after a very similar working the exposition closes over a long insistence on the dominant by the piano.

The cadence figure with which this ends is repeated at the start of the development (cf. Mozart) and thereafter the wind are given a freer individual hand than formerly. The piano's fondness for unisons in its accompanying role is maintained, and the turn into the recapitulation is long heralded, as at the end of the exposition, by an emphasis on the dominant.

The recapitulation is straightforward apart from an embryo cadenza for the piano. Beethoven yet again imitates Mozart in gay *arpeggios* for the horn near the end, but differs in adding a graceful nineteen-bar coda based on the opening of the first subject.

The *Andante cantabile* might be described as a developing *rondo*. The theme is given out at once by the piano:

and answered, as in the *Allegro*, by the wind with the clarinet stating the tune. The first episode exploits the oboe, in a four-bar phrase, and the bassoon, in a more elaborate eight-bar one, and as the four wind instruments enter at the end of these exchanges in a canonic figure, the simple chordal accompaniment grows richer, and eventually the piano emerges on its own and leads back into the theme, now decorated. The wind reply as at first. The second episode is in the minor, and is a horn solo over piano accompaniment, divided in the middle by a wind passage derived from the first four notes of the theme. The third statement of the theme is the most florid, and gives the piano a chance of brilliant display whilst the wind answer over its filigree with the same theme again. A brief coda features scale passages.

The last movement is also a *rondo*, based on a Mozartian hunting theme:

As usual, the piano gives it out and is answered by the wind. The first episode is in two halves, the first featuring piano arpeggios and a wind figure taken from (*a*) in Ex. 13, the second using a wind arpeggio in the pattern

Both play important parts in subsequent episodes.

The next opus number, 17, belongs to the Sonata in F for Horn and Piano, though it was not actually composed until four years later, in 1800. The intervening years saw the composition of, amongst other works, the first symphony, the first piano concerto, the Op. 18 quartets, and the Op. 10 piano sonatas. However, the piano answer in the first subject of the opening *Allegro* of the horn sonata bears a resemblance to the same point in the piano quintet (Ex. 10).

The movement is in a quite straightforward sonata form, and the Finale is an equally straightforward *rondo*, introduced by a brief funeral march-like *Adagio*. The work displays the horn effectively but conventionally. It was finished on 17 April, 1800, only the day before the famous Bohemian horn virtuoso Punto gave the first performance with the composer accompanying; this may in part account for the music's somewhat superficial quality.

A duet in G major for two flutes was composed in 1792, but not published until 1901; it is nowadays only played by flautists for their private enjoyment. It was written 'for friend Degenharth by L. von Beethoven, 23 August, 1792, midnight'. In her life of the composer Marion Scott adds the pleasing comment, 'What a queer feeling of sharing the warm August darkness that word "midnight" gives one.'

The same year probably saw the composition of three duos, in C, F, and B flat, for clarinet and bassoon. By their nature these works, like the flute duet, are but rarely performed, which is a pity, for though slender they contain attractive music. The B flat duo has been recorded, and consists of a full sonata form movement and a set of variations. It could hardly be expected that the writing for the instruments would be generous in the matter of rests, but Beethoven contrives to make the works playable and well worth the effort.

The problems are scarcely any less formidable in the Trio for two oboes and cor anglais (Op. 87), and so far from shirking them by writing a slender little *divertimento*, Beethoven has produced a work that goes through the complete scheme of a symphony. The first movement is in sonata form, fully worked; the second is based on a single, simple theme, and gives the cor anglais a chance to display its range and tone quality; the third is a delightful minuet and trio which turns the many rests the instruments need to witty effect; and the Finale is a lighthearted *rondo* with a perky first subject and a more melancholy second. An interesting point is that Beethoven added the word '*scherzo*' to the title *Menuetto* of the third movement; this is one of the first instances where the ever-increasing speed of the minuet seemed to demand a new definition. The whole work is an astonishing feat of composition when one considers that there is no possibility of harmony in any more than three parts nor any possibility of a major change of tone-colour. The former problem is so skilfully solved as to be unnoticeable; the latter is insoluble, and renders the work virtually unperformable. As pure sound this combination

of oboes is unexpectedly rich and attractive, but inevitably it palls quickly. Such a delightful work has, not
unexpectedly, broken its bounds; it is known in a version
for two violins and viola, which was made with Beethoven's
approval, and all in all eight transcriptions exist, including
one for piano solo.

This work was written for three players in the orchestra
of the National Court Theatre, and probably about two
years later Beethoven wrote for the same artists as set of
variations on 'Là ci darem la mano' from Mozart's *Don
Giovanni*. (Thayer provisionally dates Op. 87 as 1795 and
the variations as 1797, but a record is said to exist of the
first performance of the latter on 23 December, 1796). They
are very entertaining, enjoyable to play, and too little
known. The Trio has been recorded.

1796 probably also saw the composition of the sextet in
B flat for two each of clarinets, horns, and bassoons (Op.
71). It is a *divertimento* for *feldpartita* in spirit, cast in four
orthodox movements. The clarinets and bassoons are the
objects of interest; the dullness of the horn writing is the
work's main weakness. The first movement is in sonata
form with an *Adagio* introduction; half the first subject is
based on the notes of the chord of E flat, but, perhaps surprisingly, it is the first clarinet that pronounces it and not
the horn. Where Mozart would have seized upon the contrast of the second half of the theme to use a different instrument combination, Beethoven contents himself with providing an accompaniment for the second half and leaving
the first unaccompanied. Both this theme and the second
subject, which is similar in shape, turn the necessity for
rests to good account. A moment of glory for the first horn
occurs near the end, strongly reminiscent of the similar
passage in the piano and wind quintet.

The *Adagio* again concentrates the interest on the clarinets
and bassoons; the monotony of the horn parts is dreadful,
but their purely harmonic accompanying role does allow
the other four instruments greater melodic freedom. This
they use to full measure in an ingeniously balanced dia-

logue based on one main theme. The writing for the wood-wind instruments is admirable, evoking a rich, plummy texture while contriving ample breathing space.

The horns are given slightly more say in the Minuet, though their role is still in opposition to the others; in the Trio they remain silent. The Finale is a straightforward *rondo* on a military sounding dotted note theme.

Mention may also be made of the three *Equali* for four trombones, composed at Linz on 2 November, 1812. They are in D minor, D major, and B flat, almost entirely in block harmony with no suspicion of counterpoint, deep and sombre in tone and strangely eerie in effect. *Equali* for trombones were commonly played at funerals in Austria in Beethoven's time; the first and third of these were per-formed at his own funeral on 29 March, 1827, in an arrange-ment for four voices and four trombones by Seyfried, the *Andante* setting 'Miserere mei Deus', and the *Poco sostenuto* 'Amplius lava me' from Psalm 50 (Vulgate).

The well-known septet was such an extreme popular success on its appearance that Beethoven perversely but understandably took a strong dislike to it. Without reason – this is an ambitious but entirely successful attempt at a larger chamber music combination. It is still genuine chamber music, not a sparsely orchestrated symphony, though at times it blends its seven instruments with a sonority that is almost orchestral in richness. The wind instruments are clarinet, bassoon, and horn, with violin (one only), viola, cello, and bass. The key is as usual E flat, and in form the work lies somewhere between a *divertimento* and a symphony, tending towards the former. This conveni-ent arrangement gives it a coherence without forcing it into a structure that the instrumental arrangement would hardly suit.

The first movement is in sonata form, with a noble *Adagio* to introduce it that presents the wind with some phrasing problems. The *Adagio* unfolds its graceful theme at first on the clarinet, over one of the composer's favourite murmuring accompaniments (compare the best known example in the 'Scene by the Brook' in the Pastoral Symphony). The Minuet is very well-known, if only in arrangements, with a Trio that gives the horn some good practice in articulation. The theme of the ensuing five variations is supposed to be a Rhenish folksong, though its origin is said to have eluded all investigation. There follows a brisk *Scherzo* and Trio, which would take the place of the second minuet were this a true *divertimento*. The ensuing *Andante* is but a preface – *reculant pour mieux sauter* – before the final *Presto*, which includes quite an elaborate cadenza (written out in full) for the first violin.

With the death of Beethoven the interest in wind music lapsed for close on a century. No longer were there courts to be supplied, and a composer's vision was consciously set higher than an employer's table, though many of them must have secretly regretted the passing of an assured income by this useful and profitable form of journalism. Furthermore, the emotional range of wind instruments was too limited for the universal ideas they wished to encompass. It was the age of the orchestra, and those nineteenth-century composers who did write chamber music generally ignored the wind. Berlioz, Liszt, César Franck, Dvořák, Grieg, Mahler – in none of these composers' *oeuvre* does any wind chamber music appear, nor has any been written by Rachmaninov, Delius, Sibelius, nor Bloch. (Wagner has only an early and uninteresting *Adagio* for clarinet and string quartet.) Other romantics contented themselves with one or two wind pieces, sometimes student works written as a technical exercise for the larger orchestral works that they intended were to follow, sometimes, in an older tradition, works for a special occasion or for certain groups of players. Such are Mendelssohn's Two Concerted Pieces for Clarinet, Basset Horn, and Piano (Op. 113 and 114) (written for the distinguished clarinettist father and son Heinrich and Karl Bärmann), and Bruckner's *Aequali* for three trombones. None of these, nor many others by lesser composers, need be considered. They often fulfilled their temporary purpose smoothly enough, but they add nothing to our knowledge or appreciation of the composer or of wind instruments. Their oblivion is merciful.

Rossini's jumble of minor works includes a number of wind pieces. His six quartets for flute, clarinet, horn, and bassoon are very gay and very fetching, but they are thoughtlessly written and consequently exhausting and seldom completely effective in their rare performances. He also left some duets for two horns and a *Rondeau Fantastique* for horn and piano.

SCHUBERT

SCHUBERT wrote no wind music of importance for less than eight instruments (his great Octet uses clarinet, horn, and bassoon), unless we except his contrasting of the flute with the guitar in the quartet with viola and cello. None the less, mention should be made in passing of two wind works which hark back to Beethoven and beyond in spirit.

On 18 August 1813 he completed a Minuet and Trio for the wind section of the school orchestra of the Imperial and Royal Seminary where he studied. It is for two each of oboes, clarinets, bassoons, and horns. The Minuet has two contrasting Trios; the Finale is a *rondo*. Schubert added a postscript to the work signing himself as Imperial Chinese Director of Music at the Court of Nanking, no doubt in perpetuation of a local school joke.

Shortly after this work he wrote the *Eine Kleine Trauermusik*, in E flat, dated 9 September. It is short, elegiac, as the title suggests, and is scored for two clarinets, two bassoons, double bassoon, two horns, and two trombones (the unusual inclusion of the latter instruments into the scheme again marks their funereal association). The main melodic interest is on the horns. The legend that this work was written in memory of the composer's mother has now been exploded; Otto Erich Deutsch suggests that it commemorates the poet Theodor Körner, who had died a few weeks previously in the War of Liberation, and to whom Schubert had been introduced at the beginning of the year.

SCHUMANN AND TCHAIKOVSKY

SCHUMANN'S contribution is more slender. The original version of his Andante and Variations (Op. 46) (better known for two pianos) was scored for two pianos, two cellos, and horn. The slightness of the rescoring that took place for the piano in its translation to the second version shows that the other instruments add little to the work. Schumann thought little of it. 'I think I was rather melancholy when I composed it,' he complained.

The Märchenerzählungen (Op. 132) is scarcely more successful, and the works for wind with piano are insignificant and not particularly well written.

Tchaikovsky's offering is even less impressive, consisting of a handful of 'prentice works written in the years 1863–4 when he was studying orchestration with Rubenstein.

It will be noticed that the romantic composers who did treat wind instruments showed an especial affection for the clarinet. Understandably so; together with the horn it is the smoothest and the most expressive of the wind instruments. Thomas Willman was not far wrong, though like most enthusiasts he was overstating his case, when he wrote in his *Complete Instruction Book for the Clarinet*, in 1825 '... surely a Tone that nearly rivals the finest human Voice, and an extent of Octaves that may vie even with the ample range of the Violin, are excellencies that *must* at no very distant period share a considerable portion of popularity'. He did not foresee that in the twentieth century composers would also discover an incisive glitter in the tone that was well suited to their revolt against the very sweetness and flexibility the instrument once embodied.

BRAHMS

WITH the exception of the Trio in E Flat (Op. 40) for Violin, Horn, and Piano, all Brahms's wind chamber works made use of the clarinet. In his case it was the noted Meiningen clarinettist Richard Mühlfeld (the subject of one of Renoir's portraits) who was the immediate inspiration, though in his later years Brahms seemed, like Mozart, to find in the tone of the clarinet a sense of finding peace, of having 'grown tired of sorrow and human tears'. In 1891 he first met Mühlfeld, and during a summer holiday at Ischl that year he wrote the warm A Minor Trio for Clarinet, Cello, and Piano (Op. 114) and the famous Quintet for Clarinet and Strings. Three years later, in 1894, he composed the two sonatas (Op. 120, Nos. 1 and 2). That in F minor is the more difficult technically, but also perhaps the more rewarding musically; the E flat sonata, which is in only three movements as against its companion's four, is a more relaxed work. The first movement is especially smooth and rich; the second is an *Allegro appassionato*, in form a *scherzo* with a *sostenuto* trio; and, like the quintet, the work ends with a set of variations. Brahms later arranged both these works, and the trio, so that a viola could take the place of the clarinet, but they are first and foremost clarinet music.

Greatest of the four clarinet works is the Quintet in B Minor (Op. 115), which Mühlfeld is said to have played superlatively. The first movement, which is predominantly sombre in mood, is in sonata form. Four bars of a rather indeterminate tonality on the strings contain the essential elements of the first subject:

Ex. 15

This is taken up in an extended form by the clarinet, which, after a rhythmic bridge passage, also declares the second subject, in unison with the second violin and in mostly note-against-note counterpoint on the other strings.

Ex. 16

In the development section these elements, together with the rhythmic bridge passage, are used to weave varied textures, and the recapitulation continues to embroider upon this material. The movement ends with a gentle coda that echoes the opening of the work.

The *Adagio* opens with the main theme on the clarinet:

Ex.17

This is imitated at a distance of a bar and a half by the first violin and with a shifting accompanying figure on the other strings (all are muted here). The central *più lento* is closely derived from Ex. 16, and florid and rhapsodical in manner, returning eventually to the first section.

The *Andantino* likewise transforms its opening strain, which begins

Ex.18

into a disturbed *Presto* (compare also the *Allegretto* of the second symphony). The movement ends with a return to the original theme.

The final *Con moto* is a placid set of variations; the work is rounded off with a reference to Ex. 15, and the actual close is a slightly altered version of the end of the first movement.

After this fine work nothing else of comparable distinction was written for wind in the nineteenth century. It was, indeed, not until after the first world war that the great revival of interest in wind instruments took place. Before 1914 the orchestra had reached mammoth proportions; now post-war economics took a hand, and in the move back towards smaller ensembles a new enthusiasm was kindled for wind instruments as instruments, not merely as flecks of colour in a larger canvas.

CHAMBER WORKS WITH WIND INSTRUMENTS 311

THE TWENTIETH CENTURY

THE output has been vast, so vast that it is necessary to be drastically selective even to mention in passing some of the fine works that have appeared. One may begin by dismissing the innumerable pieces composed for the annual examinations at conservatories, both before and after the first war. Many of these have found their way into print in perpetuation of their original purpose, though seldom on to the platform. To the aspiring wind player '*Morceau imposé au Concours du Conservatoire*' are words more discouraging than ever Dante set across the mouth of Hell.

Even Debussy did not infuse much interest into his *morceaux de concours*. His *Première Rhapsodie* for clarinet and piano (there was never to be a *deuxième*) was written in 1910, and dedicated 'with feelings of sympathy' to Prosper Charles Mimart, then clarinet professor at the Paris Conservatoire. It is in one movement, marked 'dreamily slow', and it fulfils adequately its purpose of putting the soloist through his paces. Debussy later orchestrated it, in which guise it is sometimes played. Much simpler in style and less than forty bars long, is the pretty *Petite Pièce* of the same year, also for clarinet and piano (and later orchestrated) which is based exclusively, but somehow not monotonously, on one dotted figure.

Few sextets for wind exist, the most notable being Janacek's enjoyable suite *Mladi* ('Youth'), scored unusually, but cleverly and on the whole effectively, for flute (or piccolo), oboe, clarinet, bass clarinet, horn, and bassoon, which dates from 1924. The same composer also left a *Concertino* for piano with horn, clarinet, and string quartet (1925), and an ingenious *Capriccio* for piano (left hand only) and seven wind instruments (1926).

WIND QUINTETS

ONE of the discoveries, or strictly rediscoveries, of the post-war years was the wind quintet (flute, oboe, clarinet, horn, and bassoon) as an instrumental combination.

With a range of about five octaves, from the B flat below the bass stave to the C an octave and a fourth above the treble stave, and with a group of tone colours that achieve, if not a blend, certainly a happy consort, it is by far the most satisfactory combination of wind instruments. A handful of works have been written that stand out from the general run of the mill as more than mere freaks in their composers' output, but serious contributions to music.

Schönberg's massive Quintet (Op. 26) was written in 1923–4, and is a very strict twelve-note work. It is rarely heard owing to its great difficulty of preparation. The composer follows the later common dodecaphonic custom of marking the score and parts with *H* and *N* for *Hauptstimme* and *Nebenstimme* to show players which passages are to be brought out and which more subdued, but the work remains a tough nut which few ensembles are bold enough to attempt to crack. This is to be regretted, for though not one of the composer's most striking works, it contains some novel and fascinating effects, as, for example, the use of piccolo instead of flute in the second movement to impart a steely glitter to the fabric of sound. The first two movements are in fairly strict classical sonata form; the Finale is a *rondo*, and gives each of the instruments more chance of individual display in the subject, of which the most important part is the rhythmic formula first heard on the clarinet

Ex.19

(Ex. 19). This, it should be noted, is the opening pair of notes forming the row on which the whole work is based – E flat, G, A, B, C sharp, C, B flat, D, E, F sharp, A flat, F. This series is heard at once on the flute at the start of the first movement. For all its subtlety this quintet is an impractical work, relying for its effects upon a nice attention to detail, carefully expounded in a small dictionary of dynamic signs at the beginning, that would go by the board in performance. A more serious intrinsic flaw is the subduing of instrumental individuality in order to knit close patterns of sound.

Carl Nielsen's Quintet (Op. 43) is another matter altogether, a warmly personal, lyrical work of immense charm. In 1922 Nielsen met on a visit to a friend's house the members of the Copenhagen Wind Quintet, who were rehearsing there. Greatly impressed by their playing, he decided to write for them first a quintet, and then a concerto for each instrument. The flute and clarinet works are the only two of the concertos he lived to complete; in them and in this quintet he has reflected the characters of the five artists who quickly became his close friends. We learn from the music that the flautist was precise and cultured, the oboist suave, the clarinettist choleric, the horn a simple soul, and the bassoonist stolid and sober. The final variations, and indeed the whole quintet, are as much 'to my friends pictured within' as Elgar's own 'Enigma' variations.

The *Allegro* is a delightfully cool sonata form movement, followed by a Minuet that contrives an extraordinarily full effect though cast mostly in two parts. The Finale is prefaced by a strange, writhing Prelude in which the oboe is exchanged for the darker-toned cor anglais. The theme is then declared, a chorale harmonized simply and rather sanctimoniously. The ensuing eleven variations deploy the instruments with wit and great originality. Two of them are unaccompanied: the bassoon runs a course of triplets in Var. 7, and Var. 9 provides horn with dotted figures. Var. 5 is a hilarious scene between the enraged clarinet and the unperturbed bassoon, the former uttering wild shrieks without budging his companion an inch from a maddeningly obtuse position. The work ends with the chorale again, now extended to fit a 4/4 rhythm.

This use of variation form in a closing movement is psychologically sound as it provides the listener with a constantly shifting centre of interest at the moment when his ears are beginning to be sated with wind tone and his attention liable to waver. More than one composer has used the idea, which is in any case particularly suited to the medium, and some have cast their wind quintets entirely as theme and variations. Jean-Michel Damase, one of the younger French composers, has written a light-hearted quintet with seventeen variations, and Eugène Bozza's work is a well-scored set of seven variations on a rhythmically loose *thème libre*.

Milhaud solves the problem by writing a suite of movements related by external, not internal, circumstance. His *Cheminée du Roi René* is a charming conceit, neatly turned out and delightful to play and to listen to.

The most noteworthy British wind quintet is that by Peter Racine Fricker (Op. 5), originally a Clements Memorial prize work. Whilst caring for the instruments with assured craftsmanship, the composer does not deny himself a certain dry *grotesquerie* at their expense. The *Moderato* introduction makes strong use of a double-dotted figure, and leads to an *allegro moderato* that, conventionally but effectively, contrasts a fluent theme with a sharply *staccato* middle section, and makes further use of the material in the Introduction. The second movement is a *Badinerie* that gives the flute a chance of athletic display, with a strange Musette on a shifting drone.

Fricker also makes use of variation form, though in his penultimate movement, and in a more purely intellectual manner. The horn declares the angular theme unaccompanied, and there follow five short canonic variations. Var. 1 (*Adagio*, at the 4th) weaves its canon *cantabile* on the four lower instruments, with the flute adding three decorative comments. In Var. 2 (*Poco andante*, at the 5th) the horn is silent, and the oboe and clarinet wind the theme together in 5/8 with *staccato* scale passages of the bassoon and some stutters from the flute. Var 3 (at the 2nd) drops the flute and clarinet and leaves the oboe and bassoon to chatter together in Tippettesque rhythms with slow held notes on the horn between them – an interesting experiment in texture. Var. 4 (*Vivo*, at the 6th) gathers the instruments all togther in a precipitous 6/8, leading via a miniature *cadenza* between flute and clarinet into Var. 5 (*Adagio*, at the

7th), which uses the theme in the same shape as Var. 1. (The movement is really a kind of acrostic, brilliantly solved.) The finale is a headlong 12/8 split up as 3/8 + 3/4 + 3/8; a final full-scale reference to the work's introduction dissolves into a two-bar *vivo* flourish.

Hindemith's principles have naturally led him to write a large amount of wind music, but in none of his sometimes excellent sonatas for almost every conceivable instrument has he been so successful as in the *Kleine Kammermusik* (Op. 24, No. 2) for wind quintet, written in 1922. A *divertimento* in spirit, it is by no means easy on the players; with such an experienced composer at the helm nothing is made impossible, but there are effects that cause much difficulty in performance. An example is the Waltz, which requires a piccolo instead of the flute but asks this notoriously shrill instrument to play, with the others, *durchweg sehr leise*. The first three movements concern themselves with one particular rhythm each; the fourth movement is short, and stamps out an irregular rhythmic figure, separated by unaccompanied flourishes on each of the instruments in turn; the finale swings along in a very fast 6/4 varied with a bar of 9/4 at unexpected intervals.

WIND TRIOS, DUOS, AND SOLOS

THE combination of four wind instruments has for no apparent reason proved unfruitful, but there exist a number of trios. It is never a very satisfactory medium; the mixture of oboe, clarinet, and bassoon is the most effective, providing sufficient contrast of tone colour and a useful working compass. Villa-Lobos has written a trio of a staggering complexity and difficulty that is only equalled in his wind quintet; some time is needed to unravel its intricacies, but once penetrated its strange world of bumping *ostinati*, of stammering repetitions broken by swirling scales, and of thickly knotted rhythms holds a strong fascination.

Milhaud's *Suite d'après Corette* for the same instruments is a pole apart. Based on themes by the eighteenth-century organist and composer, Michel Corette, it was originally part of the incidental music to a French production of *Romeo and Juliet* in Paris in 1937; it is an amiable and smoothly written set of pieces.

The only contemporary composer to use Beethoven's combination of two oboes and cor anglais is Gordon Jacob, whose profound knowledge of instrumentation has inspired him to a number of excellently wrought wind works. The first of his Two Pieces draws a richness and sonority from the three instruments undreamt of even by Beethoven; the second is a chatty little *scherzo* with bagpipe noises interrupting.

Poulenc's Trio for Oboe, Bassoon, and Piano is a thoroughly effective work in the composer's best vein. Its dry humour is brilliantly exploited on the two dryest of the wind instruments, leading one to wonder why no one else has attempted something similar.

Reducing the count to two instruments the field narrows suddenly, as one would expect. Nothing of importance has appeared (nor, indeed, hardly could appear), though Gordon Jacob has written a lively set of Three Inventions for Flute and Oboe, and Alan Frank's Suite for Two Clarinets deserves mention for its pert wit and *insouciance*. Poulenc's Sonata, also for two clarinets, is rather too self-consciously French in a tiresome manner.

With one wind instrument at his disposal the composer is faced with an almost impossible challenge. Debussy's *Syrinx* and Honegger's *Danse de la Chèvre* are both successful programme music miniatures for flute, but as *tours de force* they pale beside Britten's astonishingly full and varied Six Metamorphoses after Ovid for oboe. The fifth uses brilliantly the difference between the ripe reedy lower register of the instrument and the sweeter high register to evoke a picture of Narcissus falling in love with his own image in the water; the extremes gradually close in until the contrasting phrases and registers lose themselves in each other and the ear can no longer distinguish original from reflection.

Stravinsky's Three Pieces for Clarinet were written in 1919, and one dedicated to Werner Reinhart, through whose generosity *L'Histoire du Soldat* had been staged during the lean years of war. It is therefore probably not a coincidence that the last of them carries echoes of the Ragtime of the earlier work. The first two are marked 'preferably A clarinet', the third 'preferably B flat clarinet', indications which suggest that Stravinsky supposed there to be a difference in the tone quality of the two instruments; none such exists. The first is a slow tranquil piece that explores the chalumeau register. The second is roughly ABA in shape in that the outside sections deal in cool arpeggios and the central one in jerky ninths. The third, the Ragtime movement, is rhythmically a virtuoso piece that needs diamond-like clarity to bring it off. All three make much play with grace-notes for extra emphasis. Eric Walter White has written that the work 'though not important in itself heralds a period of greater melodic freedom'.

MISCELLANEOUS WIND WORKS

BARTÓK's only contribution to wind chamber music is his *Contrasts*, for violin, clarinet, and piano, completed in Budapest on 24 September 1938. It was originally commissioned by Benny Goodman and Joseph Szigeti, and consists of three contrasting character pieces. The first, *Verbunkos*, is a Hungarian recruiting dance, and derives its richly ornamented figures from traditional tunes of the type often played on the *tarogato*. This is a kind of primitive conical clarinet to which the Magyars were much addicted, and which became, during the eighteenth-century Rakoczy struggles, a symbol of freedom for the Hungarians. It has a clarinet reed, but, being conical, the fingering is that of an oboe. It is, therefore, the clarinet which declares the theme of the first *Contrast*, and which retains much of the interest, including a glittering *cadenza* of scale passages.

Piheno ('relaxation') is the slow movement. Violin and clarinet move soberly in contrary motion, with *tremolo* contributions from the piano. The middle section is more agitated, and in the final section it is the piano which has the melodic interest.

Sebes is quick again. Two violins are required, one tuned G sharp D A E flat, and two clarinets, one in A and the other in B flat. The violin opens with a series of bare fifths on the open strings (but with the modified tuning two outer intervals are, obviously, diminished) through which the clarinet gives out the main tune. A middle section deals in angular skips (using the ordinarily-tuned violin), turning eventually to the first section again. There follows the central section of the whole movement, in the characteristic Bulgarian rhythm of $\frac{8+5}{8}$, divided up basically as

$3 + 2 + 3 + 2 + 3$ in each bar. The first part of the movement returns, the violin has a *cadenza* to contrast with the clarinet's *cadenza* in 'Verbunkos', and the work accelerates to a close with the skips of the middle section.

SOLO WIND INSTRUMENTS WITH STRINGS

IT is the oboe and the clarinet that have received the most attention as solo instruments with string trio or quartet, or with piano, in recent decades. Surprisingly little has been written in the way of flute quartets, though a few good sonatas exist; the horn is even more neglected with even less reason; and the bassoon has inspired less still, though Humphrey Searle has written a quintet for bassoon and strings, and Peter Warlock, of all people, once contemplated writing a work for the same combination.

The oboe owes its recent popularity to the artistry of Léon Goossens. Dedications to him head most oboe works written in the last thirty years, and he has indirectly inspired many students to take up the oboe and so create a further demand. There is a grain of truth in the criticism that he has over-refined the tone of the instrument, but he has shown that it is capable of an expressiveness and a flexibility that it has never had before, and that has been a strong attraction to composers.

Bax and Bliss have both written good quintets for oboe and strings, the former a typically warm, singing piece, the latter a more serious work of some technical difficulty. Bax's work is ripely pastoral; Bliss avoids the truly rural effects, and his quotation of a folk song in the Finale (*Connelly's Jig*) is unique for him and not in the least 'folky' in effect. Gordon Jacob's quartet is, of course, beautifully written for the instrument, and shows romantic leanings that do not here conflict with the composer's naturally crisp style.

At least two works have explored the possibilities of using a wind instrument in a string ensemble not primarily as a virtuoso solo, but as an almost equal member of the group. Britten's early Phantasy Quartet is formally very neat in construction, and uses the etching quality of oboe to good effect. Anthony Milner's quartet makes some subtle play with tone-colours, often using the oboe to supply a particular quality in accompanying passages, and it is also of considerable formal interest. Basically the first movement is in modified sonata form, the second subject deriving from the first; the second, and last, movement, is a slow fugue with a rapid middle section that does duty as *scherzo*.

Standing head and shoulders above all other chamber works for clarinet and strings in this century, and possibly above all other modern wind chamber works, is Bliss's Clarinet Quintet. Greatly underrated, this fine piece is fully worthy of its place in a line that includes the quintets by Mozart and Brahms. The opening suggests a gentle fugue, but this is not worked, and the passage forms essentially a reflective introduction to a movement of driving vitality. As in the rest of the work, the contrapuntal ingenuity is formidable; Bliss's harmony derives much of its tang from the situations brought about by the coursing of the parts in their individual manner, rather than the harmony allowing certain contrapuntal progressions to take place. The clarinet writing is indebted to Brahms, and to Mozart before him, though the brows of even Stadler and Mühlfeld might have furrowed before some of the technical problems that Bliss poses his soloist, problems brilliantly solved by Frederick Thurston.

The second movement is a long *scherzo*, more straightforward in style, and equally enthusiastic. Even the *Adagietto* does not relax the tension completely, though it evokes some wonderfully cool and rich sounds from the clarinet. The more passionate central *Allegro* section makes use of the first violin as a kind of intermediary between the clarinet and the remaining strings.

Wit returns with the Finale, a forceful *Allegro* that varies constantly between 6/8 and 3/4 (a common feature of Vaughan Williams's rhythms, though Bliss uses it with a decisiveness that is quite different in effect). Here, as throughout the work, the string writing is unusually full and sonorous. Though written in 1931, four years before *Music for Strings*, this quintet shows the same mastery of string technique and string tone that was to be exploited as an end in itself in the later work. It is not a composition of great formal interest from the analytical point of view, nor does it contain any quantity of memorable tunes. Largely rhapsodic in manner, it will have nothing to do with the angular bite that Stravinsky and other moderns have drawn from the clarinet, but returns to the nineteenth-century style of clarinet writing while employing a thoroughly contemporary idiom.

This is the modern tendency. It has been proved often enough that to write a work which pays no attention to the requirements of its medium is to write a bad work, and this is nowhere more true than with wind instruments. Having less emotional range than stringed instruments they cannot adapt themselves to an alien manner of expression so convincingly. The composer must meet them halfway, as it were. There will be little chance of him reaching the highest peak of greatness with a wind work. But one cannot always live among peaks, and the lower slopes of the mountain have had their attractions and their delights.

PART THREE

—

14

American Chamber Music

DAVID DREW

THE Americans are a cheerfully acquisitive race. Although pre-eminently amongst those that hath, much is given to them, and the rest they take. Not so long ago, a Gallup poll taken by an American periodical showed that in the opinion of the majority, Stravinsky, Schönberg, and Bloch were the greatest American composers. ... Certainly, there was good reason to be grateful to these masters – as there was to the many other Europeans who have contributed to the formation of American culture. The great exodus from Hitler's Europe to the New World completed a cycle of American cultural history that had begun with the earliest colonial settlers. Among the more musical of these settlers had been the Moravian Brethren, who paid especial attention to secular music. The most accomplished of the composers associated with the sect was Johann Friedrich Peter (1746–1813), a native of Herrendrijk, Holland, who settled in the colonies and there composed a number of pleasant if not particularly distinguished chamber works, including a set of six quintets for strings, which have proved worthy of revival. Apart from the Moravians, there were several purely secular composers. The Belgian, Joseph Gehot (1756–18–?) and the German, John Christopher Moller (c. 1750–1803) followed, like Peter, the examples of Haydn and, to a lesser extent, Mozart.

Gaetano Franceschini, a contemporary whose exact dates are unknown, wrote several trio sonatas modelled upon those of Boccherini.

However, it cannot be said that these composers established a tradition of chamber music in the New World. The Civil War gave rise to other, more stern, preoccupations and the musical activity of the first half of the nineteenth century was limited to the composition of hymns, songs, and patriotic ballads. But by the middle of the century life had become more settled, and musicians turned once more to the composition of chamber music. The London *Athenaeum* of 1853 says of a quartet by one Perkins that 'the themes appear pleasing ... and the taste of the whole laudable, as eschewing the modern defects, calling themselves romanticism, against which there is reason to warn the American musical imagination'. Reason or no, such warnings were of no avail. American composers of the second half of the nineteenth century hastened to Europe to learn the technique which they could not acquire at home. Having studied with honest minor composers like Rheinberger, Raff, and Humperdinck, they returned home and proceeded to emulate the manner of whichever of the great Romantics had caught their fancy. Brahms, Wagner, Strauss, the French Impressionists, all were laid under contribution in the works of such men as George Chadwick (1854–1931), Arthur Foote (1853–1937), John Alden Carpenter (1876–1951), and Daniel Gregory Mason (1873–1953). Of the composers of this period, only Edward Macdowell (1861–1908), with his Grieg-like talent, achieved anything of more than local interest; but unlike the others, he left no chamber music.

By 1914 there had been much music written in America, but strictly speaking there was nothing identifiable as American music. At least there was nothing known to the public. But in his New England retreat a remarkable and even to-day unclassifiable musician was writing works as ruggedly American as any poem by Walt Whitman. That musician was Charles Ives (1874–1954). Certain of his works dating from the early years of this century fore-shadow the technical innovations made by other composers many years later. That is beyond question; but their artistic worth is less certain. Ives's musical achievement is like a pathway hacked through a jungle by a primitive man armed with blunt instruments and guided by nothing more precise than instinct. It is erratic; it is clumsy: but every now and again it opens up a vista of wild and uncultivated beauty. The two piano sonatas are full of such moments, and amongst chamber, or rather, chamber-orchestral, works I would cite the nocturne, *Central Park*, with its brooding *adagio* section that might almost have been the work of Alban Berg. Ives's sense of form and sonority is often defective, and it is inevitable that his empirical methods should result in frequent calamities. Amongst the failures must be counted the Second String Quartet, which follows a programme similar to that of Sir Arthur Bliss's *Conversations*, but is so haphazard in form and style, and so ill-conceived for the medium that, apart from the typically transcendentalist finale, it has little more than the messy charm of a child's scrapbook. A *Largo* for clarinet and piano (1901–3) is more orderly and deserves to be known, whilst the *Scherzo* for wind ensemble, piano, and percussion en-titled *Over the Pavements* (1906) is almost indistinguishable in effect and quality from Milhaud's polytonal offerings of the early twenties. And amongst the piles of chaotic manu-script which Ives bequeathed to the world there are doubt-less as many works of genius (and as much nonsense) as have already been unearthed by the admirers of this, the secret father of American music.

We may date the birth of modern American music from the return to America, in 1926, of Aaron Copland (b. 1900), who had been studying composition in Paris with Nadia Boulanger. Like his predecessors, Copland took the style of a European master as the starting point for his own develop-ment. His choice was Stravinsky. But for the first time in American musical history, the European model was *only* a starting-point. Copland was too individual an artist, even in his mid-twenties, to be content with the humble role of disciple. If we examine his first important chamber work, the Sextet of 1936, we do indeed find that the harmonic idiom and the textures owe much to Stravinsky, especially the Stravinsky of the *Symphonies d'Instruments à vent*; but the articulation of each movement, the motivic-rhythmic life, is something quite distinct from the character of Stravinsky's music, something that we recognize as typically American. Yet whilst admiring the surefootedness of it all, it is difficult to avoid a sense of disquiet. The cause is not so much the lack of any melodic inspiration – the composer has indeed been forced to deny himself that luxury – as the disproportion between the outward appearance of terseness and economy, and the actual condition of the musical content, which is in fact far from compressed. There is, too, a lack of imaginative flexibility and a corresponding narrowness of procedure, which might well have boded ill for the future.

In his second important chamber work, the Piano Quartet of 1950, Copland makes a gallant attempt to broaden his field of operation. Formally, the work is most adventurous, and achieves a successful synthesis of sonata and fugue elements. The tension between form and content in the first and third movements is perfectly calculated. The expressive polyphony of the first movement would not have been possible without the experience of purely melodic writing which Copland had gained in his ballet and film scores since the sextet. The quartet makes extensive use of serial procedures – in one sense a surprising departure, though in fact it is merely the logical conclusion of the emphasis on intervallic relationships which marks Copland's work up to and including the sextet. The basic, eleven-note series is constructed in such a way as to preclude the triadic harmony which has long been the hallmark of Copland's style, and in the *vivace* central movement one becomes aware that this is an artificial restriction. The music seems painfully forced, and the imaginative impetus, feeble from the start, has petered out long before the end.

Yet for all that, the quartet is a work of distinction and individuality, which in its finest moments reaches something very like nobility.

American music owes Copland much. Not in any sense a composer of genius, he has achieved what he has by the sheer intelligence with which he has nurtured and applied a small but highly individual talent. He was the first American composer blessed with a sense of direction, and it seems likely that history will award him a place of honour, if not the crown which some disciples would like to bestow upon him.

Soon after Copland's return to his homeland in the midtwenties, he sponsored a series of concerts of modern music with a fellow composer, Roger Sessions (b. 1896). The Sessions-Copland partnership was symbolic of the two main streams in the development of modern American music. Whereas Copland has always been acutely conscious of his responsibilities as an American composer, Sessions has only been concerned with his responsibilities as a musician. His inspiration is cosmopolitan – he spent eight formative years in Europe – and although his early works owe something to Stravinsky, he has latterly turned towards a more chromatic style, influenced, at least superficially, by the Schönberg of the *Five Orchestral Pieces*. His musical thinking, unlike that of Copland, is by nature contrapuntal. It is instructive to compare his recent string quartet (the second) with Copland's Piano Quartet. Both have a fugal first movement, both reach out towards the twelve notes of the chromatic scale. But the chromaticism of the Sessions quartet is much more thoroughgoing – Copland's basic series is for the most part built from whole-tone steps – and the texture more consistently contrapuntal. If sheer professionalism is to be the yardstick, the Sessions is superior to the Copland. It is supremely well written, the unmistakable product of a firstrate musical mind. Yet in the last resort it is the Copland to which we return, finding there a sharply personal vision, in contrast to which the Sessions has nothing to offer.

The work of Wallingford Riegger resembles that of

Sessions in one respect only – its avoidance of conscious 'Americanism'. Riegger's career started academically enough, but in his mid-thirties he began to experiment with new methods of tonal organization – *vide* the *Study in Sonority* for ten violins. As could have been predicted, he soon adopted the twelve-note method. His First String Quartet (1940) might be described as a 'Plaine and Easie Introduction' to the method. As in the set of piano pieces, *New and Old* (1945), the dodecaphony is without complications. Music of so light and springy a texture is far removed from run-of-the-mill twelve-note academicism, but there are moments when the composer's anxiety to reaffirm the identity of his row overrides purely musical considerations. In his recent second quartet, Riegger is said to have achieved a true equilibrium, and to have written a work that makes a worthy companion to the much-admired Third Symphony.

As a serious and thoroughly independent artist, Riegger has, until recently, received too little attention. On the other hand, Roy Harris (b. 1898) – an independent of a very different kind – has received a great deal. There was a time when Harris was widely hailed as a genius, but as the years have passed it has become clear that he had said almost all that he had in him to say in the Piano Quintet of 1936 and the Third Symphony of 1937. In the symphony, the slowness of the musical thought had contributed to the monumental effect; in the later symphonies and chamber works it has become mere lethargy. There is always something to admire in every Harris work, even if it's only the effort which has gone into it. But the works which precede the Third Symphony and the Quintet – for instance, the early Concerto for Piano, Clarinet, and String Quartet – were in the nature of preliminary exercises, and those that followed were scarcely more than addenda. His is not a developing talent. It stands like the Statue of Liberty, solid, worthy, symbolic of much that is good in the American character, yet somehow rather unedifying.

Harris's music is predominantly modal, and in some of

his works, notably the Third String Quartet, he has attempted to enlarge his restricted harmonic vocabulary with polymodality. These preoccupations have influenced his disciple, William Schuman (b. 1910). Like Harris, whom he resembles in many respects, Schuman made his mark with a symphony (his third) and has since consolidated rather than extended his achievement. In his Fourth Quartet (1950) he has made a commendable effort to say something new, with results that have been warmly praised, perhaps too warmly, by Copland. It is a Spartan piece, and as a turning point in the career of a composer of some talent, its interest (like that of Rawsthorne's recent quartet) lies more in what the composer has rejected than in what he has gained.

Of the senior composers working within the bounds of traditional form and harmony, Samuel Barber (b. 1910) and Walter Piston (b. 1894) are the most considerable. Barber's lyrical talent is at its best when inspired by poetry. He is perhaps a trifle self-conscious about his traditionalism, and purely instrumental forms seem to encourage in him extravagances which he may regard as camouflage. The flashy rodomontade of the piano sonata and the unconvincing neo-classicism of the *Capricorn Concerto* for chamber orchestra do no credit to the composer of *Dover Beach* (for baritone and string quartet), *Knoxville, Summer 1915*, and the String Quartet, Op. 11, from which the celebrated *Adagio* is taken. Piston, on the other hand, is entirely sure of himself. Having in his youth arrived at a point comparable to that reached by the young Hindemith (see, for instance, the American's business-like Quartet No. 1 of 1930), he has latterly taken up a position similar to that of Rubbra in this country. The accomplished and musicianly Piano Quintet of 1949 does not suggest that he is an artist of Rubbra's stature, but it commands respect as the work of a convinced and convincing conservative.

So much for the leading senior composers in America. They are separated from their juniors by the war years and by the arrival in America of many distinguished composers and executants. This influx did indeed create for the younger men a situation quite different from that experienced by their elders. No longer was it necessary (or possible) to travel to Europe to absorb the benefits of a stable tradition. The final curtain had fallen on the kind of American composition – of which Arthur Berger's expertly insignificant Woodwind Quartet of 1941 is one of the last examples – associated with the Paris school of Nadia Boulanger. For a while America became the centre of musical life. The results are obvious in the music of the post-war school. The most talented composers no longer felt it necessary to assert their Americanness – which in the past had too often meant imitating Copland. Their musical language was by now naturally American, having no further need to lapse into those hearty colloquialisms – the equivalents in music of 'Hiya' and 'What d'you know' – which had sometimes betrayed the lack of confidence underlying much pre-war American music. Even the lesser talents revealed, in their imitations of the masters – whether the neo-Stravinsky of Harold Shapero, Arthur Berger, and Alexei Haieff, or the neo-Hindemith of Ellis Kohs – a technical and inventive assurance usually denied to the derivative. On a higher level we find such varied and yet unified achievements as the string quartets of Milton Babbitt, Elliott Carter, Irving Fine (whose quartet successfully fuses the lessons of serial technique with those of Stravinsky), and Leon Kirchner (a quartet that is perhaps too close to middle-period Bartók, but which is strong and convincing none the less). One notes that the first two of these composers are cosmopolitan without being anonymous, like Sessions at his best, whilst the second pair are national without being parochial, like Copland at his best. Here, and in the work of other young composers too numerous to mention, the pattern of American music continues, enriched by the European masters who have made America their home.

15

English Chamber Music (from 1700)

DAVID COX

THE richness and scope of English chamber music in the sixteenth and seventeenth centuries; the influence which English composers then had on the musical language of Europe; the great demand that there was for our instrumentalists in many countries during what has been called the golden age of our country's musical history – all this is discussed at length (with many musical illustrations) by Ernst Meyer in his book *English Chamber Music*. And it is something of a reproach to us that the job had to be done by a foreigner. He stops – understandably enough – at the end of the seventeenth century; and all we can say is: if Purcell had lived another thirty years he might have been able to assimilate the influence of Handel and yet still go on writing in the English traditions which had been built up during the previous 200 years; and he might well have indicated new paths which other English composers might have followed. But Purcell died at the age of thirty-six and he had no successors – not even (if we believe that 'genius will out' whatever the circumstances) any potential successors. And so, we rapidly became known as the 'Land without Music'.

The tremendous social and economic changes that were taking place in eighteenth-century England no doubt all played their part in producing a spiritual climate in which our own music had difficulty in flourishing. It was a time of great advances in science, of industrial revolution, imperial expansion, increasingly successful and prospering middle classes – a time when 'the Bible had a rival in the Ledger' – an Age of Reason, with so-called 'natural' theology and free-thinking, and with practical, down-to-earth values in everything.

By the eighteenth century, music – instead of being a natural and highly significant form of activity for all who could afford it, as it had been in Elizabethan times – had become an artificial, highly professional affair, and amateur cultivation had seriously declined. Not to be able to take part in music was no longer considered a serious flaw in one's education.

Before the accession of the Hanoverian Dynasty in 1714, there was already the feeling that music was a commodity which should come from abroad. With the reign of George I, the 'foreign tone and manner' was carried to extremes. The foreigner, in fact, took over. Handel – German-born, and trained as a composer in Italy – made England his home, and occupied the centre of the stage. Some of our composers tried to carry on in the old traditions – as, for example, the remarkable Thomas Roseingrave (1690–1766) – but these could make little headway against the main current.

After the Restoration, solo violin-playing had spread from Italy; and during the eighteenth century in England there were in fact many composers who wrote string sonatas – all with a strong Italian accent; but in many cases these works deserve to be better known than they are. The fact that they are known at all is largely due to the efforts and enthusiasm of a Scottish musical editor and composer, Alfred Moffat (1866–1950), who dug up works by British composers of this period and edited them – unfortunately in none too scholarly a manner – for three different publishers. Of these composers (apart from the younger Boyce, Arne, and Stanley, to whom I shall refer later), the most striking is certainly Joseph Gibbs (?1699–1788) – most of whose music seems to be lost – who may well be a composer of far greater importance than is now generally realized. At the age of fifty he published his remarkable set of eight solos (sonatas) for violin and *continuo*. Of these, the one in D minor is fairly well known, but the rest, also very fine, continue to be neglected. Another, William Babell (c. 1690–1723) was a harpsichordist, violinist, organist, and composer, whose fame spread to France, Holland, and Germany (where some sonatas of his were published). There was John Lates (?–1777) and his son – both composers and important figures in the musical world of Oxford. There was Henry Eccles (c. 1670–c. 1742), known for his twelve sonatas for violin and *continuo*; early in life, however, he decided to go to France, and joined the King's Band there. And there were many others. In 1955, the B.B.C. Third Programme broadcast an extensive series of eighteenth-century English chamber music (edited by Stanley Sadie) in which much of considerable interest was brought to light, including notable works by Charles Avison (1709–70), Stephen Storace (1763–96), and – particularly memorable – F. E. Fisher, about whom very little is known.

But in the chamber music of this time, as in other fields, it is Handel (1685–1759) who is the commanding figure – the figure of overwhelming importance in our country's musical history. John Horton has discussed the chamber music of Handel at length – in *Handel: a Symposium*, edited by Gerald Abraham – and only a brief outline of its scope and variety can be given here.

Forty-six solo and trio sonatas are published in the Handel-Gesellschaft; and there are others besides. The majority of them follow the four-movement form of the *sonata da chiesa*, as established in Italy in the late seventeenth century by Corelli: the first movement slow and prelude-like; the second quick and fugal; then a slow, lyrical movement; and finally a quick and lighthearted one. The movements are usually in the same key, but with a change to the relative or tonic minor or major for the third movement.

There are four main collections. First, the six sonatas or trios for two oboes and continuo, probably dating back to Handel's boyhood in Halle, when, as the composer said, his favourite instrument was the oboe. (Handel was, incidentally, a performer on the harpsichord, organ, oboe, and violin.)

The fifteen solos for German flute (i.e. the familiar side-blown instrument – as distinct from the English flute or

recorder), or oboe, or violin, and figured bass, first published
in Amsterdam in 1724, and later in London as Op. 1, are
miscellaneous in form and content. It is the six sonatas
or trios for two violins, flutes, or oboes, and *continuo*, Op. 2,
that are musically the most interesting of all. They are
all in four movements, and, as John Horton says, 'their
style, rich and elaborate, suggests that they are works of
Handel's maturity'. At the time it was common to use two
similar treble instruments for trio sonatas. But sometimes
composers particularly asked for two contrasting instruments, as Handel does here in No. 1 and No. 5 of Op. 2,
when he specifies flute and violin. No. 5 has been chosen as
the example of Handel's chamber music in the H.M.V.
History of Music in Sound. But musically it has not the interest,
character, and harmonic adventurousness of some of the
others in Op. 2, though the contrasting timbres of the two
instruments are most happily exploited.

No. 6 of Op. 2 – in G minor – is a particularly fine work.
The opening *Larghetto* section makes very expressive use of
imitation between the two violins. (Handel afterwards
rearranged the same material in an organ concerto.) This
leads into a fugal *Allegro*, the theme of which begins:

On that very memorable subject an extended movement is
built, which is a model of splendid craftsmanship. The
opening three crotchets are used most effectively in the
course of the movement; and in contrast, the continuo (on
equal terms with the other instruments) provides running
semiquaver passages which are taken up by the violins.
Then follows a short *Adagio*, in expressive, contrapuntal
style, starting in the relative major key (B flat) and ending
on the dominant of G minor – leading into the last movement, *Allegro*, which is in every way very characteristic of
the composer. In the words of Gerald Abraham, 'Handel
began by writing German music with an Italian accent,

and developed into a cosmopolitan composer writing Italian music with a German command of solid technique and an occasional trace of English accent, caught mainly from Purcell.' One of the most obvious Purcellian influences is the use of the hornpipe rhythm in some of Handel's movements (the hornpipe being something wholly English). It is found in the finale of this trio sonata. The main theme of the movement is a familiar one, for it occurs in several of Handel's instrumental works, including the second movement of the Organ Concerto, Op. 4, No. 3:

Of eighteenth-century composers who were younger than Handel, Thomas Arne (1710–78), William Boyce (1710–79), and John Stanley (1713–86), are the most important. All of them wrote some chamber music, all were strongly influenced by Handel, but each brought something to his style which was decidedly English. Arne's trio sonatas are pleasant, but thin; those of Boyce – an under-estimated English composer – solid and varied. Stanley (blind from the age of two), whom Dr Burney described as 'a natural and agreeable composer', had a decided freshness and individuality.

The concerts organized in London in the late seventeenth century by the violinist John Banister, and later by Thomas Britton, 'the musical small-coal man', were thought to have been the first in Europe where an audience paid for admission; these gave rise to later activity, such as the long series of chamber and orchestral concerts given by the Academy of Ancient Music from about 1710 until 1792; while in Oxford, in the Holywell music-room (the oldest room of its kind in Europe) concerts had been given since the seventeenth century.

But the increasing popularity of public and semi-public concerts did little to stimulate the composition of worthwhile British chamber music works. The end of the eighteenth century and the beginning of the nineteenth is certainly the gloomiest period of our country's musical history. Musical taste was at a very low ebb; glees and ballads were produced in profusion, but little music of lasting value.

The violinist and composer William Shield (1748–1829) was much influenced by Haydn, whose company he had shared for four days – during one of Haydn's visits to England. Shield said that in those four days he learned more than in any four years of his life. He was principally a composer of theatre music, but wrote six quite elaborate string quartets, and six duos for two violins; also, six string trios with some of the movements in the (then most unusual) time-signature of 5/4 – movements which, the composer tells us, had amused some of the most distinguished players of England and Italy. Here is the beginning of the 5/4 movement of a Trio in A by Shield:

Samuel Wesley (1766–1837) is best known as the composer of some excellent church music; but he was a prolific and important composer in many fields – said to be a pioneer of the symphonic style in England – and a list of his chamber music includes two string quartets, a string quintet, and various trios and sonatas, none of which is published. (His only published chamber music work appears to be a *Rondo* on 'Jacky Horner' for piano and flute.)

But some string quartets by his elder brother, Charles Wesley (1757–1834), have recently been republished in London, edited by Gerald Finzi, according to whom they are early and valuable examples, in both form and content, of the galant school in England. Charles Wesley was a youthful prodigy. These quartets were originally published in 1778, when the composer was twenty-one, and were followed three years later by a set of concertos for organ or harpsichord – but during his last fifty years of life he produced practically nothing. Here is the beginning of the Quartet No. 1, in F, with a theme that seems reminiscent of the beginning of Beethoven's 'Spring' Sonata:

George Onslow (1784–1853) was of an English family, a grandson of the first Lord Onslow – but it seems to have been entirely from his French mother that he inherited what musical gifts he had. He was a prolific but undiscriminating chamber-music composer, writing in a mixture of styles (C. P. E. Bach, Haydn, Clementi). His output includes thirty-four string quintets, of which Op. 34 and Op. 58 are considered the best. His music enjoyed in its day great success in the salons of both Paris and London. Some of it has recently been recorded, but its musical value is dubious, to say the least.

The enormous development of industrialism in the late eighteenth century and early nineteenth century certainly played its part in producing the cultural numbness of the time. And increasing material comforts seemed to create a need for only the most trivial kinds of music. Academic musicians were still dominated by Handel. Small wonder that John Field (1782–1837), a remarkable pianist and composer, found musical life in England intolerable and spent most of his time abroad, where he was more appreciated.

As far as chamber music is concerned, there is very little really worth mentioning at this time. William Sterndale Bennett (1816–75), as a pianist and composer, won for a time great respect abroad. He performed regularly at the Philharmonic Society's chamber and orchestral concerts in London, and between 1843 and 1856 himself organized an important series of chamber concerts. The three chamber works – the Sextet for Piano and Strings, the Piano Trio, and the Cello Sonata – are all slight and charming works in a mild way, but they are pale reflections of Spohr and Mendelssohn.

The influence of Mendelssohn became very strong in England at this time; during his short, overworked life he made several visits to this country, and both as a personality and composer was immensely popular; and with choral singing on a large scale in great vogue, *Elijah* had a success which suggested that it might be a new *Messiah*.

And so we come to the spade-work of the Renaissance of British music: the Parry Group, with its four famous knights – Sir Hubert Parry (1848–1918), Sir Charles Villiers Stanford (1852–1924), Sir Alexander Mackenzie (1847–1935), and Sir Frederick Hymen Cowen (1852–1935). The work they did was of great value, and was carried out in spite of much prejudice and apathy. None of them, however, was at his best in the field of chamber music.

Stanford, who was of Irish birth, was prolific in most branches of composition, not least in chamber music: he wrote eight string quartets, three piano trios, two string quintets, a piano quintet, a serenade-nonet for wind and strings, four violin sonatas, two cello sonatas, a clarinet sonata, and much else. Of these, perhaps the Clarinet Sonata (Op. 129) is now better known than anything else. This sonata has a most moving second movement, entitled *Caoine* (an Irish lament). Taken as a whole, his chamber music, however, is not nearly as impressive as some of his choral music; it is severely 'classical', dominated by the German masters – especially by Brahms (Stanford's senior by nineteen years). Occasionally, as in the clarinet sonata, with its

Irish lament, there are touches of nationalism in his music, as (in an English form) we find also in Parry, and (in a Scottish form) in Mackenzie. One of Stanford's best and most rewarding works is certainly his First Trio, Op. 35, dedicated to the famous pianist of those days, Hans von Bülow – who played frequently at the famous series of Popular Concerts ('Pops'), which for forty years (1858–98) gave Londoners their main opportunity of hearing chamber music. On receiving a copy of this work, von Bülow wrote to Stanford: 'Good gracious! What wonderful progress your country is making owing to your genius.' (Perhaps significantly, he went on to couple this trio with Brahms Op. 108, as the two best pieces of music that had been dedicated to him.) The spirit of Brahms is certainly obvious, right from the opening bars of the work:

The influence of Stanford as a teacher was very considerable; that there was something of genius in his method seems to be proved by the distinguished careers of so many of his pupils – Frank Bridge, Herbert Howells, John Ireland, Eugène Goossens, and many others.

The chamber-music output of Parry was also considerable, including three string quartets, a string quintet, three piano trios, a piano quartet, and a nonet for wind instruments, none of which is heard to-day. That Parry's music has sincerity, strength, and a character of its own is undeniable – but these qualities were not best expressed in his chamber compositions, but, as with Stanford, rather in his big choral works. Nevertheless, it would be interesting to hear the forgotten nonet for wind instruments, which was undertaken 'as an experiment' in 1887.

Parry is spoken of as a liberator – an important historic figure in the emancipation of British music. The real emancipation, however, came with Sir Edward Elgar (1857–1934). In composition Elgar was self-taught; he accepted the German-dominated background of musical England as he found it, just as Handel accepted the Italian style of composition; and, also like Handel, he made of his material something highly individual and significant by the sheer greatness of his musical personality. In this he outshone Stanford and Parry, whose achievement had been along similar lines, but less telling, less original.

Elgar's three chamber-music works – the Violin Sonata, the String Quartet, and the Piano Quintet – are all dated 'Brinkwells, 1918'. Written when the composer was sixty-one, they are exercises in self-discipline and economy of texture. The quintet, with 'its serious purpose and high plane of thought' (Basil Maine) is of greater importance than the other two slighter works. In the quartet, however, Elgar expresses something very English and pastoral in the second movement:

H. C. Colles tells us how he came across Vaughan Williams (b. 1872) as a student at the Royal College of Music in the nineties, and no one expected wonderful things from him; his music made no impression comparable to that of the young Coleridge-Taylor (1875–1912) and William Hurlstone (1876–1906), both of whom died too young to fulfil what promise they had – though Hurlstone's charming chamber music is still sometimes played. Music, we know, did not come easily to Vaughan Williams – which makes his achievement as a composer all the more astounding. He has laboriously evolved a personal style, which, starting from a genuine assimilation of folk-song and the early polyphony of this country, has developed and expanded magnificently, always with a clear sense of purpose, and in terms always of our national heritage and no other. A musical personality such as this has not existed since the seventeenth century, and the work done by Vaughan Williams brought new life and vigour to English music and suggested new paths. It is Vaughan Williams who is really the 'national hero', in our reawakening to 'national consciousness', rather than Elgar; and his labours resulted in the re-emergence of a relatively pure stream which had gone underground at the end of the seventeenth century. A somewhat similar path, but very isolated and reaching back to far more remote musical sources, was followed by Gustav Holst (1874–1934) – but with less positive, less integrated results. Frederick Delius (1862–1934) might be said to have avoided the issue of any national heritage by retiring into a world of his own. Bernard van Dieren (1884–1936) – who was Dutch-born, but lived in England – is also an isolated figure, whose music seems entirely personal, related to no tradition which could give it meaning for the listener; and too often (although in his later life he tended to a simpler mode of expression) the form of the music suggests a purely mathematical abstraction. Of these composers, it is certainly Vaughan Williams who has the clearest sense of direction.

As with Delius and Holst, the amount of chamber music which Vaughan Williams has written is small: two string quartets, a 'Phantasy' string quintet, and an early piano quintet and horn quintet (both of which have been scrapped). The first of the string quartets (written about 1908 and revised in 1921) is characteristic of the composer's early style, with its melodic simplicity and regularity of form, its use of the Dorian mode in the slow movement.

The second quartet belongs to a much later period of the composer's development, the late years of the second world war – the same time as the great Fifth Symphony. The second movement (characteristically called 'Romance') is in a contrapuntal style suggestive of the seventeenth-century fantasia:

It was at a National Gallery concert in 1944 that the Menges String Quartet gave the first performance of this second quartet of Vaughan Williams. The remarkable series of National Gallery Lunch-time Concerts (1939–46), organized by Dame Myra Hess, was, incidentally, one of the earliest musical ventures of the second world war, and continued into peace-time. The object was to provide daily recitals and chamber music concerts of short duration but high quality. It was said that they became symbolic of the cultural life which the nation was fighting to preserve.

Mention of Vaughan Williams's 'Phantasy' Quintet for Strings (1910) brings to mind the name of W. W. Cobbett (1847–1937), thanks to whom it was written. British chamber music of the twentieth century certainly owes a very great debt to Cobbett. A highly successful business man, he was able to retire at sixty and devote the last thirty years of his life to the cause of chamber music. 'I made propaganda for an art,' he said, 'highly considered by every true musician, yet, strange to say, somewhat neglected.' The compiling and editing of his international *Cyclopedic Survey of*

Chamber Music, published in co-operation with the Oxford University Press in 1929, was in every way a magnificent achievement. The work, as useful and interesting to-day as when it was first published, remains as a monument to his inexhaustible enthusiasm. In 1905 he instituted a series of competitions and commissions which did much to stimulate the writing of chamber music by British and other composers. The form of composition he favoured was that of the 'Phantasy' – a piece of short duration performed without a break; if the composer desired it could consist of different sections varying in tempo and character. And this was a modern analogue of the old English Fancy, an instrumental form cultivated down to Stuart times. During the first twenty-odd years of activity a large number of British chamber works in this phantasy form had been produced – composition and publication of which had been directly due to Cobbett – the list of composers' names including Vaughan Williams, Bridge, McEwen, York Bowen, Benjamin Dale, and later Howells, Armstrong Gibbs, Alan Bush, John Ireland. Cobbett's other services included the provision of a free public library of chamber music, and the founding of a Chamber Music Association under the aegis of the British Federation of Competitive Music Festivals.

Of the many British composers who established themselves during the first quarter of the twentieth century, the names of Frank Bridge (1879–1941), Sir Arnold Bax (1883–1953), Sir Arthur Bliss (b. 1891) and Herbert Howells (b. 1892) are the most important in the field of chamber music.

It was chiefly as a prolific chamber-music composer that Bridge made his reputation; but he was also well known as a fine viola player and conductor. Throughout his compositions one finds always the most excellent craftsmanship and surefootedness. His early works (composed after four years' study with Stanford) are conservative, often impetuous, fairly innocuous, always showing a tremendous facility. The 'Phantasy' Quartet for Piano and Strings (1910) sums up the early style; and according to Herbert Howells, 'there are few modern chamber works – English or other –

more fluent, more judicious in gesture and technical "behaviour"'. Ernest Walker, too, praises its originality and imaginativeness. But from 1920 onwards Bridge underwent a change to modernity, towards a more 'European' form of utterance: his work becomes full of augmented intervals, extreme chromaticism, even a feeling of polytonality, and rhythmic experiment. Here is an example taken from his Fourth String Quartet (1937):

Ex.8

Bridge's music has not yet had the recognition it deserves. Sir Arnold Bax was also a composer of tremendous natural facility, and from the beginning a prolific chamber-music composer. He was a mixture of many things: as a man of letters and a poet he was deeply influenced by Irish folklore and literature – by all things Irish; he was a wanderer in many lands absorbing many influences; his temperament was highly sensuous, as is shown in his music; he was a mystic and a pantheist; he seemed to prefer blurred outlines and unclear textures. His music is imaginative, nostalgic, decorative, picaresque, seldom subtle. Of his large chamber-music output, the Nonet for Flute, Oboe, Clarinet, Harp, and Strings (1931) is the most interesting in musical content, and has a precision and discipline which the other chamber works generally lack.

The present Master of the Queen's Musick, Sir Arthur
Bliss, started his career as an *enfant terrible*, high-spirited,
reckless, Stravinskyish, eccentric, completely on the surface.
Since then he has become more traditional and diatonic,
but with many asperities; and he is apt to be hard and
unyielding even when he is lyrical. Amongst his chamber
music we find some of his best compositions: they show a
great range of inventiveness and technical brilliance. The
Quintet for Clarinet and Strings, composed in 1931, remains
his most beautifully written chamber work. The two string
quartets – bold and vigorous in expression – are both works
of great interest. The following example, from the second
of them, in F minor, written in 1950, is typical of the composer's fine craftsmanship: it shows the rhythmical pattern
from which most of the *Scherzo* movement grows:

The work was dedicated to the members of the Griller
Quartet, as a tribute to one of our most internationally-
famous chamber-music teams on the occasion of the
twentieth anniversary of their coming-together.

Herbert Howells has shown from the start a brilliant contrapuntal technique, natural lyricism, and intellectual and emotional qualities of a highly personal kind – all of which found their most convincing early expression through the medium of chamber music. The Piano Quartet, Op. 21, written at the age of twenty-four, gained a Carnegie award and publication. It is dedicated (characteristically) 'to the Hill at Chosen and Ivor Gurney who knows it' – and the work has a hauntingly beautiful slow movement, such as one frequently finds in Howells. The piano begins:

We are told that the influences which affected Howells's early work included the associations of his native Gloucestershire, folk-songs (particularly English and Welsh), modal Tudor counterpoint, and his studies under Stanford. He stands in the same kind of relationship to our national heritage as does Vaughan Williams. But Howells's career as a composer seems to have been seriously affected by his busy life as a musical educationalist. Something has gone seriously wrong somewhere: works which followed the early period of fertility showed a disquieting over-complication, of a kind that could not come off satisfactorily in performance, though the musical content was often very fine indeed. Not so long ago, however, he seemed to start again (so to speak) as a composer, in a style which was far more integrated; and a recently published work is an excellent clarinet sonata. From earlier times also we have the impressive Piano Quartet, the Phantasy String Quartet (built on folk-song-like tunes of the composer's own invention), the String Quartet called *In Gloucestershire*, a beautiful 'Rhapsodic' Quintet for Clarinet and Strings – all of which are, as has been said, true chamber music and truly English in the best sense.

A composer who has made persistent efforts to bring his own chamber music to the notice of players and audiences is Josef Holbrooke (b. 1878); but somehow it has never caught on. His list of published works is impressively long and the titles of some are alluring – such as the Third String Quartet, which is called *The Pickwick Club* (a work, incidentally, in thirteen movements); or the Quintet for Piano and Strings called *Diabolique* (a title which, however, does not fulfil expectations). Richard Walthew describes Holbrooke's contribution as 'spontaneous, full-blooded and sincere' – all of which it may be. It is also to a large extent very miscellaneous, laboured, uncritical, unsubtle, and unrewardingly awkward for the players.

Sir Eugène Goossens (b. 1893) might be said to combine a French sensuousness, a Teutonic muddiness, and a Stravinskyish cleverness of manipulation – the whole conceived on a lighthearted level. As such he has written a good deal of exciting and quite interesting chamber music, ranging from *Five Impressions of a Holiday* for piano, flute (or violin), and cello – a most attractive work – to a nonet for wind instruments. About his 'Phantasy' String Quartet, Op. 12 (1915), Cobbett said: 'Of all the one-movement works written round the ideas promoted by the Phantasy Competition, this work realizes best my own conception of a short, concise, and essentially *fantastic* composition.' And the slow section certainly shows that Goossens is capable of writing with a warm tenderness and beauty.

Both John Ireland (b. 1879) and E. J. Moeran (1894–1950) found through the intimate medium of chamber music a more truly characteristic form of expression than in their more grandiose works. As a pupil of Stanford, Ireland acquired a solid traditional foundation on which to build, and this was noticeably absent in the case of the younger Moeran, who in London in 1920 came to John Ireland for guidance and was strongly influenced by his harmonic style, which is a combination of traditional procedures, modality, and impressionism – the 'Englishness' is that of restraint and sanity, in keeping with the uneventfulness of his outward life.

Ireland's early 'Phantasy' Trio of 1908, revised for publication, is the earliest work which the composer did not wish to suppress. This and the First Violin Sonata were both written for Cobbett competitions, and won prizes, the latter coming first out of 134 entries from all parts of the world. The later Piano Trio and the very interesting 'Phantasy' Sonata for Clarinet and Piano, written for the late Frederick Thurston, are two of Ireland's most satisfactory works.

In Moeran, however, we find far less consistency of style and purpose – and the style is sometimes rather affectedly homespun. Some of Moeran's chamber music certainly has imaginative charm and vitality, such as the early String Quartet (1921) and the more mature String Trio (1931).

A number of British composers of this time were helped in the publication of their works by the Carnegie Trust, which from 1917 to 1928 bore the cost of publishing some of their chamber-music works. Composers encouraged in this way in their early days included Walton, Howells, Bliss, Dyson, Arthur Benjamin, Alan Bush, Gerald Finzi, and many others.

During the first half of the twentieth century an immense amount of chamber music has been written by British composers; but it is probably true to say that we have produced nothing so far that is as good or striking in this field as the best of some other countries – nothing to equal, say, the string quartet of Debussy or Ravel, the quartets of Bartók, Stravinsky's *Duo Concertant*, or the chamber works of Bloch.

Of the rest of the older generation of composers who have written chamber music, it is extremely doubtful whether, in most cases, the works are of real lasting value, though many may well be revived from time to time. J. B. McEwen (1868–1948), a Scottish composer who became principal of the Royal Academy of Music, left a mass of chamber music, some of which is vital and strongly personal. Cyril Scott (b. 1879) has written works in a very limited personal idiom, influenced by oriental philosophy and theosophy. York Bowen (b. 1884), a brilliant pianist and composer, is no doubt under-rated as a composer. James Friskin and his wife, Rebecca Clarke (who were both born in the same year, 1886), have both had successes in Britain and in America with chamber-music works. And there is the scholarly, refined music of Cyril Rootham (1875–1938). Arthur Benjamin (b. 1893) always writes with slickness and vitality: his chamber music includes a charming and accomplished (though slight) sonatina for violin and piano (1925). Edric Cundell (b. 1893) won the *Daily Telegraph* chamber-music prize in 1934 with his Second String Quartet. Does his music deserve to be better known? And Armstrong Gibbs (b. 1889) won the *Daily Telegraph* prize the year before with his String Quartet in A Major, Op. 73, and was awarded the Cobbett Gold Medal for chamber music in 1934. He has written some most attractive works, especially those for string quartet. Thomas Dunhill (1877–1946) wrote an important book, *Chamber Music*, a treatise for students, in 1913. His own compositions were well written, if unadventurous. Gordon Jacob (b. 1895) has written much; and it is of most unequal quality; some of the later works are the best: the Quartet for Oboe and Strings (1938) and the Quintet for Clarinet and Strings (1942) are charming, light, and English in style. ... And the fastidious work of Charles Wood (1866–1926) – does it deserve to be neglected? ... And Ethel Smyth (1858–1944) – what has become of her Brahmsian chamber music?

Richard Walthew (1872–1951) has been quite a well-known name in British chamber music, and not only for his serious, well-written works. He is associated with that remarkable London series of Sunday concerts which started at South Place in 1887 – providing chamber music at popular prices – and still continues to-day at the Conway Hall. Walthew's compositions have been played regularly at these concerts – including his 'Phantasy' Quintet for Piano and Strings (a Cobbett commission) which was performed at the 1,000th of them. Another name associated with these South Place concerts is that of Alfred J. Clements – honorary secretary and organizer of the concerts for nearly fifty-one years, from their inception in 1887 until his death in 1938. A Clements Memorial Fund provides an important annual prize for a chamber music work. ...

We come now to the composers who have been born since 1900.

Sir William Walton (b. 1902) was born lucky. His early String Quartet (since withdrawn) was played at the first festival of the I.S.C.M. at Salzburg in 1923. Although it was not a success, it brought his name very much to the fore. An earlier Piano Quartet, however – completed when he was seventeen – survived (even after being lost for two years in the post between Italy and England), and fairly recently it stood up well to a broadcast. The judgement of the Carnegie Trust, who paid for its publication in 1924, was not far wrong when it spoke of clear texture, restraint, good writing throughout, and rising to moments of great beauty and nobility. The style, the frank romanticism, the fastidious care with which everything is done, already points towards the individuality that was to come. More than a quarter of a century later, in 1947, appeared the String Quartet which is one of Walton's finest achievements. There is here a maturity, a mellowness of expression, and, as in all Walton's best music, the feeling of high tension and purpose. The key is mostly A minor, with a slow movement in F major.

The first movement, *Allegro*, is the most extended of the four. The main theme, which is a very characteristic one, is stated right at the beginning by the viola, with an equally important counter-subject in the second violin:

Both these themes are developed in many different ways during the movement, and there is a second subject in a rhythmic pattern which we have come to associate with this composer. Later in the movement, the viola has the following version of its opening theme, and this is treated fugally:

The *Scherzo, presto*, recalls the *Scherzo* of Walton's Symphony, but is less 'malicious'. It is a short and brilliantly witty movement; biting, but without bitterness. Then follows an extended slow movement, contemplative and very personal in character, of great beauty and depth of feeling. The viola, which plays such an important part in the work as a whole, sets the tone of the discussion throughout this movement. Its first theme is:

The last movement is a short *rondo*, strongly rhythmic in character, with a contrasted lyrical section, and it brings the work to a most exciting conclusion.

Michael Tippett (b. 1905) and Edmund Rubbra (b. 1901) both dig deep into their country's musical past for inspiration. Tippett is fascinated by the counterpoint, the cross-rhythms, of the Elizabethans, bringing to them a fertile musical brain and a rich imagination, made richer by contact with Bartók, Stravinsky, Hindemith, Berg, but apt to run riot. In his excellent Second String Quartet he comes nearest to a co-ordinated form of expression which is highly individual and at times very moving. The composer tells us: 'The first movement is partly derived from madrigal technique, where each part may have its own rhythm, and the music is propelled by the differing accents, which tend to thrust each other forward'. There is a slow movement in the form of a fugue, and a brilliant *Scherzo* full of ingenious rhythmic devices. The form of the *Scherzo* is interesting, being in three sections – the second a repeat of the first a minor third higher, and the third a more extended repetition a major third higher again. The Finale (*allegro appassionato*) is rich and elaborate in texture, and of compelling intensity.

A pupil of Holst, Rubbra in his music has the same musical roots as his master, and what he is striving to express is somewhat similar in spirit and purpose. His music may well strike the listener as evocative and deeply meaningful in its solemn, mystic beauty, its melodic richness, suppleness of rhythm, and contrapuntal strength. Rubbra's Second String Quartet (commissioned by the Griller Quartet in 1950) is an excellent and important example of modern English chamber music. The key is given as E flat, which signifies a tonal centre, but without any feeling of adhering to classical usage. 'That would indeed be marking time on the spot', the composer tells us in his own analytical notes. 'But', he continues, 'it does mean that however fluid the tonal relationships are – and it is part of my purpose to get rid of rigidity in these matters – they are all seen by the analytical eye or heard by the analytical ear as controlled impulses emanating from one centre.'

The Second Quartet of Rubbra begins with a four-note motif in the second violin, which is 'mirrored' in the viola:

Ex.14

It is out of this motif and this 'mirror' idea that the material
of the first movement takes shape, developing methodically
and rhythmically, rising to a climax of great intensity.
The movement which follows (in D major – *vivace assai*) is
entitled *Scherzo polimetrico* and is a complex *moto perpetuo* in
triplets, with bar-lines that rarely coincide for all the
instruments. This is followed by a slow movement, *Cavatina*
– starting in G major – simple and song-like, in two sections;
a striking feature is the rhythmic suppleness of the music,
in spite of a regular 3/4 rhythm. In the Finale, *allegro*, the
thematic material seems to grow naturally out of material
previously heard, and brings us back to the original key,
leading to the *Chorale* coda – the *Chorale* theme being played
by each of the upper three strings in turn, with accompanying triplets.

Whether, in the music of Benjamin Britten (b. 1913), the
manner is more important than the matter, and whether
in addition to his great talents there is any particular
depth of feeling, will no doubt go on being debated. In
any case, a sensible attitude to his chamber music works
would surely be that they are interesting experiments. They
are as yet few: a Phantasy for Oboe and Strings (1932),
the Suite for Violin and Piano (1934–5), two String Quartets (1941 and 1945), and the *Lachrimae* variations for Viola
and Piano (1950).

The Second String Quartet – the most frequently played
of Britten's chamber-music works – was written to commemorate the 250th anniversary of Purcell's death, and the
last movement is in the form of a 'chacony', suggested by
Purcell.

Of British composers born since 1900 – Walton, Britten, Tippett, Rubbra, can be said to stand in a definite relationship to our musical heritage – to the traditions which petered out at the end of the seventeenth century to be revived at the end of the nineteenth century. The connection may be tenuous, but it is difficult to deny that an added significance is gained by this relationship. Some would go so far as to say that if a composer is not in some way national in his expression he cannot be a true composer – since his work can only be interpreted significantly in terms of his natural heritage. What then of Berkeley, Rawsthorne, Searle, Lutyens, Fricker, and many others, in whose music it seems impossible to trace any such relationship? Their music, as music, would appear, on the face of it, not to belong to England in any obvious way, if at all. Does it thereby fail in a fundamentally important way? Can it make up for this lack of heritage by the sheer force of its own personality? The answer may be that if one's personality is as big as (say) Handel's, that may be possible – but otherwise it is most unlikely.

The pleasant but not very striking music of such men as Gerald Finzi (1901–56) or William Wordsworth (b. 1908, a descendant of the poet's brother) is arguably 'English' in style. But in the case of Peter Racine Fricker (b. 1920) – it would only be possible, as far as national identification is concerned, to place his work 'somewhere in Europe'. Fricker is partly of French descent, and he studied with that very eclectic composer, Matyas Seiber, to whom his String Quartet (1949) was dedicated and to whom he obviously owes much. He first really attracted attention in 1947 when his wind quintet was awarded the Alfred J. Clements Prize. The style he has developed is a powerful, personal, somewhat grim and uncompromising form of 'twelve-note' technique, freely applied – and in his general outlook he seems to have much in common with the German composers of the present day. The finale of the wind quintet is a fascinating experiment in rhythm – the twelve quavers of each bar being grouped 3, 2, 2, 2, 3:

A very different kind of continental influence is shown in the music of Lennox Berkeley (b. 1903). The best-known of his various chamber music-works is a string trio (1944). He has French blood in his veins, he studied in France with the famous Nadia Boulanger, and he writes like a French composer – with elegance, refinement, lightness, and charm, in a style which is both modern and extremely attractive.

Nothing could be less English than atonality. But two English composers – Humphrey Searle (b. 1915) and Elisabeth Lutyens (b. 1906) have tried by a free and romantic use of 'twelve-note' methods to make it a natural form of expression. Searle's spiritual home seems to lie somewhere between Schönberg (or Webern, under whom he studied) and Liszt. His Intermezzo, Op. 8, for eleven instruments, is 'in memory of Webern', and his 'Passacaglietta in nomine Arnold Schönberg' for string quartet (1949) was written for Schönberg's seventy-fifth birthday. Elisabeth Lutyens's style is similar to Searle's, but less definite in its intentions. Her chamber-music output includes six string quartets, and a string quintet (1936–7) in the form of a complex five-part fantasia – a form adopted by many recent composers in preference to sonata-form. Searle and Lutyens seem to have had singularly little influence on the work of other composers.

Besides Lutyens, there are three other women composers, all of whom are fairly important names in chamber music: Priaulx Rainier (b. 1903 in South Africa), Elizabeth Maconchy (b. 1907), and Phyllis Tate (b. 1911). Priaulx Rainier's style – fragmentary and rhythmically somewhat barbaric – is certainly the most original of the three, and not at all in terms of the Royal Academy of Music, where she is a professor. But then, like Berkeley, she has been a pupil of Nadia Boulanger in Paris. Her first string quartet has been recorded under the auspices of the British Council. Maconchy's six string quartets, which were all broadcast in a series by the B.B.C. Third Programme not very long ago, are written in a free contrapuntal style, which becomes, as the composer herself says, 'a passionately intellectual and intellectually passionate discourse'. Phyllis Tate has given us something original and unusual in her Sonata for Clarinet and Cello (1947).

Of all English composers to-day, one of the most in-dividual is Alan Rawsthorne (b. 1905), who attracted considerable interest as early as 1938 when his Theme and Variations for Two Violins was given at the Festival of the I.S.C.M. in London. His careful, anything-but-fluent manner of composition is without definite key feeling, but certainly not 'atonal'. It is a highly individual style, based on rapidly-shifting tonal centres. Rawsthorne (like Bernard van Dieren) is something of a lone figure. And the same might be said of Benjamin Frankel (b. 1906), a well-known name in film music and, since the second world war, a composer of serious music also. After an early career of the most varied kind, he shows now a most eclectic versatility, with something of the yearning sadness of Bloch, with whom he shares a racial affinity.

From the racial to the ideological. Communism has played an important part in the life and work of Alan Bush (b. 1900); but whether or not one believes that social aspirations can find expression in music, it is possible to appreciate simply as a fine piece of string-quartet writing his *Dialectic*, which is probably his best piece of chamber music. (It was performed at the 1935 I.S.C.M. Festival in Prague, and has been recorded under the auspices of the British Council.) The early chamber music of Alan Bush did much to establish his reputation; the String Quartet in A Minor, Op. 4, gained a Carnegie award and publication. His style is powerful, individual, and as English as the Agincourt Song. With him is to some extent associated the name of Bernard Stevens (b. 1916), whose piano trio won the Clements Prize in 1942. Like Alan Bush, Bernard Stevens is connected with the Workers' Music Association – though his music is less ideological, just as it is less English.

In this section devoted to chamber music in England, I have been able to give little more than a general impression of the work of the more important composers in this field since Purcell. The list of composers mentioned does not, of course, pretend to be anything like complete. As far as the present day is concerned, the list could be greatly extended. I have said nothing, for example, of the impressive octet for wind instruments by the unprolific Howard Ferguson (b. 1908), nor the virile, somewhat Germanic chamber music of Arnold Cooke (b. 1906), nor the powerful and intellectual string quartets of Robert Simpson (b. 1921). And mention should also be made of three important foreign composers who have made England their home since the nineteen-thirties and written a lot of chamber music: Franz Reizenstein (born in Germany in 1911), 'the English Hindemith', has been a pupil of both Hindemith and Vaughan Williams; Matyas Seiber (born in Budapest in 1905), already mentioned as the teacher of Fricker, is certainly one of the most alive and amazingly versatile minds working amongst us; and Egon Wellesz (born in Austria, 1885), who lives and works in Oxford, 'the home of lost causes' (amongst which we may now no doubt include atonality).

It has been said that chamber music in England is a

vicious circle: not a large enough discriminating public to produce sufficient ensembles, and not sufficient ensembles to create a large enough discriminating public. Furthermore, a solo pianist who gives a recital at the Wigmore Hall is more likely to get an audience than a string quartet. The Arts Council may help with grants, as it may help also in the formation of recital and chamber music clubs in many parts of the country. Broadcasting also can be of service in giving dates to ensembles (with which comes considerable publicity) and in stimulating more general interest in chamber music by the performance of a wide range of works which can be listened to by vast numbers of people who would not otherwise hear this kind of music.

'The intimate speech of musicians' is perhaps a reasonable definition of chamber music. This kind of music is not usually written (we may suppose) with an eye to wide success – nor with monetary gain in view – but rather in response to a genuine inner compulsion. We can with truth say that no country has produced such a wide range, such a rich variety of chamber music during the present century as England has done. And amongst this variety there is certainly much that is admirable. But when are we going to produce a really outstanding chamber-music work?

16

French Chamber Music (from 1700)

EDWARD LOCKSPEISER

INTRODUCTION

THE main French contribution to chamber music is of comparatively recent date. It is a highly distinctive contribution forming part of one of the oldest musical traditions of Europe, but it is nevertheless a contribution which also has its roots in the great classical and romantic traditions of Central Europe. During the age of Mozart and Haydn, the French, in the sphere of chamber music, were learning from the Italians; later they were ready to learn from Beethoven, Schumann, and Mendelssohn; and later still there is a slight Russian influence. As opposed, therefore, to the impression, current nowadays, of the French as an insular musical nation, this shows the composers from Couperin to Ravel, whose chamber works are to be considered here, to have been, on the contrary, remarkably open and alive to vital trends in musical thought wherever they may have originated.

The seventeenth and eighteenth centuries were periods in which an Italian influence was predominant in French instrumental music. The music that made the greatest appeal were the works for small combinations of strings by the Italian violinists, Vivaldi and Corelli. To-day the subtle stylistic differences between the conceptions of the violin of the early Italian and French composers are largely lost. But broadly speaking, it may be said that the Italians showed a virtuoso-like feeling for the instrument, writing in a florid manner with many arpeggios, while the French concentrated on intricate ornamentation. The seventeenth-century French composers for the violin also wrote for the instrument with a lighter sense of vivacity and a more slender, though perhaps a more elegant, sense of lyricism.

Their melodies are more delicately shaped and sweeter in sentiment. In his trios François Couperin absorbed the Italian manner, notably in the one dedicated to Corelli, while his suites establish the French manner. The trios for strings and harpsichord by Rameau, arranged by one of his pupils for string sextet, also follow this manner, and the difference between the subtle detail of the French school and the exuberance of the Italians is apparent if these works of Rameau are contrasted with the *concerti grossi* of Vivaldi. A later development of this French style is evident in the violin sonatas, often displaying a beautiful melodic gift, by Jean-Marie Leclair.

In the eighteenth century concerts of chamber music were frequently given in Paris at the homes of the nobility, and at the Concerts Spirituels. Though many contemporary French works were played at these gatherings, the Italians held the field. After the Revolution the violinist Pierre Baillot organized the first public concerts of chamber music in Paris, but here again they were devoted not to works by native composers but mainly to the quartets of Haydn and Mozart. It was some time before the French composers attempted to imitate them. There was a vogue for a short time for the quartets of two foreign musicians settled in France, Reicha and Cherubini, and, about the middle of the century, for the chamber works for various combinations of instruments by a now almost forgotten composer, Louise Farrenc. She was considered a pioneer in her day and wrote, according to contemporary reports, in a style which was a cross between Mozart and Mendelssohn. The Anglo-French composer George Onslow, a pupil of Reicha, wrote many quartets and quintets, of little originality but which had a temporary vogue.

Baillot also introduced to France the early quartets of Beethoven. The later quartets of Beethoven were not heard in France until 1852 when they were publicly performed by the Maurin Quartet. Thereafter they were frequently given by several French ensembles, notably by the Armingaud Quartet in which the viola player, Edouard Lalo, was to be one of the founders of modern French chamber music. Beethoven's chamber works appear to have made, even at that early date, a great impression on forward-looking minds, but unlike the works of the Italian composers in France in the eighteenth century, the various styles of the Beethoven quartets were never completely absorbed by the creative musical minds. The nearest approach to the spirit of these styles is in the chamber music of César Franck. But by this time the essentially philosophical aesthetic of Beethoven was less admired in France than the romanticism of Schumann and of course Wagner.

In 1856 the *Gazette Musicale* declared that 'a new era had arrived, the era of the quartet'. Chamber-music societies abounded, their repertory, however, consisting almost exclusively of works by the German classical and romantic composers. A society formed for the performance of French works met with little success. The facts are that although chamber music was extremely popular in France throughout the nineteenth century, it was long considered to be primarily the domain of German musicians. Throughout this period the successful French composers, Berlioz, Gounod, and Offenbach were content to hold their dominating position in orchestral music or the theatre.

A reaction to all this came after the Franco-Prussian war when Saint-Saëns, César Franck, Édouard Lalo, Gabriel Fauré, and others founded a new organization, the *Société Nationale*, with the motto 'Ars Gallica'. The rules were drawn up by Alexis de Castillon, a pupil of Franck whose quintet, a powerful and original work, had earlier been performed in Paris at the Schumann Society. The aim of the new society was to encourage native composers. It had immediate and remarkable success. It was at the concerts of the *Société Nationale* that Franck's principal chamber works were first given, the violin sonata, the quintet, and the quartet. Saint-Saëns, d'Indy, Chausson, Magnard, and Florent Schmitt came forward with new chamber works; and it was at the *Société Nationale* that the first performances were given of what are still considered to be the two most original works in French chamber music, the string quartets of Debussy and Ravel.

Obviously the *Société Nationale* came into existence in response to the demands of an independent spirit that was breaking through. It is interesting to observe, however, that the very musicians who were responsible for the creation of the society were soon to become aware of its limitations. A distinctive school of French chamber music had at last emerged, but limited as it was by the framework of the *Société Nationale*, it was in danger of becoming ingrown. Foreign works, including the quartet of Strauss and chamber works by Russian composers, were accordingly given in their programmes, and in 1909 Gabriel Fauré became the president of a rival society, the *Société Musicale Indépendante*, with prominent foreign composers, including Stravinsky and Bartók, on the committee. Their aim was frankly cosmopolitan, as wide in aim in fact as the eighteenth and early nineteenth-century societies that had been ready to welcome works by composers from all over Europe. New French works were of course given at the *Société Musicale Indépendante*, notably the string quartets by Milhaud, but they had no priority. Thus the wheel had turned full circle. The two societies continue to co-exist, demonstrating in the sphere of chamber music an exemplary spirit of freedom and artistic interchange.

LALO

THE chamber works of Edouard Lalo (1823–93), though they are seldom heard nowadays, were the efforts of a pioneer. A French composer of Spanish ancestry, Lalo wrote both in the descriptive, picturesque manner, revealing affinities with Bizet and Chabrier, and also in a more severe style using the orthodox sonata forms. He was thus a composer with allegiances to two musical civilizations. As a member of the Armingaud Quartet, he had become thoroughly acquainted with their repertoire from Haydn to Schumann, and it was natural that he should have taken certain of these works as his models. Lalo's chamber music shows particularly his admiration for Weber and Schumann. Of his three trios, the last written in 1880 is by far the best, containing a splendid *scherzo* (later orchestrated) and showing in the slow movement an inspired sense of melody. Together with the first quartet by Fauré, written at about the same time, this third trio of Lalo, consistently inspired and certainly worth reviving, laid the foundations of the modern school of French chamber music. The second trio is also a pleasing work, though more derivative, and this is also true of the string quartet and the two piano and violin sonatas. The style of Lalo's chamber works, on the whole less individual than his orchestral and dramatic works, is still somewhat impure. Nevertheless they show the birth of a new spirit and some of them contain pages of real beauty.

SAINT-SAËNS

THE works by Saint-Saëns cover a much wider field. In 1865 he wrote his first quintet and the list of his chamber works continues until his death in 1921. An extremely fluent and versatile composer, Saint-Saëns easily adapted himself to the demands of any form – the string quartet, the piano trio, the piano quintet, the violin sonata, and the cello sonata – not to mention the considerable number of works he wrote for wind instruments. On the whole Saint-Saëns is at his best in his youthful works. He was blessed with an ease of writing (which some consider to have been his undoing), a stylish manner, seldom original, but always skilled and accomplished, so that almost everything he wrote leaves the impression of music neatly turned out and a joy, therefore, to listen to for its faultless workmanship. When this fluency of manner is allied to genuine inspiration he can still provide those delights of charm and elegance associated with his period. He was never a deep, nor even a warm-hearted composer: his personality was remote and frigid. Consequently people are surprised to-day to learn that Mozart was his ideal – Mozart who was also the ideal of several other seemingly un-Mozartian composers, among them Gounod, Tchaikovsky, and Richard Strauss. All these composers – and this is particularly true of Saint-Saëns – absorbed and reconstructed the spirit of Mozart in their own way; which is what, in our day, Stravinsky has similarly attempted in *The Rake's Progress*. Hence the association of Mozart and Saint-Saëns, shocking as it may seem to the purists, was a natural and also a fruitful artistic phenomenon which, as we shall see later, was to have far-reaching results. Other features in the chamber music of Saint-Saëns point to his admiration for Mendelssohn, whose lightness of touch he was sometimes able to emulate, and to Liszt whom he revered for something more than this composer's pianistic virtuosity. Beethoven and Schumann were outside his world, as was Brahms, and his knowledge of Bach was mainly a technical knowledge – Saint-Saëns was a clever writer of counterpoint. Throughout his life he greatly feared the innovations of Debussy whom he outlived and whom he never ceased to denigrate in a caustic and sardonic manner. This has redounded on Saint-Saëns – unfortunately, for his achievement has thus been unjustly belittled. His detractors amusingly maintain that what he provided was *de la mauvaise musique bien écrite*. On the other hand, he had an important influence on both Fauré and Ravel, particularly on their chamber works. The persistent figurations of Fauré and the delicate workmanship of Ravel can each be traced back to the chamber works of Saint-Saëns, rudimentary as they are in many ways. All of which is to make a plea for a revival of some of Saint-Saëns's chamber works – those of his youth particularly, like the First Cello Sonata and the First Piano Trio. These are vivacious works, spirited and alive. The lightness of his texture in the early Piano Quartet and Piano Quintet were obviously imitated by Fauré in his own works for these combinations. Among Saint-Saëns's later works it would be interesting to hear the Second String Quartet, written as late as 1919 in what looks to be a deliberate revival of an eighteenth-century manner, and also the curious *Élégie*

for violin and piano written on the composer's recollection
of a theme by Alexis de Castillon.

FRANCK

SAINT-SAËNS's contribution was by no means negligible,
but the real impetus to French chamber music came from
César Franck in three wonderfully vital and original works,
the Piano Quintet, the Piano and Violin Sonata, and the
String Quartet. In his recent book on Franck Léon Vallas
emphasizes the composer's strong Germanic origin and
associations. 'A Liégois by birth, a Netherlander, later a
Belgian, later still a Frenchman by naturalization, Walloon
by upbringing, French at heart, Franck came none the less
from Germany,' declares this author, the point being that
his ancestry, as it has now been disclosed, was predominantly German on his father's side and, on his mother's
side, purely German. Nowadays when national characteristics of style in composition are hardly discernible, we are
not greatly affected by such racial considerations, but in the
nineteenth century which held to the doctrine of *le style
c'est l'homme même*', the national or racial origin of a composer did very largely determine the stylistic features of his
music. Meyerbeer and Offenbach were naturalized French
composers who had identified themselves with the native
traditions. Theirs was the genius of assimilation: these
foreign-born composers respectively became the creators in
France of the Romantic Grand Opera and the Operetta.
Franck, on the other hand, was a naturalized Frenchman
who was able to impose on his adopted country the romantic ideals of a musical civilization which demonstrably has
its roots not in any of the masters of Latin culture but in
Beethoven, Schumann, and Liszt.

One is tempted to add to this list of Franck's musical
ancestors Schubert and Brahms, for we know that at the
time of the composition of his quartet, Franck was studying
the quartets of these masters, and it is obvious that he must
have learnt much from Schubert's modulations and probably

also from Brahms's sense of form. Weber and Mendelssohn were other sources of inspiration, possibly also Berlioz and certainly Wagner. But when all the origins of Franck's individual style have been traced and identified we are faced with the fact that the sum of all these elements still does not make the whole. By any standard Franck was a powerful and original personality. He created not only a new style; he created a new world. He was an ecstatic composer who pitched music up to an almost constant state of modulation. At the same time he galvanized the structure of his works by the reintroduction of a theme from one movement into the other movements. Form and harmony are masterly in his music; and though the sensuous and impassioned sentiment he expresses has no great variety, the impact of his music on any kind of emotional person is irresistible. Moreover, in his later works the quality of his inspiration is high. The mystical and religious associations of his art may sometimes be debatable but in the best of his music, notably the three chamber works, his inspiration never flags. The reason for this is his wonderful use of chromatic harmony. It is music that is both flexible and taut, as if he were constantly measuring the degree of tension. By this means he takes his great spans of music to the borderline of sentimentality, but unlike some of his followers he does not cross this borderline. He was one of the most sincere of composers who believed that the spirit of music was not in the notes written down on the manuscript paper, but in the actual texture and sound of harmony – he was a realist – as it creeps into the ear and into the soul.

Franck's earliest chamber music consists of a set of three piano trios dedicated to Leopold I, King of the Belgians. They date from about 1840 when the composer was still in his teens. There is a fourth trio of the same period, in a single movement, dedicated to Liszt. Apart from the first trio of the set which Franck obviously wrote spontaneously and which shows his style in embryo, these early trios, which were the outcome of an effort on the part of the composer's father to commercialize the young Franck's talents, have little musical interest for us to-day. It was not until forty years later, in 1880, that Franck's first big chamber work, the Piano Quintet, was given at the recently formed *Société Nationale*. Here Franck uses the cyclic form which he is held to have originated. The principle of this form is that there should be one or more themes common to each of the movements of the work. These themes are frequently transformed in regard to dynamics, rhythm, or harmony, yet they are recognizably the same. They are *leitmotiv* of a kind, the recurrence of which creates a mysterious association of ideas. Franck's own description of these themes which he allows to take on so many different guises was that they were 'cousins'. He allows them to germinate like the themes of the Beethoven variations. A unity of purpose, almost a philosophical unity, is thus proclaimed, and although in Franck's mind the cyclic form may have derived from a fusion of the variation form of Beethoven and the *leitmotiv* technique of Wagner, he had nevertheless produced a novel and arresting form. Here is an example of this technique of theme transformation from the piano quintet. The germinating theme appears in the opening movement in A flat:

In the second movement, which naturally uses quite different thematic material, it is suddenly introduced and most beautifully thrown into relief in this form:

Ex. 2   *Lento con molto sentimento*

And it triumphantly reappears in the Finale where it

quite clearly dominates all the other themes of the movement:

The suggestion is made in one of the latest studies of Franck, by Léon Vallas, that the passionate nature of the quintet may itself have been an expression of the composer's admiration for his pupil, the beautiful young Irish poetess and composer, Augusta Holmes. An entirely different view of Franck from the conventional portrait of him as the 'Seraphic Father' is immediately opened up by this suggestion, and indeed from the internal evidence of the music itself it is a very plausible suggestion. To-day this work, written by a devout church musician and organist, still makes its full emotional appeal. In its day, however, that appeal, so clearly bordering on erotic associations, was sufficiently alarming to shock even Liszt, the champion of the musical explorers of his time and whose own works were often inspired by emotional ideas of this order. As for Saint-Saëns, to whom the work was dedicated and who played the piano at the first performance, his attitude amounted to open hostility. He left the platform in a huff, discourteously leaving behind him the score which Franck had publicly offered to him.

The cyclic form is used again in the Piano and Violin Sonata of 1886 presented as a wedding present to the violinist Eugène Ysaÿe. An interesting story illustrating the fervour which Franck's music could arouse is told by Vincent d'Indy of the first performance of the piano and violin sonata by Ysaÿe and Madame Bordes-Pène in Brussels. The performance took place in the hall of a museum. No artificial lighting was allowed and, as the evening wore on, the players could scarcely read their music. By the end of the first movement the concert was about to be cut short, but the enthusiastic audience refused to leave. 'Ysaÿe then struck his music stand with his bow,' d'Indy recounts. ' "*Allons, allons!*" he urged his partner, and the two players plunged in gloom performed the last three movements from memory, producing music that held sovereign sway in the darkness of the night.'

Franck's last work, the String Quartet, is his most ambitious achievement. It is impossible to say whether it is predominantly a work of the heart or of the mind. Its structure, of which a detailed analysis is given by Vincent d'Indy in *Cobbett's Cyclopedic Survey of Chamber Music*, is extremely complex, and although this analysis may help the listener to find his bearings, more performances of this neglected work are nowadays required.

Constantly concerned with finding the appropriate form for his ideas, Franck goes so far in the quartet to lay out the first movement as a gigantic *lied*, the central section of which, including a big fugal development, is a sonata-movement complete in itself. The second movement is a Mendelssohnian *scherzo*; the third is a *lied* in five sections, and the Finale, like the Finale from Beethoven's Choral Symphony, successively recalls the themes of the preceding movements before deciding on the germinal theme of the opening movement as the subject for a huge contrapuntal discussion. Franck with Brahms is here revealed as one of the last composers to have renewed and kept alive the great forms of music inherited from the German Romantic composers. The date of the String Quartet is 1890. Seven months later Franck died, wrestling in his mind in a state of great agony, as we are told, with the development of a fugue that had obsessed him.

Franck had a large number of pupils and his influence persisted in France for at least a generation. It was an intense but not a lasting influence, which in view of his highly personal art is not surprising. His music is ultimately inimitable. The influence of the conservative Saint-Saëns, on the other hand, less conspicuous than the influence of Franck, was nevertheless wider and more beneficent. So, at any rate, it seems to us to-day when the musical personalities of Fauré and Ravel appear to be so much more positive than those of Franck's followers, Chausson and d'Indy.

CHAUSSON AND LEKEU

CHAUSSON is the most interesting of Franck's pupils. But his stature is slender. He lacked the virility of Franck, whom he attempted to emulate, and while much of his music has still its period attraction, it does not on the whole emerge from the lanes and by-paths of his indulgent nostalgia. A persistent mood of melancholy pervades the music of Chausson. The *Chanson perpétuelle* for soprano and piano quintet is the best of his chamber works, a sensitively written work, lush in harmony (Chausson uses the ambiguous chord of the diminished seventh rather than the taut, chromatic harmony of Franck), and attractively sentimental in the style of the minor French poets of the *fin-de-siècle*. The Piano Quartet is less inspired, while the Concerto for piano, violin, and string quartet reflects, besides the style of Franck, many a turn of phrase of Chausson's earlier master, Massenet. A much stronger personality is displayed in the Belgian composer Guillaume Lekeu, who died in 1894 at the age of twenty-four. A high-minded idealist, he studied with Franck for a short time. His remarkable correspondence and the considerable body of music he produced have left his admirers wondering how this young composer, who was inspired chiefly by the late works of Beethoven, might have developed had his life not been cut short. His Piano and Violin Sonata is the best of a series of chamber works which includes a trio, a string quartet, and two works (a cello sonata and a piano quartet) completed by Vincent d'Indy. Other chamber works worth reviving by Franck's pupils are the Piano and Violin Sonata and the powerful Piano Quintet by Gabriel Pierné; the three string quartets and particularly the piano trio by Guy Ropartz; and the *Suite Basque* for flute, two violins, violoncello, and double bass by Charles Bordes. These are works of the Franck school in which the master's manner is reproduced in a more or less personal way. We shall see the wider effects of Franck's influence when we come to consider the chamber works of Vincent d'Indy and also the string quartet of Debussy, the most original of the later French works in the cyclic form.

FAURÉ

LALO, Saint-Saëns, and César Franck had, in their different ways, laid the foundations of a native school of chamber music. The early chamber works of Gabriel Fauré antedate the great works of Franck's maturity, and show an affinity with Saint-Saëns. We now come upon the distinctive chamber-music style to which Lalo and Saint-Saëns had been groping and which finds in Fauré its full expression. For in a sense the whole of the music of Fauré, including the choral works and the piano works, and particularly the songs, is essentially music noted down for personal or private communication. When Fauré's engagement was broken off to Marianne Viardot, daughter of the famous operatic singer Pauline Viardot, he consoled himself by declaring that the proposed marriage would only have orientated his work towards the stage and the opera, for which he felt himself singularly unfitted, and that he was now free to follow his life's ideal which, as he put it, was his '*musique de chambre*'. Fauré's art – and this is particularly true of his concerted works to be considered here – has not only the quiet intimacy of a conversation between musicians; it is deliberately conceived as a sort of monochrome, hushed and suave, and excluding in its civilized manner any hint of rhetoric or romantic violence of expression. This is not to say, however, that the chamber works of Fauré are always slender; some of his later works such as the Second Quartet and the Second Quintet are, on the contrary, extremely powerful and are distinguished by the breadth of their melodies and the tenacity of their musical argument.

In England the appeal of Fauré's is of comparatively recent date. Though he was born over a hundred years ago and was a frequent visitor to this country, it is only in the last generation or so that English musicians have felt an affinity with the essentially sobre qualities of his music. Certain works of Vaughan Williams and also of Berkeley and Britten show, not an influence of Fauré, but, as we now see, similar standards of modesty, sensitiveness, and understatement. Somehow the musical civilizations of England and France seem to find a bridge in the work of Fauré.

Fauré's music was not adventurous in any technical sense, but in his chamber-music conception of what music was to be there were many new subtleties of expression. Drama or conflict is unknown to this urbane musician, but he can charm by the elegance of his discourse, by his long, beautifully sustained melodies spun out with a love of delicate detail and often with a provocative twist of phrase that unexpectedly opens up a new vista or a new layer of musical thought. Although he lived through the eras of the revolutionary works of Debussy and Stravinsky, Fauré's harmony remained predominantly diatonic, and for this reason he was long considered to have been a conservative. The fact is that he was a great traditionalist. It is true that his unobtrusive art was overshadowed by the innovations of the many forward-looking minds among his contemporaries. And it is also true that more than any other composer his master, Saint-Saëns, remained his model. But the pupil was far from a slavish imitator. He endowed the prosaic style of Saint-Saëns with a sense of poetry; the frigid manner of his conservative master is made to glow with human warmth.

Fauré's melodies are not always remarkable in themselves, but as they settle in the mind they usually become so just by the composer's subtle ability to make of the commonplace something fresh, original, and personal. This happens in several ways, but chiefly by means of Fauré's very beautiful modulations. Like Franck, Fauré earnt his living as a professional organist, and it was no doubt his long experience in improvisation at the organ that developed his individual approach to modulation. Now the art of modulation in eighteenth- and nineteenth-century music, particularly in Mozart, Chopin, and Schubert, is a highly personal aspect of the composer's technique, touching upon the whole mysterious mechanism of his harmonic language. But here the musical personality of Fauré is completely opposed to that of his contemporary, Franck, who prized modulation for its own sake, as if harmony was simply not to be maintained in any kind of static state, but was constantly to be intensified or distorted by chromatic inflections. Fauré's harmony is never chromatic in this sense: the planes of his music are broader, so to speak, and consequently when he does modulate (which is usually by the use not of adjacent notes, but of notes common to the two tonalities) the effect is less nervous and taut. He does not travel in his music in a state of agitation or confusion; his mind is organized and at peace and the vistas which his modulations disclose fall into perspective like the various planes in a picture. Here is a satisfying art to look back upon after the strains put upon music during the first half of the twentieth century – an art of conventional associations maybe, but quiet, civilized, and reassuring.

The chamber works of Fauré cover over half a century. The early A Major Violin Sonata was written in 1876; the String Quartet was written in the year of the composer's death in 1925. Between these dates Fauré produced at various intervals two piano quartets, two piano quintets, a second piano and violin sonata and two piano and cello sonatas. There is also a piano trio.

Fauré's pupil, Florent Schmitt, appropriately describes the First Piano and Violin Sonata as a *coup d'essai* which was also a *coup de maître*. Indeed, this early sonata remains one of the composer's most popular works, and deservedly so for its charming and individual character is immediately captivating. Superficially there was nothing novel. The first movement reproduces the structure, probably recommended by Saint-Saëns, of the Mozart sonatas; the second movement is a lyrical *andante* in a rocking 9/8 barcarolle rhythm; the third is a sparkling *scherzo*; and the last a finely developed finale, again after the models of Mozart. The form presents nothing new, but not one of the themes could have been written by any other composer. This beautifully flowing theme from the last movement for instance is entirely characteristic of Fauré (Ex. 4).

The Second Piano and Violin Sonata dates from 1917. The slow movement contains some of the most intensely lyrical pages Fauré ever wrote, but the work as a whole, particularly the last movement, lacks the freshness and spontaneity of the earlier work.

The first of the two Piano Quartets resembles the First Piano and Violin Sonata; the same grace and lightness, the same poise, the same purely lyrical inspiration. Fauré's method of writing for the piano in combination with the strings – a combination difficult to negotiate – is to treat the keyboard instrument in the manner of a harp. The effect in the *Scherzo* is unforgettable:

Fauré's art developed in the course of his life. He was not content merely to explore a vein of graceful charm; and a more mature stage is reached in the Second Quartet in G Minor of 1886 (dedicated to Hans von Bülow). This shows the tenuous texture of the early works replaced by a harder, more closely woven texture. The first movement opens with a theme consistently maintained in inspiration over its unusual length, but this time the three string instruments in unison proclaim their message with greater breadth and eloquence. The fiery *Scherzo*, too, has sharper outlines than the corresponding movement in the earlier quartet; and this is likewise true of the noble slow movement and the impetuous Finale. The second quartet is among the composer's more powerful works: it reveals an intensity and a diversity of sentiment that one would hardly have suspected from the composer of the graceful A Major Sonata or the early C Minor Quartet. The first D Minor Quintet of 1906 is more conventional – the *Adagio* is the most successful of the three movements – but the second C Minor Quintet of 1921, written when the composer was seventy-six is, like the Second Quartet, a work of commanding proportions, a searching work which does not easily yield its secrets, but which displays a profundity of sentiment to be found elsewhere only in the finest chamber music of Brahms. The long French neglect of Brahms, remedied only in recent years, has often puzzled foreign observers. A generation ago Brahms was so little known in Paris that when at the last moment, at one of Koussevitzky's memorable concerts at the *Opéra*, his second symphony was substituted for his fourth, none of the critics realized that a change had been made. It is understandable that two civilizations may be held to face each other in a work such as Fauré's Requiem on the one hand, music of hushes and sighs, and on the other, the unrelenting severity of the 'German Requiem' of Brahms. But in other respects the two composers had much in common, particularly their innate feeling for the various chamber-music media. An interesting point here is that in the 1890s there had been an influential circle of Brahms devotees in Paris, the chief of whom were Édouard Schuré and Hugues Imbert. Brahms was nominated an Associate Member of the French Academy in 1896 and his work certainly appears to have been known to Fauré who, together with Chausson, d'Indy, and some fifty other French musicians and music-patrons, contributed to the cost of the Brahms monument in Vienna.

The two Cello Sonatas, particularly the second, the opening theme of which:

is one of Fauré's happiest ideas, deserve to be better known, while the Piano Trio of 1924, which he called his 'little trio', is an extraordinarily fresh and alive work to have been written by a composer approaching his eightieth year. Of the same period is Fauré's only String Quartet. The fact that Fauré should have traversed the whole of his career before approaching the purity of the string quartet form shows a rare sense of modesty in this master of chamber music, for it is impossible not to suspect that some such idea must have been in his mind long before. 'You can imagine that I'm afraid of this form like everyone else,' the aged composer confides in a letter to his wife. And he describes the work he is writing as '*un quatuor pour instruments à cordes sans piano*', a curious way of putting it which cannot but remind one that the black and white sonorities of the keyboard had always first prompted Fauré's imagination, not only in his piano music, but in many of his songs and certainly in all his earlier chamber music. Here, however, in this E minor quartet he was finally able to free himself from this keyboard allegiance.

The String Quartet is an other-worldly work. As in the song cycles of the last years, the texture is extremely tenuous and elusive. Flowing melodies disappear into thin air, and the four instruments, not one of which is ever allowed to predominate, converse in long, deliberately bland dialogues. Only in the last movement is there a glimpse of a more light-hearted mood. One need not be sentimental in declaring that these last and obviously less vital pages of this beautiful composer, written with the knowledge that the end was not long to be delayed, are what one would expect them to be – a serene and happy farewell.

The chamber music of Fauré, consisting of a body of works comparable in range to the chamber works of Schumann and Brahms, was written, as we have seen, over an exceptionally long period. In all these chamber works Fauré was unaffected by his contemporaries (apart from Saint-Saëns), whether they were older men such as Franck or younger men discovering new worlds of their own such as Debussy and Ravel. In regard to Debussy, the whole spirit of his four main chamber works (the String Quartet and the three late sonatas) was especially foreign to Fauré; and understandably so, for these two figures were in a sense the classical and the romantic masters of their time. Physically, too, they were of utterly different character. Observing the two composers seated together on the board of examiners at the Paris Conservatoire, a contemporary described Fauré's white-haired figure as resembling a dignified old priest, while the sight of the swarthy Debussy suggested a one-time Italian brigand.

DEBUSSY

DEBUSSY's String Quartet was one of this composer's first works to be publicly performed. The date is 1893. Contemporary criticism, at first baffled, was soon able to glimpse the alluring strangeness of the world Debussy had entered. He is 'rotten with talent', one writer prophetically declared. And from another, apropos of a passage in the

Scherzo: 'Here is something for which I would willingly give everything that Pierre Loti ever wrote.' (The art of Debussy had sprung from the impact of so many of the literary movements of his time that the allusion to this master of Orientalism in French prose was by no means out of place. Actually Debussy had heard in Paris the music of the Javanese gamelangs, and this oriental influence in the *Scherzo* is still immediately striking to modern ears.) Another early appraisement, equally pertinent, was that of César Franck: '*C'est de la musique sur les pointes d'aiguilles*' (idiomatically, the split hairs of music or the nerves of music). Debussy was in fact greatly indebted to Franck in this work, in regard to its cyclic form at any rate, and the comment of the older composer, though meant to convey his irritated censure of Debussy's new style, defines precisely its original and essentially nervous appeal.

The quartet is unique among Debussy's works in that it shows him at the beginning of his career with one foot in the camp of Franck and his followers and the other in the revolutionary world he was about to enter – the work that immediately follows the quartet is *L'Après-midi d'un faune* which is clearly foreshadowed in the quartet's slow movement. Yet the cyclic form which Debussy inherited from Franck is used not slavishly but with great freedom. There is a minimum of thematic development (as opposed to the spacious developments of Franck); many prismatic changes of harmony; minute variations pieced together in the form of a mosaic; and constant recastings of the germinal theme, in the course of the four movements, in rhythm and mode. The impression is thus created not of a work of contrasts and logical development, but of a sort of visionary work based on the transformations of a single theme. Particularly impressive are the bold and sudden distinctions of mood: the clear-cut opening of the first movement (in the Phrygian mode), the trance-like mood of the slow movement with its moving soliloquies on the viola and cello, and the impetuous Finale driving its way through to a state of exalted tension, deriving from Franck maybe, but nevertheless entirely peculiar to this sensuous hedonist among composers.

Debussy's Quartet was the most original work to have been written in the cyclic form by any composer after Franck. Only twenty-five years later, in 1918, Debussy died in Paris, having spent the war years travelling from one country hotel to another in the hope of finding some peace of mind to work and in the hope also of consolidating the physical strength that was left to him. Afflicted with cancer, he was aware that his end was near, yet he persisted in working continuously, indeed at that feverish pace that somehow takes possession of a dying man 'in order to give proof' as he put it 'that French thought will not be destroyed'. Usually hesitant in the gradual exteriorization of his ideas, he now announced a series of six sonatas for various combinations of instruments. On the handsome title page of the first, under the composer's name, appeared, as a natural assertion of pride during those war years, the words *Musicien Français*. Only three of the sonatas were completed, the Cello Sonata, the Sonata for Flute, Viola, and Harp, and the Violin Sonata. (The fourth sonata was to have been written for the unusual combination of oboe, horn, and harpsichord.)

These sonatas of Debussy are not abstract conceptions. They are written in the spirit of the eighteenth-century philosopher who, having admired the formal proportions of a classical work, was nevertheless driven to proclaim at the end: '*Sonate que me veux-tu?*' Debussy's sonatas are full of symbolic associations. The Cello Sonata was originally to have been entitled *Pierrot fâché avec la lune*. Although the composer was returning in this work to the form and spirit of the eighteenth-century sonata he was also haunted, as in fact he had been throughout his life, by the symbolic figure of Harlequin. The work opens with a prologue in the form of a noble soliloquy. This first movement occupies no more than four pages of the score and what is remarkable within this tiny framework is the extraordinary eloquence of the cello part. The ideas follow each other naturally, as in a narrative. There is some kind of ghostly rumbling in a

short passage introduced to provide a dramatic interruption, and the prologue closes as it began in a mood of serenity. The second movement is a bitter, almost tragic serenade in which the cello is called upon to imitate a guitar, a mandoline, a flute, and even the tambourine. It is one of the many serenades in Debussy's work which recaptures the spirit of an eighteenth-century elegance, but which belong clearly enough to our day, for these old-world pastiches are not pastiches as we usually understand the term at all; they are shot through with some kind of anxious foreboding and are often dramatically interrupted by strange questionings and doubts. The original *pizzicati* and *portando* effects in the cello writing are extremely expressive and leave one amazed at the vivacious character Debussy was able to impart to this normally slow-moving instrument of the string family. The last movement is a high-spirited piece, but here again the pathetic figure of Harlequin seems to peer through the jovial proceedings and is unmistakably evoked in these few bars of heart-rending desolation.

RAVEL

AT Debussy's death the ideals of his later years had only partly been realized, for this genius among twentieth-century composers had foreseen a return to a classical spirit in music, and in his late sonatas had laid the foundations of the neo-classical style of Stravinsky. Like Stravinsky, he was inspired in these last works not by the creation of a new style, but by the re-creation of earlier styles (in this case the styles of Rameau and Couperin). Ravel was similarly concerned to endow the music of these eighteenth-century composers with a new spirit – he does so most successfully in the piano suite *Le Tombeau de Couperin*. But as a pupil of Fauré, Ravel, in his relatively few chamber works, was also concerned to develop a virtuoso capacity for solving the most knotty technical problems. These composers take delight in performing in their music astonishing technical feats which, if one were to look at them objectively, would seem almost impossible of execution without sacrificing the essential artistic impulse. These feats of Fauré and Ravel, in which mind and heart are one, have always, however, their artistic *raison d'être*. Fauré, for instance, master of the art of modulation, wrote a long series of variations for the piano to show that this form (in which modulation plays an all-important part) could be negotiated without modulation. Similarly Ravel, convinced, as he declared, that the piano and the violin were 'essentially incompatible instruments', thereupon decided to write a piano and violin sonata apparently to prove that the contrary was equally true. From which one sees that the music of Ravel is, in a sense, the music of paradox. It is also the music of an ironist, a tragic ironist, some sort of Baudelaire of music whose ancestry is rooted in Mozart and Liszt.

Of much greater value is Ravel's Quartet, written in 1902, the date of the first production of Debussy's opera *Pelléas et Mélisande*. The relations between the two composers had up to that time been friendly; and since Ravel was the younger man, hardly known beyond a circle of intimate friends, there was a natural reverence for Debussy who by that time had produced several of his major works. This friendship, however, was not to last – on account of no personal differences but simply because there had been much distasteful publicity on the rival merits of their two string quartets. Ravel's laconic comment on the unfortunate situation was that 'it's probably better for us after all to be on frigid terms for illogical reasons'. To the younger composer, harassed as he was by misplaced criticisms of his remarkable achievement, Debussy declared: 'In the name of the gods of music and in mine do not touch a single note of what you have written in your quartet.' What is significant here is that this F Major Quartet is one of the few works of Ravel that show signs of a Debussyan influence. It is evident particularly in the second movement which has a distinct resemblance to the *Scherzo* of the earlier Debussy quartet. Other stylistic elements in this work of the youthful Ravel derive from his master Fauré, to whom the work is dedicated, but who was frankly censorious of the fourth movement which he found 'stunted, badly balanced, in fact a failure'. In regard to the form of the finale this was no doubt a legitimate criticism. At the same time one cannot help suspecting that the aged master of Ravel was among those who, like Saint-Saëns, were constantly fearful of the inroads of Debussy's adventurous art.

There was in fact no cause for any such fear. The young Ravel knew very well what he was about: his individuality had been completely declared in his earliest music and the quartet similarly shows an instinctive grasp of a new and entirely personal idiom. It is one of the most spontaneous of Ravel's works – a fact of which the composer was well aware when years later he declared that he would willingly exchange his technical mastery for the artless strength of this early string work. Not that it is altogether artless. The opening movement is in strict ternary form, neat, logical, and precise, on the model of the early Piano Quartet of Fauré. Trills, tremolos, and *pizzicati* effects give a beautiful sheen to the instrumental writing of the *Scherzo*. This movement also displays a wonderfully alive and pointed rhythmic ingenuity with elaborate cross-rhythms and an almost orchestral sense of the string combination. The slow movement is a free rhapsody, and the Finale is a lively movement in 5/8 time inspired perhaps by Ravel's admiration for Borodin, but revealing that essentially Gallic sense of vivacity which Ravel was later to develop in his orchestral works.

The spirits of Mozart and of Liszt are revived and somehow made to merge into each other in the prosaically entitled Introduction and Allegro for harp, string quartet, flute and clarinet of 1906. The title may be formal and cumbersome, but this happily inspired little work is one of the most poetic of Ravel's scores. Almost every bar has some exquisite piece of detail to linger over. It is sometimes called a Septet, but it is really a virtuoso concert piece in the form of a miniature Concerto for harp and a small chamber ensemble. The form is based on the Rhapsodies of Liszt, but the wonderfully clear texture is never in any way showy or bombastic despite the highly arresting and effective writing for the harp. Here Ravel adapts for the harp Liszt's grand manner at the keyboard—he adapts it and he refines upon it with just that Mozartian sense of balance, precision, and sensitiveness of musical phrasing. Particularly lovely, to the type of listener with an immediate nervous response to music, are the ravishing harp *glissandi* in chords of the seventh. For sheer sound – the unadulterated pleasure of sound without any of music's more remote intellectual or scientific associations – this little rhapsody is one of the most delectable of musical experiences. The harmony is very simple – it is a work belonging to an earlier style of Ravel, rather like his *Shéhérazade* – the themes are melodious and easily recognized, and the charming instrumentation is a dream. People who are becoming acquainted with the delights of French music should compare this work with the later Trio for flute, viola, and harp by Debussy, where, again, the harp is wonderfully treated – these composers understood the genius of the harp in the way that Chopin understood the genius of the piano. The Debussy work happens to be a much more sophisticated example of his work, but both display the very beautiful ranges of colour to be obtained from the plucked strings of the harp in contrast with wind and string instruments.

At the beginning of the first world war, Ravel wrote his Piano Trio. Themes from the composer's native Basque country are used in the first movement of this broad and powerful work. The second, entitled *Pantoum* (after the verse form of this name), is another example of Ravel's unique sense of vivacity; the third movement is a *passacaglia* and the work concludes with an elaborate finale built on an inversion of the opening theme of the first movement. The Trio is remarkable for its themes of Spanish association and also for the many novel solutions of the problem of the contrast of sonorities as between the essentially percussive piano and the singing tone of the string instruments. In the sonata for violin and cello, written at the time of the opera *L'Enfant et les Sortilèges*, Ravel set himself the solution of yet other problems. He refers to this work, dedicated to the memory of Debussy, as marking a turning point in his evolution. It is indeed an extremely severe work to have come from the composer of the *Spanish Rhapsody* and the *Mother Goose Suite*, an experiment in a deliberately lean and harsh style which Ravel was to develop in many unexpected ways in his last works. The little *Berceuse on the name of Fauré* for violin and piano is a more serene and heartfelt example of Ravel's chamber music, the last example of which, to be considered here, is the piano and violin sonata of 1927 with its wry slow movement entitled *Blues*, reminiscent of the sardonic jazz music in *L'Enfant et les Sortilèges*.

D'INDY

RAVEL was not averse to the principles of the cyclic form – movements in his chamber works frequently recall or transform earlier ideas – though the fine-spun texture of these works of Ravel owe, of course, nothing whatever to the lush, emotional art of César Franck. Two civilizations similarly appear to face each other if one compares the chamber works of Ravel with those of another pupil of Fauré, Florent Schmitt, notably his gigantic piano quintet. In the meantime, Franck's pupil, Vincent d'Indy, was proclaiming the traditions of his master to his pupils at the Schola Cantorum, the school which he founded in Paris with Charles Bordes. These traditions d'Indy developed into a cult, over-emphasizing, as we see now, the mystical and religious aspects of Franck's work. As Léon Vallas points out in his authoritative study of the life and works of this composer, d'Indy was a complex figure full of strange contradictions who almost literally worshipped the music of Franck, the spirit of which, however, hardly persists in his own works for the reason that he lacked Franck's characteristic warmth and fervour. Nor was the purely intellectual passion which d'Indy brought to the composition of his works a compensation for the fantasy and originality which he saw about him in Fauré, Debussy, and Ravel. Consequently he persisted in making a virtue of erudition – he was a remarkable teacher and scholar – not to say pedantry. Perfection of form was his ideal – the cyclic form which he perceived not only in Beethoven, but even in Brahms, and the variation form for which his model was Beethoven's *Diabelli Variations*. In his own works, however, the use of these forms was seldom inspired by any kind of glowing musical imagination. Of his three string quartets, the third, in D flat, of 1929, presents some interesting problems of construction (discussed at length by the composer in the published preface to the work). The violin and the cello sonatas are seldom played, but the string sextet is worth reviving, particularly for the *Quodlibet alla Schumann* at the end of the last movement.

ROUSSEL

LITTLE by little d'Indy's pupil, Albert Roussel, has emerged since his death in 1937 as the most impressive figure in recent French music. There is a granite-like quality in the texture of his music, not immediately seductive like the art of Debussy nor refined in detail like the be-jewelled patterns of Ravel, but usually stern and rough-hewn. Roussel was d'Indy's pupil only for a short time, in his youth. Except in some of his early works he was never one of d'Indy's followers. Perhaps it was because Roussel was always a great traveller, especially in Africa and the Far East – he was for many years an officer in the French Navy – that he was little affected by the sophisticated art of the Parisians. However this may be, he wrote certain pages of dramatic grandeur which are like nothing else in French music of that period. He was an unsentimental and powerful figure, pursuing his ideal of 'music that should be satisfying in itself, music that shall be homeless, of no particular place'. There was always something of the peasant in this native of French Flanders. But he was a sailor too, and one has to reckon with the explorer in him. It is not surprising, therefore, that French critics have sought a parallel between the music of Roussel and the art of Joseph Conrad. The second of the two Piano and Violin Sonatas shows Roussel's chamber music at its best. The String Quartet is remarkable for its gay, pointed *Scherzo* and for its finely developed fugue in the last movement. The String Trio, written in 1937, shows Roussel to have been in full possession of his powers at the time of his death.

MAGNARD

ANOTHER pupil of d'Indy is the little-known composer, Albéric Magnard – little-known even in his own country, for he lived as a recluse, refusing anything that would approach self-advertisement and even refusing to have certain of his works commercially published. At the beginning of the 1914–18 war, living as a civilian at his country home at Baron, he courageously fired on the invading German troops with the result that his home, containing many of his unpublished works, was burnt to the ground. A cello sonata, a piano trio, and a string quartet are the main chamber works of this composer whose admiration in instrumental music went principally to the string quartets of Beethoven.

MILHAUD, POULENC, AND MESSIAEN

THE inspiring influence of Beethoven on French chamber music which, as we have seen, dates back to the middle of the nineteenth century, has been fruitful in many different ways and is alive still in the work of contemporary composers. Darius Milhaud, one of the most prolific composers of our time, has set himself the task of producing the same number of quartets as Beethoven; he has so far written fifteen, the last two designed to be played either separately or together as an octet. The musical quality of this series is uneven, but there are some charming pages in the first quartet, dedicated to the memory of Cézanne, and some bold harmonic experiments in the fifth, dedicated to Schönberg. The Second Violin Sonata of Milhaud, dedicated to André Gide, has a delightful pastoral feeling not unlike the music in this vein of Vaughan Williams. Milhaud is one of the last stylists in French music. The chamber music produced in France in recent years is abundant, but it is almost impossible to see any significant or salient trends: in France as in other countries stylistic features among composers have become less discernible than they were. Two composers, however, who have written chamber music may be singled out for the clear-cut profiles they unmistakably offer. They are Francis Poulenc – to be mentioned here in connexion with his Piano and Violin Sonata, a work of considerable melodic originality and charm – and the controversial figure of Olivier Messiaen, a composer of deep religious inspiration whose sincere and novel style, disconcerting at first by reason both of its garishness and its complexity, is gradually commanding more and more respect.

17

Modern German Chamber Music

ANDREW PORTER

THIS chapter could have been filled entirely with the list of the compositions that fall within the scope of the heading above. Alternatively, it might have considered in rapid succession, with but a few sentences on each, the principal works of the principal composers. Instead it deals, in the main, with three works: Arnold Schönberg's string sextet *Verklärte Nacht*, Alban Berg's Lyric Suite, and Hindemith's First String Trio. A reason for choosing these is that good recordings are available of the first and last, while a recording of the Lyric Suite cannot be long delayed (America has two). A more cogent reason is the opportunity afforded for discussing Schönberg's development from *Verklärte Nacht*, through the First and Second String Quartets, to the twelve-note system which Alban Berg employed, albeit not strictly, in his Lyric Suite; and one of the aims here was to provide some introduction to that system, whose influence on modern German chamber music has been almost all-pervading. Had space been limitless, we might have gone on to attempt some notes on Schönberg's later chamber music, and on Anton Webern's. But what there is is scrappy enough already, and full commentaries are available – though not always in English – for those who are interested. Hindemith, Schönberg, and Stravinsky are the triple pillars of contemporary music; and Hindemith's First String Trio (1924) is a characteristic enough work from his most influential period.

SCHÖNBERG

ARNOLD SCHÖNBERG'S approach to composition was by way of chamber music. At the age of twelve he learnt the violin, and wrote duos which he performed with his teacher. Soon afterwards he used to join with his fellow-pupils in making chamber music, and produced for them trios and quartets. Then he taught himself the cello, and composed sonatas for this instrument. The musical content of this juvenilia was probably undistinguished; 'up to the age of seventeen,' Schönberg said, 'all my compositions were merely imitations of such music as I had access to. They were violin duets and arrangements of operatic pot-pourris for two violins, plus the music I heard played by military bands in the public gardens.'

The importance of this early self-schooling in chamber music has often been stressed. It encouraged a predilection for linear writing, which must have been confirmed in the composer's counterpoint lessons with Alexander von Zemlinsky – the only formal instruction Schönberg ever received. A glance at Schönberg's most opulently scored passages – in the *Gurrelieder*, or the Dance round the Golden Calf in *Moses und Aron* – will show that his harmony is built up polyphonically; like Hindemith, he prefers to write notes that are necessary, and serve a structural function. In *Verklärte Nacht* there are *tremolos*, *arpeggio* figures, and other pieces of 'colouring'; but one of the lushest passages of all (letter Q) yields itself up as a strict canon between four of the six parts, accompanied by an *ostinato* from the other two. This 'lean, athletic style' of Schönberg was to develop from work to work. In later years he described his first quartet as 'thick', and each successive one as coming nearer to the Mozartian ideal of 'transparency'.

In 1897 Schönberg composed a String Quartet in D major, which was performed at a Vienna Tonkünstlerverein concert the following year. The work was successful, and praised for its 'melodic warmth', but the score, alas, has been lost. And so the first chamber work to survive to us is the string sextet, *Verklärte Nacht* ('Transfigured Night'), Op. 4, composed in three weeks in 1899. To-day *Verklärte Nacht* may strike someone hearing it for the first time as a late-Romantic offshoot of *Tristan*; but in Vienna it was refused performance because in it the composer had used a chord of the ninth with the dissonant ninth in the bass part, a procedure that was strictly forbidden:

Ex.1

(The quotation is from eight bars after C; Schönberg speaks of '*one* single uncatalogued dissonance', but the progression occurs again, even more strikingly – but with the harmonies too widely flung to make a tidy short-score – at a climatic point seven bars after J.) 'Evidently,' said Schönberg, 'an inverted ninth does not exist; and so there was no performance, for after all one can't perform something which doesn't exist. I had to wait for a few years' ... until 1903, when *Verklärte Nacht* was played in Vienna, and condemned as 'radical' and cacophonous!

Verklärte Nacht was novel in its conception – a full-length tone-poem for string sextet. The literary inspiration came from a poem by Richard Dehmel, which is printed as a preface to the score. The poet overhears a conversation between a woman and a man she has met and fallen in love with. Already married, she is bearing her husband's child – she married not for love, but for security and because she wished for children. Now, by the side of the man she truly loves, she is ashamed of this. Tenderly he consoles her; their love will transfigure the unborn child and make it as if it were entirely their own. The glory of the moonlit night reflects and is commingled with the radiance of his love. Since the form of this poem determines that of the sextet, and an English translation is hard to come by, it may be worth giving one here:

Two people go through the bare, cold wood;
The moon accompanies them, they gaze at it.
The moon accompanies them above the high oaks —
no cloud obscures the light of heaven,
which the black tree-tops reach up to.
The voice of a woman speaks:

I bear a child which is not yours
In sin I am walking beside you.
I have transgressed against myself.
I no longer believed in happiness
and yet had a great longing
for life, for the happiness of being a mother,
and duty; therefore I dared,
and shuddering, yielded my body
to the embraces of a strange man,
and have counted myself blessed for doing so.
No life has taken its revenge,
now I have met you, ah you.

She goes on with awkward pace.
She looks upward; the moon accompanies them.
Her dark glance is bathed in light.
The voice of a man speaks:

The child that you have conceived,
let it be no burden to your soul.
O see, how brightly the whole world shines!
There is a glory on everything here,
You are drifting with me on a cold sea,
But a mutual warmth flickers
from you to me, from me to you.
That will transfigure the strange child;
You will bear it for me, and from me;
You have brought glory to me,
You have made of me myself a child.

He takes her by the strong hips.
Their breath commingles in the gentle breeze.
Two people go through the lofty, clear night.

The speeches of the woman and the man are framed by
description of the scene; and the moonlit night is pictured in
this theme, played very softly over a pedal D:

Impassive, tranquil, and beautiful, it rises to a climax only
to introduce the woman's speech (when the situation as
well as the scene is to be revealed), taking in as it does so
the characteristic 'turn' which in *Tristan* is associated with
mounting passion (this turn is used frequently in *Verklärte
Nacht*). Over a tremolo bass, the grief-laden accents of Ex.
3(*a*) are heard. Ex. 3*b* is a further development of this
phrase, which mounts to an anguished climax.

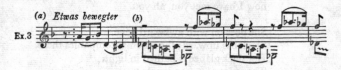

There is a moment of respite, a broad, tender E major
melody softly launched by the first violin over warm, full
harmonies:

The earlier phrases return, and break into a frenzy of self-
reproach. The third 'stanza' presents Ex. 1 again (the
moonlit night), now played strongly and richly harmonized,
dying away to a low B flat as if musing, with the poet, what
the man's answer will be. This answer is generous and
warm. The tonality lights up in D major, and the themes of
the woman's speech are transfigured in a series of glorious

pages, rich and glowing. Finally, Ex. 1 returns, no longer noncommittal, but personalized, in D major.

There are at least three long-playing recordings of *Verklärte Nacht* available, one of them played by string sextet, and the other two in the arrangement for string orchestra which the composer made in 1917 and revised in 1943. Perhaps the orchestral version, when sensitively played, strikes more deeply at the emotions; but the original score makes the contrapuntal mastery more apparent. Rather than break into coloured prose about this very approachable work, let us look at the themes a little more closely. This will prepare us for the chamber music to follow.

Anyone who essays analysis of a highly developed piece of music is struck, again and again, by the truth in the notion of a *Grundgestalt*, or 'basic shape', underlying much composition. Hermann Scherchen, in *The Nature of Music* (Dobson), has given us an impressive demonstration of Schubert's 'Unfinished' Symphony stemming, in all its main features, from one 'basic idea', the seven notes of the opening. This could hardly have been conscious. But what Scherchen calls 'an act of volition' must lie behind Beethoven's permeating his Fifth Symphony with echoes of its opening bars, or unifying his Seventh Symphony with a basic rhythmic pattern of long-short-long. The first reaction of a reader to such analysis tends to be that the writer has over-ingeniously discovered something not intended by the composer, nor, indeed, important. Take, for example, Schönberg's own account of the motifs of the last movement of Beethoven's F Major Quartet, Op. 135:

Ex.5

(*a*) the *Muss es sein?* phrase with which the movement opens, in the major and in inversion (*d*), yields *Es muss sein* (*b*).

Reversed (*e*), and then with this reversion inverted (*f*), we get the shape which when filled out with passing notes (*g*) produces the secondary motif (*c*). If this seems unbearably involved, then the simpler statement that Beethoven has given us every 'combination and permutation' of the three notes concerned in the interval of a third lying within a fourth (the 'basic shape') may be more acceptable. 'Whether this device was used consciously by Beethoven,' says Schönberg, 'does not matter at all. From my own experience I know that it can also be a subconsciously received gift from the Supreme Commander!'

In this connexion Schönberg's essay on 'Heart and Mind in Music', reprinted in *Style and Idea* (Williams and Norgate) should be read, and also the third chapter of Josef Rufer's *Composition with Twelve Notes related only to one another* (Rockliff; translated by Searle. This book is the 'classical' exposition of Schönberg's method). Sometimes one can distinguish between ideas 'received' and ideas worked out. In the essay referred to, Schönberg quotes a bar of *Verklärte Nacht* which took 'a full hour' to compose – letter H, where a theme derived from Ex. 3 and its inversion are woven in elaborate counterpoint. 'This combination was not the product of a spontaneous inspiration but of an extra-musical intention [i.e. to express an idea in the poem], of a cerebral reflection.' But it was only years after the composition of *Verklärte Nacht*, during a sleepless night after he had conducted the work in Barcelona, that the composer realized a subtle harmonic point which lent strength to the structure (see Dika Newlin's *Bruckner, Mahler, and Schoenberg*, pp. 214–5).

To show that the diverse themes of *Verklärte Nacht* are developments from the basic shape of Ex. 2, no further words are needed: we need only place the examples already quoted one below the other (the two motives of Ex. 3*b* are hown on separate staves) as in Ex. 6.

Schönberg's next chamber composition was the String Quartet No. 1 in D Minor, Op. 7 (1904–5). Played without break, it comprises four movements (first movement,

Ex. 6

Scherzo, *Adagio*, and *Rondo-Finale*), in which the development sections are fused in the structure. The first major
development is deliberately patterned on that of Beethoven's 'Eroica' Symphony. The energetic principal theme
(Ex. 7a shows the start of it) has been the subject of an
extensive study by Alban Berg (in the essay 'Why is Schönberg's music so difficult to understand?'). This theme, in
the major, closes the quartet with some of the most beautiful pages in modern chamber music. In our example (7b)
only the first violin and cello parts are shown (notice that
the bass is an inversion of that to Ex. 7a):

Ex. 7

Fundamental to Schönberg's music, from the earliest to
the last, is the notion of a clear *shape*. There is a story of
Schönberg's picking up a hat, turning it about in front of
his pupils, and explaining: 'You see, this is a hat, whether I
look at it from above, from below, from the front, from
behind, from the left, from the right, it always remains a

hat, though it may look one thing from above and another from below.' This idea of a shape, the basic idea of a composition from which all the rest is generated, is not difficult to accept. In his Second String Quartet in F sharp minor, Op. 10 (1907–8, revised 1921), Schönberg omitted development sections from his first two movements (the first a sonata-form without its centre, the second a *scherzo*) and used instead the third movement to 'work out' the material of the earlier ones. There is a well-known analysis of the first nine bars of this movement, originally made by Webern, and also quoted by Egon Wellesz in his book on the composer, and by René Leibowitz in his *Introduction à la Musique de Douze Sons* (pp. 41–2). Anyone who wishes to work this out for himself should compare the viola part with the opening of the quartet, and its second strain with bars 15–6 of the *Scherzo*; the first violin part with bars 24–5 of the first movement, and the minim figure with bars 58–9 (the second subject) of the first movement. Schönberg has been denting that hat about a bit, so to speak; each of these melodies, which weave in smooth counterpoint, is a motive from the earlier movements altered only in respect of note-values. The relation between the motives themselves, incidentally, is quite easily discovered. This slow movement is also a theme and variations in E flat minor, and a setting (for soprano voice and string quartet) of Stefan George's *Litanei*.

The Finale, a setting for soprano of George's *Entrückung* (Ecstasy), compels us to consider the harmonic aspects of Schönberg's development. The uproar with which the first performance of the quartet was greeted is by now a well-known story (see, for example, Alma Mahler's Reminiscences or Erwin Stein's account in *Orpheus in Many Guises*, p. 48). And no wonder, for this last movement loses touch with any recognizable key, and is pulled back into F sharp minor only at the very close. The soprano's words must have sounded all too appropriate when she sang, at the start of this movement, 'I feel air from another planet,' and then 'I dissolve in sounds':

Here the first violin doubles the voice part. The progression is not too strange for anyone who has analysed harmonic progressions in *Tristan*; but in his succeeding works Schönberg was to suspend identifiable tonality altogether. For the next ten years or so the composer and his pupils, notably Berg and Webern, wrote the sort of music they felt impelled to do, carrying the 'emancipation of the dissonance' far further than Wagner, Strauss, Debussy, Mahler, and Reger had done. These years produced at least one undisputed masterpiece – Berg's opera *Wozzeck*; gradually these composers were finding their way to what eventually crystallized in Schönberg's 'method of composing with twelve notes related only to one another'. Related to no tonic and dominant, that is, and in no key! Gone were the traditional ways of marking musical paragraphs, sentences, and phrases, by means of tonal planes, with consonances for commas. That this should happen was the logical consequence of the gradual acceptance of more and more dissonances in music. (And contrapuntists are generally more harmonically daring than harmonists: a fairly oft-quoted passage from Gesualdo's *Moro lasso*, published in 1611, anticipates Wagner, and is certainly in no recognizable key, although the individual parts move naturally and singably; and Bach's subject for his F minor Fugue in the first book of the Forty-Eight is a nine-note theme which caused some puzzled head-shaking when it was used for the opening of Hans Werner Henze's ballet, *Der Idiot*.)

The constructive values of the new chords remained undiscovered, and so atonal pieces had either to be very brief, or to be given shape by a text. Finally a constructive principle emerged: the basic shape of a composition should contain all twelve notes of the chromatic scale. Like Schönberg's hat, or a Bach fugue subject, this shape could be viewed from above or from below (i.e. in inversion), or from either side (i.e. in retrograde motion), or even backwards and inverted together. From this shape all the features of the piece were to be derived – much as the themes of *Verklärte Nacht* and the earlier quartets grew from a basic shape. Since the note-row contained all twelve notes of the scale, it would not (or at any rate need not) gravitate towards any tonality; but it would contain distinctive features – principally intervals – from which the music would take shape. 'You might,' writes Mosco Carner, 'call the note-row the chrysalis of the future theme or themes'; and readers should consult Dr Carner's account of it on pp. 365–6 of the Pelican volume, *The Concerto*.

The idea of a twelve-note theme was not startlingly novel. As early as 1895 Richard Strauss had used one as the fugue-subject for the 'Of Science' section of his tone poem *Also sprach Zarathustra*. There are several examples in Reger's chamber music, and Bartók's First String Quartet contains one. Schönberg was the first to set it up as a constructive principle for composition; and the last number of his Five Piano Pieces (1923) is the first piece to be written in the 'strict' twelve-note method. Schönberg never claimed it as *the* method ('There is plenty of good music still to be written in C major!'). But it was, and is, eagerly embraced by many composers, and it soon bore fruit in the very beautiful Lyric Suite of Alban Berg.

BERG

ALBAN BERG became a pupil of Schönberg's in 1904. In 1910 he composed a String Quartet, Op. 3; the Lyric Suite for String Quartet dates from 1925–6. Before embarking on its composition Berg followed the example of Wagner, who had written the songs *Im Treibhaus* and *Träume* as preliminary studies for *Tristan*. Berg composed a song, *Schliesse mir die Augen beide*, to words by Theodor Storm, in which he explored some of the possibilities of the note-row which he had chosen for the Lyric Suite. He had already in 1900 set these same words in C major; he dedicated the two songs to Emil Hertzka, founder of Universal Edition, to mark the twenty-fifth anniversary of the firm. They have recently been published by Universal, and anyone interested in the Lyric Suite should study also the song. The note-row which Berg chose has a number of interesting features. Here it is, with its inversion:

Ex.9
Note-row
(a)

1 2 3 4 5 6 7 8 9 10 11 12

Inversion
(b)

Berg never fully accepted Schönberg's serial technique in its purest form (this is in no way a criticism of the *musical* value of his compositions). He varied the note-row from movement to movement, as we shall see below, and as any-one who has studied *Lulu* knows (for there the note-rows 'derived' from one another are really new rows). Moreover his rows generally have tonal implications – this is one of the reasons why his music is enjoyed by people who can 'make nothing' of Schönberg's. The row of *Der Wein* (1920) starts with a scale of D minor; that of the Violin Concerto (1935) with a chain of ascending thirds. And here 2, 3, and 4 give us an A minor triad (F sharp major in the inversion), while 9, 10, and 11 yield E flat minor (C major in inversion). Divided into pairs, the row is seen as a series of falling intervals: a second, third, fourth, fifth, sixth, and seventh in turn; while the rising intervals bring up the total to the eleven possible within the octave (no interval occurs twice). When we write the row backwards, as in the black notes below, we get this curious symmetrical pattern:

Ex.10

In fact, the row is a sort of palindrome, which yields itself in a diminished fifth transposition when reversed. Moreover when it is exposed entirely in one direction, from a high note downwards or a low one upwards, it forms a chord containing all the eleven intervals possible within the octave (this chord had been published by F. W. Klein in 1924, and was named the *Mutterakkord*).

The Lyric Suite has six movements, alternately fast and slow, the fast ones growing ever faster, and the slow ones slower:

I. *Allegretto gioviale* (12)
II. *Andante amoroso*
III. *Allegro misterioso* (12) ... *Trio estatico*
IV. *Adagio appassionato*
V. *Presto delirando* ... *Tenebroso* (12)
VI. *Largo desolato* (12)

Only the four sections marked (12) are in the twelve-note system; the others are 'atonal'. The work is rightly called *Lyric* Suite: as Willi Reich writes in the new *Grove*, 'No unprejudiced hearer ... can deny the great expressive power of the music.' Those who are not interested in music's structure should pursue this chapter no further; knowing nothing of the ground-plan, one can enjoy Berg's contrasting moods and emotions: the violent outbursts of the *Trio estatico*, the broad lyrical climax in the *Adagio appassionato*, the mysterious whispers of the *Tenebroso*, and the inconsolable sadness of the ending. The music, like that of *Wozzeck* or the Violin Concerto, speaks to everyone. The commentary that follows is only for readers who, possessing the miniature score, feel curious to see how the work is put together.

A kind of cyclic form is given to the work by the fact that each movement contains a passage which is caught up and developed in the subsequent one. To point out these details would be a waste of space, since to anyone without a score they would be meaningless, and the score itself has a preface by Erwin Stein which makes the correspondence clear. Mr Stein also analyses the form of the movements. We shall attempt something else: by dissecting a few characteristic bars, to show how the note-row can yield not only the main theme (which anyone can see) but also the subsidiary voices.

Berg casts his main theme (bars 2–4) in a form which gives prominence to the descending pairs of notes, and special emphasis to the fifth, A flat to D flat:

His first bar presents the twelve notes of the chromatic scale as raw material, grouped mainly into fifths, with this interval further accentuated by a decorative swoop over the open strings of the cello. The first violin, Ex. 11, orders the chromatic chaos. Its next entry (bar 7) starts on 9, runs through the row to 12, and again on from 1 to 6. At bar 13 there is a bridge-passage (the movement, like that in Schönberg's Second Quartet, is in sonata form without development), and here the successive chords may be seen to consist of 12, 1, 2, 3, 4; 5, 6, 7; 8, 9, 10, 11; 12 in the cello. 12, the B, is the same in both the row and its inversion, and here it forms the pivot for the last three chords of the bar, which present, in retrograde form, the inversion of the row (Ex. 9*b*): 12, 11, 10, 9; 8, 6, 5, then 7; 3, 2, 1, with 5 held by the cello and yielding to 4 just after the fourth beat. To lead into the second subject the first violin plays a long theme (bars 15 [second beat]–22) consisting of 1–7 (with 6 strongly sounded in the second violin as a turning-point), 5, 4, 3, 2, 1; 1–12 in inversion; and then 1–12 in the main form. This becomes a theme of melodic beauty.

Here and in the other movements Berg has defined his paragraphs with changes of tempo, so that the structure is easy to follow even though the themes may wriggle into new shapes. The second subject is marked *poco più tranquillo*, and as can be seen below, it starts with the second violin closing its basic row (this row started at the beginning of bar 21), and pivoting on the B natural to the retrograde inversion, from 12 to 5, taken up on 4 by the first violin, who then pivots on the F and goes on to a complete statement of the original row. Berg masks the pivotal points by a pleasing rhythmic motif; and the viola, inserting *forte* notes in a *pianissimo* line, supplies the 'missing' numbers of the series (these viola notes are ringed in the example below):

These are cumbersome things to explain!

The *rondo* form of II, the *Andante amoroso*, is clearly defined by Mr Stein in his preface to the score. III, the *Allegro misterioso*, will puzzle people until they realize that Berg has altered his row by exchanging notes 4 and 10:

This yields a note-row ending with three rising semitones, which form a useful motif. We quote it at the pitch at which the first violin gives it out at bars 2–3. The viola responds at the original pitch (a fourth lower) starting with 4 and ending with 3; and the second violin at the same pitch but starting with 10 and ending with 9. The introduction to this theme presents notes 1–4 in three different orders (1, 2, 3, 4; 2, 1, 4, 3; 2, 1, 3, 4), and with the stress falling in a different place each time (cf. Ex. 5 above); at bars 6–9 the cello arranges these motifs to form a melodic theme.

The next twelve-note section, the *Tenebroso* episode which twice casts its shadow over the *Presto delirando*, is again puzzling until we realize that it is based on yet another note-row, Ex. 9b rearranged in the order 1, 2, 3,

10, 4, 8, 7, 6, 9, 5, 11, 12. Here it is, transposed down a semitone as Berg uses it in this movement, and re-numbered:

and here is the start of the *Tenebroso* episode:

To save space I have written four of Berg's bars as one, and cannot show the elaborate expression marks. These chords drift in and out of one another, each one sounded so gently as to be inaudible until its predecessor has finished – a shadow cast on a shadow, and bewitching to listen to!

The Finale is built on the same row, Ex. 14, now at its 'normal' pitch, i.e. starting on F. The cello gives it out four times at the start, each time in slightly shorter note-values. This movement is a free, rhapsodic construction, much of which defies a clear twelve-note analysis; the creeping semitones of the first violin's first entry, for example, seem written rather for their expressive connotations than for any structural purpose. On the other hand, such features as the new row (in the cello) played simultaneously with its inversion (in the second violin) will be quite apparent (bar 6). At bars 26–7 there is a citation from *Tristan*; in the *Adagio appasionato* there was one from the Lyric Symphony of Alexander von Zemlinsky (to whom Berg's Lyric Suite is dedicated).

Berg wrote no more chamber music. In 1924 Schönberg composed a Wind Quintet (see p. 313 of this volume); in 1926 a Suite for three clarinets and piano quartet; in the same year his Third String Quartet, and ten years later his

Fourth. Finally, in 1946 came a String Trio of great beauty. Novices should perhaps start with the Suite, which is light and witty, easy on the ear, and brilliantly written for the instruments. The second movement of this twelve-note work, *Tanzschritte*, uses the syncopations and dotted rhythms of jazz. The third is a set of variations on the German folk-song *Aennchen von Tharau*, which moves forward in E major through the twelve-note texture. The Fourth String Quartet is also a work to make converts; its continuously beautiful sounds, clear form, and poise and elegance should prove of compelling interest and fascination to any listener.

Before leaving the subject of twelve-note music, we must at any rate mention Anton Webern's later chamber works: a String Trio (1927), a Quartet for violin, saxophone, clarinet, and piano (1930), a Concerto for nine instruments (1934), and a String Quartet (1938). These are economical, almost to the point of unintelligibility at times: it is as if one were in a dark room in which just single objects were illuminated one after another. With familiarity the shape of the room becomes clearer. Webern handles and places sounds and notes as if they were precious objects. We may be reminded of an exquisite jade: cold to the touch, warming to the spirit, beautiful, and mysterious.*

HINDEMITH

From 1922 to 1929 Paul Hindemith was the viola player in the Amar Quartet, and his chamber works of this period were generally performed for the first time by this group. It is not surprising then that the composer shows the most intimate knowledge of the medium; one of the first things we note when we look into his chamber scores – and even more when we hear them performed – is the virtuosity with which he handles the strings. An early String Quartet, Op.

* Much interesting material about Schönberg, Berg, and Webern may be found in *Schönberg and His School* by René Leibowitz (Philosophical Library, New York).

1, is withdrawn, according to the official Hindemith catalogue (and so the numbers in *Grove* need pushing one back).
No. 1 dates from 1919; from the Amar Quartet period we
have Nos. 2, 3, and 4 (all first performed by this quartet),
the last dated 1923. Then there is a twenty-year gap before
Nos. 5 and 6 (both first played by the Budapest Quartet in
Washington) appear. The Second String Trio intervened
in 1933.

Hindemith's First String Trio, Op. 34, followed the
Fourth Quartet, and was played by members of the Amar
Quartet at Salzburg in August 1924. It is dedicated to
Alois Haba, the Czech quarter-tone composer; it does not
contain any quarter-tones, but is a fine example of Hinde-
mith's style at its most energetic and brilliant.

The first movement is a Toccata in D, whose principal
theme is rapped out by the three instruments in three
octaves:

Then the violin sails away with this theme a semitone higher
while the other instruments propose snatches of free inversions and variants of it. The viola has some particularly
insistent remarks to make on the subject of the motif marked
(*a*) above. After fifty bars the violin comes to a halt, or rather
to activity confined to one spot, with a trill on F, while the
lower instruments try the theme out a tone down. Another
statement in full octaves, and we reach this secondary
theme:

This is played in octaves by violin and cello, but is in fact
subsidiary to the viola part, which is now moving in fierce
and dramatic semiquavers (hitherto the quaver triplets

have afforded the fastest motion). Another climax, and it is the cello's turn to dominate the ensemble. Each instrument has a brief solo cadenza, and the movement ends with the theme once more, landing on a firm chord of D major.

The second movement is marked: slow and very peaceful. In B minor, it offers one of those melodies which, like Japanese paper flowers in water, slowly release petal after petal. As soon as one flower is open, another one, of a different hue, begins – the viola, silent for the first six bars, starts the melody a sixth lower. Later the order is reversed: the viola accompanies the violin's unfolding (now in A minor) with the same counter-melody that formerly the cello had had, and the cello enters six bars later, down in C minor.

The brief *Scherzo* is in strong contrast. The instruments are muted, and played *pizzicato* throughout, except for the cello on the last page, which darts to and fro like a fish on a line. Motif (*a*) from Ex. 16 is called into play, and its fourths are extended in a chain reaching upwards: C, F, B flat, E flat, A flat. So brilliantly is this exuberant movement written (with plenty of triple stopping) that often it sounds as if the whole string section of an orchestra were engaged on it.

The Finale is a lively fugue, the exposition of whose subject is accompanied by this curious little figure derived from it:

The movement is a dazzling display of contrapuntal ingenuity. The headlong rush is pulled up by a silent pause, and there follows a quieter section where the three instruments are barred in three different metres. The fugue returns, proceeding to a resolute climax, after which the first violin starts a two-and-a-half-bar *ostinato* lasting for thirty-six bars, *pp* to *fff*. The movement ends with the sub-sidiary motif of Ex. 18, a tone higher, played six times by the first violin, and each time differently harmonized, in a very odd bold progression. The final statement seems to be leading inevitably to a close in E flat, but instead lands resolutely on the curious chord of E flat, B flat; C, F; B flat, F.

18

Russian Chamber Music (from 1800)

ANDREW PORTER

THE great nineteenth-century Russians seem to have had comparatively little natural feeling for chamber music; there are only two string quartets from the period which can be said to form part of the international repertory: Tchaikovsky's First (1871) and Borodin's Second (1881–5), both in D major. This is not to say that chamber music was not written. The circle around Belayev created a great deal of it, much of it light in character.

Belayev, music publisher, concert promoter, Maecenas to Russian composers, was an amateur viola-player, and passionately devoted to chamber music. In the late 1880s a circle comprising Borodin and Rimsky-Korsakov and, among the younger members, Liadov, Glazunov, Ippolitov-Ivanov, and Arensky, would meet on Fridays at Belayev's house for chamber music. Three composite works for string quartet commemorate these meetings. No less than ten composers joined in the set of quartet movements called *Fridays*. Rimsky-Korsakov, Liadov, Borodin, and Glazunov collaborated in producing a string quartet based on the three musical letters of their host's name (B–la–F), with which Belayev's name-day in November 1886, was celebrated. Borodin died the following year, so the corresponding quartet of 1887, *Jour de Fête*, had only three movements.

In its light, pleasant way this quartet is probably characteristic of most of the chamber music produced in the Belayev circle. The opening *Allegro* is by Glazunov, and entitled 'Christmas Singers'; it uses traditional Christmas themes. The central movement, by Liadov, is called 'Glorification', and its principal theme recalls one in

Rimsky-Korsakov's *Russian Easter Overture*. Rimsky-Korsakov's finale is sub-titled *Khorovod*, which is a Russian circular dance.

TCHAIKOVSKY

BUT back to Tchaikovsky. His catalogue for the student years 1863–4 shows him getting his hand in with a dozen chamber works for various combinations of instruments. Opp. 1–10 (excluding Op. 3, *The Voyevode*) are piano pieces, and then Op. 11 is the String Quartet of which the *Andante cantabile*, at the least, is known to all who listen to music.

Early in 1871, Tchaikovsky wished to raise money by giving a concert, and in February he produced a new work to be played at it, this rather hurriedly written String Quartet. It is hard to know just what models the composer had in mind, but it is not uninteresting to recall that the previous year he had been present at the Beethoven Centenary Festival in Mannheim. There is a certain freedom, boldness, and invention in the writing, in the last movement particularly, which point, perhaps, to a study of Beethoven. Most of the material, however, is distinctively Russian. The actual string-writing is highly competent, but without any very individual characteristics.

Pedal basses mark much of the Quartet. All but the last note of our first quotation below is heard over a pedal D and A, sustained by cello and viola. This is the first subject, which illustrates the fascinating combination of simplicity with subtle, even elusive, rhythmic inflexion, that runs through all four movements:

After the theme has been heard twice, its rhythm persists, while against it decorative counterpoints are spun out in semiquavers. Two 'get-ready' bars for the viola – the most conventional ones in the Quartet – lead to the second subject:

Ex.2

Again the rhythm is elusive, partly because of the 'springing' in the last beat of the first two bars, partly because the inserted bar of 12/8 confuses an ear which does not have the score to guide it. This melody is repeated at once by the cello, but this time with the third bar adapted so that it stays in 9/8; against it the first violin spins out counterpoints in the same semiquaver rhythm as those to the first subject. A *poco più mosso* hurries us to the close of the exposition.

The development is of an extraordinary richness. Rhythmically, it makes subtle play among the elements of the lilting syncopation in Ex. 1, the 'sprung' last beat of Ex. 2, even quavers, and the semiquavers of the countermelodies. The rising third which opens Ex. 2 is expanded to larger intervals, and a point to watch out for, near the beginning of the development, is the treatment of this new form of the second subject as if it were a fugal *stretto* – first as a rising fourth, and then a rising sixth (bars 68 and 78 ff. for those who have the score).

There is much preparation for return of Ex. 1. The cello sounds its rhythm in a sequence of monotone bars which climb by semitones: C, D flat, D, E flat, E, then a climax on F; B flat, then three bars of dominant, heralding the theme on the second violin, while the first continues its bold semiquaver figuration. The remainder of the movement holds no real surprises, though the *poco più mosso* goes on to an *allegro giusto* section, and then further with *poco accel* – a section enlivened by the same rhythmic play as the rest of the movement.

Tolstoy was among the earliest admirers of the second movement, the *Andante cantabile*. 'I never felt so flattered in my life,' Tchaikovsky confessed, 'or so proud of my creative power, as when L. Tolstoy, sitting beside me, listened to my *Andante* while the tears streamed from his eyes.' The well-known melody is quoted only because those who know it by ear alone tend to find the accents surprisingly hard to scan:

Ex.3

The single bar of 3/4 lends an extraordinary fluidity to the phrase. As waltz tune which underlies the melody of Tchaikovsky's song, 'At the Ball', becomes infinitely haunting and sweet by reason of its rhythmic variation – broken as if by so many catches of the breath – so the slight expansion here seems to give the melody a power to span vast, bleak horizons. It is with something of a shock that we learn that Tchaikovsky had heard this tune while staying with his sister in the summer of 1869; he was orchestrating *Undine*, and a carpenter outside his room had been singing – to ribald words! – the lovely melody which brought tears to Tolstoy's eyes.

The tune is heard through against simple harmonies, yet even here we can detect the careful craftsman – at the first repetition the cello expands the bass into a subtle 'rhythmic canon'. An enharmonic modulation, by way of F on the second violin, takes us into D flat, an ingenious *pizzicato ostinato* for the cello, and the second theme, which is of the composer's own invention:

Ex.4

At its first hearing second violin and viola supply a very simple accompaniment, just two chords. Second time through, the cello expands its *ostinato* and the harmonies are richer. Ex. 3 returns, also more richly clad: and then, after some dramatic pauses, Ex. 4 re-enters in the expressive G-string register of the first violin. The first theme starts, dies away after a suggestion, then drifts off and disappears, like a wisp of cloud, in a plagal cadence.

Rhythmic vitality again marks the *Scherzo* (*Allegro non tanto*). Here the departures from convention are more vigorous; the structure is 4+4+4. The Trio is heavily syncopated, and for the greater part of it the cello buzzes away at B flat–A–B flat–A, in semiquavers. From a melodic point of view this is a slightly disappointing movement.

But the Finale (*Allegro giusto*) is again highly inventive. The main theme is:

This repeats exactly as above, except that the last note is a close on D. Tchaikovsky uses elements from this theme – almost as Haydn might – to make up his movement. The rhythm of the first bar plays an important part, and the drop is often expanded to an octave (the cello has a rising octave, d – d', as bass to this bar). The falling fourth of the first bar, and the rising fourth of the fourth bar, both recur in all sorts of contexts. They make a bass to the tune itself (in bars 2, 3, and 8); here they are again in the second subject:

Notice, too, how the various rhythmic units of the main theme are here reshuffled. This very Russian-sounding theme is almost sneaked in by the viola.

When the first theme returns, *ff* and an octave higher, it is supported by an unflinching foundation of pedal D and A, rising and falling an octave, double-stopped by the cello. Ex. 6 is given to the cello this time (it never reaches the upper strings). In a coda, *Allegro vivace*, Ex. 5 skitters away divided into semiquavers.

Tchaikovsky had little interest in chamber music, and although this string quartet was succeeded by two others, in

F major (1874) and E flat minor (1876), neither of them recaptured the peculiar intimacy and freshness of the D major work. For the rest, there is only the String Sextet entitled *Souvenirs de Florence*, which gets an occasional hearing, and the A Minor Piano Trio, Op. 50.

In October 1880 Tchaikovsky's patroness, Nadejda von Meck, urged him to compose something for her private piano trio (whose pianist was then Debussy!). In 1881, in Rome, Tchaikovsky began a work for the medium, although he had once described it as 'torture' to listen to. He was prompted not only by Mme von Meck, but also by a desire to compose something more or less intimate, with an important piano part, in memory of Nicholas Rubinstein, who had died in March 1881. The piece was completed in January of the following year, and was dedicated 'To the Memory of a Great Artist'. The theme of the lengthy variations has some personal association with Rubinstein, and each variation is said to have some connexion with an episode in his career.

BORODIN

STUDENT works apart, Borodin's short catalogue of chamber music opens with a string sextet in D minor in Mendelssohnian vein, which he wrote in 1860 at Heidelberg 'to please the Germans'. Then, in 1862, during an idyllic summer at Viareggio with his bride, he composed a pianoforte quintet in C minor. In the spring of 1875, 'to the great distress of Stassov and Mussorgsky', he sketched a string quartet in A major 'suggested by a theme of Beethoven's' (from the B Flat Quartet, Op. 130); and it is this work, completed only in August 1879, which Calvocoressi described as 'the earliest of first-rate chamber music to be written by a Russian composer, and, in the opinion of many competent judges, the very finest in the output of the whole school'. The work, now recorded, hardly seems to merit such praise, but it was performed with success; and in a letter written a few months before his death the composer

noted that 'my first quartet pleased not only many European audiences, but also American. During the past season it
was played four times at the Buffalo Philharmonic Concerts.'

It is not very likely that Buffalonians hear much of the
A Major Quartet to-day. The Second String Quartet in D
Major has decisively ousted it – and almost all other Russian chamber music besides – from public favour. This
quartet was written the following year; it is dedicated to
the composer's wife, and was not published until after his
death. Like Tchaikovsky's D Major Quartet, it contains a
movement – the Nocturne – which has been detached from
its context, and arranged for several combinations. Sir
Malcolm Sargent's version for string orchestra is one of the
best known. Lately, in a horrid vocal arrangement as 'And
this is my beloved', it has figured in the musical show *Kismet*.

Borodin's actual string-writing in this work is far more
individual than in the Tchaikovsky D Major Quartet considered above. The texture has been likened, not inappro-
priately, to a string quartet equivalent of Chopin's piano
style, where a melody threads its way over an accompaniment of broken chords, or more intricate arabesques. The
harmony, too, is touched with that sweet, delicate individual
flavouring which was peculiarly Borodin's.

The first movement, *Allegro moderato*, is entirely lyrical,
and although examination of the score soon reveals that the
movement is carefully shaped, it has the spontaneous
character of an improvisation. The first subject is given out
by the cello, and repeated by the first violin a fourth higher,
in the more extended form quoted below:

First violin and cello are the solo singers; the inner voices
have nothing to do but supply accompanying chords while

this melody passes from top line to bottom line, until it moves without 'bridge passage' to a dominant chord, and yields at once to:

The close kinship between this and the sixth bar of Ex. 7 is apparent; we seem to be dealing less with a new theme than with a development of the old one. The first violin plays it, with *pizzicato* accompaniment. A slightly more strenuous passage is based on the rising fourth which opens Ex. 8, transformed to rhythm marked (*b*), then the cello takes over the second subject, and the section closes with a few *animato* bars in which the rhythm marked (*a*) in the two examples above predominates. A short development, mainly in F, gives second violin and viola occasional fleeting chances to play a melody; but the viola really comes into its own only when, after a regular recapitulation of the first subject, it introduces the second – in E flat, a semitone above the expected key. The more strenuous rising fourth theme succeeds, and then first violin and cello sail out with the second subject, in octaves, in its proper key. The *animato* section slackens to *tranquillo*, and through the slow close-shifting harmonies over a pedal D the viola murmurs in chromatic semitones.

The *Scherzo* is an enchanting movement, as light in touch as one of Mendelssohn's, but harmonically far more interesting. Nothing is laboured, and the modulations are fleeting. The first theme, *Allegro*, consists of dancing quavers, supported by broken chords. After twenty-one bars during which the first violin holds full sway, the cello turns the theme backwards, and launches us into this lilting waltz, played in thirds by the violins:

It is not long before we are shown that the dancing quavers can well accompany this tune. Next, we have the quavers running from part to part. Skipping out every second quaver gives a quasi-trio section in crotchet motion, after which quavers and waltz return, till the movement flickers away in light *pizzicati*.

The musical arrangers of *Kismet* must have known they had a hit-number on their hands when they turned to the *Notturno* of Borodin's Quartet. Above an accompaniment of syncopated chords from second violin and viola, the cello launches this melody, whose surpassing sweetness is surprisingly uncloying:

It lasts for twenty-four bars, gradually sinking below the accompaniment chords. Then it reappears high on the first violin (the second A above the stave), unfolding its full heavenly length once again. A point of technical interest lies in the different accompaniments which Borodin has devised for each repetition of the tune; one of the most striking is at bars 133 ff., where the viola trembles across thirds above a light arpeggio *pizzicato* from the cello – a passage Chopin might have written had he composed for string quartet instead of piano. There are two other important thematic elements. One is simply a rising scale of semiquavers, which is used to lead into important solo entries; the other is as follows:

At the forty-eighth bar the first violin mounts, by way of the ascending scale, to this theme; and while the theme is descending, step by step, the second violin uses the scale to rush up past and start the theme at the top again (the entry is shown in our example). In the central section of the movement these two themes alternate. In the third, Ex. 10 appears as a unison or octave canon, at one beat's distance, adjusted at the fourth bar to two beats; first this is heard between first violin and cello, then between the two violins, against the fascinating accompaniment already referred to. The effect seems wonderfully uncontrived. Finally (as if to end up with 'something plain'), the violin plays the tune over a bass line, with nothing but a pedal A from the viola to enrich the two-part harmony. A series of imitative entries on bar 7 of the main theme (not quoted, but all too familiar from *Kismet*), closes the movement.

After so much harmony, Borodin gives us a contrapuntal Finale. The opening recitative is quoted below:

It seems very likely that the composer had Beethoven's F Major Quartet, Op. 135, and its similar introductory statements to the Finale ('*Muss es sein? Es muss sein!*') in mind when he prefaced his movement with these. (Perhaps one day words will turn up to fit the notes.) After this introduction the tempo changes to *vivace*, and the two components are handled as subjects of a quasi-double fugue, which soon gives way to a very long tune, the beginning of which is quoted below. Apart from the falling sixths, it moves entirely by semitones.

These are the materials of the movement, which is twice broken by the return of the *Andante*, and also by some heavy dramatic statements whose significance we are left to guess at.

PROKOFIEV

THE lack of interest in chamber music seems to have persisted among Russian composers. Beyond the early Three Pieces for String Quartet (1914) and the one-movement Concertino for String Quartet (1920), Stravinsky has avoided the medium, except in his Wind Octet (1923) and the recent Septet (1952) – both works which lie outside this chapter, as do the two most popular chamber works by Prokofiev, the Overture on Hebrew Themes (1919) for clarinet, string quartet and piano, and the Quintet (1924) for oboe, clarinet, violin, viola, and double bass. Both were commissioned works: the first a gay, straightforward piece based on two contrasting melodies, the second spiky, and perhaps more interesting as a study in sonorities than as musical thought. It was composed in Paris, to accompany a ballet dealing with circus life.

Prokofiev also wrote two string quartets, again both to a commission. The First (1930) was composed to a commission from the Library of Congress during Prokofiev's American tour of 1930; the Second, and more interesting, dates from 1941, when Prokofiev and several other artists were evacuated from Moscow to escape the German air raids. In the Caucasus he encountered a kind of folk music he had not heard before, and determined to combine this regional idiom with classical form. The slow movement is based on a hauntingly beautiful melody, decorated in the composer's most elegant manner, and the finale is vivid and bright.

SHOSTAKOVICH

THE outstanding example of modern Russian chamber music, however – and perhaps the finest composition to come out of Soviet Russia – is Shostakovich's Piano Quintet, Op. 57. The composer has also written two piano trios, two string quartets and a string octet, which do not seem to be on the same level; the Piano Quintet has captivated listeners both inside Russia (where it won a Stalin prize) and in the West. Its five movements span a wide range of mood and emotion. The idiom is neo-classical, but unaffectedly so. Pages of the first movement recall a Bach toccata; the second is a broad fugue, the third a *Scherzo* in which the high spirits sound genuine and not 'manufactured to order'. An Intermezzo is elegiac, but not in the least sentimental; a steady crotchet tread lends Bachian dignity to the emotion; and the Finale is light and sparkling – within strict sonata form. There are few Soviet compositions at once so sincere, so untrivial, and musically so satisfying.

SELECTED BIBLIOGRAPHY*

THE appropriate volumes of *The Master Musician* series, edited by Eric Blom (Dent), all contain valuable material as also, and at greater length, do the volumes of *Symposiums*, edited by Gerald Abraham (O.U.P.) (of which the following, up to this date, have appeared: *Handel, Schubert, Schumann, Tchaikovsky, Grieg, Sibelius*), and Alfred Einstein's *Mozart* (Cassell), Karl Geiringer's *Haydn*, and *Brahms* (Allen and Unwin), and Halsey Stevens's *Bartók* (O.U.P.).

The following volumes in the *Musical Pilgrim* series of booklets (O.U.P.) are still in print and will prove most useful: *Beethoven, Quartets, Op. 18* (Hadow); *Second Period Quartets* (Abraham); *Brahms, The Chamber Music* (Colles); *Debussy and Ravel* – but dealing only with Debussy's quartet (Shera); *Walton*, Book 1 – the pianoforte quartet (Howes). Vaughan Williams's chamber music is fully treated in Frank Howes's large book on the composer (O.U.P.). Britten's in the Mitchell-Keller *Commentary* on his works (Rockcliff). An excellent little book, *Chamber Music*, by A. Hyatt King, in *The World of Music* series (Parrish), now out of print, may be sought in second-hand music shops, as also may Thomas Dunhill's practical treatise for students with the same title (Macmillan).

There is much of interest in Tovey chamber music volume in his *Essays in Musical Analysis* (O.U.P.), although only six of the twenty works discussed by Tovey are chamber music in the sense defined in my introduction to the present volume; the rest are works for piano, voice, and solo violin.

Paul Lang's *Music in Western Civilisation* (Dent), one of the finest books on music written in our time, naturally surveys the whole subject in the course of its pages, and much can be learnt from it. Chamber music from the death of Berlioz to Fauré is admirably treated in Martin Cooper's book on French Music (O.U.P.).

It is hardly necessary to mention *Grove V* (Macmillan) for general information and I only wish that could be said of the particular information in W. W. Cobbett's *Cyclopaedic Survey of Chamber Music* (O.U.P.), first published in 1930 and long since out of print. A reissue of this invaluable work, brought up to date, is an urgent necessity. It is rumoured to be on the way. Very welcome too would be the publication in this country of Homer Ulrich's

* A number of books mentioned in the text are not again listed here.

Chamber Music, the Growth and Practice of an Intimate Art (1948) and Ruth Halle Rowen's *Early Chamber Music* (1949) – taken up to the end of the eighteenth century – both of which are published by Columbia University Press and available from O.U.P.

How to Read a Score, by Gordon Jacob (Boosey and Hawkes), provides clear instruction on this subject, and *The Well-Tempered String Quartet*, by Bruno Aulich and Ernst Heimeran (translated by D. Millar Craig), will delight amateur players (Novello). They will find much valuable advice in *The Playing of Chamber Music* by George Stratton and Alan Frank (Dobson).

INDEX OF COMPOSERS MENTIONED
IN THE TEXT

MORE ABOUT PENGUINS
AND PELICANS

Penguin Book News, an attractively illustrated magazine which appears every month, contains details of all the new books issued by Penguins as they are published. Every four months it is supplemented by *Penguins in Print*, which is a complete list of all books published by Penguins which are still available. (There are well over two thousand of these.)

A specimen copy of *Penguin Book News* can be sent to you free on request, and you can become a regular subscriber at 3s for twelve issues (with the complete lists). Just write to Dept EP, Penguin Books Ltd, Harmondsworth, Middlesex, enclosing a cheque or postal order, and your name will be added to the mailing list.

Two other books published by Penguins are described on the following pages.

Note: *Penguin Book News* and *Penguins in Print* are not available in the U.S.A. or Canada.

Edited by Robert Simpson

THE SYMPHONY

(in two volumes)

This completely new work in two volumes provides a comprehensive introduction to the whole symphonic scene from Haydn to the present day.

Robert Simpson – himself a well-known symphonist – has done more than compile programme notes of the great symphonies: he has, in his two introductions, analysed the essence of symphonic form. By identifying the elements of rhythm, melody, harmony, and – vitally important – tonality as *all* being present in full measure in any successful symphony, he has provided a frame of reference which binds together symphonists from Haydn to Holmboe, from Mozart to Martinů.

His team of distinguished contributors, which includes Deryck Cooke, Hans Keller, and Hugh Ottaway, has thus been able to provide a connected, unified study of all major composers who have 'attempted to achieve in an orchestral work the highest state of organization of which music is capable'.

Volume 1: HAYDN TO DVORÁK
Volume 2: ELGAR TO THE PRESENT DAY

Also available

THE CONCERTO

Edited by Ralph Hill

Arthur Jacobs

A NEW DICTIONARY OF MUSIC

A New Dictionary of Music is a basic reference book for all who are interested in music. It covers orchestral, solo, choral, and chamber music; it likewise covers opera and (in its musical aspects) the ballet. There are entries for Composers (with biographies and details of compositions); Musical Works well known by their titles, such as operas and symphonic poems; Orchestras, Performers, and Conductors of importance to-day; Musical Instruments (not forgetting those of the dance band and brass band); and Technical Terms. English terms and names are used whenever possible, but foreign terms in general use are cross-referenced. Particular importance has been attached to bringing the reader abreast of new musical developments: there are entries for Concrete Music and Electronic Music as well as references to several recent works.

What is a fugue? What is the difference between a saxophone and a saxhorn? When was Sir Thomas Beecham made a knight and when a baronet? Who, besides Puccini, wrote an opera 'La Boheme'? These and thousands of similar questions are answered in this book.

Also available
CHORAL MUSIC